INTERACTIVE EPISTEMOLOGY

World Scientific Series in Economic Theory

(ISSN: 2251-2071)

Series Editor: Eric Maskin *(Harvard University, USA)*

Published

Vol. 10 *Interactive Epistemology*
by Robert J Aumann

Vol. 8 *Learning and Intertemporal Incentives*
by Dirk Bergemann and Juuso Välimäki

Vol. 7 *Models of Bounded Rationality and Mechanism Design*
by Jacob Glazer and Ariel Rubinstein

Vol. 6 *Uncertainty within Economic Models*
by Lars Peter Hansen and Thomas J Sargent

Vol. 5 *The Language of Game Theory: Putting Epistemics into the Mathematics of Games*
by Adam Brandenburger

Vol. 4 *Simple Adaptive Strategies: From Regret-Matching to Uncoupled Dynamics*
by Sergiu Hart and Andreu Mas-Colell

Vol. 3 *Case-Based Predictions: An Axiomatic Approach to Prediction, Classification and Statistical Learning*
by Itzhak Gilboa and David Schmeidler

Vol. 2 *Robust Mechanism Design: The Role of Private Information and Higher Order Beliefs*
by Dirk Bergemann and Stephen Morris

Vol. 1 *Equality of Opportunity: The Economics of Responsibility*
by Marc Fleurbaey and François Maniquet

Forthcoming

Selected Contributions to Game Theory
Robert J Aumann *(The Hebrew University, Israel)*

Decision Theory
Wolfgang Pesendorfer *(Princeton University, USA)* &
Faruk Gul *(Princeton University, USA)*

Leverage and Default
John Geanakoplos *(Yale University, USA)*

Leverage Cycle, Equilibrium and Default
Vol. 2: Collateral Equilibrium and Default
John Geanakoplos *(Yale University, USA)*

World Scientific Series in Economic Theory – Vol. 10

INTERACTIVE EPISTEMOLOGY

Robert J Aumann
The Hebrew University of Jerusalem, Israel

World Scientific

NEW JERSEY • LONDON • SINGAPORE • BEIJING • SHANGHAI • HONG KONG • TAIPEI • CHENNAI • TOKYO

Published by

World Scientific Publishing Co. Pte. Ltd.
5 Toh Tuck Link, Singapore 596224
USA office: 27 Warren Street, Suite 401-402, Hackensack, NJ 07601
UK office: 57 Shelton Street, Covent Garden, London WC2H 9HE

Library of Congress Cataloging-in-Publication Data
Names: Aumann, Robert J., author.
Title: Interactive epistemology / Robert J. Aumann, The Hebrew University of Jerusalem, Israel.
Description: New Jersey : World Scientific, [2024] | Series: World Scientific series in economic theory, 2251-2071 ; vol. 10 | Includes bibliographical references and index.
Identifiers: LCCN 2022007211 | ISBN 9789811227325 (hardcover) | ISBN 9789811227332 (ebook) | ISBN 9789811227349 (ebook other)
Subjects: LCSH: Game theory. | Epistemic logic. | Economics--Mathematical models.
Classification: LCC HB144 .A947 2024 | DDC 519.3--dc23/eng/20220512
LC record available at https://lccn.loc.gov/2022007211

British Library Cataloguing-in-Publication Data
A catalogue record for this book is available from the British Library.

For any available supplementary material, please visit
https://www.worldscientific.com/worldscibooks/10.1142/12019#t=suppl

Typeset by Stallion Press
Email: enquiries@stallionpress.com

Contents

Introduction

Epistemology is the philosophy of knowledge. Interactive epistemology (IE) is the philosophy of knowledge about knowledge; it provides conceptual and formal tools for studying what people know about what other people know.

Game theory (GT) studies situations — *games*[1] — in which several "players" (individuals, households, sports teams, corporations, nations, etc.) interact, the outcome depending on the actions of all. When deciding how to act, rational players strive to achieve their goals as best they can, given their information. In particular, given what they know about other players' actions, which in turn, depend on the information of those other players. Thus, IE is fundamental to GT.

This book comprises all our published contributions to IE up to the present. It is divided into four parts. The first concerns "pure" IE, not explicitly related to games. Though historically, IE grew out of GT, it is convenient to present the "pure" theory first, not least because the basic IE concepts are essential to the GT applications.

The second part deals with the role of IE in GT; specifically, in sorting out and understanding notions of strategic equilibrium. The games here are in *strategic* (aka normal or matrix) form, so the sequential process of play is not explicitly laid out. This simplifies the decription of the game, enabling us to focus on strategic equilibrium

[1]Italics are used for emphasis and for terms being defined.

and its epistemic characterizations. It was this that led to my involvement in IE, and perhaps also that of others.

The third part treats games in *extensive* form — where the sequential process of play *is* explicitly laid out. Specifically, it treats several epistemic characterizations of the backward induction outcome in perfect information games.

Some of this material engendered controversy; this is laid out in the fourth part, which comprises the original comments as well as my replies.

A lively overview of the book is Chapter 1 — an interview conducted in 2009.

Originally, we planned on calling this book *Contributions to Interactive Epistemology*, but then decided to call it simply *Interactive Epistemology.* Indeed, it is not a series of disparate contributions on various aspects of this large discipline. Rather, it forms a coherent whole, can be read without much or indeed any background in IE, and only basic background in GT. To be sure, it has important intellectual roots, notably Harsanyi's monumental 1967–1968 series on games of incomplete information, cited in many of our chapters.[2] But it stands on its own; may be considered a monograph on the basics of IE, its relation with GT, and the history of that relation.

Part 1: "Pure" Interactive Epistemology

Chapter 2, *Agreeing to Disagree* — the shortest (and arguably most influential) in this book — features four fundamental ideas: (i) common knowledge,[3] (ii) the semantic interactive knowledge formalism, (iii) common priors, and (iv) the agreement theorem. All four refer to a fixed set of people: the *individuals.* Specifically:

(i) An event is *commonly known* if all individuals know it, all know that all know it, all know that all know *that*, and so on without

---

[2]Harsanyi, J. C., "Games with Incomplete Information Played by 'Bayesian' Players," Parts I–III, Management Sci. 14 (1967–1968), pp. 159–182, 320–334, and 486–502.

[3]First introduced by David Lewis in 1969. See Chapter 1, pp. 5–6.

end. For example, if all are in a room and reliably testify that an event occurred, then that event becomes common knowledge.

(ii) The *semantic interactive knowledge formalism* consists of (a) a space, whose points represent all conceivable states of the world and whose subsets represent events; (b) for each individual, an *information partition* of the state space, where two states are separated by an individual's partition if and only if he[4] knows in each that the other does not obtain[5]; and (c) for each state, the probability distribution of each individual on the state space.[6]

(iii) A *common prior* is a single probability distribution on the state space from which all individuals can calculate their probability distributions at all states by conditioning on their knowledge. Conceptually, existence of a common prior means that differences in probability assessments between the individuals are due *only* to differences in what they know.[7]

(iv) The *agreement theorem* says that if the individuals have a common prior and commonly know each other's probability assessments for some event, then those assessments coincide; and that is so even though their information may be entirely different. In short, individuals cannot agree to disagree about probabilities.

The theorem is formally stated and proved in this chapter, using the semantic interactive knowledge formalism. The proof implicitly assumes that though each individual's private information is not commonly known, his information *partition* — what he gets to know in each state of the world — *is* commonly known. In the chapter, we argue informally that this is legitimate, as it involves no substantive knowledge.

---

[4]Masculine pronouns refer to indeterminate as well as masculine antecedents, as was customary in the past.

[5]Thus, each agent knows the atom of his partition that contains the true state — no more and no less.

[6]For simplicity, the state space is here taken to be finite. Relaxations of this restriction are considered in subsequent chapters.

[7]For a thorough discussion, see Chapter 22.

Chapters 3 and 4 — simply entitled *Interactive Epistemology I and II: Knowledge and Probability* — formalize the argument for common knowledge of the information partitions by explicitly constructing the state space and information partitions. In principle, the construction is straightforward: A state of the world is identified with its description, i.e., the list of all sentences that hold in that state. Each such list is logically consistent and *complete:* for each sentence, either it or its negation is in the list — otherwise, the list does not fully describe the state. Conversely, any logically consistent and complete list describes a possible state of the world. The information partitions are implicit in these descriptions, as the sentences in each such list explicitly say what each individual knows.

The construction is carried out in detail in these chapters. In particular, they set forth the two dual IE formalisms: the *syntactic,* based on sentences, and the *semantic,* based on state spaces and partitions.

Chapter 5, co-authored with Aviad Heifetz and originally published in the *Handbook of Game Theory,* surveys several approaches to IE. Of particular interest are two characterizations of the existence of a common prior.

Chapter 6 is an informal discussion of information and knowledge dealing mostly with subjects with which theory has not adequately dealt. Among them are awareness (or rather unawareness), logical omniscience, and the cost of calculation. The matter of common knowledge of the model is also informally discussed.

Part 2: Interactive Epistemology and Game Equilibrium

A *strategy* (or *pure strategy*) of a player in a game G is a complete plan of that player for playing that game, taking all possible contingencies into account. The notion of strategy enables (i) a vast conceptual simplification of the description of a game and (ii) a unified way of viewing all games. First, note that specifying each player's strategy determines the outcome of play completely. Next, with each possible outcome, we may associate a profile[8] of real numbers, representing the players' *payoffs*.[9] Thus, one may think of a game as a mapping from profiles of strategies to profiles of payoffs. This is called the *strategic*[10] *form* of the game; it totally abstracts away from the manner in which the game is actually played.[11]

A *pure strategy Nash equilibrium* of a game is a profile of pure strategies, known to all players, in which it is optimal[12] for each player to play his pure strategy in that profile, given that the others play theirs.

A *mixed strategy* of a player i is a random pure strategy[13]; mixed strategies of different players are assumed independent. A *mixed strategy Nash equilibrium* of a game is a profile of mixed strategies in which it is optimal[14] for each player to play his mixed strategy in that profile, given that the others play theirs.

In analyzing games, one is naturally led — almost forced — to generalize the idea of "strategy" from pure to mixed; just as in analyzing algebraic equations, one is naturally led — almost forced — to generalize the idea of "number" from real to complex. Indeed, algebraic equations need not have real roots, but they do always have complex roots; similarly, games need not have pure strategy Nash equilibria, but they do always have mixed strategy Nash equilibria.

---

[8]A *profile* is a list of items, one for each player.

[9]The payoff of player i for outcome o may be thought of as i's von Neumann–Morgenstern (NM) utility for o.

[10]Aka *normal*.

[11]In symbols, a game in *strategic form* consists of a set N (the *players*), a set S_i for each player i (i's *pure strategies*), and a function from $\times_{i\in N}S_i$ to $\mathbb{R}^N$ (the *payoff function*).

[12]Yields highest payoff.

[13]That is, a pure strategy that is randomly chosen in accordance with prescribed probabilities. (Formally, a random variable whose values are pure strategies i.e., a measurable function from a probability space (Ω, p) to the set of i's pure strategies.) In particular, a pure strategy s may be viewed as a mixed strategy in which s has probability 1.

[14]Yields highest expected payoff. As payoffs are NM utilities, the utility of a random outcome is the expected payoff of its realizations.

Chapter 7, published in 1974, introduced two generalizations of the basic notion of mixed strategy: *subjectivity* and *correlation.* Both were seminal, in diametrically opposed senses: The first because it led nowhere — for fundamentally important reasons. The second because it led to a large, rich literature and to a deep understanding of the nature of optimal play as set forth in Chapters 8 and 9.

Mixing *subjectively* means that rather than randomizing with "objective" devices like roulette wheels, the players use "subjective" devices, like horse races, where different players may ascribe different probabilities to the same outcome. Thus, a *subjective equilibrium* is defined as a profile of subjectively mixed strategies in which it is optimal for each player to play his strategy, given that the others play theirs. For this to make sense, it is not enough that different players ascribe different probabilities to the same event; they must also in some sense be mutually aware of those probabilities. Section 9j grapples with this issue inconclusively; *inter alia*, it says, "Though the players may know each other's probability, they may not know on precisely what observations it is based. Thus, each player would not know if his own information is or is not more reliable than the other player's, and might be inclined to stick with his own information. Of course, some revision of probabilities would certainly be called for even in such a case, but whether such a revision must always ultimately lead to equal probabilities ... is not clear."

Two years later, the issue was settled with the publication of Chapter 4, which sets forth the idea of common knowledge and establishes the agreement theorem. These imply that subjective equilibrium can occur only when players have different priors, and so is not very interesting.[15] As a result, the idea of subjective equilibrium had no substantial echo, led nowhere; but the reason for its leading nowhere became a cornerstone of IE.

The other generalization considered in Chapter 7 is *correlation,* in which one foregoes the requirement that the randomizations of different players be independent; thus, different players may get

[15]See, e.g., Section 5 of Chapter 8, and Chapter 22.

different information about the pure strategies played by all, and play accordingly. Specifically, a *correlated equilibrium* is a random profile of pure strategies with distribution known to all players, in which, when each player is informed only of his own pure strategy, it is optimal for him to play it, given that the others play theirs.

Underlying all three equilibrium notions — Nash, subjective, and correlated — is the notion of a player's *rationality*: that he does the best he can for himself — plays a pure strategy that is best for him,[16] given his beliefs. Chapters 8 and 9 establish intimate connections between correlated equilibrium and common knowledge of the players' rationality (CKR). Both chapters look not only at the game G itself but also at the context in which it is played, which informs the beliefs of the players — regarding the strategies that will be played and regarding those beliefs themselves.

Specifically, let Ω be the set of states of the world, where a state specifies which pure strategy each player plays, the beliefs of each player about the pure strategies played by the others, the beliefs of each player about those beliefs, and so on. In addition to CKR, assume that the players' beliefs are *consistent*,[17] i.e., that there is a common prior on Ω, from which each player derives his beliefs by conditioning on his information. Chapter 8 then shows that the strategy profiles chosen by the players constitute a correlated equilibrium. Chapter 9, coauthored with Jacques Dreze, shows that the possible expectations of a player i are precisely his expected payoffs to correlated equilibria of the *doubled* game $2G$, in which each of i's pure strategies appears twice.[18]

Both the above assumptions — CKR and belief consistency — play central roles in this volume, but they are vastly different. CKR is substantive, indeed very strong: an ideal[19] condition, unlikely to

[16]Yields highest expected payoff; see Footnote 14.

[17]The terminology is due to Harsanyi, *op. cit.*

[18]The notation 2_iG might be more appropriate, as only i's pure strategies must appear twice. Those of the other players may appear once or twice; it makes no difference.

[19]This is not a value judgment; "ideal" is meant as in "ideal gas."

be met in practice, that describes a fully rational world, in which any possibility of irrationality, no matter how remote, is ruled out. On the other hand, belief consistency is essentially a modeling assumption, has little or no real substance. It says only that differences in probabilities should be attributed to differences in information; that players who have always been fed precisely the same information[20] do not entertain different probabilities.

Chapters 8 and 9 shed light on an important debate that took place in the last century between Joseph Kadane and Patrick Larkey (KL), on one side, and John Harsanyi, on the other.[21] KL maintained that the problem facing a player in a game is no different from any one-person decision problem under uncertainty. Thus, following Savage,[22] each player should simply form subjective probabilities on the unknowns — in this case, the strategies of the others — and act to maximize his utility given those probabilities. In particular, they said, he should not assume that the other players are rational; rather, each player should turn to psychology to understand how the others might play in the particular situation at hand.

Harsanyi argued that games differ in principle from one-person decisions, in that the players' decisions are interdependent. Therefore, it is a *priori* unclear what each player "should" do to advance his interests even when rationality is assumed, or even what precise meaning this has. That is the question that game theory addresses; it answers it via "solution concepts" (such as Nash equilibrium) that shed light in various different ways on rational play. Only after exploring what it means to behave rationally can one meaningfully address the possibility of irrational behavior.

By Chapter 8, correlated equilibrium expresses KL's approach, in that following Savage, each player forms subjective probabilities on the strategies of the others and then maximizes utility given those

[20]Including their genetic endowments.

[21]KL, "Subjective Probability and the Theory of Games," *Management Science* 28 (2), 1982, pp. 113–120; Harsanyi, "Comments," pp. 120–124; KL, "Reply," p. 124; Harsanyi, "Rejoinder," pp. 124–125.

[22]*The Foundations of Statistics*, New York: John Wiley, 1954.

probabilities. It expresses Harsanyi's approach in that it assumes CKR, ruling out any possibility of irrationality.

Chapter 10, coauthored with Adam Brandenburger, returns to the epistemics of Nash equilibrium, pure and mixed. In the pure case, the condition is simple: A pure strategy profile played by the players in a game is a Nash equilibrium if the players are rational,[23] know their own payoff function, and know which strategies the others play. This holds also for mixed strategies if understood as conscious randomizations, in which the player i is uncertain of his own pure strategy. But it is also possible to view i's mixed strategy as expressing the uncertainty of others as to i's pure strategy. Thus, when there are just two players, the mixed strategy of each player i is understood as the other player's *conjecture re i* — his belief regarding the pure strategy that i plays. We show that if both players know the game,[24] know that both are rational, and know both conjectures, then the conjectures constitute a Nash equilibrium.

With more than two players, matters are more complex, as, in general, different players may have different conjectures re a given player i. But if the conjectures are commonly known, then by the agreement theorem, all players other than i have the same conjecture re i. We show that if all players know the game, know that all are rational, and commonly know all the conjectures, then the conjectures constitute a Nash equilibrium.[25]

These epistemic assumptions sound — and are — very strong. How would the players know what the others plan to do, not to speak of what the others believe? Perhaps more than any other analytic tool, Nash equilibrium is widely applied in economic theory, as well as in other social sciences; but its conceptual underpinnings are murky. Possibly, it can be understood as applying to social and economic

[23] Just R; the far stronger CKR is not needed.

[24] That is, both players' payoff functions.

[25] These conditions are "tight:" Examples show that if any are weakened, the conclusion may be false. In particular, it is not enough to assume outright that for each player i, the conjectures of all other players re i coincide; they must be commonly known.

norms. It would appear that such a norm cannot survive if it does not constitute a Nash equilibrium, though we know of no formal treatment of this matter. Note that with this viewpoint, the game underlying the situation to which the social norm applies may have several Nash equilibria; what is needed for the norm to survive is that it represent *a* Nash equilibrium, not necessarily *the* Nash equilibrium.

Part 3: Interactive Epistemology and Backward Induction

In games *of perfect information* (PI), players move one at a time, in full knowledge of the moves previously made.[26] Examples of PI games are chess, checkers, go, and hex. Battleship is not PI, as neither player knows where the other placed his ships. PI games represent games of strategy in their "purest" form: The considerations are strategic only, there are no informational issues, everything is open and above board.

Formally, a PI game is modelled as a rooted tree. The nodes are histories; the root is the null history. Except at the root, one of the edges at each node comes from the previous history; the other edges are the alternatives available to the player at that node. When the leaves (terminal nodes) are reached, play is finished, and the payoff profile at that leaf is specified. The tree[27] is assumed finite, commonly known, and generic.[28] For simplicity, chance moves are ruled out, though in principle they occasion no difficulty.

---

[26]Including by chance.

[27]Including the assignment of nodes to players and the payoffs at the leaves.

[28]That is, the payoffs to each player at different leaves of the game tree are different. This condition (called "in general position" in Chapter 11) is excessively strong; for example, it is not satisfied by chess, which can end in only three ways, but has more leaves than there are electrons in the universe. Moreover, it is not really needed. Chapter 13 dispenses with it altogether; and in Chapter 11, while genericity renders both the statement of the result and its proof simpler and more transparent, it plays no essential role. In Chapters 12 and 14, it plays no role at all.

Of fundamental importance in PI games is the *backward induction* (BI) process: Each player at a preterminal node chooses what is best for him; taking this as given, each player at a prepreterminal node[29] chooses what is best for him; and so on, until the root is reached. This process determines an action at each node; and so, a path from the root to a leaf (the *BI path*), the leaf at the end of this path (the *BI outcome*), and for each player, a complete plan for playing the game — his *BI strategy*. Kuhn (1953) shows that the BI strategies constitute a pure strategy Nash equilibrium. Just as in Part 2, we identified the epistemic circumstances yielding various forms of equilibrium, so here we seek to identify the epistemic circumstances yielding the BI process.

As in Part 2, the notion of rationality is central here, but it is not quite the same notion as there. That is because the strategic form studied in Part 2 obliterates the game's fine structure; one can relate only to strategies taken as a whole. In PI games, one can relate to choices at individual nodes.

Specifically, a player is *irrational at* a node v if he chooses an alternative there while knowing that a different alternative would yield him a larger payoff if v is reached. He is *rational at* v if he is not irrational there. A *strategy* of a player is a function that associates with each of his nodes the choice of an alternative at that node; he is *rational* if his strategy calls for a rational choice at each of his nodes.

The main result of Chapter 11 is that in every PI game, CKR — common knowledge of the players' rationality — entails using the BI strategies, and so reaching the BI outcome. This is easily seen by induction: If there is just one decision node, then by CKR, the player there is rational, so chooses a leaf that is best for him; that starts the induction. Now assume the assertion when there are up to n decision nodes, and suppose there are $n+1$. Whichever alternative the root player chooses leads to a subtree with at most n decision nodes. By CKR and the induction hypothesis, this entails the BI

[29] Where all subsequent nodes are preterminal or terminal, and some are preterminal.

outcome for that subtree. By CKR, the root player is rational, so chooses the alternative leading to the subtree with the BI outcome that is best for him. That is precisely what his BI strategy dictates, so the induction is complete. The rigorous proof follows the same lines, using the semantic interactive knowledge formalism.[30]

The significant contribution of Chapter 11 lies more in the result's formulation than in its proof. First, the chapter identifies CKR as the natural rationality condition underlying BI in PI games. Second, it clarifies that the notion of conditional[31] used here is the *substantive* notion: What a player *would* do at a given node *if* reached, though in fact it may not be reached; as distinguished from *material* conditionals, commonly used in mathematics, where it suffices that the antecedent be false — the node not be reached — for the conditional to be correct. Indeed, all decision-making rests on substantive conditionals — what the decision maker would get if (substantive!) he makes this or that decision. PI games — indeed all extensive games — are nested decisions, so rest on nested substantive conditionals. First, what would result if (substantive!) the player at the root chooses this or that alternative; next, what would result if (substantive!) the player at the resulting node chooses this or that alternative; and so on. In our case, the definition (above) of irrationality at a node essentially involves a substantive conditional: The "if" in the phrase "if v is reached" is substantive.

It is worthy of note that if we substitute a material "if" for the substantive "if" in the definition of rationality, then not only does the result's proof break down, but also the result itself actually becomes incorrect. Explicitly, with the above definition of rationality at a node, call a player *materially rational* if his strategy calls for a rational choice at each of his *reached* nodes. Then CK that all players are materially rational does *not* imply the BI outcome; a very simple counterexample — just two moves — is Game 1 in Section 4.1

[30]See (ii) in Part 1 of this introduction.

[31]A *conditional* is a statement of the form "if p then q."

of Chapter 11 (p. 277); this example also shows why substantive rationality is a natural condition.

The material conditionals of mathematics have a straightforward formal definition: "If p then q" means "q or not p," no more and no less. We know of no similar formal definition of substantive conditionals in general. In the current context, the idea of substantive conditional is formally expressed by the concept of conditional payoff. Namely, the *conditional payoff at* a node v to a player i for a strategy profile s is i's payoff if starting at v, the players play s. If v is not reached under s, the conditional payoff may well differ from the actual payoff.

At the end of the chapter, there are two important disclaimers, which we repeat here for emphasis.

(i) The chapter says nothing about the behavior of players at vertices off the BI path that are actually reached. Under CKR, vertices off the BI path *cannot* be reached; and the chapter deals only with the case in which CKR obtains.

(ii) The chapter does *not* assert that playing the BI strategy is rational. It says only that if[32] CKR obtains, then all players play the BI strategy. It might well be highly irrational for a player to play the BI strategy if at some level he attributes irrationality to another player. Thus, in the game examined in Chapter 14, even minute departures from CKR may make it incumbent for rational players to depart radically from the BI strategy. CKR is an ideal[33] condition, which expresses the idea that all irrationality is ruled out: Not only are all players themselves rational, but they cannot conceive of irrationality on the part of any other player.

Chapter 12, coauthored with Itai Arieli, addresses the following conceptual conundrum: A player i on the BI path must either continue on the BI path or go off. If he goes off, the player j who is reached is unreachable under CKR, and j knows this as commonly known propositions are *a fortiori* known by all players. Since j bases

[32] *This* "if" is of course material.

[33] Meant as in "ideal gas," not as a value judgment.

his choice on what he thinks subsequent players will do, and his "knowledge" has been contradicted, it is not clear what he (j) will do. But i must base his choice on what he thinks j will do, so it is not clear what i should do either. Specifically, it is not clear that the BI action is indeed rational for i — that he could not do better by leaving the BI path.

To avoid grappling with this conundrum, Chapter 12 replaces "knowledge" by "strong belief", where a player *strongly* believes a proposition p if he believes it unless it is logically inconsistent with his node being reached. *Common* strong belief of p signifies that p holds, all players strongly believe p, all strongly believe the foregoing, all strongly believe the foregoing, and so on. It is then shown that an outcome of a simple[34] PI game is consistent with the common strong belief of rationality iff it is a BI outcome.

Chapter 13 concerns a particularly enigmatic PI game, Bob Rosenthal's *centipede,* played as follows: There are two players, Ann and Bob. At the first move, Ann may "leave" — end play — immediately; if she does, she gets 2 and Bob gets 1. If not, it is Bob's turn, and *he* may then leave; if he does, he gets 4 and Ann gets 1. If not, it is again Ann's turn; if she then leaves, she gets 4 and he gets 3. And so on. At each move, the payoff to the player at that move increases by 3 if play ends there, while the payoff to the other player decreases by 1; thus every two moves, the payoff to each player increases by 2. If Bob does not leave at his n'th move, where $n = 1{,}000{,}000$, then at the next move, Ann *must* leave[35] (see the figure[36] on p. 326).

[34]In a *simple* PI game, each player moves at only one node. Any PI game may be thought of as simple if one splits each player i into several independent "agents," one for each of i's vertices, each with the same payoff as i. This does have non-trivial conceptual implications, which are discussed in the chapter.

[35]The particular numerical payoffs in the above description are unimportant; for each player, only the ordinal relation between the payoffs is important. And of course, the choice of n is also unimportant; the result holds for any n.

[36]The payoffs in the figure corresponding to Bob's horizontal choice at his last move are those when Ann ends the game — as she must — at her last move.

Note that at each move, it is optimal for the player at that move to "stay in" — refrain from ending the game — if and only if the player at the subsequent move also stays in.

Now, if her last move is reached, Ann *must* leave. So if Bob's last move is reached, it is optimal for *him* to leave, and this is CK. So under CKR, it is optimal for Ann to leave at the move previous to Bob's last, if that move is reached, and *that* is CK. Continuing in this way, we conclude that under CKR, Ann leaves at her first move.

But in that way, she gets only 2; whereas if she had stayed in, she might well have gotten up to 2,000,000.

Note that Ann's leaving at her first move is the game's BI outcome; so, that CKR implies her leaving at her first move is a consequence of Chapter 11. What is new here is that Chapter 13, unlike Chapters 11 and 12, uses material rationality only; it shows that specifically in the centipede game, CK of material rationality already yields the BI outcome.

Finally, we must say that we find this result on the centipede game to be conceptually extremely puzzling. Not only are both players rational — i.e., payoff maximizers — but it is commonly known between them that they are; nevertheless, they willingly settle for small change, when there are millions to be had. For example, by staying in at her first move, Ann could signal to Bob that she does not buy the BI logic and invites him to stay in as well; and then they could both make a lot of hay. What does she risk thereby? In the worst case, Bob would not bite. But then she has lost only 1, which is negligible compared to what she could be making. It seems to us that properly understanding the centipede game is an important challenge for game theory.

Chapter 14 treats a variant of the centipede game — ordinally equivalent to that described above — in which the payoffs increase exponentially very rapidly; at the end of only three rounds (six moves), the payoffs are in the millions of dollars. Of course, here too CKR yields BI; that is, Ann exits at her first move and gets only \$10. We show that in this particular game, a very small breakdown in the commonality of the knowledge of rationality enables the players to hold beliefs (about each others' strategies and beliefs) that justify "staying in" for a fairly long time. It remains to be seen whether and how this can be generalized to arbitrary centipede games.

Part 4: Discussion

Chapter 15, by Ken Binmore, and Chapter 17, by Binmore and Larry Samuelson, question our result that in games of perfect information, common knowledge of rationality (CKR) implies that the backward induction (BI) outcome is reached (Chapter 11). We reply (Chapters 16 and 18) that their arguments undermine not the implication $CKR \Rightarrow BI$, but rather the reasonableness of the BI outcome; and on this we agree with them.

In Chapter 19, Avishai Margalit and Menachem Yaari express discomfort with the "pure" theory laid out in Chapters 2 and 3. While some of their points are well taken, others are due to misunderstandings (Chapter 20). There is also a difference in emphasis and direction between us. They are interested in the sources and meaning of knowledge. Our approach is less philosophical; we wish only to provide a coherent formalization of those aspects of knowledge that are relevant to Game Theory.

In Chapter 21, Faruk Gul questions the conceptual foundations of the Common Prior Assumption (CPA). This affords us an excellent opportunity to discuss the CPA and the underlying information model in detail, and provide formal and conceptual underpinnings for them (Chapter 22).

Chapter 1

Interview with Robert Aumann*

Interviewed by Oliver Roy on January 23rd, 2010, in Bonn, Germany.

O.R.:
Professor Aumann, many thanks for accepting our invitation to give us an interview. First question: What initially drew you to epistemic logic?

R.A.:
It was a natural outgrowth of work in game theory. The beginning came with work on common knowledge, the *Agreement Theorem.* This states that when two people have common priors and common knowledge about each other's probability assessments, then these probability assessments must be the same. The moment you start talking about common knowledge you get drawn into all kinds of epistemic considerations. The question is, what led to *that*? What led to the interest in common knowledge?

*Reprinted from *Epistemic Logic: 5 Questions* (2010), edited by V. F. Hendricks and O. Roy, with permission from *Automatic Press.*

I wrote a paper in the very early '70s called 'Subjectivity and Correlation in Randomized Strategies'.[1] Randomised strategies go back to von Neumann and Morgenstern. These are mixed strategies based on some kind of coin toss, roll of the dice or spin of the roulette wheel. On the other hand there was the work of Savage, going back to Ramsey and de Finetti. This concerned *subjective* probabilities, which started to bloom in the '50s and early '60s. So the next step seemed obvious: what happens when you try to apply subjective — rather than objective — probabilities to randomisation? This question led to the paper about subjectivity and correlation in randomised strategies, which was also the beginning of *correlated* equilibria. In this paper, I show that you can have subjective mixing and that subjective mixing leads to different equilibria, called in the paper *subjective* equilibria. You even get different pure equilibria from those you get with just objective mixing. At the end of the paper I discuss how this can occur. Why would people have different subjective evaluations? At that time it was an open question.

One summer I was at the Stanford Institute for Mathematical Studies in the Social Sciences. Sitting with Kenneth Arrow and Frank Hahn in Frank's office, we were discussing the question, and I recall that the idea somehow arose from that discussion. I went back to my office and started thinking about it, and that's how the agreement theorem was born. At the time it actually seemed too simple to publish. As you know, the proof only takes two lines; but I think the main thing is the *formulation* of the idea: it's not the proof itself. The proof seemed so simple that it somehow seemed beneath my dignity to publish it. I explained the theorem to Arrow and Hahn, and at first they didn't want to believe it. Finally they became convinced, and then actually convinced me that this was worth publishing. It became one of the two papers in my oeuvre that are cited most widely, and that was the beginning of my interest in epistemic logic.

Then one tries to develop, to get at the foundations, and this is how I became especially interested in the *syntactic* part.

[1] *Journal of Mathematical Economics,* 1(1), pp. 67–96, 1974.

One question that is very puzzling to people who read the Agreeing to Disagree paper is: where does the partition *come from*? Somehow the knowledge partitions are assumed to be known to the players. In fact they're *common* knowledge to the players. This is built into the system. Where does it come from? These are the questions that most often arise with regard to that paper. How do people know each other's partitions? Why is this sort of given? Why is the partition a *given*? And that got me interested in the syntactic angle. In some sense, when you talk about partition spaces, when you talk about a semantic representation in epistemic logic, you want to say: Hey, let's put it in English! You are making some kind of assertion about agreement or whatever it is that you're talking about. Establish this assertion and don't give me partition spaces and state spaces and stuff like that. Say it in English! And that's what the syntactic approach is all about: saying it in English.

I became obsessed with the idea of *deriving* a semantic representation from *plain English,* which is what syntactics is all about. 'Syntactic epistemic logic' is just saying it in English. Dov Samet, an outstanding expert in epistemic logic, especially interactive epistemic logic, who did a PhD with me, put it this way, very picturesquely: If you want to explain it to your mother, you had better say it syntactically. Your mother won't understand if you try to say it semantically.

That sounds right. In semantics there's more grease, which allows you to work more easily. But you don't know where the foundations come from. Syntactic logic is more awkward, but it is simply logic. You derive one thing from another. You have certain axioms and you can argue about the axioms if you wish, but at least one thing follows from another. You don't have these sets and states of the world. What is a state of the world, anyway?

This is where the idea arose to view the semantic approach as *deriving* from the syntactic approach. You build a semantic approach *from* the syntactic approach.

This is how the whole thing started. I never see something and say: hey, this looks interesting, let's work on that. That's not the way it works. Rather, you have some problem and you say: we need to develop a tool to solve it. It is not 'this looks interesting and let's work on it'. People often ask me, why did I go into game theory? Well, I was faced with a problem, a specific problem that called for the use of game theory. So I said 'We have to study games.' It was a very specific problem. It's not like when you're a student at the university, you say: this subject looks attractive, that subject looks attractive, let's go into that subject. At least it was never that way in *my* research. Research is always very specifically purpose-oriented; one thing leads to another.

O.R.:
How did the semantic representation of epistemic logic come about, at the very beginning, at the origin of the Agreeing to Disagree paper?

R.A.:
I don't remember *exactly* the genesis of it, but it comes from Harsanyi's work. A type structure is essentially a partition structure. I think Harsanyi didn't think of it in *quite* that way, in terms of a state space with a partition. I don't know exactly how I came across that. I think it's already in the paper about subjectivity and correlation, in the first issue of JME.[2] So I think it was '72, or thereabouts, fooling around with the Harsanyi type-space structure, that led to the structure of states and partitions. That's where it comes from; it's already in there. 'Agreeing to Disagree', as I said, sort of grew out of the problem left open in that paper about subjectivity and correlation. So it was a natural progression. It's a *restatement* of the Harsanyi structure. Not a very deep restatement but some sort of restatement. A type determines what each person thinks about the other person's types and payoffs. So everything is an n-tuple of types, and a slight restatement gives you a partition structure.

O.R.:
After Agreeing to Disagree, there's been a convergence between the work that you initiated on the semantic side about partition

[2] *Journal of Mathematical Economics,* 1(1), pp. 67–96, 1974.

structures, and the work that was done by David Lewis in philosophy, for example. How did this convergence come about?

R.A.:
The David Lewis matter is really very, very interesting. I'll tell you my side of the story.

I wrote this paper and called this concept 'common knowledge'. This was published in 1976. Now around 1979 I ran across a paper in a philosophical journal which quoted my paper, I think. I'm not sure, though. It certainly quoted Lewis's book *Convention*,[3] which was published in '69. Perhaps it discussed a citation from my paper, too: I don't remember now, but it certainly quoted Lewis's book. I opened my eyes and said: 'Hey! What's going on here? This chap had the concept of common knowledge already in '69?' And, yes, it turned out that he did! I went back and bought the book or took it out of the library, and there it was. In 1969! And the amazing thing was that we used the *same word* for it, the same word that I thought I had invented. So from then on, when I wrote about this I started quoting Lewis.

Now, a year or two later Lewis sent a letter to the provost of Princeton University. In his PhD thesis, Sergio Ribeiro da Costa-Werlang had quoted me on common knowledge. Somehow the thesis was passed on to David Lewis as a reader. Lewis was furious because the thesis didn't quote him at all. It made believe that common knowledge was my concept. So I think Lewis wrote a letter to the provost in which he said ... well, he complained about this in fairly strong language. I don't remember the exact language. He sent a copy to Hugo Sonnenschein and a copy to me. So I got this copy and immediately wrote back saying: 'you know, Prof. Lewis, this is your concept. No question about it. I was not *aware* of your contribution to this when writing the '76 paper. I simply did not know. You might find this difficult to believe because we use the *same word*, we use the word 'common knowledge'. But it's true. And as

[3] *Convention: A Philosophical Study*, Cambridge, MA: Harvard UP, 1969.

soon as I became aware, which is a year or two ago now, I started citing you. Please accept my abject apologies. I'm not even saying that this is independent work. You can talk about independent work when you're talking about something that is done at approximately the same time or even a year or two later, but not when there's a hiatus of seven years. Because, you know, people talk at lunch or they talk in seminars and things filter through, very often without attribution. Both the idea itself and the name could have filtered through somehow without my being aware of it. So I'm not claiming independence. It's your contribution. The idea of common knowledge is your contribution and there's no question about it. This is all yours. I've been saying it for a while now, and I'll say it again. And let's meet.'

I was in Stony Brook at that time. I went down to Princeton, and I met Lewis and Kripke. We had a nice conversation. By that time there was a kosher dining club in Princeton. I'll have to tell you some stories about Princeton when I was originally there in the fifties. It was a hotbed of anti-Semitism. But you know, the world progresses, and by 1981–82 there was a kosher dining club; and in fact Hugo Sonnenschein became provost of Princeton. He's Jewish, of course. And then afterwards there was even a Shapiro who became President of Princeton University. He is also Jewish. So we're making progress. I had a nice day in Princeton and made it up with Lewis and Kripke, and everything was fine. And at every opportunity, including this one, I've been acknowledging that the idea of common knowledge is Lewis's idea. Period. No independence, nothing.

However, let me just add this: Lewis had the idea of common knowledge, and this is very clear. What he did *not* have is the agreement theorem. He did not have the agreement theorem, he had no glimpse of the agreement theorem, nothing like that. So I still lay claim to the agreement theorem.

O.R.:
You met both Lewis and Kripke. Were you already interested at that time in the syntactic part of epistemic logic?

R.A.:
I'm not sure I got into the syntactic thing at that point. No, I don't think so, no. I was bothered by this question of where the partition structure comes from. That was in the early '80s: it bothered me even then. But I sort of finessed it. I said, well, *descriptively*, not *formally*: a state of the world includes everything that is relevant about that state, including what people know about that state. It's rather like a dictionary. It's nothing substantive, it's like a dictionary. And that statement occurs in my '87 paper 'Correlated Equilibria as an Expression of Bayesian Rationality'.[4] But actually to *describe* that dictionary, to do that and carry through this idea formally, I didn't see how to do it. I didn't see how to do it and therefore I can't say I was actively looking for it. I don't think so.

And then came a paper by Samet,[5] whom I have already mentioned. That's where I got this idea that we have a syntax, we have a set of statements, a list of statements; this list has to be complete and consistent. By complete we mean that every sentence — either the sentence itself or its negation — is in the list. Consistent means there are no logical contradictions in the list. A beautiful idea. You take a language and you say everything that can be said in that language. Everything. And then you look at lists, complete and consistent in this sense. And you say: that list *is* a state of the world. It's a beautiful idea. And this came out of Samet's paper.

I took that, developed it and formalised it. In some respects it was already formal. The fruition of this was the paper which was published in the *International Journal of Game Theory* in 1999, 'Interactive Epistemology',[6] which takes that and actually builds a semantic space out of this 'dictionary'. I was at Yale University for six weeks in '89, where I gave a course on interactive epistemology, and presented that idea. It took another ten years to publish it because

[4] *Econometrica,* 55(1), pp. 1–18, 1987.
[5] D. Samet. Ignoring Ignorance and Agreeing to Disagree. *Journal of Economic Theory,* 52, pp. 190–207, 1990.
[6] *International Journal of Game Theory,* 28(3), pp. 263–300, 1999.

I'm very slow to publish. Other stuff is going on and there's family and grandchildren, all kinds of stuff happening. It took ten years, but eventually I did publish, basically, the notes from the six weeks in '89 at Yale on interactive epistemology. So that's how that came about. I'm convinced now that semantic game theory is fine, but the syntactic is more basic. Say it in English! If you have something to say, say it in English.

O.R.:
What is the relevance of epistemic logic? To what kind of topic is it best geared to contribute?

R.A.:
It's for exploring the foundations of game theory. You want to ask yourself: why do we look only at the objective mixed equilibria? Then one thing leads to another, you get the agreement theorem and then you have to ask yourself where this comes from. It's foundational work. It also develops a toolkit that enables you to think precisely about these things. It allows you to formulate precise questions.

Let me give you another application. I published this paper in 1995, 'Backward Induction and Common Knowledge of Rationality'.[7] People raised their eyebrows about it, and said: this is open to question, because according to Aumann's definition of rationality, people also have to behave rationally at nodes of the game tree that they themselves have excluded by previous actions. So they know they're not going to get there, but they still have to behave rationally. I wrote a lengthy discussion in that paper and I do think it makes sense and I think people should read the discussion part very, very carefully. Part of what ails the world is that people only look superficially at a paper. I really thought carefully about these problems. And I think the criticism is *not* justified.

But I always like to look at the other side of the coin. I said, OK, people don't like this idea that you have to behave rationally at nodes of the game tree that you yourself have excluded. They call these 'counterfactual conditionals'. In order to avoid using counterfactual

[7] *Games and Economic Behavior,* 8(1), pp. 6–19, 1995.

conditionals, Adam Brandenburger and I replaced the idea of *knowledge* of something by *belief,* by the idea of *strong* belief. This means I continue to believe that everybody is rational until it becomes *logically* impossible to do so, until it's obvious we've reached a node of the game tree where somebody had to behave irrationally. And then we developed this idea of common strong belief of rationality. It seemed intuitive that this should lead to backward induction. Adam and I worked on this for five or six years and we couldn't prove it.

Then one day a paper crossed my desk written by Battigalli and Siniscalchi.[8] They did exactly that. Fantastic! It is a wonderful piece of work; it's very deep and it's very roundabout, but they did it! It's very good.

Battigalli and Siniscalchi did it using a very complex *semantic* model. In a semantic model it's difficult to express what it means for something to be logically impossible. In a semantic model, something that is logically impossible is represented by an empty set; but if an event is represented by an empty set, that doesn't mean it's logically impossible. You have to have a *universal* semantic model to say that, and these models are large and clumsy.

Now I have a student who is just completing his doctorate. His name is Itai Arieli, a very bright and deep young man. He managed to overcome this difficulty with a syntactic proof. 'Logically impossible' has a very transparent meaning in a syntactic model. Itai has a straightforward — well, straightforward may not be the right word — but he has a largely syntactic proof of this which solves the problem without encountering the conceptual difficulties of the semantic approach.

How does this relate to your question? The syntactic and the semantic models provide a *toolkit* for thinking about these problems. You want to fix some system, you need the screwdrivers. This is the toolkit for dealing with these problems and for attacking them, and thinking about them logically.

---

[8]P. Battigalli and M. Siniscalchi, Strong Belief and Forward Induction Reasoning. *Journal of Economic Theory,* 106(2), pp. 356–391, 2002.

O.R.:
So if I understand correctly, you see this work in the characterisation of solution concepts as foundational for game theory. Could you think of it in the same way as the work in the foundations of decision theory or subjective probability, for example?

R.A.:
I think maybe it's less important in one-person decision theory. It does not play much of a role there. Savage,[9] Anscombe–Aumann,[10] it's not *essential*, I don't see applications there.

But let me say it's not just foundational stuff. I wrote a paper with Jacques Dreze[11] about rational expectations in games. In some sense this grew out of the epistemic approach, which as I say started with the paper in the JME about subjectivity and correlation. This is more or less the latest development there; not the latest development in foundational terms but in *practical* terms.

In this paper with Jacques what we're really trying to promote is a revolution. We haven't been too successful yet. We're saying: Listen! Equilibrium is not the way to look at games. Nash equilibrium is *king* in game theory. Absolutely king. We say: No! Nash equilibrium is an interesting concept, it's an important concept, but it's not the most basic concept. The most basic concept should be: *to maximise your utility given your information*, in a game just like in any other situation. What does that imply when you make strong assumptions like common priors and common knowledge of rationality? Does it imply Nash equilibrium? No, it does not! It implies something else, and we can write formulas for it. That's the way to go.

In some sense the epistemic world of ideas led to this. This work started with a remark Jacques made. Jacques visited Israel in '96, and we went on a trip to Petra in Jordan with a whole group of economists who were visiting Israel at that time. I was sitting next to Jacques

[9] L. J. Savage, *The Foundations of Statistics,* New York: John Wiley, 1954.
[10] F. J. Anscombe and R. J. Aumann. A Definition of Subjective Probability. *The Annals of Mathematical Statistics,* 34(1), pp. 199–205, 1963.
[11] R. J. Aumann and J. H. Dreze, Rational Expectations in Games, *American Economic Review,* 98(1), pp. 72–86, 2008.

in the bus and he said to me: 'Bob, how would you define values in games that are not zero-sum?' We started thinking about it, and a year or two later I went to Louvain-la-Neuve. We thought about it some more, and eventually it grew into this paper. So in one sense the *question* didn't come from epistemic roots, but the *answer* came from epistemic roots. In two-person zero-sum games, common knowledge of rationality and common priors imply the value. That's it. You don't need the equilibrium concept. This gives a solid foundation to the value of two-person zero-sum games, which was missing before. Then you take that and you extend it to other games. I think that should replace Nash equilibrium as the fundamental concept of game theory. But it hasn't yet...

So epistemic considerations also lead to conclusions *outside* their own domain, which is the test of any important scientific theory or development. It's got to lead some place outside, not just inside.

O.R.:
In this paper with Dreze you make a strong case for analysing interaction in terms of common priors and common knowledge of rationality. Do you think these are fundamental assumptions?

R.A.:
Yes, I do. Let me put it this way: common priors is in my opinion a very reasonable assumption, *more* reasonable than common knowledge of rationality. People usually take it the other way around. They think that common knowledge of rationality is something they can buy; it's a strong assumption but it's something they can buy. But common priors? They ask 'Where did these come from?' *I* think common priors are more reasonable, because in some very basic sense you want somehow to account for differences in probability assessments. Why do people differ in their probability assessments? It seems reasonable that at *some* level it's because they had different inputs. So they got to know different things, and this is what accounts for the different posteriors. When you say that differences in probability assessments are due to different information, that is the common prior assumption. So this is really something very basic and very important.

Common knowledge of rationality is not that kind of thing at all. It's a very far-fetched assumption. I don't even know if *I'm* rational, but let's say I am. I'm willing to assume you're rational, but do I *know* that you *know* that I'm rational? It's not that common knowledge of rationality is something basic; it's some sort of *benchmark.*

The way we put it in the paper is: tic-tac-toe is a draw. What does that mean, that it *is* a draw? What it means is that under common knowledge of rationality the result will be a draw. It doesn't mean that a smart kid would not lose the game, because a smart kid might play for a win, or try, because that kid does not assume the other one knows that he is rational and so might play for some kind of trap and might lose as a result. Common knowledge of rationality is not something about the real world, it's a sort of a benchmark. It says: this is the way things work out when there's no irrationality in the system. If there is no irrationality in the system at all, this is how things work out. Everything else is calculated as a *departure* from the benchmark. It's like a no-friction assumption in physical systems, or the no-air-resistance assumption. When you have the formula for acceleration of a body under gravity, you let something fall, it assumes no air resistance. But there *is* air resistance. Does that make the formula for no air resistance unimportant? No, it's very important; you start out with the assumption that under *ideal* conditions, you have no air resistance, and then from there you can go and calculate what happens *with* air resistance. I don't think common knowledge of rationality is at all a reasonable assumption about the real world. I believe common priors *is* a reasonable assumption about the real world. Common priors is much more basic than CKR. But if you don't buy CKR, you won't get the value of a two-person zero-sum game.

So in order to answer Jacques' question, we do need CKR because he wants to generalize the value. The value of the game is the outcome when people play *correctly.* So when people play correctly, you have CKR in some sense. That's the *definition* of correct play.

O.R.:

You mention in that paper that the notion of value was something that was more or less forgotten, but it returns when you look at a game from the perspective of common priors and common knowledge of rationality. Do you think there are other topics, especially in epistemic logic, that have been somewhat relegated to the background and should be given more prominence?

R.A.:
One should probably try to look at relaxing these conditions of CKR or of common priors. Shmuel Zamir spoke with me about 'approximately common priors'. One could try to look at rational expectations in specific classes of games. I can't think at the moment about something really foundational but my research, as far as I've experienced, never worked that way. Something seizes you and then you go in that direction. If you don't, then it hasn't seized you. Some kind of approximation to these ideal conditions is one question that can be asked. It's important to keep the application in mind, keep your purpose in mind. But to point to something specific, no, I don't know.

O.R.:
You mentioned the common knowledge of rationality assumption as a benchmark. Would you think the same of the assumption or the fact that agents in most epistemic logic systems are so-called logically omniscient?

R.A.:
Logical omniscience, that is a very important problem. It's a problem I've thought about a little. Not that I've gotten anywhere with it. I really don't know what to do with it. It is a very important problem, which does need treatment, but I don't know what to do with it.

O.R.:
Do you think recent work on unawareness could...

R.A.:
Unawareness, yes, those two: logical omniscience and unawareness, those are the two big open problems as far as I know. I think there's been work on them recently, though, but I haven't studied it. *Mea culpa.* I cannot venture an opinion as to whether the recent work

really gets to the foundations of the problem. But those *are* the two outstanding problems. Maybe somebody has solved them in the meantime. Unawareness and logical omniscience: even though I am not omniscient – I do not claim to be omniscient — I'm unaware of satisfactory solutions to those two problems. But they are two very important problems, which do cry out for satisfactory treatment.

In that connection maybe I should mention something else which is maybe not particularly logical, but it has to do with logic. That is the problem of how much to calculate when you're optimising something. Most work that I know of, all the work I know of, does not take the cost of calculation into account. So the question is, how much do you calculate? If you really want to optimise the solution to something, how much should you calculate in order to find that solution? You want to get the cheapest possible solution without knowing what to expect. In order to even calculate the *time* it would take to optimise, you have to do a calculation, and that calculation in itself may not be worthwhile. When you're playing chess and the clock is ticking, how much do you calculate? It's not at all clear. Deep Blue had to solve this problem somehow. I don't know how they solved it. This is a very important problem, which has not been solved satisfactorily. It's in the same league as unawareness and logical omniscience.

O.R.:
So you say that the big issue or the big challenges for us now are about relaxing the fundamental assumptions?

R.A.:
No, I think logical omniscience and unawareness and how much to calculate, those are the three big outstanding issues at this time. The matter of relaxing, I don't think it's *that* important. It's not that basic. Those other things are more basic and I think they'll be more difficult to achieve. Relaxing is also relaxing the focus, in some sense: you see things more blurred. I like focus.

O.R.:
Are you optimistic about progress on these three questions?

R.A.:
Who knows? *Que sera, sera.* Those are Hilbert's three problems for epistemic game theory or logic. The third question is not really epistemic but it's also there and it has philosophical sides to it. But the unawareness and the logical omniscience, absolutely. Whether I'm optimistic, I don't know. It will be very nice if somebody solves them.

Part 1

"Pure" Interactive Epistemology

Chapter 2

Agreeing to Disagree*,†

Abstract: Two people, 1 and 2, are said to have *common knowledge* of an event E if both know it, 1 knows that 2 knows it, 2 knows that 1 knows it, 1 knows that 2 knows that 1 knows it, and so on.

Theorem. *If two people have the same priors, and their posteriors for an event A are common knowledge, then these posteriors are equal.*

If two people have the same priors, and their posteriors for a given event A are common knowledge, then these posteriors must be equal. This is so even though they may base their posteriors on quite different information. In brief, people with the same priors *cannot agree to disagree.*

We publish this observation with some diffidence, since once one has the appropriate framework, it is mathematically trivial. Intuitively, though, it is not quite obvious; and it is of some interest in areas in which people's beliefs about each other's beliefs are of

*Reprinted from *Annals of Statistics* (1976), 4(6), 1236–1239, with permission from Institute of Mathematical Statistics and Wiley.

†This work was supported by National Science Foundation Grant SOC74-11446 at the Institute for Mathematical Studies in the Social Sciences, Stanford University.

importance, such as game theory[1] and the economics of information.[2] A "concrete" illustration that may clarify matters (and that may be read at this point) is found at the end of the paper.

The key notion is that of "common knowledge." Call the two people 1 and 2. When we say that an event is "common knowledge," we mean more than just that both 1 and 2 know it; we require also that 1 knows that 2 knows it, 2 knows that 1 knows it, 1 knows that 2 knows that 1 knows it, and so on. For example, if 1 and 2 are both present when the event happens and see each other there, then the event becomes common knowledge. In our case, if 1 and 2 tell each other their posteriors and trust each other, then the posteriors are common knowledge. The result is not true if we merely assume that the persons know each other's posteriors.

Formally, let $(\Omega, \mathscr{B}, p)$ be a probability space, $\mathscr{P}_1$ and $\mathscr{P}_2$ partitions of Ω whose join[3] $\mathscr{P}_1 \vee \mathscr{P}_2$ consists of nonnull events.[4] In the interpretation, $(\Omega, \mathscr{B})$ is the space of states of the world, p the common prior of 1 and 2, and $\mathscr{P}_i$ the information partition of i; that is, if the true state of the world is ω, then i is informed of that element $\mathbf{P}_i(\omega)$ of $\mathscr{P}_i$ that contains ω. Given ω in Ω, an event E is called *common knowledge at* ω if E includes that member of the meet[5] $\mathscr{P}_1 \wedge \mathscr{P}_2$ that contains ω. We will show below that this definition is equivalent to the informal description given above.

Let A be an event, and let $\mathbf{q}_i$ denote the posterior probability $p(A|\mathscr{P}_i)$ of A given i's information; i.e., if $\omega \in \Omega$, then $\mathbf{q}_i(\omega) = p(A \cap \mathbf{P}_i(\omega))/p(\mathbf{P}_i(\omega))$.

---

[1]Cf. Harsanyi (1967–1968); also Aumann (1974), especially Section 9j (page 92), in which the question answered here was originally raised.

[2]Cf. e.g., Radner (1968) and (1972); also the review by Grossman and Stiglitz (1976) and the papers quoted there.

[3]Coarsest common refinement of $\mathscr{P}_1$ and $\mathscr{P}_2$.

[4]Events whose (prior) probability does not vanish.

[5]Finest common coarsening of $\mathscr{P}_1$ and $\mathscr{P}_2$.

Proposition. *Let $\omega \in \Omega$, and let q_1 and q_2 be numbers. If it is common knowledge at ω that $\mathbf{q}_1 = q_1$ and $\mathbf{q}_2 = q_2$, then $q_1 = q_2$.*

Proof. Let P be the member of $\mathscr{P}_1 \wedge \mathscr{P}_2$ that contains ω. Write $P = \cup_j P^j$, where the P^j are disjoint members of $\mathscr{P}_1$. Since $\mathbf{q}_1 = q_1$ throughout P, we have $p(A \cap P^j)/p(P^j) = q_1$ for all j; hence $p(A \cap P^j) = q_1 p(P^j)$, and so by summing over j we get $p(A \cap P) = q_1 p(P)$. Similarly $p(A \cap P) = q_2 p(P)$, and so $q_1 = q_2$. This completes the proof.

To see that the formal definition of "common knowledge" is equivalent to the informal description, let $\omega \in \Omega$, and call a member ω' of Ω *reachable from* ω if there is a sequence $P^1, P^2, \ldots, P^k$ such that $\omega \in P^1, \omega' \in P^k$, and consecutive P^j intersect and belong alternatively to $\mathscr{P}_1$ and $\mathscr{P}_2$. Suppose now that ω is the true state of the world, $P^1 = \mathbf{P}_1(\omega)$, and E is an event. To say that 1 "knows" E means that E includes P^1. To say that 1 knows that 2 knows E means that E includes all P^2 in $\mathscr{P}_2$ that intersect P^1. To say that 1 knows that 2 knows that 1 knows E means that E includes all P^3 in $\mathscr{P}_1$ that intersect P^2 in $\mathscr{P}_2$ that intersect P^1. And so on. Thus all sentences of the form "i knows that i' knows that i knows ... E" (where $i' = 3 - i$) are true if and only if E contains all ω' reachable from ω. But the set of all ω' reachable from ω is a member of $\mathscr{P}_1 \wedge \mathscr{P}_2$; so the desired equivalence is established.

The result fails when people merely know each other's posteriors. Suppose Ω has 4 elements $\alpha, \beta, \gamma, \delta$ of equal (prior) probability, $\mathscr{P}_1 = \{\alpha\beta, \gamma\delta\}$, $\mathscr{P}_2 = \{\alpha\beta\gamma, \delta\}$, $A = \alpha\delta$, and $\omega = \alpha$. Then 1 knows that $\mathbf{q}_2$ is $\frac{1}{3}$, and 2 knows that $\mathbf{q}_1$ is $\frac{1}{2}$; but 2 thinks that 1 may not know what $\mathbf{q}_2$ is ($\frac{1}{3}$ or 1).

Worthy of note is the implicit assumption that the information partitions $\mathscr{P}_1$ and $\mathscr{P}_2$ are themselves common knowledge. Actually, this constitutes no loss of generality. Included in the full description of a state ω of the world is the manner in which information is imparted to the two persons. This implies that the information sets $\mathbf{P}_1(\omega)$ and

$\mathbf{P}_2(\omega)$ are indeed defined unambiguously as functions of ω, and that these functions are known to both players.

Consider next the assumption of equal priors for different people. John Harsanyi (1968) has argued eloquently that differences in subjective probabilities should be traced exclusively to differences in information — that there is no rational basis for people who have always been fed precisely the same information to maintain different subjective probabilities. This, of course, is equivalent to the assumption of equal priors. The result of this paper might be considered evidence against this view, as there are in fact people who respect each other's opinions and nevertheless disagree heartily about subjective probabilities. But this evidence is not conclusive: even people who respect each other's acumen may ascribe to each other errors in calculating posteriors. Of course we do not mean simple arithmetical mistakes, but rather systematic biases such as those discussed by Tversky and Kahneman (1974). In private conversation, Tversky has suggested that people may also be biased because of psychological factors, that may make them disregard information that is unpleasant or does not conform to previously formed notions.

There is a considerable literature about reaching agreement on subjective probabilities; a recent paper is DeGroot (1974), where a bibliography on the subject may be found. A "practical" method is the Delphi technique (see, e.g., Dalkey (1972)). It seems to me that the Harsanyi doctrine is implicit in much of this literature; reconciling subjective probabilities makes sense if it is a question of implicitly exchanging information, but not if we are talking about "innate" differences in priors. The result of this paper might be considered a theoretical foundation for the reconciliation of subjective probabilities.

As an illustration, suppose 1 and 2 have a uniform prior on the parameter of a coin, and let A be the event that the coin will come up H (heads) on the next toss. Suppose that each person is permitted to make one previous toss, and that these tosses come up H and T (tails) respectively. If each one's information consists precisely of the outcome of his toss, then the posteriors for A will be $\frac{2}{3}$ and $\frac{1}{3}$ respectively. If each one then informs the other one of his posterior, then they will both conclude that the previous tosses came up once H and once T, so that both posteriors will be revised to $\frac{1}{2}$.

Suppose now that each person is permitted to make several previous tosses, but that neither one knows how many tosses are allowed the other one. For example, perhaps both make 4 tosses, which come up $HHHT$ for 1, and $HTTT$ for 2. They then inform each other that their posteriors are $\frac{2}{3}$ and $\frac{1}{3}$ respectively. Now these posteriors may result from a single observation, from 4 observations, or from more. Since neither one knows on what observations the other's posterior is based, he may be inclined to give more weight to his own observations. Some revision of posteriors would certainly be called for even in such a case; but it does not seem clear that it would necessarily lead to equal posteriors.

Presumably, such a revision would take into account each person's prior on the number of tosses available to him and to the other person. By assumption these two priors are the same, but each person gets additional private information — namely, the actual number of tosses he is allotted. By use of the prior and the information that the posteriors are, respectively, $\frac{2}{3}$ and $\frac{1}{3}$, new posteriors may be calculated. If the players inform each other of these new posteriors, further revision may be called for. Our result implies that the process of exchanging information on the posteriors for A will continue until these posteriors are equal.

References

Aumann, R. J., 1974, Subjectivity and correlation in randomized strategies, *J. Math. Econom.* 1, 67–96. [Chapter 7]

Dalkey, N. C., 1972, *Studies in the Quality of Life*, Lexington Books, Lexington, Mass.

DeGroot, M. H., 1974, Reaching a consensus, *J. Amer. Statist. Assoc.* 69, 118–121.

Grossman, S. J. and J. E. Stiglitz, 1976, Information and competitive price systems, *Amer. Econom. Rev.* 46, 246–253.

Harsanyi, J., 1967–1968, Games of incomplete information played by Bayesian players, Parts I–III, *Management Sci.* 14, 159–182, 320–334, 486–502.

Radner, R., 1968, Competitive equilibrium under uncertainty, *Econometrica* 36, 21–58.

Radner, R., 1972, Existence of equilibrium plans, prices, and price expectations in a sequence of markets, *Econometrica* 40, 289–304.

Tversky, A. and D. Kahneman, 1974, Judgment under uncertainty: Heuristics and biases, *Science* 185, 1124–1131.

Chapter 3

Interactive Epistemology I: Knowledge*,†

Abstract: Formal Interactive Epistemology deals with the logic of knowledge and belief when there is more than one agent or "player." One is interested not only in each person's knowledge about substantive matters, but also in his knowledge about the others' knowledge. This paper examines two parallel approaches to the subject. The first is the *semantic* approach, in which knowledge is represented by a space Ω of *states of the world*, together with partitions $\mathscr{I}_i$ of Ω for each player i; the atom of $\mathscr{I}_i$ containing a given state ω of the world represents i's knowledge at that state — the set of those other states that i cannot distinguish from ω. The second is the *syntactic* approach, in which knowledge is embodied in sentences constructed according to certain syntactic rules. This paper examines the relation between the two approaches, and shows that they are in a sense equivalent.

*Reprinted from *International Journal of Game Theory* (1999), 28, 263–300, with permission from Springer.

†This paper is based on notes originally distributed in connection with a sequence of six lectures on Interactive Epistemology given at the Cowles Foundation for Research in Economics, Yale University, in the spring of 1989, and expanded and corrected several times since then. Previous versions were distributed in connection with the tutorial and workshop on "Knowledge and Game Theory" held at the Summer Institute in Game Theory, State University of New York at Stony Brook, July 20–24, 1992, and in connection with the Fifth Jerusalem Summer School in Economic Theory, on "Rationality of Action and Belief in the Economy," June 13–23, 1994. The author is grateful to Prof. Dov Samet for important help in preparing the current version. Research support from the USNSF under grant SES-9209277 and previous grants is gratefully acknowledged.

In game theory and economics, the semantic approach has heretofore been most prevalent. A question that often arises in this connection is whether, in what sense, and why the space Ω and the partitions $\mathscr{I}_i$ can be taken as given and commonly known by the players. An answer to this question is provided by the syntactic approach.

0. Introduction

In interactive contexts like game theory and economics, it is important to consider what each player knows and believes about what the other players know and believe. Here we discuss and relate two formalisms — the *semantic* and the *syntactic* — for analyzing these matters. The current paper treats knowledge only; probability is left to a companion paper (Aumann 1999).

The semantic formalism consists of a "partition structure:" a space Ω of *states of the world*, together with a partition of Ω for each player, whose atoms represent *information sets*[1] of that player; Ω is called the *universe*. Like in probability theory, *events* are subsets of Ω; intuitively, an event is identified with the set of all those states of the world at which the event obtains. Thus an event E obtains at a state ω if and only if $\omega \in E$, and a player i "knows" E at ω if and only if E includes his information set at ω. For i to know E is itself an event, denoted K_iE: it obtains at some states ω, and at others does not. The knowledge operators K_i can therefore be concatenated; for example, K_jK_iE denotes the event "j knows that i knows E."

The syntactic formalism, on the other hand, is built on propositions, expressed in a formal language. The language has logical operators and connectives, and also operators k_i expressing knowledge: If e is a sentence, then k_ie is also a sentence, whose meaning is "i knows e." The operators k_i can be iterated: The sentence

[1]I.e., he can distinguish between states ω and ω' if and only if they are in different atoms of his partition.

$k_j k_i e$ means "j knows that i knows e." Logical relations between the various propositions are expressed by formal rules.

There is a rough correspondence between the two formalisms: Events correspond to sentences, unions to disjunctions, intersections to conjunctions, inclusions to implications, complementation to negation, and semantic knowledge operators K_i to syntactic knowledge operators k_i. But the correspondence really *is* quite rough; for example, only some — not all — events correspond to syntactically admissible sentences.

While the semantic formalism is the more convenient and widely used of the two, it is conceptually not quite straightforward. One question that often arises is, what do the players know about the formalism itself? Does each know the others' partitions? If so, from where does this knowledge derive? If not, how can the formalism indicate what each player knows about the others' knowledge? For example, why would the event $K_j K_i E$ then signify that j knows that i knows E?

Another point concerns the interpretation of the concept "state of the world." In game theoretic applications, for example, the state of the world often specifies the players' actions. Some feel that this restricts the freedom of action of a player, by "forcing" him, at the state ω, to choose the action that ω specifies for him. Why, they ask, should he not be allowed, if he wishes, to choose a different action at that state?

More generally, the whole idea of "state of the world," and of a partition structure that accurately reflects the players' knowledge about other players' knowledge, is not transparent. What *are* the states? Can they be explicitly described? Where do they come from? Where do the information partitions come from? What justifies positing this kind of model, and what justifies a particular partition structure?

One may also ask about the global properties of the partition structure. We have seen that there is a rough correspondence between the semantic and syntactic models. Do global properties of the partition structure correspond to anything syntactic? For example, if the partition structure is finite, does this correspond to anything in the syntactic formalism? Can finiteness of the partition structure be formulated in syntactic terms — that is, in plain English?

A related point is that the semantic formalism is not *canonical*: There are many essentially different partition structures. Which is the "right" one?

These questions are not unanswerable. For example, an answer to the last question (which is the "right" partition structure?) is that it usually doesn't matter; proofs using the semantic formalism generally work with *any* partition structure. We also hold that the issue of the players' "freedom of action," while superficially puzzling, poses no real problem (Aumann and Brandenburger 1995, Section 7a, p. 1174). Yet all in all, there is little doubt that conceptually and philosophically, the semantic formalism is comparatively subtle.

In contrast, the syntactic formalism is entirely straightforward. One reasons from explicit hypotheses to explicit conclusions using explicit, transparent rules of deduction. There are no philosophical subtleties, no problems with the meaning of the sentences that enter the syntactic formalism. And *this* formalism *is* canonical.

Thus the semantic formalism appears to involve nontrivial conceptual issues. There are two approaches to these issues. One is to deal with them on the verbal, conceptual level, while retaining the semantic formalism as a formal primitive. In the other, the semantic formalism — the partition structure — is no longer taken as primitive, but is explicitly constructed from another formalism.

In the past, such explicit constructions have employed a hierarchical procedure (see Section 10c). While perfectly coherent, these hierarchical procedures are cumbersome and far from transparent. Here, we construct a canonical semantic partition structure in a more straightforward way, directly in terms of the syntactic formalism. In this construction, the states are simply lists of propositions. Each state ω is *defined* by specifying those propositions that hold at ω; any list of propositions that is complete, coherent and consistent in the appropriate sense constitutes a state.

Before presenting this construction, we set forth both the semantic (Sections 1, 2, 3) and the syntactic (Sections 4, 5) formalisms in detail. Section 1 presents the foundations of the semantic formalism for the fundamental case of one player, including an axiomatic development of the knowledge operator. Section 2 develops the many-player case, concentrating on a succinct presentation of the fundamental properties of common knowledge. Section 3 is a conceptual discussion of the semantic formalism, presenting in more detail some of the issues discussed above, and setting the stage for the subsequent canonical construction in terms of the syntactic formalism. Section 4 formally presents the syntactic formalism, and Section 5 discusses it. Section 6 constructs the canonical semantic partition structure in terms of the syntactic formalism, and Section 7 is a conceptual discussion of this construction. Section 8 establishes in precise terms the above-discussed "rough" correspondence between the syntactic and the semantic formalisms. In Section 9, this is used to show that a list of sentences in the syntactic formalism is logically consistent if and only if it has a semantic "model." Section 10 is devoted to additional discussion, including discussion of the relationship between the "direct" construction of the canonical semantic partition structure that is presented here, and the hierarchical construction to which we alluded above. An appendix discusses the cardinality of the canonical universe (which, when there is more than one player, is at least that of the continuum).

This paper originated in notes for a series of lectures given at Yale University in 1989, and informally circulated, in various forms, for many years thereafter. Much of the material is basically due to others, and has been known for some time,[2] though perhaps not in the form presented here. Nevertheless, this is not a review; there is no attempt to cover any significant part of the literature, nor even to cite it. Rather, it is largely expository; the purpose is to make the basic facts of interactive epistemology accessible in a succinct form that should be useful for game theorists and economists.

---

[2]E.g., Fagin *et al.* (1995); Hintikka (1992); Kripke (1959); Lewis (1969).

Doing justice to all the relevant previous work would take more effort, time and space than we can afford here. However, we do wish to cite one particular work to which we owe the greatest immediate debt: Dov Samet's "Ignoring Ignorance and Agreeing to Disagree" (1990), from which we drew the simple but ingenious and fundamental idea of formally characterizing a state of the world by the sentences that hold there.

1. The Semantics of Knowledge for a Single Individual

In this section we present and examine the relationships between five different but equivalent semantic formalizations of knowledge: knowledge functions, information functions, information partitions, knowledge operators, and knowledge ufields (universal fields).

We start with a set Ω whose members are called *states of the world*, or simply *states*. An *event* is defined as a subset of Ω; the family of all events is denoted $\mathscr{E}$. This formalism may be familiar to some readers from probability theory; an event in the ordinary sense of the word, like "it will be sunny tomorrow," is identified in the formalism with the set of all states at which it is sunny tomorrow. Union of events corresponds to disjunction, intersection to conjunction, and complementation ($\sim$) to negation. For example, the event "it will snow or rain tomorrow" is the same as the union of the event "it will snow tomorrow" with the event "it will rain tomorrow." When E and F are events with $E \subset F$, we will say that *E entails F*.

We will assume given a function κ on Ω, which we call the *knowledge function*. The range of κ is an abstract set, whose members represent different possible "states of knowledge" of some fixed individual i. Thus, $\kappa(\omega)$ represents the knowledge that i possesses when the true state of the world is ω. For example, this knowledge might include today's weather, but not tomorrow's. A related way of thinking about $\kappa(\omega)$ is as the signal that i receives from the outside world when the true state of the world is ω.

Define a function $\mathbf{I}$ on Ω by

$$\mathbf{I}(\omega) := \{\omega' \in \Omega : \kappa(\omega') = \kappa(\omega)\}. \tag{1.1}$$

In words, $\mathbf{I}(\omega)$ is the set of all those states that i cannot distinguish from ω. Thus if ω is the true state of the world, i will usually not know this; he will know only that *some* state in $\mathbf{I}(\omega)$ is the true one. $\mathbf{I}(\omega)$ consists of those states ω' that i considers possible.

The reader may verify that for any states ω and ω',

$$\omega \in \mathbf{I}(\omega), \text{ and} \tag{1.11}$$

$$\mathbf{I}(\omega) \text{ and } \mathbf{I}(\omega') \text{ are either disjoint or identical.} \tag{1.12}$$

Any function $\mathbf{I}$ on Ω satisfying 1.11 and 1.12 is called an *information function.* From 1.11 and 1.12 it follows that the distinct $\mathbf{I}(\omega)$ form a *partition* of Ω; that is, they are pairwise disjoint and their union is Ω. We call this partition i's *information partition*, and denote it $\mathscr{I}$; atoms of $\mathscr{I}$ are called *information sets.* The family of all unions of events in $\mathscr{I}$, denoted $\mathscr{K}$, is a *universal field*, or *ufield* for short; that is, it is closed under complementation and under arbitrary (not necessarily finite or denumerable) unions, and therefore also under arbitrary intersections. It is called i's *knowledge ufield.*

Now define an operator $K : \mathscr{E} \to \mathscr{E}$ as follows: for any event E,

$$KE \text{ is the union of all the events in } \mathscr{I} \text{ that are included in } E. \tag{1.2}$$

Equivalent forms of this definition are

$$\omega \in KE \text{ if and only if } \mathbf{I}(\omega) \subset E, \text{ and} \tag{1.21}$$

$$KE \text{ is the largest element of } \mathscr{K} \text{ that is included in } E. \tag{1.22}$$

In words, KE is the event that i knows that the event E obtains;[3] more explicitly, the set of all states ω at which i knows that E contains ω (he usually will not know the true ω).

[3]By "obtains" we mean "happened, is happening, or will happen." Time is irrelevant; we want to avoid tenses. If the reader wishes, he can think of a state ω of the world as a complete possible history, from the big bang until the end of the world. Thus "it will snow tomorrow" and "it snowed yesterday" are both events, which may or may not "obtain" at a given ω.

From 1.22 it follows that $KE \in \mathscr{K}$ for all E. Conversely, if $E \in \mathscr{K}$, then 1.22 yields $E = KE$, so each member of $\mathscr{K}$ has the form KE. Thus we conclude that

$$\mathscr{K} = K\mathscr{E} := \{KE : E \in \mathscr{E}\}. \tag{1.23}$$

In words, $\mathscr{K}$ is the family of events that express i's knowing some particular event.

The reader may verify, directly from its definition, that the operator K has the following properties (for all events E and F):

$$KE \subset E \tag{1.31}$$

$$E \subset F \text{ implies } KE \subset KF \tag{1.32}$$

$$\sim KE \subset K \sim KE. \tag{1.33}$$

In words, 1.31 says that a person can only know something if it is true; and 1.33, that if he does *not* know something, then he knows that he does not know it. 1.32 expresses the intuition that if E entails F, and i knows that E, then he may conclude that F, so he knows F. Any operator $K : \mathscr{E} \to \mathscr{E}$ satisfying 1.31 through 1.33 is called a *knowledge operator.*

Note also that

$$K\left(\bigcap_{\alpha} E_{\alpha}\right) = \bigcap_{\alpha} K(E_{\alpha}), \tag{1.4}$$

where the intersection may be over an arbitrary index set; this, too, follows directly from 1.2. In words, 1.4 says that i knows each of several events if and only if he knows that they all obtain.

Rather than starting with the knowledge function κ as a primitive, and deriving from it the information function $\mathbf{I}$, the information partition $\mathscr{I}$, the knowledge operator K, and the knowledge ufield $\mathscr{K}$, one can start from any other one of these five and derive the other four from it. The only one of these derivations that is not entirely straightforward[4] is that starting with K; we show below how to do this. To have a term for the relationship between the objects κ, $\mathbf{I}$, $\mathscr{I}$, K, $\mathscr{K}$ defined in this section, call any two of them *associated.*

We now show how $\mathbf{I}$, κ, $\mathscr{I}$ and $\mathscr{K}$ can be derived if we start with a knowledge operator K as a primitive. So suppose we are given such a K, i.e., an operator $K : \mathscr{E} \to \mathscr{E}$ satisfying 1.31 through 1.33. It is enough to define $\mathbf{I}$, as we have already noted that $\mathscr{I}$, κ, and $\mathscr{K}$ can be derived from $\mathbf{I}$. We define

$$\mathbf{I}(\omega) := \sim K \sim \{\omega\}. \tag{1.5}$$

In words, 1.5 defines $\mathbf{I}(\omega)$ as the set of all those states at which i does not know that ω did not occur; i.e., those he cannot distinguish from ω, the ones he considers possible. This is precisely the intuitive meaning of $\mathbf{I}$ that is embodied in the original definition 1.1. To justify the definition (1.5), we must show

Proposition 1.6. *As defined from K by 1.5, $\mathbf{I}$ is an information function and satisfies 1.21.*

Indeed, by proving that $\mathbf{I}$ satisfies 1.21, we show that it is associated with K in the sense explained at the end of Section 1. Thus if we start with $\mathbf{I}$, define K from it by means of 1.2, and then apply the definition (1.5), we get back an information function identical to that with which we started.

Proof of Proposition 1.6. In this proof, we may use only 1.5 and 1.31 through 1.33, not formulas derived from the definitions in the body of the text.

To show that $\mathbf{I}$ is an information function, we must establish 1.11 and 1.12. To prove 1.11, note that $\sim\{\omega\} \supset K \sim \{\omega\}$ by 1.31, so $\{\omega\} \subset \sim K \sim \{\omega\} = \mathbf{I}(\omega)$. 1.12 will be established below.

---

[4]Starting from $\mathscr{K}$, we call two states *equivalent* iff they are not separated by $\mathscr{K}$, and define $\mathscr{I}$ to consist of the equivalence classes.

Now *define* $\mathscr{K}$ by 1.23 (remember that K is now the primitive); we then assert that

$$\mathbf{I}(\omega) \in \mathscr{K}, \text{ and} \tag{1.61}$$

$$\mathbf{I}(\omega) \text{ is the intersection of all members of } \mathscr{K} \text{ containing } \omega. \tag{1.62}$$

To prove 1.61, note that by 1.33, $\mathbf{I}(\omega) = {\sim}K \sim \{\omega\} = K \sim K \sim \{\omega\} \in K\mathscr{E} = \mathscr{K}$. To prove 1.62, suppose $\omega \in F \in \mathscr{K}$. Then $F = KE$ for some E in $\mathscr{E}$. Thus ${\sim}KE = {\sim}F \subset {\sim}\{\omega\}$. So by 1.33 and 1.32, ${\sim}KE \subset K \sim KE \subset K \sim \{\omega\}$. Hence $\mathbf{I}(\omega) = {\sim}K \sim \{\omega\} \subset KE = F$. Thus $\mathbf{I}(\omega)$ is included in every member F of $\mathscr{K}$ that contains ω, and so in their intersection. For the reverse inclusion, note that by 1.11 and 1.61 (which we have already proved), $\mathbf{I}(\omega)$ itself is an element of $\mathscr{K}$ containing ω, and therefore it includes the intersection of all such elements.

To prove 1.12, note that either ω is contained in precisely the same members of $\mathscr{K}$ as ω', or not. If yes, then 1.62 yields $\mathbf{I}(\omega) = \mathbf{I}(\omega')$. If not, then w.l.o.g. there is an F in $\mathscr{K}$ with $\omega \in F$ and $\omega' \in {\sim} F$; then by 1.62, $\mathbf{I}(\omega) \cap \mathbf{I}(\omega') = \emptyset$.

To prove 1.2, we first show

$$KE \text{ is the disjoint union of those events } \mathbf{I}(\omega) \text{ that are included in } E. \tag{1.63}$$

Indeed, that the union is disjoint follows from 1.12. Next, if $\mathbf{I}(\omega) \subset E$, then by 1.5, 1.33, and 1.32, $\mathbf{I}(\omega) \subset K\mathbf{I}(\omega) \subset KE$. Hence the union in question is included in KE. On the other hand, if $\omega \in KE$, then by 1.11 and 1.62, $\omega \in \mathbf{I}(\omega) \subset KE$, so every element of KE is in the union in question, so the union includes KE.

1.2 now follows from 1.11, 1.12, and 1.63.

1.1. *Notes to Section 1*

(i) An alternative for 1.32 is the intuitively more transparent

$$K(E \cap F) = K(E) \cap K(F), \tag{1.64}$$

which says that i knows two things if and only if he knows each. Note that 1.64 implies[5] 1.32; indeed, if $E \subset F$ then 1.64 yields $KE = K(E \cap F) = KE \cap KF \subset KF$. But from Note (i) it follows that in the presence of the other two conditions, 1.32 implies 1.4 and a fortiori 1.64, so that the two systems (with 1.32 and with 1.64) are equivalent.

(ii) Note that

$$K\Omega = \Omega. \tag{1.7}$$

Indeed, $K\emptyset = \emptyset$, by 1.31; so $\Omega \supset K\Omega = K \sim \emptyset = K \sim K\emptyset \supset \sim K\emptyset = \sim\emptyset = \Omega$, by 1.33, and 1.7 follows. In words, 1.7 says that if an event obtains at all states of the world, then i knows it.

(iii) Condition 1.33 is sometimes called *negative introspection.* A related condition is

$$KE = KKE, \tag{1.8}$$

sometimes called *positive introspection*, which says that if a person knows something, then he knows that he knows it. 1.8 follows from 1.31 and 1.33, as follows: $\sim KE = K \sim KE$, so $KE = \sim K \sim KE$, so $KKE = K \sim K \sim KE = \sim K \sim KE = KE$. From 1.8 and 1.23 it follows that

$$\mathscr{K} = \{E : E = KE\}. \tag{1.9}$$

2. Common Knowledge

Let N be a collection of several individuals i, each with his own knowledge function κ_i, knowledge operator K_i, knowledge ufield $\mathscr{K}_i$, information partition $\mathscr{I}_i$, and information function $\mathbf{I}_i$; the space Ω of states of the world and the ufield $\mathscr{E}$ of events remain the same for all individuals. We call N the *population.*

Call an event E *common knowledge* (in the population) if all know E, all know that all know it, all know that all know that all

[5]The converse is false (as a referee pointed out): take $\Omega := \{1, 2, 3\}, KE := E\backslash\{\min E\}$.

know it, and so on ad infinitum. Formally, define operators K^m from $\mathscr{E}$ to $\mathscr{E}$ by

$$K^1E := \bigcap_{i\in N} K_iE,\ K^{m+1}E := K^1K^mE, \tag{2.1}$$

then define K^∞ by

$$K^\infty E := K^1E \cap K^2E \cap \cdots . \tag{2.2}$$

If $\omega \in K_iE$, we say that "i knows E at ω." Thus K_iE is the set of all states of the world at which i knows E; in other words, K_iE is the event that i knows E. If $\omega \in K^\infty E$, we say that "E is commonly known at ω;" and $K^\infty E$ is the event that E is commonly known. Similarly, K^1E is the event that E is *mutually* known (between the individuals in N), and K^mE that E is *m'th level mutual* knowledge. Thus m'th level mutual knowledge of E means that all relevant individuals know E, all know that all know it, and so on, but only m times; and an event is common knowledge iff it is mutual knowledge at all levels.

Lemma 2.3. *$K_iK^\infty E = K^\infty E$ for all i.*

Proof. The inclusion $\subset$ follows from 1.31. For the opposite inclusion, 2.1 and 1.4 yield $K_iK^\infty E = K_i\bigcap_{m=1}^\infty K^mE = \bigcap_{m=1}^\infty K_iK^mE \supset \bigcap_{m=1}^\infty K^1K^mE = \bigcap_{m=2}^\infty K^mE \supset \bigcap_{m=1}^\infty K^mE = K^\infty E$.

Lemma 2.4.

$$K^\infty E \subset E, \text{ and} \tag{2.41}$$

$$E \subset F \text{ implies } K^\infty E \subset K^\infty F. \tag{2.42}$$

Proof. Follows from 2.1, 2.2, 1.31, and 1.32.

Call an event F *self-evident* if $K_iF = F$ for all i; that is, if the event itself entails everyone knowing it (in other words, whenever it obtains, everyone knows that it obtains). For example, if two people enter into a contract,[6] then it is self-evident to them that they do. From 1.9 we get

$$\text{An event is self-evident if and only if it is in } \bigcap_{i\in N} \mathscr{K}_i. \tag{2.5}$$

Theorem 2.6. *$K^\infty E$ is the largest event in $\bigcap_{i\in N} \mathscr{K}_i$ that is included in E.*

In words: E is commonly known if and only if some self-evident event that entails E *obtains.*

Proof. By 2.3, 1.8, and 2.41, $K^\infty E$ is in $\bigcap_{i\in N} \mathscr{K}_i$ and is included in E. If $E \supset F \in \bigcap_{i\in N} \mathscr{K}_i$, then $F \in \mathscr{K}_i$, so $K_i F = F$ by 1.8, so $K^\infty F = F$ by 2.1, so $F = K^\infty F \subset K^\infty E$ by 2.42.

Corollary 2.7. *K^∞ is a knowledge operator, and the associated knowledge ufield is $\bigcap_{i\in N} \mathscr{K}_i$.*

Remark. The events in $\bigcap_{i\in N} \mathscr{K}_i$ are those that are in all the $\mathscr{K}_i$; those that are *common* to them all. This provides an additional rationale for the term "common knowledge;" it is knowledge that is, in a sense, common[7] to the protagonists. Of course, the main rationale for the term "common knowledge" is that its everyday meaning[8] corresponds nicely to the formal definition at 2.1.

---

[6]In common law, a contract is sometimes characterized as a "meeting of the minds." Interpreted more broadly — i.e., epistemically only, without necessarily involving the element of mutual commitment — the idea of "a meeting of the minds" nicely encapsulates the notion of a self-evident event.

[7]To be sharply distinguished from the knowledge that results if the protagonists share (tell each other) what they know. The latter corresponds to the ufield, sometimes denoted $\bigvee_{i\in N} \mathscr{K}_i$, comprising unions of events of the form $\bigcap_{i\in N} E_i$, where $E_i \in \mathscr{K}_i$ for each i. This is quite different from $\bigcap_{i\in N} \mathscr{K}_i$; in particular, $\bigcap_{i\in N} \mathscr{K}_i$ is included in (represents less information than) each of the $\mathscr{K}_i$, whereas $\bigvee_{i\in N} \mathscr{K}_i$ includes each of them (represents more information).

[8]Suppose you are told "Ann and Bob are going together," and respond "sure, that's common knowledge." What you mean is not only that everyone knows this, but also that the announcement is pointless, occasions no surprise, reveals nothing new; in effect, that the situation after the announcement does not differ

Proof. Each ufield $\mathscr{K}$ is associated with a unique information partition $\mathscr{I}$, and so by 1.2, with a unique knowledge operator K (given by 1.22). By 2.6, K^∞ is the knowledge operator associated with the ufield $\bigcap_{i\in N} \mathscr{K}_i$.

Corollary 2.8. $K^\infty E \subset K^\infty(K^\infty E)$, *and* $\sim K^\infty E \subset K^\infty(\sim K^\infty E)$.

In words: If an event is commonly known, then it is commonly known that it is commonly known; if it is not commonly known, then it is commonly known that it is not commonly known.

Proof. A consequence of 2.7, using 1.8 and 1.33.

Remark 2.9. $K^\infty \Omega = \Omega$.

In words: An event obtaining at all states is commonly known at each state.

Proof. 1.7 and 2.7.

The information partition and information ufield corresponding to the knowledge operator K^∞ are denoted $\mathscr{I}^\infty$ and $\mathscr{K}^\infty$ respectively. Ω is called the *universe*. The members of $\mathscr{K}^\infty$ are called *common knowledge subuniverses*, or simply *subuniverses*; they are the self-evident events. The atoms of $\mathscr{I}^\infty$ are called *common knowledge components* (of Ω); they are the minimal non-empty subuniverses. The structure consisting of the universe Ω, the population N, and the knowledge functions κ_i of the individuals i is called a *semantic knowledge system*.

from that before. This is precisely what is described in 2.6; the event "Ann and Bob are going together" — call it E — is common knowledge if and only if some event — call it F — happened that entails E and also entails all players' knowing F (like if all players met Ann and Bob at an intimate party). Contrast the familiar missionary story, in which announcing the facts changes the situation dramatically, in spite of everybody's knowing the facts, knowing that everybody knows them, and so on up to the 36'th order. If the facts had been common knowledge, in the everyday meaning of the phrase, the announcement would have changed nothing.

In the sequel, we sometimes consider common and mutual knowledge among the individuals in a specified proper subset N' of N. Thus in Section 10a, we treat a world with three individuals, and consider common and mutual knowledge among two out of the three. In that case, the same definitions and notation as above apply, with N replaced by N'.

3. Discussion

When we come to interpret the model introduced in Section 2, an inevitable question is, "what do the participants know about the model itself?" Does each "know" the information partitions $\mathscr{I}_i$ of the others? Are the $\mathscr{I}_i$ themselves in some sense "common knowledge"? If so, how does this common knowledge come about — how does each individual get to know what the others' partitions are? If not, how does the model reflect each individual's information — or lack of information — about the others' partitions? To do this right, doesn't one need to superpose another such model over the current one, to deal with knowledge of (or uncertainty about) the $\mathscr{I}_i$? But then, wouldn't one need another and yet another such model, without end even in the transfinite domain?

Addressing this question in 1976, we wrote as follows: "... the implicit assumption that the information partitions ... are themselves common knowledge ... constitutes no loss of generality. Included in the full description of a state ω of the world is the manner in which information is imparted to the two persons. This implies that the information sets $\mathbf{I}_1(\omega)$ and $\mathbf{I}_2(\omega)$ are indeed defined unambiguously as functions of ω, and that these functions are known to both players."

In 1987, we were more expansive: "While Player 1 may well be ignorant of what Player 2 knows — i.e., of the element of $\mathscr{I}_2$ that contains the 'true' state ω of the world — 1 cannot be ignorant of the *partition* $\mathscr{I}_2$ itself.... Indeed, since the specification of each ω includes a complete description of the state of the world, it includes also a list of those other states ω' of the world that are, for Player 2, indistinguishable from ω. If there were uncertainty about this list on the part of Player 1 (or any other player), then the description of ω would not be complete; one should then split ω into several states, depending on which states are, for 2, indistinguishable from ω. Therefore the very description of the ω's implies the structure of $\mathscr{I}_2$, and similarly for all the $\mathscr{I}_i$. The description of the ω's involves no 'real' knowledge; it is only a kind of code book or dictionary. The structure of the $\mathscr{I}_i$ also involves no real knowledge; it simply represents different methods of classification in the dictionary."

That is all well and good as far as it goes; but it leaves some important questions unanswered.

Can such a "dictionary" actually be constructed? Isn't there some kind of self-reference implicit in the very idea of such a dictionary? If it can nevertheless be constructed, is the construction in some sense unique, "canonical"? If not, which of the possible "dictionaries" would the participants use?

The most convincing way to remove all these questions and doubts is to construct Ω and the $\mathscr{I}_i$ — or equivalently, the κ_i — in an explicit, canonical, manner, so that it is clear from the construction itself that the knowledge operators are "common knowledge" in the appropriate sense. This will be done in Section 6, making use of the syntactic formalism. But first, we introduce the syntactic formalism for its own sake.

4. The Syntactic Knowledge Formalism

As in Section 2, we assume given a set N of *individuals*, called the *population*. We start by constructing a certain "language", in purely formal terms; afterwards we interpret it. The building blocks of the language are the following symbols, constituting the *keyboard*:

> *Letters* from an *alphabet* $\mathfrak{X} := \{x, y, z, \ldots\}$, taken as fixed throughout; and the symbols $\vee$, $\neg$, (,), and k_i(for all i in N).

A *formula* is a finite string of symbols obtained by applying the following three rules in some order finitely often:

$$\text{Every letter in the alphabet is a formula.} \tag{4.11}$$

$$\text{If } f \text{ and } g \text{ are formulas, so is } (f) \vee (g). \tag{4.12}$$

$$\text{If } f \text{ is a formula, so are } \neg(f) \text{ and } k_i(f) \text{ for each } i. \tag{4.13}$$

In the sequel, we often omit parentheses when the intended meaning is clear, and we use $f \Rightarrow g$ as an abbreviation for $(\neg f) \vee g$.

A *list* is a set of formulas. A list $\mathfrak{L}$ is called *logically closed*, or simply *closed*, if

$$(f \in \mathfrak{L} \text{ and } f \Rightarrow g \in \mathfrak{L}) \text{ implies } g \in \mathfrak{L}. \tag{4.2}$$

It is called *epistemically closed* if

$$f \in \mathfrak{L} \text{ implies } k_i f \in \mathfrak{L}, \tag{4.3}$$

and *strongly closed* if it is both logically and epistemically closed. The *strong closure* of a list $\mathfrak{L}$ is the smallest strongly closed list[9] that includes $\mathfrak{L}$. A *tautology*[10] is a formula in the strong closure of the list of all formulas having one of the following seven forms (for some f, g, h and i):

$$(f \vee f) \Rightarrow f \tag{4.41}$$

$$f \Rightarrow (f \vee g) \tag{4.42}$$

$$(f \vee g) \Rightarrow (g \vee f) \tag{4.43}$$

$$(f \Rightarrow g) \Rightarrow ((h \vee f) \Rightarrow (h \vee g)) \tag{4.44}$$

$$k_i f \Rightarrow f \tag{4.51}$$

$$k_i(f \Rightarrow g) \Rightarrow ((k_i f) \Rightarrow (k_i g)) \tag{4.52}$$

$$\neg k_i f \Rightarrow k_i \neg k_i f. \tag{4.53}$$

A formula g is a *consequence* of (or *follows* from) a formula f if $f \Rightarrow g$ is a tautology.

The set of all formulas with a given population N and alphabet $\mathfrak{X}$ is called a *syntax*, and is denoted $\mathfrak{S}(N, \mathfrak{X})$, or just $\mathfrak{S}$.

[9]The intersection of all strongly closed lists including $\mathfrak{L}$; it is itself strongly closed, and is included in all strongly closed lists that include $\mathfrak{L}$.

[10]See the next section for an informal explanation of this concept.

For convenience,[11] assume that N and $\mathfrak{X}$ are finite or denumerable; it follows that $\mathfrak{S}$ is denumerable.

5. Interpretation of the Syntactic Formalism

The syntactic formalism is subject to different interpretations; for now, we present only one. The letters of the alphabet represent what may be called "natural occurrences": substantive happenings that are not themselves described either in terms of people knowing something, or as combinations of other natural occurrences using the connectives of the propositional calculus.[12] Such a "natural" occurrence might be, "it will snow tomorrow." Not all possible natural occurrences need be represented in the alphabet; normally, one restricts oneself to natural occurrences that are "relevant" to the matter under discussion. In many cases of interest these constitute a finite set, perhaps even with just one element.

The symbol "k_i" means "i knows that ...". So if x stands for "it will snow tomorrow," then $k_i x$ stands for "i knows that it will snow tomorrow." The symbol "$\neg$" means "it is not true that", and the symbol "$\vee$" means "or". Parentheses have their usual meaning. Thus a formula is a **finite** concatenation of natural occurrences, using the operators and connectives[13] of the propositional calculus, and the knowledge operators k_i.

In ordinary discourse, a "tautology" is a statement that is logically necessary, one that embodies no empiric knowledge, nothing substantive about the real world, one whose truth is inherent in the

---

[11]This is used only twice — in 8.7 and in the appendix — and even there can be circumvented.

[12]The distinction between "natural occurrences" and arbitrary "occurrences" is analogous to that between "states of nature" and "states of the world" that one sometimes sees in the literature. We ourselves don't like this distinction; in the context of the current general treatment, we consider it artificial. But it is often used by economists, game theorists, and others who treat knowledge formally, and for the present we go along (but see Section 10b).

[13]As is well known, all the connectives of the propositional calculus can be defined in terms of $\vee$ and $\neg$.

meaning of the terms involved (like "a circle is round"). That is the meaning intended here. For example, formulas of the form 4.4·, which embody the axioms of the propositional calculus, are tautologies; so are formulas of the form 4.5·, which embody fundamental properties of knowledge.[14]

A logical deduction from a tautology is also a tautology. This is embodied in the condition that the set of tautologies be logically closed, i.e., obeys 4.2 (called the rule of *modus ponens*): if f and $f \Rightarrow g$ are tautologies, so is g.

In addition, the set of tautologies is epistemically closed, i.e., obeys 4.3 (this is called the rule of *necessitation*[15]): if f is a tautology, so is $k_i f$. In effect, this says that each individual knows each tautology, and that this is a logical necessity. Thus it is part of the logical infrastructure that the individuals are logically consistent. It follows that everybody knows this itself as a logical necessity, so that, for example, if f is a tautology, then so are $k_j k_i f$, $k_i k_j k_i f$, and so on. In this sense, one might say that it is "commonly known" that all individuals reason logically, though in the syntactic formalism, common knowledge has not been formally defined.

---

[14]Substantively, the knowledge "axioms" 4.5· correspond roughly to the defining properties 1.3· of the semantic knowledge operator K; but there is a noteworthy difference between 1.32 and 4.52. Both have the same conclusion — that if i knows the hypothesis of an implication, then he knows the conclusion — but their hypotheses are different. The hypothesis of 1.32 is the implication itself; that of 4.52, that i knows the implication, which seems stronger. To reconcile the two, note that the set inclusion used in the semantic formalism denotes *logical* — or better, *tauto*logical — implication; to say that $E \subset F$ means that by the very definitions of E and F, it cannot be that F happens unless E does. Indeed, $E \subset F$ is not an event, and so cannot hold at only some states of the world; it is either true — a logical necessity — or false. On the other hand, the formula $f \Rightarrow g$ — which simply stands for $\neg f \vee g$ — is not a logical necessity; it may hold *sometimes* — under certain circumstances — and sometimes not. Unlike with $E \subset F$, therefore, it makes sense to talk of i's knowing $f \Rightarrow g$; and then one cannot conclude that i knows g from his knowing f unless $f \Rightarrow g$ is not merely true, but in fact i *knows* $f \Rightarrow g$.

[15]This term is inherited from modal logic, where "necessity" plays a role like that of "knowledge" in epistemic logic. In that context, the rule of necessitation says that tautologies are not just true, but "necessarily" true.

The formal definition of tautology in Section 4 embodies precisely these principles: A tautology is *defined* as a formula that follows from the axioms of logic (including the logic of knowledge) by repeated use of modus ponens and the rule of necessitation.

In applications, the semantic and the syntactic formalisms have similar functions: Either may be used formally to analyze interactive situations — such as games or economies — in which the knowledge of the protagonists plays a role. In principle, the syntactic formalism is the more straightforward; it simply represents the usual methods of logical deduction. Thus given a hypothesis f, we may conclude that g if and only if $f \Rightarrow g$ is a tautology. The semantic formalism is more roundabout. In it, sentences are replaced by "events" — sets of states of the world. Specifically, a sentence f is replaced by the set of those states of the world at which f obtains. To conclude g from f, one shows that the corresponding events G and F satisfy $F \subset G$; i.e., that F entails G, that g obtains at each state of the world at which f does.

What we here call a "tautology" is in formal logic sometimes called a "theorem," the term "tautology" being reserved for sentences that "hold at" each state of each semantic knowledge system. Actually, the two meanings are equivalent, as will be shown below (9.4). Using the term "theorem" in this connection would cause confusion with the more usual kind of theorem — the kind that appears in papers like this, and in particular in this paper itself.

Though in principle the syntactic formalism is more straightforward, in practice the semantic formalism is often more useful.[16] On the other hand, the semantic formalism is beset by the conceptual difficulties discussed in Section 3 and in the introduction. To overcome these difficulties, we now construct an explicit canonical

[16]This is an empirical observation; we are not sure of the reason. Part of it may be that the semantic formalism is set theoretic, and set theory has more immediacy and transparency than formal logic. For example, a syntactic tautology, no matter how complex, corresponds in the semantic formalism simply to the set Ω of all states.

semantic knowledge system, using the syntactic formalism introduced in Section 4.

6. The Canonical Semantic Knowledge System

As in Section 4, assume given a finite population N and an alphabet $\mathfrak{X}$. Call a list $\mathfrak{L}$ of formulas *coherent* if

$$\neg f \in \mathfrak{L} \text{ implies } f \notin \mathfrak{L}, \tag{6.1}$$

complete if

$$f \notin \mathfrak{L} \text{ implies } \neg f \in \mathfrak{L}. \tag{6.2}$$

Define a *state* ω *of the world*, or simply a *state*, as a closed, coherent, and complete list of formulas that contains all tautologies. Denote the set of all states $\Omega(N, \mathfrak{X})$, or simply Ω. For all individuals i, define a knowledge function κ_i on Ω by specifying that for all states ω,

$$\kappa_i(\omega) \text{ is the set of all formulas in } \omega \text{ that start with } k_i. \tag{6.3}$$

The system comprising Ω, N, and the κ_i is called the *canonical semantic knowledge system* for the population N and the alphabet $\mathfrak{X}$ (or simply the *canonical system*).

7. Interpretation of the Canonical System

Intuitively, once a state ω of the world has been specified, there can be no remaining uncertainty, or at least no "relevant" uncertainty. This means that at ω, each of the denumerably many possible formulas is either definitely true or definitely false. Our device is formally to *define* a state ω as the list of those formulas that are true at ω.

Thus for each formula f, either f itself or its negation $\neg f$ must be in the list that defines ω (completeness), and only one of these two alternatives can obtain (coherence). Also, the ordinary processes of logical deduction are assumed valid at each state; anything that follows logically from formulas true at a certain state is also true at that state. This is embodied in two conditions. The first is that each state ω is logically closed, which means that *modus ponens* (4.2) is satisfied at ω ($\Rightarrow$ stands for "implies"). The second is that all tautologies are true at each state.

At a given state ω, which formulas does individual i know? Well, it is all written in the list that defines ω. He knows exactly those formulas that it says in the list that he knows: namely, those formulas f such that $k_i f$ is in the list. The list of all such $k_i f$ is $\kappa_i(\omega)$. So an individual can distinguish between two states ω and ω' if and only if $\kappa_i(\omega) \neq \kappa_i(\omega')$, i.e., if and only if he knows something at one state that he does not know at the other. The other representations of knowledge — $\mathbf{I}_i, \mathscr{I}_i, K_i$ and $\mathscr{K}_i$ — are then defined from κ_i as in Section 1.

We can now address the question raised in Section 3, whether each individual "knows" the information partitions $\mathscr{I}_i$ of the others. The $\mathscr{I}_i$ are defined in terms of the information functions κ_i, and so in terms of the operators k_i (which, in the formulation of Section 6, replace the κ_i, as primitives of the system). Thus the question becomes, does each individual "know" the operators k_i of the others (in addition, of course, to his own)?

The answer is "yes." The operator k_i operates on formulas; it takes each formula f to another formula. Which other formula? What is the result of operating on f with the operator k_i? Well, it is simply the formula $k_i f$. "Knowing" the operator k_i just means knowing this definition. Intuitively, for an individual j to "know" k_i means that j knows what it means for i to know something. It does not imply that j knows any specific *formula* $k_i f$.

Suppose, for example, that f stands for "it will snow tomorrow." For j to know the operator k_i implies that j knows that $k_i f$ stands for "i knows that it will snow tomorrow;" it does *not* imply that j knows that i knows that it will snow tomorrow (indeed, i may not know this, and perhaps it really will not snow).

In brief, j's knowing the operator k_i means simply that j knows what it means for i to know something, not that j knows anything specific about what i knows.

Thus the assertion that each individual "knows" the knowledge operators k_i of all individuals has no real substance; it is part of the framework. If j did not "know" the operators k_i, he would be unable even to consider formulas in the language of Section 4, to say nothing of knowing or not knowing them.

From this we conclude that all individuals indeed "know"[17] the functions κ_i, as well as the partitions $\mathscr{I}_j$.

We conclude this section by recalling the end of Section 3, where we said that "the description of the ω's involves no 'real' knowledge; it is only a kind of code book or dictionary." We have now explicitly constructed this "dictionary;" the construction is canonical (given the set N of individuals and the alphabet $\mathfrak{X}$); no self-reference is involved; and all individuals "know" the description of the model, including the partitions $\mathscr{I}_i$.

8. The Relationship between the Syntax and Semantics of Knowledge

In the foregoing we developed two related but distinct approaches to interactive epistemology. The states-of-the-world construction presented in Sections 1 and 2 embodies the *semantic* approach. The approach of Section 4, involving a formal "language," is *syntactic*. In our development, the syntactic approach is the more fundamental: In Section 6, we define semantics (states ω and knowledge functions κ_i) in terms of syntax (the formal language).

There are some obvious correspondences between the two approaches. Formulas (syntactic) correspond to events (semantic); disjunction, conjunction, and negation correspond to union, intersection, and complementation; the knowledge operators k_i to the knowledge operators K_i. By "correspond", we mean "have similar

[17]It should be recognized that "knowledge" in this connection has a meaning that is somewhat different from that embodied in the operators k_i and K_i; that is why we have been using quotation marks when talking about "knowing" an operator or a partition. That an individual i knows an event E or a formula f can be embodied in formal statements ($\omega \in K_iE$ or $k_if \in \omega$) that are well defined within the formal systems we have constructed, and whose truth or provability can be explicitly discussed in the context of these formal systems. This is not the case for "knowing" an operator or a partition. For discussion of a related point, see Section 10a.

substantive content". Thus "i knows that it will snow or rain tomorrow" is expressed by $k_i(x \vee y)$ in the syntactic formalism and by $K_i(E_x \cup E_y)$ in the semantic formalism, where x and E_x stand for "it will snow tomorrow", and y and E_y for "it will rain tomorrow". Formally, $k_i(x \vee y)$ and $K_i(E_x \cup E_y)$ are distinct objects; the first is a string of letters, connectives, operators and parentheses, the second a set of states. But substantively, they express the same thing.

The purpose of this section is to formalize the correspondence between syntactic and semantic entities, to embody it in precise theorems. We will see that the correspondence is not complete; whereas every formula f corresponds to a unique event E_f, it is not the case that every event corresponds to some formula. Roughly, the reason is that formulas are finite concatenations, whereas events can also express infinite concatenations (e.g., infinite unions). But subject to this caveat (i.e., if one considers events of the form E_f only), we will see that there is a perfect "isomorphism" between the syntactic and semantic approaches.

Unless otherwise stated, the population N and the alphabet $\mathfrak{X}$ — and so also the syntax $\mathfrak{S} = \mathfrak{S}(N, \mathfrak{X})$ — will be taken as fixed, as in Section 4.

In the sequel, we use the following standard notations (for arbitrary formulas f and g):

$$f \wedge g := \neg(\neg f \vee \neg g), \tag{8.01}$$

$$f \Leftrightarrow g := (f \Rightarrow g) \wedge (g \Rightarrow f). \tag{8.02}$$

The following syntactic formulation of "positive introspection" will be needed in the sequel:

Proposition 8.1. *Any formula of the form $k_i f \Leftrightarrow k_i k_i f$ is a tautology.*

Proof. Analogous to the proof of 1.8.

We proceed now to a precise formulation of the "isomorphism" between the syntactic and semantic approaches. If f is a formula, define

$$E_f := \{\omega \in \Omega : f \in \omega\}. \tag{8.2}$$

In words, E_f is the set of all states of the world containing the formula f, i.e., the set of all states at which f is true; in other words, it is the event that f obtains.

The "isomorphism" is embodied in the following three propositions (f and g denote arbitrary formulas, i an arbitrary individual):

Proposition 8.3.

$$\sim E_f = E_{\neg f}; \tag{8.31}$$

$$E_f \cup E_g = E_{f \vee g}; \tag{8.32}$$

$$E_f \cap Eg = E_{f \wedge g}. \tag{8.33}$$

Proposition 8.4. $K_i E_f = E_{k_i f}$.

Proposition 8.5. $E_f \in E_g$ *if and only if* $f \Rightarrow g$ *is a tautology.*

Though 8.4 is analogous to the components of 8.3, we have stated it separately because its proof lies considerably deeper. From 8.4 we will deduce that for *any* event E (not necessarily of the form E_f),

$$\omega \in K_i E \text{ iff } E \supset \bigcap_{k_i f \in \omega} E_f. \tag{8.51}$$

In words, 8.51 says that $K_i E$ is the event that E follows logically[18] from the formulas f that i knows. For a discussion of this result, see Section 10a.

From 8.5 it follows[19] that

$$E_f = E_g \text{ if and only if } f \Leftrightarrow g \text{ is a tautology.} \tag{8.52}$$

In words, 8.52 says that logically equivalent formulas correspond to the same event.[20]

[18] $E \supset F$ means that E is a *logical* consequence of F. Compare Proposition 8.5 and Footnote 15.

[19] A formal derivation is given below.

[20] The term "isomorphism" usually denotes a one–one correspondence that preserves the relevant operations. In our case, the correspondence between formulas

The proofs require some preliminary work. Call a formula f *elementary* if it contains no k_i. A *theorem of the propositional calculus* is defined as an elementary formula that yields the truth value T for each assignment of truth values to the letters appearing in it (using the usual rules for calculating truth values).

Lemma 8.61. *Let e be a theorem of the propositional calculus, possibly in a syntax different from the given one.*[21] *Let f be a formula (in the given syntax) that is obtained by substitution*[22] *from e. Then f is a tautology, and so is in each state ω.*

Proof. Let $\mathfrak{S}$ be the given syntax, $\mathfrak{S}'$ a syntax containing e. Since e is a theorem of the propositional calculus, it can be derived[23] by repeatedly applying *modus ponens* to formulas of the form 4.4. (Recall that the rule of *modus ponens* allows one to derive h from g and $g \Rightarrow h$). The formal expression of modus ponens is 4.2, so e is in the closure of the list of formulas of the form 4.4· in $\mathfrak{S}'$. Now f is obtained from e by substituting appropriate formulas in $\mathfrak{S}$ for the letters in e. If we make these substitutions already in the original formulas of the form 4.4· in $\mathfrak{S}'$ from which e was derived, then we obtain formulas of the form 4.4· in $\mathfrak{S}$. If we then follow

and events is not one–one, even when one considers events of the form E_f only. But from 8.52, it follows that there is a one–one correspondence between events of the form E_f and *equivalence classes* of formulas (under logical equivalence); and by 8.3 and 8.4, this correspondence indeed preserves the relevant operations.

[21] I.e., with a different alphabet. The reason for this caveat is that we may need more letters than are available in the given alphabet for which to substitute different formulas, though each of these formulas is in the given syntax. For example, let there be two individuals 1, 2, and let the given alphabet have only one letter x. Then 8.61 implies that $k_1x \wedge k_2x \Rightarrow k_1x$ is a tautology, but this would not be so if the e of the lemma had to be in the given syntax.

[22] Of course, if the substitutes (the formulas being substituted for the letters in e) are elementary, then f itself is a theorem of the propositional calculus. Our lemma applies to the more general case in which the substitutes may contain knowledge operators k_i.

[23] See, e.g., Hilbert and Ackermann (1928), p. 22ff. They use the rule of substitution as well as modus ponens; our approach obviates the need for the rule of substitution, by using axiom schemas (families of axioms obtained by substituting arbitrary formulas for f, g, and h) rather than axioms.

exactly the same derivation step by step, we obtain f. Thus f is in the closure of the list of formulas of the form 4.4· in $\mathfrak{S}$. A fortiori it is in the strong closure of the list of formulas of the form 4.4· and 4.5·, i.e., the set of tautologies.

Remark 8.62. If f and $f \Rightarrow g$ are both in a state ω, then $g \in \omega$.

Proof. Follows from 4.2, since each state is by definition closed.

The following proposition is important in its own right, and also as a lemma for 8.3.

Proposition 8.63. *For all states ω and formulas f and g,*

$$\neg f \in \omega \textit{ if and only if } f \notin \omega, \tag{8.631}$$

$$f \vee g \in \omega \textit{ if and only if } (f \in \omega \textit{ or } g \in \omega), \tag{8.632}$$

$$f \wedge g \in \omega \textit{ if and only if } (f \in \omega \textit{ and } g \in \omega), \tag{8.633}$$

$$f \Rightarrow g \in \omega \textit{ if and only if } (f \in \omega \textit{ implies } g \in \omega), \textit{ and} \tag{8.634}$$

$$f \Leftrightarrow g \in \omega \textit{ if and only if } (f \in \omega \textit{ if and only if } g \in \omega). \tag{8.635}$$

Proof. 8.631 restates the coherence (6.1) and completeness (6.2) of ω. Next, by 8.61, $f \Rightarrow (f \vee g)$ and $g \Rightarrow (f \vee g)$ are in each state, so "if" in 8.632 follows from 8.62. To prove "only if," suppose that on the contrary, $f \vee g \in \omega$ and $f \notin \omega$ and $g \notin \omega$. Since ω is complete, it follows that $\neg f \in \omega$ and $\neg g \in \omega$. Now by 8.61, $(\neg f \Rightarrow (\neg g \Rightarrow \neg (f \vee g))) \in \omega$. So $\neg f \in \omega$ and 8.62 yield $(\neg g \Rightarrow \neg(f \vee g)) \in \omega$. So $\neg g \in \omega$ and 8.62 yield $\neg(f \vee g) \in \omega$. So the coherence of ω yields $(f \vee g) \notin \omega$, contrary to what we assumed. This proves 8.632, and the other assertions follow from it, from 8.631, and from the definitions of $\wedge, \Rightarrow$, and $\Leftrightarrow$.

Proof of Proposition 8.3. Let $\omega \in \Omega$. By the meaning of the symbol $\sim$ (complementation), 8.2, 8.631, and again 8.2, we have

$$\omega \in {\sim}E_f \text{ iff } \omega \notin E_f \text{ iff } f \notin \omega \text{ iff } \neg f \in \omega \text{ iff } \omega \in E_{\neg f};$$

this proves 8.31. The proofs of 8.32 and 8.33 are similar; instead of 8.631, we use 8.632 and 8.633 respectively.

Proposition 8.4 requires more preparation. Denote the list of all tautologies by $\mathfrak{T}$. If $\mathfrak{L}$ is any list, denote by $\mathfrak{L}^*$ the smallest closed list that includes[24] $\mathfrak{L} \cup \mathfrak{T}$.

Lemma 8.64. *If $f \in \mathfrak{L}$ and $g \in \mathfrak{L}$, then $f \wedge g \in \mathfrak{L}^*$.*

Proof. $\mathfrak{L}^*$ contains $f \Rightarrow (g \Rightarrow (f \wedge g))$, which is a tautology by 8.61, and by hypothesis it contains f. So since it is closed (4.2), it contains $(g \Rightarrow (f \wedge g))$. But it also contains g. So since it is closed, it contains $f \wedge g$.

Corollary 8.641. *If f and g are tautologies, so is $f \wedge g$.*

Proof. Since $\mathfrak{T}$ is by definition strongly closed, it is closed. So $\mathfrak{T}^* = \mathfrak{T}$. The corollary now follows by setting $\mathfrak{L} := \mathfrak{T}$ in 8.64.

Lemma 8.65. *$\mathfrak{L}^*$ consists of all consequences of finite conjunctions of formulas in $\mathfrak{L}$.*

Proof. By 8.64, all finite conjunctions of formulas in $\mathfrak{L}$ are in $\mathfrak{L}^*$. Also all tautologies are in $\mathfrak{L}^*$, so since $\mathfrak{L}^*$ is closed, all consequences of finite conjunctions of formulas in $\mathfrak{L}$ are in $\mathfrak{L}^*$.

It remains to show that the set of all such consequences is closed. So suppose that f is a finite conjunction of formulas in $\mathfrak{L}$, that g is a consequence of f, and that $g \Rightarrow h$ is a tautology; it is sufficient to show that h is also a consequence of f. But g being a consequence of f means that $f \Rightarrow g$ is a tautology. So by 8.641, $(f \Rightarrow g) \wedge (g \Rightarrow h)$ is a tautology. By 8.61, $((f \Rightarrow g) \wedge (g \Rightarrow h)) \Rightarrow (f \Rightarrow h)$ is a tautology. So since $\mathfrak{T}$ is closed, $f \Rightarrow h$ is a tautology. So h is a consequence of f.

Call $\mathfrak{L}$ *consistent* if for all formulas f,

$$f \in \mathfrak{L}^* \text{ implies } \neg f \notin \mathfrak{L}^*. \tag{8.66}$$

Lemma 8.67. *If $\mathfrak{L}_1 \subset \mathfrak{L}_2 \subset \cdots$ is a nested sequence (possibly finite) of consistent lists, then its union $\mathfrak{L}_\infty := \bigcup_m \mathfrak{L}_m$ is consistent.*

[24]The intersection of all closed lists including $\mathfrak{L} \cup \mathfrak{T}$; it is itself closed, and is included in all closed lists that include $\mathfrak{L} \cup \mathfrak{T}$.

Proof. By 8.65, $\mathfrak{L}_\infty^* = \bigcup_m \mathfrak{L}_m^*$. So if 8.66 is false, then there are m, n, and f with $f \in \mathfrak{L}_m^*$ and $\neg f \in \mathfrak{L}_n^*$. W.l.o.g. $n \leq m$, so $\mathfrak{L}_n \subset \mathfrak{L}_m$, so $\mathfrak{L}_n^* \subset \mathfrak{L}_m^*$, so $f \in \mathfrak{L}_m^*$ and $\neg f \in \mathfrak{L}_m^*$, contrary to the hypothesis that $\mathfrak{L}_m$ is consistent.

Lemma 8.68. *Let $\mathfrak{L}$ be a consistent list, f a formula with $\neg f \notin \mathfrak{L}^*$. Then $\mathfrak{L} \cup \{f\}$ is consistent.*

Proof. If not, then by 8.65, there are formulas $g_1, g_2, \ldots, g_m$ and $h_1, h_2, \ldots, h_n$ in $\mathfrak{L}$, and a formula e, such that $(g \wedge f) \Rightarrow e$ and $(h \wedge f) \Rightarrow \neg e$ are tautologies, where $g := g_1 \wedge g_2 \wedge \cdots \wedge g_m$ and $h := h_1 \wedge h_2 \wedge \cdots \wedge h_n$. Hence by 8.641, $((g \wedge f) \Rightarrow e) \wedge ((h \wedge f) \Rightarrow \neg e)$ is a tautology. By 8.61, $(((g \wedge f) \Rightarrow e) \wedge ((h \wedge f) \Rightarrow \neg e)) \Rightarrow ((g \wedge h) \Rightarrow \neg f)$ is a tautology. Since the set of tautologies is closed, we deduce that $(g \wedge h) \Rightarrow \neg f$ is a tautology. Now $g \wedge h$ is a finite conjunction of formulas in $\mathfrak{L}$, so we deduce that $\neg f \in \mathfrak{L}^*$, contrary to our hypothesis.

Lemma 8.69. *Every state ω is consistent.*

Proof. By definition, ω is closed and includes $\mathfrak{T}$, so $\omega = \omega^*$. But then the consistency of ω follows from its coherence.

Proposition 8.7. *A list $\mathfrak{L}$ is consistent if and only if there is a state ω with $\mathfrak{L} \subset \omega$.*

Proof. If: Follows from 8.69.

Only if: Suppose that $\mathfrak{L}$ is consistent. We must find a state that includes $\mathfrak{L}$. Let $(f_1, f_2, \ldots)$ be an enumeration of all formulas. We will define a nested sequence $\mathfrak{L}_1 \subset \mathfrak{L}_2 \subset \ldots$ (possibly finite) such that $\mathfrak{L}_\infty^*$ is a state, where $\mathfrak{L}_\infty := \bigcup_m \mathfrak{L}_m$. Set $\mathfrak{L}_1 := \mathfrak{L}$. Suppose $\mathfrak{L}_1, \mathfrak{L}_2, \ldots, \mathfrak{L}_m$ have been defined. If for each formula f, either $f \in \mathfrak{L}_m^*$ or $\neg f \in \mathfrak{L}_m^*$, then the sequence ends with $\mathfrak{L}_m$. Otherwise, let f^m be the first f_n such that $f \notin \mathfrak{L}_m^*$ and $\neg f \notin \mathfrak{L}_m^*$, and define $\mathfrak{L}_{m+1} := \mathfrak{L}_m \cup \{f^m\}$. An induction using 8.68 then shows that all the $\mathfrak{L}_m$ are consistent. So by 8.67, their union $\mathfrak{L}_\infty$ is consistent. Now $\mathfrak{L}_\infty^*$ contains all the $\mathfrak{L}_m^*$, so by construction, it contains, for each formula f_n, either f_n or $\neg f_n$; i.e., it is complete. Moreover, since $\mathfrak{L}_\infty$ is consistent, $\mathfrak{L}_\infty^*$ cannot contain both. Thus $\mathfrak{L}_\infty^*$ is complete and coherent. Moreover it is closed and contains all tautologies, so it is a state; denoting it ω completes the proof.

Lemma 8.71. *Let e be a theorem of the propositional calculus, possibly in a syntax different from the given one.*[25] *Let f be a formula (in the given syntax) that is obtained by substitution from e. Then $k_i f$ is a tautology for all i.*

Proof. By 8.61, f is a tautology; since the set $\mathfrak{T}$ of tautologies is by definition strongly closed, 4.3 yields $k_i f \in \mathfrak{T}$.

Lemma 8.72. $k_i(f \wedge g) \Leftrightarrow (k_i f) \wedge (k_i g)$ *is a tautology.*

Proof. By 8.71, $k_i((f \wedge g) \Rightarrow f)$ is a tautology, and so a member of each ω. So by 4.52 and 4.2, $k_i(f \wedge g) \Rightarrow k_i f$ is a tautology. Similarly, $k_i(f \wedge g) \Rightarrow k_i g$ is a tautology, and it follows that

$$k_i(f \wedge g) \Rightarrow (k_i f) \wedge (k_i g) \text{ is a tautology.} \qquad (8.721)$$

For the other direction, note first that by 8.61, $f \Rightarrow (g \Rightarrow (f \wedge g))$ is a tautology. So by 8.71, $k_i(f \Rightarrow (g \Rightarrow (f \wedge g)))$ is a tautology. So by 4.52, $(k_i f) \Rightarrow k_i(g \Rightarrow (f \wedge g))$ is a tautology. Again by 4.52, $(k_i(g \Rightarrow (f \wedge g))) \Rightarrow ((k_i g) \Rightarrow k_i(f \wedge g))$. Combining the last two observations, we deduce that $(k_i f) \Rightarrow ((k_i g) \Rightarrow k_i(f \wedge g))$ is a tautology, and from this it follows that $((k_i f) \wedge (k_i g)) \Rightarrow k_i(f \wedge g)$ is a tautology. The proof may be completed by applying 8.641 to this and to 8.721.

Lemma 8.73. *Let ω and ω' be states, and let $\kappa_i(\omega) \subset \omega'$. Then $\kappa_i(\omega') = \kappa_i(\omega)$.*

Proof. Any formula in either $\kappa_i(\omega)$ or $\kappa_i(\omega')$ has the form $k_i f$. Suppose, therefore, that $k_i f \in \kappa_i(\omega)$. Then since $\kappa_i(\omega) \subset \omega'$,

[25] See Footnote 21.

it follows that $k_i f \in \omega'$, so by the definition of $\kappa_i(\omega')$, we get $k_i f \in \kappa_i(\omega')$. Conversely, suppose that $k_i f \in \kappa_i(\omega')$. If $k_i f \in \omega$, then also $k_i f \in \kappa_i(\omega)$, and we are done. Otherwise, $\neg k_i f \in \omega$, by 6.2. So by 4.53 and 4.2, $k_i \neg k_i f \in \omega$. So $k_i \neg k_i f \in k_i(\omega)$. Since $\kappa_i(\omega) \subset \omega'$, we deduce $k_i \neg k_i f \in \omega'$. So by 4.51 and 4.2, $\neg k_i f \in \omega'$. Since ω is coherent, it follows that $k_i f \notin \omega'$, contradicting $k_i f \in \kappa_i(\omega') \subset \omega'$.

Proof of Proposition 8.4. We start with the inclusion $\supset$. Let $\omega \in E_{k_i f}$, which means that $k_i f \in \omega$ (by 8.2). We must show that $\omega \in K_i E_f$, i.e. (by 1.21) that $\mathbf{I}_i(\omega) \subset E_f$. So let ω' be a state with $\kappa_i(\omega') = \kappa_i(\omega)$. Since $k_i f \in \omega$, it follows from 6.3 that $k_i f \in \omega'$. So $f \in \omega'$ by 4.51 and 4.2; so again by 8.2, $\omega' \in E_f$. This holds for all ω' with $\kappa_i(\omega') = \kappa_i(\omega)$, i.e., for all ω' in $\mathbf{I}_i(\omega)$. Thus $\mathbf{I}_i(\omega) \subset E_f$, as asserted. This demonstrates $\supset$.

To demonstrate $\subset$, let $\omega \in K_i E_f$. Then by 1.21,

$$\mathbf{I}_i(\omega) \subset E_f. \tag{8.74}$$

We wish to show that $\omega \in E_{k_i f}$, which by 8.2 is the same as $k_i f \in \omega$. Setting $\mathfrak{L} := \kappa_i(\omega)$, we obtain from 8.74, 1.1, 8.2, and 8.73 that for all states ω',

$$\mathfrak{L} \subset \omega' \text{ implies } f \in \omega'. \tag{8.75}$$

From this it follows that $f \in \mathfrak{L}^*$. For if not, then by 8.68, $\mathfrak{L} \cup \{\neg f\}$ is consistent. So by 8.7, there is a state ω' including $\mathfrak{L} \cup \{\neg f\}$, which contradicts 8.75 (because of the coherence of ω').

Since $f \in \mathfrak{L}^*$, it follows from 8.65 that f is a consequence of a finite conjunction of formulas in $\mathfrak{L}$. Since $\mathfrak{L}$ is defined as $\kappa_i(\omega)$, all formulas in $\mathfrak{L}$ start with k_i. Thus there are formulas $k_i f_1, k_i f_2, \ldots, k_i f_m$ in $\mathfrak{L}$ such that $(k_i f_1 \wedge k_i f_2 \wedge \cdots \wedge k_i f_m) \Rightarrow f$ is a tautology. So by 4.3 and $\mathfrak{T}$ being strongly closed, $k_i((k_i f_1 \wedge k_i f_2 \wedge \cdots \wedge k_i f_m) \Rightarrow f)$ is a tautology. So by 4.52 and 4.2, $k_i(k_i f_1 \wedge k_i f_2 \wedge \cdots \wedge k_i f_m) \Rightarrow k_i f$ is a tautology. Using 8.72 and that $k_i k_i g \Leftrightarrow k_i g$ is a tautology (8.1), we deduce that $(k_i f_1 \wedge k_i f_2 \wedge \cdots \wedge k_i f_m) \Rightarrow k_i f$ is a tautology. So $k_i f \in \mathfrak{L}^*$, by 8.65. Now $\mathfrak{L} = \kappa_i(\omega) \subset \omega$, and ω is closed, so ω includes the smallest closed list $\mathfrak{L}^*$ that includes $\mathfrak{L}$. So $k_i f \in \omega$, as was to be proved.

We proceed next to prove 8.5. First, an auxiliary proposition that is of interest on its own.

Proposition 8.8. *A formula is a tautology if and only if it is in every state.*

Proof. "Only if" is part of the definition of state. To prove "if", suppose that $g \in \omega$ for all states ω. Then $\neg g \notin \omega$ for all ω, so by 8.7, the list $\{\neg g\}$ is not consistent. So by 8.66, there is an f in $\{\neg g\}^*$ with $\neg f \in \{\neg g\}^*$. By 8.65, it follows that both f and $\neg f$ are consequences of $\neg g$. Thus both $\neg g \Rightarrow f$ and $\neg g \Rightarrow \neg f$ are tautologies, so $(\neg g \Rightarrow f) \wedge (\neg g \Rightarrow \neg f)$ is a tautology. Now $(\neg y \Rightarrow x) \wedge (\neg y \Rightarrow \neg x) \;\Rightarrow\; y$ is a theorem of the propositional calculus, so by 8.61, $(\neg g \Rightarrow f) \wedge (\neg g \Rightarrow \neg f) \Rightarrow g$ is a tautology. But the list of all tautologies is closed, since it is strongly closed; so g is a tautology.

Proof of Proposition 8.5. Suppose first that $f \Rightarrow g$ is a tautology. Then it is in every state ω. Hence if $f \in \omega$, then since ω is closed, it follows that $g \in \omega$. Hence $E_f = \{\omega \in \Omega : f \in \omega\} \subset \{\omega \in \Omega : g \in \omega\} = E_g$. This proves "if".

Conversely, suppose that $f \Rightarrow g$ is not a tautology. Then by 8.8, there is a state ω that does not contain $f \Rightarrow g$, so contains $\neg(f \Rightarrow g)$. Now $\neg(f \Rightarrow g) \Rightarrow (f \wedge \neg g)$ is a tautology by 8.61, so it is in ω. Since ω is closed, it follows that $f \wedge \neg g \in \omega$; so by 8.633, $f \in \omega$ and $\neg g \in \omega$, so $g \notin \omega$. So E_f is not included in E_g. This proves "only if".

We come now to the proofs of 8.51 and 8.52; it is convenient to start with 8.52.

Proof of 8.52. $f \Leftrightarrow g$ is a tautology iff $f \Rightarrow g$ and $g \Rightarrow f$ are tautologies, which is iff $E_f \subset E_g$ and $E_g \subset E_f$, i.e., $E_f = E_g$.

For the proof of 8.51, two more lemmas are needed (again of interest in their own right).

Lemma 8.81. $\mathbf{I}_i(\omega) = \bigcap_{g \in \kappa_i(\omega)} E_g$.

Proof. To show $\subset$, suppose $\omega' \in \mathbf{I}_i(\omega)$ and $g \in \kappa_i(\omega)$; we must prove $\omega' \in E_g$. By 1.1, $\kappa_i(\omega') = \kappa_i(\omega)$, so $g \in \kappa_i(\omega') \subset \omega'$, so $\omega' \in E_g$ by 8.2.

To show $\supset$, suppose $\omega' \in E_g$ for all $g \in \kappa_i(\omega)$. Thus by 8.2, $g \in \omega'$ for all $g \in \kappa_i(\omega)$; i.e., $\kappa_i(\omega) \subset \omega'$. Hence by 8.73, $\kappa_i(\omega') = \kappa_i(\omega)$, so by 1.1, $\omega' \in \mathbf{I}_i(\omega)$.

Lemma 8.82. $\bigcap_{g \in \kappa_i(\omega)} E_g = \bigcap_{\kappa_i f \in \omega} E_f$.

Proof. To show $\subset$, note that by 1.4 and 8.4, $K_i \bigcap_{k_i f \in \omega} E_f = \bigcap_{k_i f \in \omega} K_i E_f = \bigcap_{k_i f \in \omega} E_{k_i f} = \bigcap_{g \in \kappa_i(\omega)} E_g$, and then use 1.31. To show $\supset$, note that $\bigcap_{k_i f \in \omega} E_f \subset \bigcap_{k_i k_i h \in \omega} E_{k_i h} = \bigcap_{h: k_i h \in \omega} E_{k_i h} = \bigcap_{g \in \kappa_i(\omega)} E_g$, where $\subset$ follows from the intersection of a smaller family being larger, and the first $=$ sign from 8.1 and 8.52 (which has already been proved).

Proof of 8.51. If: Assume $E \supset \bigcap_{f: k_i f \in \omega} E_f$; from 1.32, 1.4, 8.4, and 8.2 we get $K_i E \supset K_i \bigcap_{f: k_i f \in \omega} E_f = \bigcap_{f: k_i f \in \omega} K_i E_f = \bigcap_{f: k_i f \in \omega} E_{k_i f} \supset \bigcap_{f: k_i f \in \omega} \{\omega\} = \{\omega\}$. Only if: Assume $\omega \in K_i E$. Then by 1.21, $\mathbf{I}_i(\omega) \subset E$. So by 8.82 and 8.81, $\bigcap_{f: k_i f \in \omega} E_f = \bigcap_{g \in \kappa_i(\omega)} E_g \subset E$.

We conclude this section with

Proposition 8.9. *A list is a state if and only if it is complete and consistent.*

Proof. By 8.69, every state is complete and consistent. Conversely, let $\mathfrak{L}$ be a complete consistent list. By 8.7, there is a state ω with $\mathfrak{L} \subset \omega$. If the inclusion is strict, there is a formula f with $f \in \omega$ and $f \notin \mathfrak{L}$. Since $\mathfrak{L}$ is complete, $\neg f \in \mathfrak{L}$, so $\neg f \in \omega$, so $f \notin \omega$ by the coherence of ω, contradicting $f \in \omega$.

9. Representations and Models

This section treats the notion of "model." The idea is to "interpret" syntactic formulas as events in a semantic knowledge system $\mathscr{S}$

(not necessarily the canonical system). The letters $x, y, z, \ldots$ of the alphabet are interpreted as certain distinguished events $X, Y, Z, \ldots$ in $\mathscr{S}$; the syntactic knowledge operators k_i as semantic knowledge operators K_i; and disjunctions, conjunctions, and negations as unions, intersections, and complements respectively. Thus each formula f corresponds to a unique event F in $\mathscr{S}$, constructed from the distinguished events $X, Y, Z, \ldots$ like f is constructed from the alphabet letters $x, y, z, \ldots$.

Substantively, f and F have similar content; to say them in English, one uses the same words. There is, however, a subtle difference between them. A syntactic formula f is, so to speak, "context-free;" the semantic system $\mathscr{S}$ provides the context, the environment. Thus, f entails *nothing* except the formula itself and its logical consequences — strictly in the sense of Section 4. The corresponding event F may entail much more, depending on the system $\mathscr{S}$ in which F is imbedded. Specifically, F entails all those events G that include F, although G may correspond to a formula g that does not follow from f "logically" — in the sense of Section 4 — but only, so to speak, in the "context" of $\mathscr{S}$.

A formula f is said to *hold at* a state ω in $\mathscr{S}$ if ω is a member of the event F corresponding to f. A *model* of a list $\mathfrak{L}$ of formulas is a state ω in a semantic knowledge system $\mathscr{S}$ at which each formula in $\mathfrak{L}$ holds. The main result of this section, Proposition 9.2, is that a list is consistent if and only if it has a model. In practice, pointing to a model is the major practical tool for proving consistency of lists — or indeed, proving that an individual formula is not tautologically false; proving consistency directly, by syntactic methods only, is notoriously cumbersome. The other side of the same coin is Corollary 9.3, which says that a formula g "follows" from a list $\mathfrak{L}$ if and only if g holds in *every* model of $\mathfrak{L}$. This, too, is a major tool in practical applications. As promised in Section 5, we also show that the tautologies are precisely those formulas that hold at each state of each semantic knowledge system (Corollary 9.4).

One simple application of these ideas is Corollary 9.5 — that the canonical knowledge system Ω defined in Section 6 is non-empty, i.e., that there exists at least one complete coherent list for every population and alphabet. Obvious as this may sound, it is not easily established by purely syntactic methods. But using the idea of model, it is immediate. One need only point to a state (*any* state) in a semantic knowledge system (*any* such system — for example, the system with one state only). The set of all formulas holding at that state is closed, complete and coherent, and contains all tautologies (Lemma 9.21).

A more substantial application is to issues of cardinality. Using 9.2, one may show that when there are at least two players, the canonical system has a continuum of states, even when the alphabet has just one letter. Two proofs are known. One is by Hart, Heifetz, and Samet (1996) — henceforth HHS; the other is in the appendix to this paper. Both are based on Proposition 9.2. HHS prove that there is a continuum of states by exhibiting a continuum of lists, each of which is consistent in itself, but any two of which are mutually inconsistent; by 8.7, each of these lists can be expanded to a state. HHS's proof is shorter and more elegant than ours; we adduce the latter here "for the record," and because its method, though clumsier than HHS's, may sometimes be applicable where theirs is not (needless to say, the opposite is also true).

To complete the picture, we will show in the appendix that when there is only one individual (and the alphabet is finite), then Ω is finite. This underscores the relative complexity of many-person epistemology when compared with one-person epistemology.

We proceed now to the formal treatment. Fix a population N and an alphabet $\mathfrak{X} := \{x, y, \ldots\}$; let $\mathfrak{S} := \mathfrak{S}(N, X)$ be the corresponding syntax. Recall (from Section 2) that a *semantic knowledge system* (or simply *knowledge system* for short) consists of a population, a universe $\hat{\Omega}$, and knowledge functions[26] $\hat{\kappa}_i$ for each individual i; denote the knowledge operators in such a system by $\hat{K}_i$, and the ufield of events by $\hat{\mathscr{E}}$. For brevity, we will sometimes denote the whole knowledge system simply by $\hat{\Omega}$, rather than $(\hat{\Omega}, N, (\hat{\kappa}_i)_i)$. This is

[26]The carets (hats) are to distinguish these objects from the specific universe Ω and knowledge functions κ_i defined in Section 6.

standard mathematical usage: A group is defined as a pair consisting of a set G and a multiplication, but the group (i.e., the pair) is itself often denoted G; a metric space is a set together with a metric, but the space and the set are often denoted by the same letter; and so on.

Define a *representation* of $\mathfrak{G}$ as a knowledge system $(\hat{\Omega}, N, (\hat{\kappa}_i)_i)$, together with a function $\varphi : \mathfrak{G} \to \hat{\mathscr{E}}$ satisfying

$$\begin{aligned} &\varphi(\neg f) = {\sim}\varphi(f), \quad \varphi(f \vee g) = \varphi(f) \cup \varphi(g), \text{ and} \\ &\varphi(k_i f) = \hat{K}_i \varphi(f). \end{aligned} \tag{9.1}$$

We will slightly abuse our terminology by using "representation" to refer also to just $\hat{\Omega}$ itself, or just φ itself (not just to the pair consisting of the knowledge system and φ). Given φ and a particular formula f, we will also call $\varphi(f)$ the "representation of f."

Remark 9.11. For each knowledge system $\hat{\Omega}$, each function from the alphabet $\mathfrak{X}$ into $\hat{\mathscr{E}}$ has a unique extension to a representation of $\mathfrak{G}$.

Proof. Follows from 9.1, as each formula f results from a *unique* sequence of operations $\neg$, $\vee$, and k_i.

Remark 9.11 implies that one can think of a representation of $\mathfrak{G}$ simply as an (arbitrary) knowledge system $\hat{\Omega}$, together with an (arbitrary) specification of events $\varphi(x), \varphi(y), \ldots$ corresponding to the letters of the alphabet. Intuitively, the events $\varphi(x), \varphi(y), \ldots$ may be thought of as the "natural" events.

Given a representation φ of $\mathfrak{G}$ and a state $\hat{\omega}$ in $\hat{\Omega}$, define

$$\phi(\hat{\omega}) := \{f \in \mathfrak{G} : \hat{\omega} \in \varphi(f)\}. \tag{9.12}$$

In words, $\phi(\hat{\omega})$ is the list of all formulas that *hold* at $\hat{\omega}$, i.e., whose representation $\varphi(f)$ obtains at $\hat{\omega}$.

Let $\mathfrak{L} \subset \mathfrak{G}$ be a list. Define a *model* for $\mathfrak{L}$ as a representation $(\hat{\Omega}, \varphi)$ of $\mathfrak{G}$ together with a state $\hat{\omega}$ in $\hat{\Omega}$ at which all formulas in $\mathfrak{L}$ hold (i.e., $\hat{\omega} \in \varphi(f)$ for all f in $\mathfrak{L}$).

Proposition 9.2. *A list $\mathfrak{L}$ of formulas is consistent if and only if it has a model.*

We first prove

Lemma 9.21. *Let $(\hat{\Omega}, \varphi)$ be a representation of the syntax $\mathfrak{S}$, and let $\hat{\omega} \in \hat{\Omega}$. Then $\phi(\hat{\omega}) \in \Omega$.*

In words: For a fixed representation, the list of all formulas that hold at a given state $\hat{\omega}$ is closed, coherent, complete, and contains all tautologies; i.e., it is a state in the canonical knowledge system.

Proof. Set $\omega := \phi(\hat{\omega})$. We must prove that the list ω is closed, coherent, complete, and contains all tautologies.

To say that ω is closed means that it satisfies 4.2; i.e., that ($f \in \omega$ and $f \Rightarrow g \in \omega$) implies $g \in \omega$; i.e., that

$$(\hat{\omega} \in \varphi(f) \text{ and } (\hat{\omega} \in \varphi((\neg f) \vee g))) \text{ implies } \hat{\omega} \in \varphi(g). \tag{9.22}$$

Now

$$\hat{\omega} \in \varphi(f) \text{ and } \hat{\omega} \in \varphi((\neg f) \vee g) \text{ iff } \hat{\omega} \in \varphi(f) \cap \varphi((\neg f) \vee g), \tag{9.23}$$

and since $\varphi(f) \cap \varphi(h) = \varphi(f \wedge h)$ by 9.1, we have

$$\varphi(f) \cap (\varphi(\neg f) \cup \varphi(g)) = \varphi(f) \cap (\sim\varphi(f) \cup \varphi(g)) \subset \varphi(g); \tag{9.24}$$

putting together 9.23 and 9.24 yields 9.22.

We prove next that ω contains all tautologies. First we show

$$\text{if } e \text{ is a tautology, then } \varphi(e) = \hat{\Omega}. \tag{9.25}$$

Indeed, let $\hat{\mathfrak{T}}$ be the list of all formulas e such that $\varphi(e) = \hat{\Omega}$. Using 9.1 and 1.31 through 1.33, we verify directly that every formula with one of the seven forms 4.41 through 4.53 is in $\hat{\mathfrak{T}}$. Moreover, if $f \in \hat{\mathfrak{T}}$ and $f \Rightarrow g \in \hat{\mathfrak{T}}$ then $\hat{\Omega} = \varphi(f)$ and $\hat{\Omega} = \varphi(f \Rightarrow g)$, so $\hat{\Omega} = \varphi((\neg f) \vee g) = = (\sim\varphi(f)) \cup \varphi(g) = (\sim\hat{\Omega}) \cup \varphi(g) = \emptyset \cup \varphi(g) = \varphi(g)$, so $g \in \hat{\mathfrak{T}}$; thus $\hat{\mathfrak{T}}$ is closed. Finally, if $f \in \hat{\mathfrak{T}}$, then $\varphi(k_i f) = \hat{K}_i \varphi(f) = \hat{K}_i \hat{\Omega} = \hat{\Omega}$ (by 1.7), so $\hat{\mathfrak{T}}$ is strongly closed. Thus $\hat{\mathfrak{T}}$ is strongly closed and contains all formulas of the form 4.41 through 4.53, so it includes the strong closure of the list of all formulas of this form, i.e., the list of all tautologies; this proves 9.25. It follows that $\hat{\omega} \in \hat{\Omega} = \varphi(e)$ for all tautologies e, so ω contains all tautologies, as asserted.

Finally, to verify completeness (6.2) and coherence (6.1), note that

$$\neg f \in \omega \text{ iff } \hat{\omega} \in \varphi(\neg f) \text{ iff } \hat{\omega} \in {\sim}\varphi(f) \text{ iff } \hat{\omega} \notin \varphi(f) \text{ iff } f \notin \omega.$$

Thus ω is a closed, coherent, complete list that contains all tautologies; i.e., $\omega = \phi(\hat{\omega})$ is a state.

Proof of Proposition 9.2. Only if: Let the knowledge system consist of the state space Ω together with N and the knowledge functions κ_i constructed in Section 6. Define $\varphi(f) := \{\omega \in \Omega : f \in \omega\}$ ($=E_f$, by 8.2). By 8.3 and 8.4, φ satisfies 9.1. Since $\mathfrak{L}$ is consistent, there is a state ω that includes $\mathfrak{L}$ (8.7). So each formula f in $\mathfrak{L}$ is in ω, so ω is in all the corresponding $\varphi(f)$.

If: Let the model be $(\hat{\Omega}, \varphi, \hat{\omega})$. Then $\mathfrak{L} \subset \phi(\hat{\omega})$. By 9.21, $\phi(\hat{\omega})$ is a state, so by 8.7, $\mathfrak{L}$ is consistent.

Corollary 9.3. *Let $\mathfrak{L}$ be a list, g a formula. Then g is a consequence of a finite conjunction of formulas in $\mathfrak{L}$ if and only if every model for $\mathfrak{L}$ is also a model for $\{g\}$. (In words, a formula "follows" from a list if and only if it holds in* ***every*** *model of that list.)*

Proof. Recall that $\mathfrak{L}^*$ denotes the list of all consequences of finite conjunctions of formulas in a list $\mathfrak{L}$ (8.65). If g is *not* in $\mathfrak{L}^*$, then by 8.68, $\mathfrak{L} \cup \{\neg g\}$ is consistent, so by 9.2 has a model, which by 9.13 is not a model for $\{g\}$. In the opposite direction, if it is not the case that every model for $\mathfrak{L}$ is also a model for $\{g\}$, then $\mathfrak{L}$ has a model that is *not* a model for $\{g\}$, and so by 9.21 *is* a model for $\{\neg g\}$, hence also for $\mathfrak{L} \cup \{\neg g\}$. So by 9.2, $\mathfrak{L} \cup \{\neg g\}$ is consistent, so by 8.68, $g \notin \mathfrak{L}^*$.

Corollary 9.4. *A formula f is a tautology if and only if for any representation, $\varphi(f) = \hat{\Omega}$ (in words, if and only if f holds at each state in each representation).*

Proof. "Only if" follows from 9.21. To show "if," note first that by 8.3 and 8.4, the canonical semantic knowledge system Ω, together with the function φ on $\mathfrak{S}$ defined by $\varphi(f) := E_f$, constitute a representation of $\mathfrak{S}$. So by hypothesis, $E_f = \varphi(f) = \Omega$, which means that f is in every state of Ω. So by 8.8, f is a tautology.

Corollary 9.5. *The canonical knowledge system Ω is non-empty.*

Proof. By Lemma 9.21, $\phi(\hat{\omega})$ is always in Ω; so it is enough to show that there exists *some* semantic knowledge system, and that is obvious (for example, the one with one state only).

Note to Section 9

In this note we show that every representation of $\mathfrak{S}$ can be thought of as a common knowledge subuniverse of Ω. More precisely, for every representation there is a common knowledge subuniverse of Ω such that the given representation is isomorphic, in a natural sense, to this common knowledge subuniverse.

Given a representation $(\hat{\Omega}, \varphi)$ of the syntax $\mathfrak{S}$, denote $\hat{\mathscr{S}} := \varphi(\mathfrak{S}) \subset \hat{\mathscr{E}}$, and call the events in $\hat{\mathscr{S}}$ *syntactic*. In words, a syntactic event is one of the form $\varphi(f)$; one that corresponds, under the representation φ, to a formula in the syntax $\mathfrak{S}$.

Now let $(\hat{\Omega}_1, \varphi_1)$ and $(\hat{\Omega}_2, \varphi_2)$ be two representations of $\mathfrak{S}$; set $\hat{\mathscr{S}}_j := \varphi_j(\mathfrak{S})$, $j = 1, 2$. Call φ_1 and φ_2 *isomorphic* if there is a one–one mapping F (an *isomorphism*) from $\hat{\mathscr{S}}_1$ onto $\hat{\mathscr{S}}_2$ such that $\varphi_2 = F \circ \varphi_1$ (see the diagram at 9.6).

$$\begin{array}{ccc} & \mathfrak{S} & \\ {}^{\varphi_1}\swarrow & & \searrow^{\varphi_2} \\ \hat{\mathscr{S}}_1 & \xrightarrow[F]{} & \hat{\mathscr{S}}_2 \end{array} \tag{9.6}$$

Let $(\hat{\Omega}, \varphi)$ be a representation of $\mathfrak{S}$. By 9.21, for each state $\hat{\omega}$ in $\hat{\Omega}$, the list $\phi(\hat{\omega})$ is a state ω in Ω. The set of all ω obtained in this way is a subset of Ω, which we denote Ω^{φ}. Formally, $\Omega^{\varphi} := \phi(\hat{\Omega})$. In words, a state in Ω is in Ω^{φ} iff it corresponds to some $\hat{\omega}$ in $\hat{\Omega}$ under the representation φ; i.e., iff it consists of precisely those formulas f for which the representation $\varphi(f)$ holds at $\hat{\omega}$.

Denote by Γ^φ the smallest common knowledge subuniverse[27] of Ω that includes Ω^φ. By associating with Γ^φ the population N and the knowledge functions $\kappa_i|\Gamma^\varphi$, we obtain a knowledge system; denote the set of events in this system by $\mathscr{E}^\varphi$. Define $\varphi^* : \mathfrak{S} \to \mathscr{E}^\varphi$ by

$$\varphi^*(f) := E_f \cap \Gamma^\varphi. \tag{9.61}$$

Proposition 9.7. *$(\Gamma^\varphi, \varphi^*)$ is a representation of $\mathfrak{S}$, which is isomorphic to $(\hat{\Omega}, \varphi)$.*

For the proof of 9.7, we need several lemmas. In the statements of these lemmas, f, g, and h denote arbitrary formulas.

Lemma 9.71. $\phi(\varphi(f)) = E_f \cap \Omega^\varphi$.

Proof. We have $\phi(\varphi(f)) = \{\phi(\hat{\omega}) : \hat{\omega} \in \varphi(f)\}$, so $\omega \in \phi(\varphi(f))$ iff there is an $\hat{\omega} \in \varphi(f)$ with $\omega = \phi(\hat{\omega}) = \{g : \hat{\omega} \in \varphi(g)\}$, and this is so iff $f \in \omega \in \Omega^\varphi$; thus $\phi(\varphi(f)) = \{\omega \in \Omega^\varphi : \omega \in f\} = E_f \cap \Omega^\varphi$.

Lemma 9.72. *$\Omega^\varphi \subset E_f$ iff $\hat{\Omega} = \varphi(f)$.*

Proof. $\Omega^\varphi \subset E_f$ iff $f \in \omega$ for all ω in Ω^φ; that is, iff for each $\hat{\omega}$ in $\hat{\Omega}$, we have $f \in \phi(\hat{\omega}) = \{g : \hat{\omega} \in \varphi(g)\}$; that is, iff $\hat{\omega} \in \varphi(f)$ for all $\hat{\omega}$ in $\hat{\Omega}$; i.e., $\hat{\Omega} = \varphi(f)$.

Corollary 9.73. *If $\Omega^\varphi \subset E_f$, then $\Omega^\varphi \subset K_i E_f$.*

Proof. By 9.72, $\Omega^\varphi \subset E_f$ yields $\hat{\Omega} = \varphi(f)$. Hence by 9.1, $\hat{\Omega} = \hat{K}_i\hat{\Omega} = \hat{K}_i\varphi(f) = \varphi(k_i f)$. So again by 9.72, $\Omega^\varphi \subset K_i E_f$.

Lemma 9.74. *If $\Omega^\varphi \subset E_f$, then $\Gamma^\varphi \subset E_f$.*

Proof. Set $F := \bigcap E_f$, where the intersection is over all f with $\Omega^\varphi \subset E_f$. From 1.4, 8.4, and 9.73, it follows that $K_i F = F$ for all i. Thus F is self-evident, and so a subuniverse of Ω. By definition, $F \supset \Omega^\varphi$. Hence F includes the smallest subuniverse that includes Ω^φ,

[27] See the end of Section 2.

namely Γ^φ. But by its definition, F is included in each E_f for which $\Omega^\varphi \subset E_f$, so the lemma is proved.

Lemma 9.75. $\varphi^*(g) = \varphi^*(h)$ *iff* $\varphi(g) = \varphi(h)$.

Proof. If: Assume $\varphi(g) = \varphi(h)$. Then by 9.71, $E_g \cap \Omega^\varphi = \phi(\varphi(g)) = = \phi(\varphi(h)) = E_h \cap \Omega^\varphi$. Thus for each ω in Ω^φ, we have $g \in \omega$ iff $h \in \omega$, which, by 8.635, is equivalent to $(g \Leftrightarrow h) \in \omega$. Now set $f := (g \Leftrightarrow h)$. Then $f \in \omega$ for each ω in Ω^φ; that is, $\Omega^\varphi \subset E_f$. So by 9.74, $\Gamma^\varphi \subset E_f = E_{g\Leftrightarrow h}$. Thus $(g \Leftrightarrow h) \in \omega$ for each ω in Γ^φ; that is, $g \in \omega$ iff $h \in \omega$ for each such ω; that is, $\varphi^*(g) = E_g \cap \Gamma^\varphi = E_h \cap \Gamma^\varphi = \varphi^*(h)$.

Only if: Suppose $\varphi(g) \neq \varphi(h)$; w.l.o.g. let $\hat{\omega} \in \varphi(g) \backslash \varphi(h)$. Set $\omega := \phi(\hat{\omega}) = \{f : \hat{\omega} \in \varphi(f)\}$. Then $\omega \in \phi(\hat{\Omega}) = \Omega^\varphi \subset \Gamma^\varphi$, and $g \in \omega$ but $h \notin \omega$. Hence $\omega \in E_g \cap \Gamma^\varphi = \varphi^*(g)$ but $\omega \notin E_h \cap \Gamma^\varphi = \varphi^*(h)$, so $\varphi^*(g) \neq \varphi^*(h)$.

Proof of 9.7. To prove that $(\Omega^\varphi, \varphi^*)$ is a representation of $\mathfrak{S}$, we establish 9.1 for φ^*. From 9.61 and 8.31 we get

$$\begin{aligned}\varphi^*(\neg f) &= E_{\neg f} \cap \Gamma^\varphi = (\sim E_f) \cap \Gamma^\varphi = \Gamma^\varphi \backslash (\Gamma^\varphi \subset E_f)\\ &= \Gamma^\varphi \backslash \varphi^*(f).\end{aligned} \tag{9.76}$$

From 9.61 and 8.32 we get

$$\varphi^*(f \vee g) = E_{f\vee g} \cap \Gamma^\varphi = (E_f \cup E_g) \cap \Gamma^\varphi = \varphi^*(f) \cup \varphi^*(g). \tag{9.77}$$

From 9.61, 8.4, 1.4, and Γ^φ being a subworld, we get

$$\begin{aligned}\varphi^*(k_i f) &= E_{k_i f} \cap \Gamma^\varphi = K_i E_f \cap \Gamma^\varphi = K_i E_f \cap K_i \Gamma^\varphi =\\ &= K_i(E_f \cap \Gamma^\varphi) = K_i \varphi^*(f).\end{aligned} \tag{9.78}$$

Combining 9.76 through 9.78, we conclude[28] that φ^* is indeed a representation of $\mathfrak{S}$.

That φ^* is isomorphic with φ follows from 9.75.

[28]The conclusion from 9.38 uses the fact that the knowledge operator for the universe Γ^φ is $K_i|\mathscr{E}^\varphi$; this follows from Γ^φ being a subuniverse.

10. Discussion

(a) *The meaning of the knowledge operators K_i*

Proposition 8.4 says that when K_i is applied to a syntactic event E_f, its meaning corresponds precisely to that of the knowledge operator k_i on the formula f. But the domain of K_i includes *all* events — all subsets of Ω — not just syntactic events. Thus one may ask how to interpret K_iE for events E that are not syntactic (e.g., infinite unions of syntactic events). Specifically, is it still correct that K_iE means "i knows E"?

This question is in the interpretive realm; the answer depends on how we think about it. On the straightforward intuitive level, the answer is "no." With the definition in Section 6, the correct interpretation of K_iE is not that "i knows E", but that "E follows logically from the syntactic events that i knows" (see 8.51). An individual i may know something without its following logically from the syntactic events (formulas) that he knows; in that case, K_iE does not obtain, though it is the case that "i knows E".

For example, i might know an infinite disjunction without knowing any of the partial finite disjunctions. Thus suppose that the alphabet contains infinitely many letters $x_1, x_2, \ldots$. The event $E_{x_1} \cup E_{x_2} \cup \cdots$ signifies that "at least one of the x_m obtains". But $K_i(E_{x_1} \cup E_{x_2} \cup \cdots)$ does *not* signify that "i knows that at least one of the x_m obtains"; rather, it signifies the stronger statement that "it follows from the *formulas* known to i that at least one of the x_m obtains." For this, i must know some *finite* disjunction $x_1 \vee x_2 \vee \cdots \vee x_m$.

More generally, we have

Proposition 10.1. *If $f_1, f_2, \ldots,$ are formulas, then*

$$K_i(E_{f_1} \cup E_{f_2} \cup E_{f_3} \cup \cdots) = E_{k_i f_1} \cup E_{k_i(f_1 \vee f_2)} \cup E_{k_i(f_1 \vee f_2 \vee f_3)} \cdots .$$

Proof. That the right side is included in the left follows from 1.32, 8.3 and 8.4. To prove the opposite inclusion, let $\omega \in K_i(E_{f_1} \cup E_{f_2} \cup E_{f_3} \cup \cdots)$. Then by 1.21,

$$\mathbf{I}_i(\omega) \subset E_{f_1} \cup E_{f_2} \cup E_{f_3} \cup \cdots . \tag{10.11}$$

Setting $\mathfrak{L} := \kappa_i(\omega)$, we obtain from 8.74, 1.1, 8.2, and 8.73 that for all states ω',

$$\mathfrak{L} \subset \omega' \quad \text{implies} \quad f_1 \in \omega' \quad \text{or } f_2 \in \omega' \quad \text{or} \cdots . \tag{10.12}$$

Therefore the list $\mathfrak{L} \cup \{\neg f_1, \neg f_2, \ldots\}$ is not consistent; for if it were, then by 8.7, it would be included in a state, contrary to 10.12. So by 8.67, already one of the lists $\mathfrak{L} \cup \{\neg f_1, \ldots, \neg f_m\}$ is not consistent. Therefore $\mathfrak{L} \cup \{\neg f_1 \wedge \cdots \wedge \neg f_m\}$ — and so also $\mathfrak{L} \cup \{\neg(f_1 \vee \cdots \vee f_m)\}$ — are not consistent. So $\neg(f_1 \vee \cdots \vee f_m)$ is not in any state ω' that includes $\mathfrak{L}$. So $f_1 \vee \cdots \vee f_m$ is in every state ω' that includes $\mathfrak{L}$. In particular, $f_1 \vee \cdots \vee f_m$ is in every state ω' with $\kappa_i(\omega') = \kappa_i(\omega)$. Thus $\mathbf{I}_i(\omega) \subset E_{f_1 \vee \cdots \vee f_m}$. So by 1.21 and 8.4,

$$\begin{aligned}\omega \in K_i(E_{f_1 \vee \cdots \vee f_m}) &= E_{k_i(f_1 \vee \cdots \vee f_m)} \\ &\subset E_{k_i f_1} \cup E_{k_i(f_1 \vee f_2)} \cup E_{k_i(f_1 \vee f_2 \vee f_3)} \cdots .\end{aligned}$$

For another illustration,[29] consider an alphabet with just one letter x. Let $N = \{1, 2, 3\}$ (three individuals). The statement "x is common knowledge between 1 and 2" describes the event[30] $K_{12}^{\infty} E_x$. But "3 knows that x is not common knowledge between 1 and 2" does *not* describe the event $K_3 \sim K_{12}^{\infty} E_x$. Indeed, "3 knows that x is not common knowledge between 1 and 2" means that 3 knows that mutual knowledge of x between 1 and 2 (Section 2) fails at some level, but he (3) need not know at *which* level it fails.[31] On the other hand, $K_3 \sim K_{12}^{\infty} E_x$ signifies that mutual knowledge of x between 1 and 2 fails at some specified level m that 3 knows.

Formally, $K_{12}^{\infty} E_x := K_{12}^1 \cap K_{12}^2 E_x \cap \cdots$, where K_{12}^m denotes m'th level mutual knowledge between 1 and 2. Thus $\sim K_{12}^{\infty} E_x = \sim K_{12}^1 E_x \cup \sim K_{12}^2 E_x \cup \cdots$. So as before, $K_3 \sim K_{12}^{\infty} E_x$ signifies that 3 knows some finite disjunction $\sim K_{12}^1 E_x \cup \sim K_{12}^2 E_x \cup \cdots \cup \sim K_{12}^m E_x$. Since this disjunction equals[32] $\sim K_{12}^m E_x$, it follows that $K_3 \sim K_{12}^{\infty} E_x$

[29] Communicated by Moshe Vardi.

[30] See Section 2; we do not distinguish between K_{12}^{∞} and $K_{\{1,2\}}^{\infty}$.

[31] For example, this could happen if 2 tells 3, "x is not common knowledge between 1 and me," and 3 knows that 2 tells the truth.

[32] If x is mutual knowledge at the m'th level, it certainly is at any lower level.

signifies that mutual knowledge of x between 1 and 2 fails at a level known to 3, as asserted.

Note that there is *no* event $E \subset \Omega$ that signifies "3 knows that x is not common knowledge between 1 and 2". Events can only represent statements that are constructed from (finite) formulas by means of negation, conjunction and disjunction (possibly infinite or even non-denumerable). The statement "3 knows that x is not common knowledge between 1 and 2" is not of this kind. In contrast, "x is common knowledge between 1 and 2" does describe an event (i.e., a subset of Ω), though not a syntactic event; and of course, the same holds for "x is not common knowledge between 1 and 2". Also, "3 knows that x is common knowledge between 1 and 2" describes an event, namely the event $K_3 \sim K_{12}^{\infty} E_x$; this is because knowledge operators commute with intersections (1.4), but not with unions.

Up to now in this section, we have taken the "intuitive" view: that there is some informal notion of knowledge, not embodied in the syntactic knowledge operators k_i, that enables us to speak of, say, "knowing" an infinite disjunction even when we don't know any of the partial finite disjunctions. But it is possible also to take a different, more formal view: that in an essay of this kind, it is not appropriate to discuss concepts that are not given formal, mathematical expressions. With this view, all relevant knowledge is embodied in formulas; the term "knowledge" is *meaningful* only when it is derived from knowledge of formulas.

If we take this view, we must adjust our answer to the question that begins this section, "does K_iE mean 'i knows E'?" The answer now becomes "yes." Substantively, nothing has changed; as before, K_iE still means "E follows logically from the formulas that i knows." But with the new view, there *is* no other knowledge; *all* knowledge is embodied in formulas; you *can't* know something *unless* it follows logically from the finite formulas that you know.

Under this view, 10.1 may be stated verbally as follows: "i knows an infinite disjunction of formulas if and only if he knows the disjunction of some finite subset of these formulas."

One may take this view as representing a procedural position only, according to which one should not discuss a concept (such as knowledge of infinite disjunctions) that is not part of the formal framework. But one can also take it as representing a deeper philosophical position, somewhat reminiscent of the intuitionistic school of mathematics that was popular at the beginning of this century. According to this position, the infinite is at best a useful abstraction — a shorthand for avoiding complex, cumbersome formulations. Substantively, all real knowledge must, in the end, be finitely describable.

While we find this position attractive, we do not take an unequivocal stand on these matters. We are pragmatists; our purpose is to develop epistemic machinery that will be useful in the applications. When all is said and done, there is little real difference between the views and positions we have described; they only represent different "angles," different ways of looking at the same thing. The reader may choose the approach he prefers — or supply his own.

(b) *An alternative interpretation of the letters of the alphabet*

In Section 5, we interpreted the letters in the alphabet as "natural occurrences": substantive happenings that are not themselves described either in terms of people knowing something, or as combinations of other natural happenings using the connectives of the propositional calculus. An alternative interpretation is that a letter of the alphabet may represent any occurrence whatsoever. Usually, the letters will represent occurrences in which one is particularly interested, the objects of the analysis. If they happen to refer to an individual knowing something, or to involve logical connectives, that is alright.

A basic rationale for the first interpretation is to avoid logically inequivalent representations of the same occurrence, which would lead to "states of the world" that are in practice impossible. Thus if x denotes "it will snow tomorrow", and y denotes "2 knows it will snow tomorrow," then formally there is a state ω at which both k_2x and $\neg y$ hold, and this is nonsensical. By restricting the alphabet to "natural" occurrences, we seek to avoid this awkwardness.

The trouble with this is that though a natural occurrence is most directly described without knowledge operators or logical connectives, it may have practical implications that do involve them; and then we are back with the original problem. For example, "Alice and Bob played a game of chess" implies that "Bob knows that Alice won or Bob knows that Alice did not win", and this implication is commonly known. A formal system that always avoided this awkwardness would be quite cumbersome, and it does not seem worthwhile to try to construct one.

We have seen that in the alternative interpretation, where a letter may represent any occurrence whatsoever, there may well be "impossible" states: states that conform to the formal consistency requirements of Section 6, but that cannot occur when the meaning of the letters is taken into account (like the state ω discussed above, containing both $\neg y$ and k_2x, even though y and k_2x have the same meaning). Differently put, it may happen that in a specific application, there are logical connections between the formulas constituting a syntax; connections that are inherent in the interpretations of the letters of the alphabet within the application — and so are commonly known — but that do not follow from the axioms of the propositional calculus (4.4) and of knowledge (4.5). In such an application, we will wish to reserve the term "state" for those states that are actually "possible" — states at which the logical connections that are inherent in the interpretations of the letters are satisfied and are commonly known. The states that are in this sense "possible" constitute a common knowledge subuniverse of Ω.

(c) *Knowledge hierarchies*

The first explicit constructions[33] of canonical semantic formalisms were hierarchical. For simplicity, suppose there are just two players. Start with a set $\mathfrak{H}$ of mutually exclusive and exhaustive "states of nature," which describe some aspect of reality (like tomorrow's temperature in Jerusalem) in terms not involving knowledge. Let $\mathfrak{H}^1$

[33]Which were in the probabilistic context; see the companion paper to this one (Aumann 1999).

be the set of non-empty subsets of $\mathfrak{H}$, $\mathfrak{H}^2$ the set of non-empty subsets of $\mathfrak{H} \times \mathfrak{H}^1$, $\mathfrak{H}^3$ the set of non-empty subsets of $\mathfrak{H} \times \mathfrak{H}^1 \times \mathfrak{H}^2$, and so on. A *knowledge hierarchy* h_i of a player i has infinitely many levels. Level 1 describes i's information about the true state s of nature; formally, it is a member h_i^1 of $\mathfrak{H}^1$ (the set of members of $\mathfrak{H}$ that i thinks could be the true s). Level 2 describes i's information about the state of nature *and* the information h_j^1 of the *other* player j about the state of nature;[34] formally, it is a member h_i^2 of $\mathfrak{H}^2$ (the set of members of $\mathfrak{H} \times \mathfrak{H}^1$ that i thinks could be the true $(s,\ h_j^1)$). Level 3 describes i's information about the triple consisting of the state of nature, j's information h_j^1 about the state of nature, and j's information h_j^2 about i's information h_j^1 about the state of nature; formally, it is a member h_i^3 of $\mathfrak{H}^3$ (the set of members of $\mathfrak{H} \times \mathfrak{H}^1 \times \mathfrak{H}^2$ that i thinks could be the true $(s,\ h_j^1,\ h_j^2)$). Proceeding in this way, we generate the entire hierarchy $h_i := (h_i^1,\ h_i^2,\ \ldots)$; it embodies i's information about the state of nature, about the players' knowledge about the state of nature, about the players' knowledge about *that*, and so on.

Not all sequences h_i in $\mathfrak{H}^1 \times \mathfrak{H}^2 \times \cdots$ are feasible hierarchies of i; some consistency conditions must be met. For h_i to be feasible, it must be that (i) i's information at each level is consistent with his information at all previous levels, (ii) i knows that j considers i's information possible, and (iii) i knows that j's hierarchy h_j is feasible. Formally, we first define feasibility for *finite* sequences $(h_i^1, \ldots, h_i^m)$, using induction on the level m. At level 1, all nonempty subsets of $\mathfrak{H}$ are feasible. For $m > 1$, call $(h_i^1, \ldots, h_i^m)$ *feasible* if

(i) h_i^{m-1} is the projection of h_i^m on $\mathfrak{H}^{m-1}$,
(ii) if $(s,\ h_j^1, \ldots, h_j^{m-1})$ is in h_i^m, then $(s,\ h_i^1, \ldots, h_i^{m-2})$ is in h_j^{m-1}, and
(iii) if $(s,\ h_j^1, \ldots, h_j^{m-1})$ is in h_i^m, then $(h_j^1, \ldots, h_j^{m-1})$ is feasible.

[34]Though i's information about the state of nature is already embodied in his Level 1, it is not enough at Level 2 to specify just his information about j's Level 1; we need his information about the *pair* $(h^0,\ h_i^1)$.

Define a *hierarchy for* i as a sequence h_i in $\mathfrak{H}^1 \times \mathfrak{H}^2 \times \cdots$ with $(h_i^1, \ldots, h_i^m)$ feasible for each m.

Call a pair (h_i, h_j) of hierarchies of i and j *mutually consistent* if each player considers the other's hierarchy possible; formally, if $(h_j^1, \ldots, h_j^{m-1})$ is in h_i^m, and $(h_i^1, \ldots, h_i^{m-1})$ is in h_j^m, at each level m.

This yields an explicit construction of a canonical semantic formalism, where a state is identified with a mutually consistent pair of hierarchies, the universe is the set of all states, and i's partition of the universe separates between two such pairs g and h if and only if $g_i \neq h_i$.

While this construction looks quite different from that of Section 6, they are in fact equivalent. If, say, the alphabet has r letters $x_1, \ldots, x_r$, then $\mathfrak{H}$ consists of 2^r "states of nature," corresponding to the 2^r possible specifications of x_j or $\neg x_j$ for each $j = 1, \ldots, r$. At each ω in Ω, a unique such state of nature obtains. Moreover, ω determines, for each player i, the states of nature that i considers possible at ω; for example, if $k_i x_1$ is in ω, then i can exclude any state of nature with $\neg x_1$. Thus h_i^1 — and so also h_j^1 — can be read off from ω; similarly, $h_2, h_3, \ldots$ can be read off from ω. One can reason similarly in the opposite direction, and conclude that the two constructions are equivalent.

Though they are equivalent, the construction in Section 6 above is far simpler, more transparent and more straightforward.[35]

Note that two states of the world ω and ω' are in the same element of i's partition of Ω if and only if they correspond to the same knowledge hierarchy of i. Thus i's knowledge hierarchies correspond precisely to the atoms of his information partition; each can be read off from the other. In particular, it follows that the knowledge hierarchy of any *one* player determines precisely the common knowledge component of the true state of the world.

[35]In fact, the hierarchy construction is so convoluted that we present it here with some diffidence. Specifically, we have not checked carefully that the three conditions (i), (ii), (iii) really are the "right" conditions for feasibility.

Appendix: Cardinality of the Canonical State Space

Here we show that when there are at least two players, the canonical system has at least a continuum of states, even when the alphabet has just one letter. By contrast, with only one player (and finitely many letters), the number of states is finite. For background, see the beginning of Section 9.

Define a *context* as a pair consisting of a population N and an alphabet $\mathfrak{X}$. Call a context $(M, \mathfrak{Y})$ *larger* than a context $(N, \mathfrak{X})$ if they are not the same and each component of $(M, \mathfrak{Y})$ includes the corresponding component of $(N, \mathfrak{X})$. Proposition 9.2 yields:

Remark A.1. A list $\mathfrak{L}$ that is consistent in a context $(N, \mathfrak{X})$ is also consistent in any larger context.

Proof. Since $\mathfrak{L}$ is consistent in $(N, \mathfrak{X})$, it has a model in that context. This can be converted to a model for $\mathfrak{L}$ in the larger context by defining $\hat{\kappa}_j$ and $\varphi(z)$ in an arbitrary fashion when j is not in N and z is a letter not in $\mathfrak{X}$ (e.g., one can define the $\hat{\kappa}_j$ as constants and the $\varphi(z)$ as $\hat{\Omega}$).

Proposition A.2. *If* $2 \leq |N| \leq \aleph_0$ *and* $1 \leq |\mathfrak{X}| \leq \aleph_0$, *then* $|\Omega| = 2^{\aleph_0}$.

Before proving A.2, we develop some machinery. Let $\hat{\Omega}$ be a universe, i an individual. We shall say that two states $\hat{\omega}$ and $\hat{\eta}$ in $\hat{\Omega}$ are *i-adjacent* if $\hat{\omega} \in \hat{\mathbf{I}}_i(\hat{\eta})$, *adjacent* if they are i-adjacent for some i. By 1.1, adjacency is symmetric and reflexive. Define the *distance* $d(\hat{\omega}, \hat{\eta})$ as the minimal length of a chain from $\hat{\omega}$ to $\hat{\eta}$ in which successive members are adjacent; formally, as the smallest integer $m \geq 0$ for which there exist states $\hat{\omega}_0, \hat{\omega}_1, \ldots, \hat{\omega}_r$ in $\hat{\Omega}$ with $\hat{\omega} = \hat{\omega}_0, \hat{\omega}_r = \hat{\eta}$, and $\hat{\omega}_{j-1}$ adjacent to $\hat{\omega}_j$ for $j = 1, \ldots, r$. Note that the distance between a state and itself is 0, between different adjacent states 1, and between states in different common knowledge components ∞; and that d is a metric on $\hat{\Omega}$. Denote by $B(\hat{\omega}, r)$ the ball with center $\hat{\omega}$ and radius r, i.e., the set $\{\hat{\eta} : d(\hat{\omega}, \hat{\eta}) \leq r\}$.

Recall (Section 2) that $\hat{K}^1\hat{E} : \bigcap_{i \in N} \hat{K}_i\hat{E}$, $\hat{K}^m E := \hat{K}^1(\hat{K}^{m-1}\hat{E})$.

Lemma A.31. *$\hat{\omega} \in \hat{K}_i\hat{E}$ iff all states i-adjacent to $\hat{\omega}$ are in E.*

Proof. By 1.23, $\hat{\omega} \in \hat{K}_i\hat{E}$ iff $\hat{\mathbf{I}}_i(\hat{\omega}) \subset \hat{E}$; but $\hat{\mathbf{I}}_i(\hat{\omega})$ consists of precisely those states that are i-adjacent to $\hat{\omega}$, so it follows that $\hat{\omega} \in \hat{K}_i\hat{E}$ iff all states i-adjacent to $\hat{\omega}$ are in $\hat{E}$.

Corollary A.32. *$\hat{\omega} \in \hat{K}^1\hat{E}$ iff $\hat{E} \supset B(\hat{\omega},\ 1)$ (i.e., iff each state adjacent to $\hat{\omega}$ is in E).*

Proof. We have $\hat{\omega} \in \hat{K}^1\hat{E}$ iff $\hat{\omega} \in \hat{K}_i\hat{E}$ for all i; by A.31, this holds iff for all i, all states i-adjacent to $\hat{\omega}$ are in E; and this, in turn, holds iff each state adjacent to $\hat{\omega}$ is in E.

Lemma A.33. *$\hat{\omega} \in \hat{K}^n\hat{E}$ iff $\hat{E} \supset B(\hat{\omega},\ n)$.*

Proof. By induction on n. For $n = 1$ this is A.32. Suppose the lemma true up to $n - 1$. Then $\hat{\omega} \in \hat{K}^n\hat{E}$ iff $\hat{\omega} \in \hat{K}^1(\hat{K}^{n-1}\hat{E})$; by A.32, this is so iff $\hat{K}^{n-1}\hat{E} \supset B(\hat{\omega},\ 1)$, which means that

$$d(\hat{\eta}, \hat{\omega}) \leq 1 \Rightarrow \hat{\eta} \in \hat{K}^{n-1}\hat{E}. \tag{A.331}$$

But by the induction hypothesis, $\hat{\eta} \in \hat{K}^{n-1}\hat{E}$ iff $\hat{E} \supset B(\hat{\eta},\ n-1)$, i.e., iff $d(\hat{\xi},\ \hat{\eta}) \leq n - 1 \Rightarrow \hat{\xi} \in \hat{E}$. Thus A.331 holds iff

$$d(\hat{\eta},\ \hat{\omega}) \leq 1 \Rightarrow (d(\hat{\xi},\ \hat{\eta}) \leq n - 1 \Rightarrow \hat{\xi} \in \hat{E}),$$

which is the same as

$$((d(\hat{\eta},\ \hat{\omega}) \leq 1) \wedge (d(\hat{\xi},\ \hat{\eta}) \leq n - 1)) \Rightarrow \hat{\xi} \in \hat{E}. \tag{A.332}$$

We thus conclude that

$$\hat{\omega} \in \hat{K}^n\hat{E} \text{ iff A.332 holds for all } \hat{\eta} \text{ and } \hat{\xi}. \tag{A.333}$$

Now it is a theorem of the first order predicate calculus (and may be verified directly) that

$$(\forall\hat{\xi})\,(\forall\hat{\eta})\,(P(\hat{\eta},\ \hat{\xi}) \Rightarrow Q(\hat{\xi})) \Leftrightarrow (\forall\hat{\xi})\,((\exists\hat{\eta})\,(P(\hat{\eta},\ \hat{\xi})) \Rightarrow Q(\hat{\xi})) \tag{A.334}$$

for any predicates P and Q. Also, it may be verified that

$$(\exists\hat{\eta})\,((d(\hat{\eta},\,\hat{\omega}) \leq 1) \wedge (d(\hat{\xi},\,\hat{\eta}) \leq n-1)) \Leftrightarrow d(\hat{\xi},\,\hat{\omega}) \leq n. \quad \text{(A.335)}$$

Together, A.333, A.334, and A.335 yield

$$\hat{\omega} \in \hat{K}^n\hat{E} \quad \text{iff } (\forall\hat{\xi})\;(d(\hat{\xi},\,\hat{\omega}) \leq n \Rightarrow \hat{\xi} \in \hat{E}). \quad \text{(A.336)}$$

Corollary A.34. *$\hat{\omega} \in \sim\ \hat{K}^n \ \sim\ \hat{E}$ iff $\hat{E} \cap B(\hat{\omega},\,n) \neq \emptyset$ (i.e., iff there is a state in $\hat{E}$ whose distance from $\hat{\omega}$ is at most n).*

Proof. $\hat{\omega} \in \sim\ \hat{K}^n \ \sim\ \hat{E}$ iff $\hat{\omega} \notin \hat{K}^n \ \sim\ \hat{E}$; by A.33, this holds iff it is not the case that $\sim\hat{E} \supset B(\hat{\omega},\,n)$, i.e., iff $\hat{E} \cap B(\hat{\omega},\,n) \neq \emptyset$.

Proof of Proposition A.2. Since $|N| \leq \aleph_0$ and $|\mathfrak{X}| \leq \aleph_0$, the set of formulas is at most denumerable, so the set of sets of formulas has cardinality $\leq 2^{\aleph_0}$. Since a state ω is a set of formulas, it follows that $|\Omega| \leq 2^{\aleph_0}$.

To prove $|\Omega| \geq 2^{\aleph_0}$, we will construct a continuum of different lists, each of which is consistent, but any two of which contradict each other. Since any consistent list can be extended to a state (8.7), it will follow that there is a continuum of states. To show that the lists are indeed consistent, we construct models for them (9.2).

By A.1, we may assume w.l.o.g. that $|N| = 2$ and $|\mathfrak{X}| = 1$. The models we construct all use the same universe $\hat{\Omega}$. This universe has $\aleph_0$ states, denoted $\hat{\omega}_0, \hat{\omega}_1, \hat{\omega}_2, \ldots$. The information partition $\hat{\mathscr{I}}_1$ of individual 1 consists of the events $\{\hat{\omega}_0,\ \hat{\omega}_1\}, \{\hat{\omega}_2, \hat{\omega}_3\}, \{\hat{\omega}_4, \hat{\omega}_5\}, \ldots$. The information partition $\hat{\mathscr{I}}_2$ of individual 2 consists of $\{\hat{\omega}_0\}$, $\{\hat{\omega}_1, \hat{\omega}_2\}, \{\hat{\omega}_3, \hat{\omega}_4\}, \ldots$. One can think of $\hat{\Omega}$ as a sequence of lattice points in the plane, (0, 0), (0, 1), (1, 1), (1, 2), (2, 2), (2, 3), . . . ; then $\hat{\kappa}_1$ is the first coordinate (the vertical projection), and $\hat{\kappa}_2$ the second coordinate (the horizontal projection). Note that $\hat{\omega}_n$ is adjacent only to itself, to $\hat{\omega}_{n-1}$ and to $\hat{\omega}_{n+1}$, and that therefore the distance $d(\hat{\omega}_n,\ \hat{\omega}_m)$ between states $\hat{\omega}_n$ and $\hat{\omega}_m$ is $|n - m|$.

Since there is only one letter x in the alphabet, in order to define a representation, we need only specify to which $\hat{\omega}_n$ we assign x and to which $\neg x$ (9.11). Start out by assigning $\neg x$ to $\hat{\omega}_0$ and x to $\hat{\omega}_1$. After that, define a sequence of blocks with successive lengths $3, 3^2, 3^3, \ldots$. The last state in the ℓ'th block D_ℓ is thus $\hat{\omega}_{1+3+3^2+\cdots+3^\ell} = \hat{\omega}_{(3^{\ell+1}-1)/2}$, the first state in D_ℓ is $\hat{\omega}_{1+3+3^2+\cdots+3^{\ell-1}+1} = \hat{\omega}_{(3^\ell+1)/2}$, and the middle state in D_ℓ is $\hat{\omega}_{((3^\ell+1)/2)+((3^\ell-1)/2)} = \hat{\omega}_{3^\ell}$. Hence

$$B(\hat{\omega}_{3^\ell},\ (3^\ell - 1)/2) = D_\ell. \tag{A.35}$$

For each ℓ, define an operator $Q^\ell : \hat{\mathscr{C}} \to \hat{\mathscr{C}}$ (i.e., from events in $\hat{\Omega}$ to events in $\hat{\Omega}$) by $Q^\ell(\hat{E}) := {\sim}\hat{K}^{3^\ell} \sim \hat{K}^{(3^\ell-1)/2}(\hat{E})$. From A.33 and A.34 it follows that

$$\begin{aligned}&\hat{\omega} \in Q^\ell(\hat{E}) \text{ iff there is a ball of radius } (3^\ell - 1)/2 \text{ included}\\ &\text{in } \hat{E} \text{ whose center is within a distance } 3^\ell \text{ of } \hat{\omega}.\end{aligned} \tag{A.36}$$

Now suppose given an arbitrary infinite sequence $\delta := (\delta_1, \delta_2, \ldots)$ of 0's and 1's. Denote by φ_δ the representation that assigns x to each $\hat{\omega}$ in D_ℓ if $\delta_\ell = 1$, and assigns $\neg x$ to each $\hat{\omega}$ in D_ℓ if $\delta_\ell = 0$. From A.35 and A.36 it follows that

$$\hat{\omega}_0 \in Q^\ell \varphi_\delta(x) \quad \text{if } \delta_\ell = 1; \tag{A.37}$$

the ball required by A.36 is simply D_ℓ. Next, we assert

$$\hat{\omega}_0 \in {\sim}Q^\ell \varphi_\delta(x) \quad \text{if } \delta_\ell = 0. \tag{A.38}$$

Contrariwise, suppose that $\delta_\ell = 0$ and $\hat{\omega}_0 \in Q^\ell\varphi_\delta(x)$. Since $\hat{\omega}_0 \in Q^\ell\varphi_\delta(x)$, it follows from A.36 that within a distance at most 3^ℓ from $\hat{\omega}_0$, there lies the center of a ball — say C_ℓ — of radius $(3^\ell - 1)/2$, all states in which are assigned x. But since $\delta_\ell = 0$, the entire ℓ'th block D_ℓ is assigned $\neg x$; since ω_0 is also assigned $\neg x$, C_ℓ must be included in $\{\omega_1\} \cup D_1 \cup D_2 \cup \cdots \cup D_{\ell-1} = \{\omega_1, \ldots, \omega_{(3^\ell-1)/2}\}$. This set has diameter[36] $(3^\ell - 3)/2$, so the diameter of C_ℓ is $\leq (3^\ell - 3)/2$. But C_ℓ has radius $(3^\ell - 1)/2$, and so diameter $\geq (3^\ell - 1)/2$; this contradiction proves A.38.

---

[36]The *diameter* of a set in a metric space is defined as the maximum (or supremum) distance between two points.

Define an operator $k^1 : \mathfrak{G} \to \mathfrak{G}$ (i.e., from formulas to formulas) by $k^1 f := k_1 f \wedge k_2 f$. Define k^m inductively by $k^m f := k^1(k^{m-1} f)$, and define $q^\ell := \neg k^{3^\ell} \neg k^{(3^\ell - 1)/2}$. From 9.1 we get

$$Q^\ell \varphi_\delta(x) = \varphi_\delta(q^\ell x) \quad \text{and} \quad {\sim} Q^\ell \varphi_\delta(x) = \varphi_\delta(\neg q^\ell x). \tag{A.39}$$

For each sequence δ, let $\mathfrak{L}_\delta$ be the list $(f_\delta^1,\ f_\delta^2,\ \ldots)$, where $f_\delta^\ell := q^\ell x$ if $\delta = 1$, and $f_\delta^\ell := \neg q^\ell x$ if $\delta = 0$. From A.37, A.38, and A.39, it follows that for each δ, the intersection of the events $\varphi_\delta(f_\delta^\ell)$ contains $\hat{\omega}_0$, and so is non-empty. Hence $(\hat{\Omega},\ \varphi_\delta)$ is a model for $\mathfrak{L}_\delta$, and so $\mathfrak{L}_\delta$ is consistent (9.2). But any two lists $\mathscr{L}_\delta$ contradict each other. For, there must be some ℓ such that $\delta_\ell = 1$ for one of the lists whereas $\delta_\ell = 0$ for the other; and for that ℓ, the two corresponding formulas f_δ^ℓ are precisely the negatives of each other. Since there is a continuum of different δ, we have constructed a continuum of lists, each of which is consistent, but any two of which contradict each other.

In contrast to A.2, we have

Proposition A.4. *If there is only one individual ($|N| = 1$) and the alphabet $\mathfrak{X}$ is finite, then Ω is finite.*

To prove A.4, we need some lemmas. Since there is only one individual, we write k for k_i.

Lemma A.41. *$k(f \vee kg) \Leftrightarrow (kf \vee kg)$ is a tautology for all f and g.*

Proof. This is most quickly proved directly from the definitions in Section 4; but we prefer verbal reasoning,[37] which makes the proof more transparent. We use 8.8, which says that a formula is a tautology iff it is in every state. Thus given an arbitrary state ω, we must show $(k(f \vee kg) \Leftrightarrow (kf \vee kg)) \in \omega$. To this end, we use 8.63, which enables us to replace symbols like $\vee, \neg$, and $\Rightarrow$ by the corresponding words. The process is facilitated by writing "f" for the more cumbersome $f \in \omega$; thus "f" means "f holds at ω".

We wish to prove that "$k(f \vee kg)$" iff "$kf \vee kg$". To show "if", assume "$kf \vee kg$". If "kf", then "$k(f \vee kg)$" (4.52), so we are done.

[37] E.g., using words like "or" and "not".

If "kg", then "$k(kg)$" (8.1), so "$k(f \vee kg)$" (4.52), and again we are done.

To show "only if", assume "$k(f \vee kg)$". Then "$f \vee kg$" (4.51). If "kg", then "$kf \vee kg$", so we are done. Otherwise "$\neg kg$", so "$k \neg kg$" (4.53), so "$k(f \vee kg)$" and "$k \neg kg$", so "$k(f \vee kg) \wedge k(\neg kg)$", i.e., "$k((f \vee kg) \wedge \neg kg)$" (8.72), i.e., "$k(f \wedge \neg kg)$", so "$kf$" (4.52), so "$kf \vee kg$", and again we are done.

Corollary A.42. *$k(kf \vee kg) \Leftrightarrow (kf \vee kg)$ is a tautology.*

Proof. A.41 and 8.1.

Corollary A.43. *$k(f \vee \neg kg) \Leftrightarrow (kf \vee \neg kg)$ is a tautology.*

Proof. A.41, 4.51, and 4.53.

Call a formula *fundamental* if it is either a letter in the alphabet or has the form kg, where g is elementary (contains no knowledge operators). Say that a formula has *depth* 1 if it is constructed from atomic formulas by using the symbols $\vee$, $\neg$,), and (only. Thus a formula has depth 1 if and only if the knowledge operator is not concatenated.

Lemma A.44. *If $|N| = 1$, every formula is equivalent*[38] *to a formula of depth* 1.

Proof. Define a formula of *depth* n inductively by specifying that it be constructed from formulas of the form h and kh, where h is a formula of depth $n-1$, by using the symbols $\vee$, $\neg$,), and (only. Clearly, each formula is of depth n for some n. Thus it suffices to prove that a formula of depth 2 is equivalent to one of depth 1; and for this, it suffices to prove that if h is of depth 1, then kh is equivalent to a depth 1 formula.

[38]Recall that f is *tautologically equivalent* to g — or simply *equivalent* for short — if $f \Leftrightarrow g$ is a tautology.

So let h be a formula of depth 1. Thus h is constructed from letters and from formulas of the form kg — where g is an elementary formula — by using the symbols of the propositional calculus only. Replace each occurrence in h of a formula of the form kg by a new letter, one that does not occur in the original alphabet. We thus get a new formula h' which does not contain any knowledge operators. Write h' in its conjunctive normal form, i.e., as a conjunction of disjunctions of letters and their negatives.[39] Now replace the new letters — those that replaced formulas of the form kg — by the original formulas that they replaced. We thus conclude that

$$h \sim (f_1 \vee \pm kg_{11} \vee \pm kg_{12} \vee \cdots) \wedge (f_2 \vee \pm kg_{21} \vee \pm kg_{22} \vee \cdots) \wedge \cdots,$$

where $\sim$ stands for equivalence, $\pm$ stands for either nothing or $\neg$, and in this instance, three dots $(\cdots)$ indicate a *finite* sequence. From 8.72, A.41, A.42 and A.43 we then get

$$kh \sim (kf_1 \vee \pm kg_{11} \vee \pm kg_{12} \vee \cdots) \wedge (kf_2 \vee \pm kg_{21} \vee \pm kg_{22} \vee \cdots) \wedge \cdots,$$

and the right side is a formula of depth 1.

Proof of Proposition A.4. From the conjunctive normal form it follows that with a given finite alphabet, there are at most finitely many inequivalent elementary formulas (only finitely many inequivalent disjunctions, so only finitely many inequivalent conjunctions of these disjunctions). Since $f \sim g$ implies[40] $kf \sim kg$, it follows that there are only finitely many formulas of the form kf where f is elementary. Hence there are only finitely many inequivalent first order formulas. The proposition now follows from A.44.

References

Aumann, R. J., 1976, Agreeing to disagree, *Annals of Statistics* 4, 1236–1239. [Chapter 2]

[39] Every elementary formula can be written in this way. See, for example, Hilbert and Ackermann (1928), p. 9ff.

[40] This follows from 4.52 and the set of tautologies being epistemically closed.

Aumann, R. J., 1987, Correlated equilibrium as an expression of Bayesian rationality, *Econometrica* 55, 1–18. [Chapter 8]

Aumann, R. J., 1999, Interactive epistemology II: Probability, *International Journal of Game Theory* 28, 301–314. [Chapter 4]

Aumann, R. J., Brandenburger, A., 1995, Epistemic conditions for Nash equilibrium, *Econometrica* 63, 1161–1180. [Chapter 10]

Fagin R., Halpern, J. Y., Moses, M., Vardi, M. Y., 1995, *Reasoning about Knowledge*, MIT Press, Cambridge.

Hart, S., Heifetz, A., Samet, D., 1996, "Knowing whether", "knowing that", and the cardinality of state spaces, *Journal of Economic Theory* 70, 249–256.

Hilbert, D., Ackermann, W., 1928, *Grundzüge der theoretischen Logik*, Springer, Berlin.

Hintikka, J., 1962, *Knowledge and Belief*, Cornell University Press, Ithaca.

Kripke, S., 1959, A completeness theorem in modal logic, *J. Symbolic Logic* 24, 1–14.

Lewis, D., 1969, *Convention*, Harvard University Press, Cambridge.

Samet, D., 1990, Ignoring ignorance and agreeing to disagree, *Journal of Economic Theory* 52, 190–207.

Chapter 4

Interactive Epistemology II: Probability*,†

Abstract: Formal Interactive Epistemology deals with the logic of knowledge and belief when there is more than one agent or "player." One is interested not only in each person's knowledge and beliefs about substantive matters, but also in his knowledge and beliefs about the others' knowledge and beliefs. This paper examines two parallel approaches to the subject. The first is the *semantic*, in which knowledge and beliefs are represented by a space Ω of *states of the world,* and for each player i, partitions $\mathscr{I}_i$ of Ω and probability distributions $\pi_i(\cdot;\omega)$ on Ω for each state ω of the world. The atom of $\mathscr{I}_i$ containing a given state ω represents i's knowledge at that state — the set of those other states that i cannot distinguish from ω; the probability distributions $\pi_i(\cdot;\omega)$ represent i's beliefs at the state ω. The second is the *syntactic* approach, in

*Reprinted from *International Journal of Game Theory* (1999), 28, 301–314, with permission from Springer.

†This paper is based on notes originally distributed in connection with a sequence of six lectures on Interactive Epistemology given at the Cowles Foundation for Research in Economics, Yale University, in the spring of 1989, and expanded and corrected several times since then. Previous versions were distributed in connection with the tutorial and workshop on "Knowledge and Game Theory" held at the Summer Institute in Game Theory, State University of New York at Stony Brook, July 20–24, 1992, and in connection with the Fifth Jerusalem Summer School in Economic Theory, on "Rationality of Action and Belief in the Economy," June 13–23, 1994. The author is grateful to Prof. Dov Samet for important help in preparing the current version. Research support from the USNSF under grant SBR-9730205 and previous grants is gratefully acknowledged.

which beliefs are embodied in sentences constructed according to certain syntactic rules. This paper examines the relation between the two approaches, and shows that they are in a sense equivalent.

In game theory and economics, the semantic approach has heretofore been most prevalent. A question that often arises in this connection is whether, in what sense, and why the space Ω, the partitions $\mathscr{I}_i$, and the probability distributions $\pi_i(\cdot;\omega)$ can be taken as given and commonly known by the players. An answer to this question is provided by the syntactic approach.

11. Introduction

In interactive contexts like game theory and economics, it is important to consider what each player knows and believes about what the other players know and believe. Two different formalisms — the *semantic* and the *syntactic* — are available for this purpose. A companion paper (Aumann 1999, Chapter 2, henceforth [A]) discusses and relates the two formalisms in the context of *knowledge*. Here we extend that analysis to include issues of belief — i.e., probability.

The semantic formalism consists of a "partition structure." For knowledge only [A], this consists of a space Ω of *states of the world* (or simply *states)*, together with a partition of Ω for each player i. To deal with probability as well, one adds a probability distribution $\pi_i(\cdot;\omega)$ on Ω for each player i and each state ω. The atoms of i's partition are his *information sets*[1]; Ω is called the *universe*. Like in probability theory, *events* are subsets[2] of Ω; intuitively, an event E is identified with the set of all those states at which the event obtains. Thus E obtains at a state ω if and only if $\omega \in E$. Player i's probability for event E at state ω is represented by $\pi_i(E;\omega)$. If α is between 0 and 1 and E is an event, then "i's probability for E is at

[1]I.e., he can distinguish between states ω and ω' if and only if they are in different atoms of his partition.

[2]But unlike in [A], not *every* subset of Ω is an event; certain measurability conditions must be met. See Section 1.

least α" is itself an event, denoted $P_i^\alpha E$; explicitly, it is the set of all states ω at which $\pi_i(E;\omega) \geq \alpha$. Similarly, "$i$ knows E" is an event, denoted $K_i E$; explicitly, ω is in $K_i E$ if and only if the information set of i containing ω is included in E.

The syntactic formalism, on the other hand, is built on propositions, expressed in a formal language. The language has logical operators and connectives, operators k_i expressing knowledge, and operators p_i^α expressing beliefs. If e is a sentence, then $k_i e$ and $p_i^\alpha e$ are also sentences; $k_i e$ means "i knows e," and $p_i^\alpha e$ means "i has a probability of at least α for e." The operators k_i and p_i^α can be iterated: The sentence $k_j p_i^\alpha e$ means "j knows that i's probability for j knowing e is at least α." Logical relations between the various propositions are expressed by formal rules.

There is a rough correspondence between the two formalisms: Events correspond to sentences, unions to disjunctions, intersections to conjunctions, inclusions to implications, complementation to negation, semantic knowledge operators K_i and belief operators P_i^α to syntactic knowledge operators k_i and belief operators p_i^α. But the correspondence really *is* quite rough; for example, only some — not all — events correspond to syntactically admissible sentences.

While the semantic formalism is the more convenient and widely used of the two, it is conceptually not quite straightforward. One question that often arises is, what do the players know about the formalism itself? Does each know the others' partitions, and does he know the others' probability measures as functions of ω? If so, from where does this knowledge derive?

For the case of knowledge, this question is answered by constructing a unique *canonical* semantic partition structure, in terms of the syntactic formalism; see [A]. The main purpose of this paper is to do the same in the expanded context that includes also probability.

The underlying idea is as in [A]. A state ω in the canonical semantic formalism is *defined* as a list of (syntactic) sentences that is complete and consistent in the appropriate senses; intuitively, the list is the set of all sentences that "hold at" ω. Also as in [A], the concept of a semantic *model* for a list of sentences plays a central role; a list is consistent if and only if it has a model.

But there are some significant divergences from [A]. For one thing, probability involves measurability; though this offers no particular difficulty, it must be dealt with. More important, in [A] the definition of "consistency" is syntactic, and one *proves* that a list of sentences is consistent if and only if it has a model. Here — in the context of probability — we did not succeed in formulating a satisfactory syntactic definition of consistency that would enable the proof of such a result. We therefore *define* a consistent list of sentences as one that has a model. This and other conceptual issues will be discussed in Sections 15 and 17.

While we have tried to make this paper self-contained, it does have important ties to [A], both conceptual and formal. To make it easier to refer to [A], we continue [A]'s numbering system here: The current paper starts with Section 11, so that a reference to 1.8, say, refers to [A]. For notations that are not explained here, the reader is referred to [A].

The remaining sections are numbered roughly as in [A], with the number 10 added. Thus Section 12 here describes the semantic knowledge-belief formalism, whereas Section 2 in [A] describes the (multi-player) semantic knowledge formalism. Sections 13 and 3 are conceptual discussions of the semantic formalisms. Sections 14 and 4 respectively set forth the syntactic knowledge-belief formalism, and the syntactic knowledge formalism; Sections 15 and 5 discuss these constructions. Sections 16 and 6 respectively construct the canonical semantic knowledge-belief and knowledge systems; again, Sections 17 and 7 discuss these constructions. Like Sections 8 and 9, Sections 18 and 19 explore and justify the foregoing material, using mathematical tools. Specifically, we show that there is a rough "isomorphism" between the two formalisms, similar to that established in Section 8 for the case of knowledge. Also, we show that the canonical system constructed in Section 16 is indeed a knowledge-belief system as defined in Section 12 (the corresponding statement for knowledge systems is immediate). The paper closes with a discussion in Section 20, roughly parallel to the discussion of knowledge formalisms in Section 10.

12. Semantic Knowledge-Belief Formalisms

Recall that a *semantic knowledge system* (Section 2) consists of a *universe* Ω, a *population* N, and a *knowledge function* κ_i for each individual i in N. Define a *finite semantic knowledge-belief system* to consist of a semantic knowledge system with a finite universe, and, for each individual i and state ω, a probability measure $\pi_i(\cdot;\omega)$ on the field $\mathscr{E}$ of subsets of Ω (called *events*). The interpretation is that at state ω, individual i ascribes probability $\pi_i(E;\omega)$ to event E. Set

$$P_i^\alpha E := \{\omega : \pi_i(E;\omega) \geq \alpha\}; \tag{12.1}$$

$P_i^\alpha E$ is the event that i ascribes a probability of at least α to E. Assume that

$$K_i E \subset P_i^1 E, \text{ and} \tag{12.2}$$

$$P_i^\alpha E \subset K_i P_i^\alpha E. \tag{12.3}$$

Intuitively, 12.2 says that if i knows something, then he assigns it a probability of 1; 12.3, that he knows the probabilities that he assigns to events. Technically, 12.2 says that $\pi_i(\cdot;\omega)$ is concentrated on i's information set $\mathbf{I}(\omega)$; 12.3, that $\pi_i(E;\cdot)$ is $\mathscr{K}_i$-measurable.[3]

In the general (not necessarily finite) case, define a *knowledge-belief system* as a knowledge system $\{\Omega, N, \{\kappa_i\}_{i\in N}\}$, together with a sigma-field $\mathscr{F}_\sigma$ of sets in Ω (called *events*), and, for each individual i and state ω, a probability measure $\pi_i(\cdot;\omega)$ on $\mathscr{F}_\sigma$ such that

$$\text{the atoms of the } \mathscr{I}_i \text{ are } \mathscr{F}_\sigma\text{-measurable, and} \tag{12.4}$$

$$\pi_i(E;\omega) \text{ is } \mathscr{F}_\sigma\text{-measurable in } \omega \text{ for each fixed } E \text{ in } \mathscr{F}_\sigma. \tag{12.5}$$

[3]This means that if ω' and ω are in the same atom of the information partition $\mathscr{I}_i$, then $P_i(F,\omega') = P_i(F,\omega)$.

As before, $\pi_i(E;\omega)$ signifies i's probability for E at ω; and we assume 12.2 and 12.3, where P_i^α is defined by 12.1.

For future reference, note that

$$\pi_i(E;\omega) = \sup\{\text{rational } \alpha : \omega \in P_i^\alpha E\}. \tag{12.6}$$

Indeed, fix ω, i and E. By 12.1, for any α (not necessarily rational) we have

$$\omega \in P_i^\alpha E \text{ iff } \pi_i(E;\omega) \geq \alpha. \tag{12.7}$$

Therefore $\pi_i(E;\omega)$ is $\geq$ any rational α for which $\omega \in P_i^\alpha E$, which establishes $\geq$ in 12.6. On the other hand, if a rational β is $\leq \pi_i(E;\omega)$, then by 12.7, $\omega \in P_i^\beta E$, so $\beta \leq \sup\{\alpha : \omega \in P_i^\alpha E\}$; this establishes $\leq$ in 12.6.

13. Discussion

First, note that as presented here, the beliefs of the players depend explicitly on their information; in effect, each player's probability is concentrated on his information set. This is in contrast to formulations (e.g., Aumann (1987)) in which the probability distributions are initially given on the entire state space Ω, and then the players compute posterior probabilities, conditional on their information. Proceeding as we do here emphasizes that we are analyzing a single moment of time, at which the players have the information that they have; we are interested in the beliefs of the players at that time, and at that time only.

Next, the conceptual issues discussed in Section 3 arise here also. Basically, the problem is to justify the implicit assumption that the players know the model itself, including the partitions of the other players and their probability distributions (for each of their information sets). The problem could be resolved by presenting an explicit canonical semantic formalism, with explicit descriptions of the states, partitions, and probabilities. This, indeed, is what we do in Section 16.

14. The Syntactic Knowledge-Belief Formalism

Start with a finite population N, and a *keyboard* consisting of an alphabet $\mathfrak{X} := \{x, y, z, \ldots\}$ and the symbols $\vee, \neg,), (, k_i$, and p_i^α, where i ranges over the individuals in N and α over the rationals between 0 and 1 inclusive. A *formula* is defined as a finite string of symbols obtained by applying finitely often, in some order, the following rules:

$$\text{Every letter in the alphabet is a formula.} \tag{14.1}$$

$$\text{If } f \text{ and } g \text{ are formulas, so is } (f) \vee (g). \tag{14.2}$$

$$\begin{aligned}&\text{If } f \text{ is a formula, so are } \neg(f), k_i(f), \text{ and } p_i^\alpha(f)\\ &\text{for each } i \text{ and each } \alpha.\end{aligned} \tag{14.3}$$

We often omit parentheses, and in particular write $p_i^\alpha f$ for $p_i^\alpha(f)$; intuitively, $p_i^\alpha f$ means "i ascribes a probability of at least α to f." Adding the probability operators p_i^α to the language enables us to refer to the players' beliefs, in addition to the elements treated in Section 4.

The set of all formulas with the given population N and alphabet $\mathfrak{X}$ is called a *syntax*, and is denoted $\mathfrak{S}(N, \mathfrak{X})$, or just $\mathfrak{S}$. Assume that N and $\mathfrak{X}$ are finite or denumerable; it follows that $\mathfrak{S}$ is denumerable. Define a *representation* of $\mathfrak{S}$ as a knowledge–belief system, $\hat{\Pi}$, together with a function $\varphi : \mathfrak{S} \to \hat{\mathscr{F}}_\sigma$ such that for all f, g, i, and α,

$$\begin{aligned}&\varphi(\neg f) = \sim \varphi(f), \quad \varphi(f \vee g) = \varphi(f) \cup \varphi(g),\\ &\varphi(k_i f) = \hat{K}_i \varphi(f), \quad \text{and} \quad \varphi(p_i^\alpha f) = \hat{P}_i^\alpha \varphi(f),\end{aligned} \tag{14.4}$$

where $\hat{\mathscr{F}}_\sigma$ is the σ-field of events in $\hat{\Pi}$, and $\hat{K}_i, \hat{P}_i^\alpha$, are the corresponding semantic knowledge and belief operators. Given a representation $(\hat{\Pi}, \varphi)$ and a state $\hat{\omega}$ in $\hat{\Pi}$, a formula f is said to *hold at* $\hat{\omega}$ if $\hat{\omega}$ is in $\varphi(f)$. A *list* $\mathfrak{L}$ is a set of formulas. A *model* for $\mathfrak{L}$ is a representation φ and a state $\hat{\omega}$ in $\hat{\Pi}$ such that every formula in the list holds at $\hat{\omega}$. A formula f is a *consequence* of (or *follows* from) $\mathfrak{L}$ if every model for $\mathfrak{L}$ is also a model for $\{f\}$.

15. Discussion

In Section 5 we discussed and interpreted the syntax of pure knowledge, as set forth in Section 4; much of that discussion applies, mutatis mutandis, to the knowledge-belief syntax set forth in Section 14.

Each of these two syntaxes provides both a *grammar* and a *logic.* The grammar tells us how to construct "well-formed formulas," i.e., meaningful sentences; the logic, how to deduce formulas from one another.

The two grammars are entirely analogous. Both are embodied in the descriptions of the keyboards, and in the rules for constructing formulas from keyboard elements (14.1 through 14.3 for knowledge-belief, 4.1 through 4.3 for knowledge). Indeed, the only difference is that the knowledge-belief grammar has probability operators p_i^α in addition to the other elements.

But the two logics are quite different, in several ways. In Section 4 — which treats knowledge only — the fundamental notion of consequence is defined in purely syntactic terms: g is a *consequence* of f if it follows from f by repeated use of certain axioms and rules of deduction.[4] Moreover, it is finitary, in that the hypothesis comprises just one formula f; and though one *can* speak of g following from a list $\mathfrak{L}$ of formulas, that is tantamount to g following from a conjunction of *finitely* many formulas in $\mathfrak{L}$.

In contrast, in Section 14 the notion of consequence is infinitary: A formula can follow from a list $\mathfrak{L}$ without following from any finite sublist. For example, $p^{1/2}x$ follows from all the $p^\alpha x$ with $\alpha < 1/2$, but not from any finite number of them. Moreover, the definition is no longer purely syntactic; it involves "models," which are essentially semantic.

While these differences are conceptually significant, their practical effect is limited. Though infinitary deductions are in principle possible, we know of none in actual game-theoretic or economic applications of epistemological formalisms. As for the issue of syntax

[4]That is what "strong closure" amounts to.

versus semantics in defining "consequence," practically speaking it shouldn't matter. In the case of knowledge, it indeed doesn't matter; by 9.4, the two approaches are equivalent. In the case of probability (knowledge-belief), we have not succeeded in developing a deductive logic that allows us to establish such a result formally. Conceptually, it would certainly be desirable to do so; and for a "purely" syntactic logic, without any semantic component, it is indispensable. But even without this, the definition of tautology in Section 14 does, practically speaking, provide a coherent logic for the syntactic grammar.

Section 16 uses the syntactic formalism of Section 14 to construct an explicit canonical semantic knowledge-belief system. But it should be remembered that the syntactic formalism is important not only as a tool for constructing the canonical semantic formalism, but also in its own right, as a formalism of deduction. In this formalism, there are no explicit states; one simply deduces true statements from other true statements. As noted in the introduction, this mode of deduction is in a sense more compelling — has more immediacy — than the semantic mode.

16. The Canonical Semantic Knowledge-Belief System

As in Section 14, assume given a finite population N and an alphabet $\mathfrak{X}$. Call a list $\mathfrak{L}$ of formulas *closed* if it contains all its consequences; *coherent*, if

$$\neg f \in \mathfrak{L} \text{ implies } f \notin \mathfrak{L}; \tag{16.1}$$

and *complete* if

$$f \notin \mathfrak{L} \text{ implies } \neg f \in \mathfrak{L}. \tag{16.2}$$

A *state* is a closed, coherent, and complete list. Denote the set of all states $\Pi(N, \mathfrak{X})$, or simply Π. For all individuals i, define a knowledge function κ_i on Π by specifying that for all states ω,

$$\kappa_i(\omega) \text{ is the set of all formulas in } \omega \text{ that start with } k_i. \tag{16.3}$$

For each formula f, define an event E_f (a subset of Π) by

$$E_f := \{\omega \in \Omega : f \in \omega\}. \tag{16.4}$$

Let $\mathscr{F}_\sigma$ be the σ-field generated[5] by the events E_f. For each f, i, and ω, define

$$\pi_i(E_f; \omega) := \sup(\alpha : p_i^\alpha f \in \omega). \tag{16.5}$$

We will show below (Section 18) that $\pi_i(\cdot; \omega)$ is well-defined on the events E_f for each ω and i, and extends uniquely to a σ-additive probability measure on $\mathscr{F}_\sigma$, which is also denoted $\pi_i(\cdot; \omega)$; moreover (Section 19), that the system comprising Π, the κ_i, the σ-field $\mathscr{F}_\sigma$, and the probability measures $\pi_i(\cdot; \omega)$ satisfies 12.2 through 12.5, and so is a knowledge-belief system. We call it the *canonical semantic knowledge-belief system* for $(N, \mathfrak{X})$, or simply the *canonical system.*

17. Discussion

As before, much of the discussion of the canonical semantic knowledge formalism applies, mutatis mutandis, also here; see Section 7.

We have seen (Section 15) that the logic of the syntactic knowledge-belief formalism depends on the notion of a semantic model, and so is not "purely" syntactic. This raises the question as to whether there is not some kind of circularity implicit in our construction of the canonical semantic formalism.

The answer is "no". Our aim, as stated at the end of Section 13, is to present an explicit canonical semantic formalism, with explicit descriptions of the states, partitions, and probabilities. The construction in Section 16 accomplishes this in a coherent and valid manner.

18. The Canonical Probabilities Are Well-Defined and Superadditive

Throughout this section and the next, ω denotes a state in the canonical system. In this section we prove that $\pi_i(\cdot; \omega)$ is well-defined

[5]The smallest sigma-field containing all the E_f.

on the events E_f (18.32), that it is finitely additive (18.4), that it extends uniquely to a sigma-additive measure on $\mathscr{F}_\sigma$ (18.56), and that it is a probability measure (18.6). In the process, we will begin, in the current knowledge-belief context, to establish a correspondence between syntax and semantics analogous to that established in Section 8 in the context of knowledge (18.1).

Let x be in the alphabet. Since ω is coherent, either $\neg x \notin \omega$ or $x \notin \omega$. Suppose w.l.o.g. that $x \notin \omega$. Since ω is closed, x is not a consequence of ω. Thus it is not true that every model for ω is also a model for x. So there is a model for ω that is not a model for x. In particular, there is a model for ω; denote it $(\hat{\Pi}, \varphi, \hat{\omega})$. Let $\hat{\pi}_i(\cdot;\hat{\omega})$ be the probabilities of i in $\hat{\Pi}$ at $\hat{\omega}$. Call an event of the form E_f *syntactic*, and denote the family of syntactic events by $\mathscr{F}$.

Proposition 18.1.

$$\sim E_f = E_{\neg f}, \tag{18.11}$$

$$E_f \cup E_g = E_{f\vee g}, \text{ and} \tag{18.12}$$

$$E_f \cap E_g = E_{f\wedge g}. \tag{18.13}$$

Proof. Analogous to that of 8.3, and so omitted.

Corollary 18.14. *The family $\mathscr{F}$ of syntactic events is a field; that is, it is closed under complementation, finite unions, and finite intersections.*

Lemma 18.2.

$$\text{If } E_f \subset E_g, \text{ then } \varphi(f) \subset \varphi(g), \tag{18.21}$$

$$f \in \omega \text{ iff } \hat{\omega} \in \varphi(f), \text{ and} \tag{18.22}$$

$$\hat{\pi}_i(\varphi(f);\hat{\omega}) = \sup\{\alpha : p_i^\alpha f \in \omega\}. \tag{18.23}$$

Proof. Suppose it is not the case that $\varphi(f) \subset \varphi(g)$; i.e., that there is an element $\hat{v}$ of $\varphi(f)\backslash\varphi(g)$. Let v be the list of all formulas that hold at $\hat{v}$. Then v is a consistent and complete list — i.e., a state in the canonical system Π. By construction, $f \in v$ and $g \notin v$, and the existence of such a state is incompatible with $E_f \subset E_g$. This establishes 18.21.

The "only if" part of 18.22 is what we mean by saying that $(\hat{\Pi}, \varphi, \hat{\omega})$ is a model for ω. For the "if" part, let $f \notin \omega$. Then $\neg f \in \omega$ by completeness (16.2). So by the "only if" part, $\hat{\omega} \in \varphi(\neg f) = {\sim}\varphi(f)$; that is, $\hat{\omega} \notin \varphi(f)$. This proves the contrapositive of the "if" part.

Finally, by 12.6 and 18.22, $\hat{\pi}_i(\varphi(f); \hat{\omega}) = \sup\{\alpha : \hat{\omega} \in \hat{P}_i^\alpha \varphi(f)\} = \sup\{\alpha : \hat{\omega} \in \varphi(p_i^\alpha f)\} = \sup\{\alpha : p_i^\alpha f \in \omega\}$, as asserted in 18.23.

Lemma 18.3. *If $E_f \subset E_g$, then $\sup(\alpha : p_i^\alpha f \in \omega) \leq \sup(\alpha : p_i^\alpha g \in \omega)$ for all i and ω.*

Proof. By 18.21, $\varphi(f) \subset \varphi(g)$, so $\hat{\pi}_i(\varphi(f), \hat{v}) \leq \hat{\pi}_i(\varphi(g), \hat{v})$; the lemma then follows from 18.23.

Corollary 18.31. *If $E_f = E_g$, then $\sup(\alpha : p_i^\alpha f \in \omega) = \sup(\alpha : p_i^\alpha g \in \omega)$ for all i and ω.*

Corollary 18.32. *The $\pi_i(\cdot; \omega)$, as defined by 16.5, are well-defined on the events E_f.*

Corollary 18.33. $\pi_i(E_f; \omega) = \hat{\pi}_i(\varphi(f); \hat{\omega})$.

Proof. Follows from 16.5 and 18.23.

Lemma 18.4. *The $\pi_i(\cdot; \omega)$ are finitely additive; that is, if $E_f \cap E_g = \emptyset$, then $\pi_i(E_f; \omega) + \pi_i(E_g; \omega) = \pi_i(E_f \cup E_g; \omega)$.*

Proof. $E_f \cap E_g = \emptyset$ and 18.1 yield $E_f \subset E_{\neg g}$. So by 18.21, $\varphi(f) \subset \varphi(\neg g) = {\sim}\varphi(g)$, so $\varphi(f) \cap \varphi(g) = \emptyset$, so by 18.12, 18.33, and 14.4, $\pi_i(E_f \cup E_g; \omega) = \pi_i(E_{f \vee g}; \omega) = \hat{\pi}_i(\varphi(f \vee g); \hat{\omega}) = \hat{\pi}_i(\varphi(f) \cup \varphi(g); \hat{\omega}) = \hat{\pi}_i(\varphi(f); \hat{\omega}) + \hat{\pi}_i(\varphi(g); \hat{\omega}) = \pi_i(E_f; \omega) + \pi_i(E_g; \omega)$.

Lemma 18.5. *Let $g, f_1, f_2, \ldots$ be an infinite sequence of formulas such that*

$$E_{f_1} \subset E_{f_2} \subset \cdots \textit{and} \tag{18.51}$$

$$E_{f_1} \cup E_{f_2} \cup \cdots = E_g. \tag{18.52}$$

Then for each individual i and state ω,

$$\pi_i(E_g; \omega) = \lim_{n\to\infty} \pi_i(E_{f_n}; \omega). \tag{18.53}$$

Proof. By 18.21,

$$\varphi(f_1) \subset \varphi(f_2) \subset \cdots \subset \varphi(g). \tag{18.54}$$

We claim that

$$\varphi(f_1) \cup \varphi(f_2) \cup \cdots = \varphi(g). \tag{18.55}$$

If not, then the last inclusion in 18.54 is strict; that is, there is a $\hat{v}$ in $\varphi(g)$ that is not in any of the $\varphi(f_n)$. Set $v := \{f : \hat{v} \in \varphi(f)\}$. Then v is a consistent and complete list of formulas — i.e., a state in Π. This state contains g but none of the f_n, contradicting 18.52; so 18.55 is proved. Then by 18.33, 18.54, 18.55, and the countable additivity of the $\hat{\pi}_i(\cdot; \hat{\omega})$,

$$\lim_{n\to\infty} \pi_i(E_{f_n}; \omega) = \lim_{n\to\infty} \hat{\pi}_i(\varphi(f_n); \hat{\omega}) = \hat{\pi}_i(\varphi(g); \hat{\omega}) = \pi_i(E_g; \omega).$$

Corollary 18.56. *The definition (16.5) of $\pi_i(\cdot; \omega)$ extends uniquely to a σ-additive measure on $\mathscr{F}_\sigma$.*

Proof. By 18.14, the events E_f form a field. So, by Caratheodory's theorem, it suffices to show that $\pi_i(\cdot; \omega)$ is countably additive when restricted to events of the form E_f; i.e., that if $E_{g_1} \cup E_{g_2} \cdots = E_g$

and the E_{g_m} are mutually disjoint, then

$$\pi_i(E_{g_1};\omega) + \pi_i(E_{g_2};\omega) + \cdots = \pi_i(E_g;\omega).$$

To this end, set $f_n := g_1 \vee \cdots \vee g_n$, apply 18.5, 18.12, and 18.4, and conclude that

$$\begin{aligned}\pi_i(E_g;\omega) &= \lim_{n\to\infty} \pi_i(E_{f_n};\omega) = \lim_{n\to\infty} \pi_i\left(\bigcup_{m=1}^{n} E_{g_m};\omega\right)\\ &= \lim_{n\to\infty} \sum_{m=1}^{n} \pi_i(E_{g_m};\omega) = \sum_{m=1}^{\infty} \pi_i(E_{g_m};\omega).\end{aligned}$$

Lemma 18.6. $\pi_i(\Pi;\omega) = 1.$

Proof. By completeness (16.2), each state contains x or $\neg x$, and so in any case $x \vee \neg x$. Therefore $\Pi = \mathrm{E}_{x\vee\neg x}$, so by 11.9 and 13.23,

$$\begin{aligned}\pi_i(\Pi;\omega) &= \pi_i(\mathrm{E}_{x\vee\neg x};\omega) = \sup\{\alpha : p_i^\alpha(x \vee \neg x) \in \omega\} =\\ &= \hat{\pi}_i(\varphi(x \vee \neg x);\hat{\omega}) =\\ &= \hat{\pi}_i(\varphi(x) \cup \varphi(\neg x);\hat{\omega}) = \hat{\pi}_i(\varphi(x) \cup \varphi(\neg x);\hat{\omega}) =\\ &= \hat{\pi}_i(\varphi(x) \cup \sim \varphi(x);\hat{\omega}) = \hat{\pi}_i(\hat{\Pi};\hat{\omega}) = 1.\end{aligned}$$

19. The Canonical System Satisfies the Conditions for a Knowledge-Belief System

In this section we show that the canonical system satisfies the conditions set forth in Section 4 for knowledge-belief systems: That an individual's probabilities are concentrated on his information set (19.5); that he knows his own probabilities (19.6); and that everything in sight is $\mathscr{F}_\sigma$-measurable (19.7 and 19.9). These four propositions establish Conditions (12.2) through (12.5) respectively.

We will also finish establishing, in the current knowledge-belief context, the correspondence between syntax and semantics (19.2 and 19.4).

The knowledge and probability operators of i in the canonical system will be denoted K_i and P_i^α (see 12.1). As in the previous section, ω denotes a state in the canonical system, $(\hat{\Pi}, \varphi, \hat{\omega})$ a model for $\omega, \hat{\pi}_i(\cdot;\hat{\omega})$ the probabilities of i in $\hat{\Pi}$ at $\hat{\omega}$, $\hat{K}_i$ and $\hat{P}_i^\alpha$ the knowledge and probability operators in $\hat{\Pi}$.

We use 18.22 and 14.4 repeatedly in this section, without explicit mention.

Lemma 19.1.

$$\textit{If } k_i f \in \omega \textit{ then } f \in \omega, \tag{19.11}$$

$$\textit{if } \alpha \leq \beta \textit{ and } p_i^\beta f \in \omega \textit{ then } p_i^\alpha f \in \omega, \textit{ and} \tag{19.12}$$

$$\textit{if } p_i^\alpha f \in \omega \textit{ then } k_i p_i^\alpha f \in \omega. \tag{19.13}$$

Proof. If $k_i f \in \omega$, then by 1.31, $\hat{\omega} \in \varphi(k_i f) = \hat{K}_i \varphi(f) \subset \varphi(f)$, so $f \in \omega$, proving 19.11. Next, let $p_i^\beta f \in \omega$, where $\alpha \leq \beta$. Then $\hat{\omega} \in \varphi(p_i^\beta f) = \hat{P}_i^\beta \varphi(f) = \{\hat{v} : \hat{\pi}_i(\varphi(f);\hat{v}) \geq \beta\}$, so $\hat{\pi}_i(\varphi(f);\hat{\omega}) \geq \beta \geq \alpha$, so $\hat{\omega} \in \{\hat{v} : \hat{\pi}_i(\varphi(f);\hat{v}) \geq \alpha\} = \hat{P}_i^\alpha \varphi(f) = \varphi(p_i^\alpha f)$, so $p_i^\alpha f \in \omega$, proving 19.12. Finally, if $p_i^\alpha f \in \omega$, then $\hat{\omega} \in \varphi(p_i^\alpha f) = \hat{P}_i^\alpha \varphi(f) \subset \hat{K}_i \hat{P}_i^\alpha \varphi(f) = \varphi(k_i p_i^\alpha f)$, by 12.3 applied to $\hat{\Pi}$; so $k_i p_i^\alpha f \in \omega$, proving 19.13.

Proposition 19.2. $K_i E_f = E_{k_i f}$.

Proof. We have $\omega \in K_i E_f$ iff $\mathbf{I}_i(\omega) \subset E_f$, and $\omega \in E_{k_i f}$ iff $k_i f \in \omega$. So we must show that $\mathbf{I}_i(\omega) \subset E_f$ iff $k_i f \in \omega$. If indeed $k_i f \in \omega$, then $k_i f$ is in each member of $\mathbf{I}_i(\omega)$, so f is in each member of $\mathbf{I}_i(\omega)$ (by 19.11, when applied to arbitrary states in $\mathbf{I}_i(\omega)$), so indeed $\mathbf{I}_i(\omega) \subset E_f$. For the opposite direction, suppose $k_i f \notin \omega$, so $\hat{\omega} \notin \varphi(k_i f) = \hat{K}_i \varphi(f)$. So $\hat{\mathbf{I}}_i(\hat{\omega})$ is not included in $\varphi(f)$. So there is an element $\hat{v}$ of $\hat{\Pi}$ with $\hat{\kappa}_i(\hat{v}) = \hat{\kappa}_i(\hat{\omega})$ and $\hat{v} \notin \varphi(f)$. Set

$$v := \{g : \hat{v} \in \varphi(g)\}; \tag{19.21}$$

in words, v is the list of all formulas that are true "at" $\hat{v}$. If $k_i h \in \omega$, then $\hat{\omega} \in \varphi(k_i h) = \hat{K}_i \varphi(h)$. Since $\hat{\kappa}_i(\hat{v}) = \hat{\kappa}_i(\hat{\omega})$, it follows that also $\hat{v} \in \hat{K}_i \varphi(h) = \varphi(k_i h)$, so $k_i h \in \nu$ by 19.11. If $k_i h \in \nu$, it may be seen similarly that $k_i h \in \omega$. So $\kappa_i(v) = \kappa_i(\omega)$. So $\mathbf{I}_i(v) = \mathbf{I}_i(\omega)$.

But $\hat{v} \notin \varphi(f)$ and 19.21 yield $f \notin v$, so $v \notin E_f$. But by definition, $v \in \mathbf{I}_i(v) = \mathbf{I}_i(\omega)$. So it is not the case that $\mathbf{I}_i(\omega)$ is included in E_f. This completes the proof of the opposite direction.

Proposition 19.3. *If $p_i^\beta f \in \omega$ for all $\beta < \alpha$, then $p_i^\alpha f \in \omega$.*

Proof. By hypothesis, $\hat{\omega} \in \varphi(p_i^\beta f) = P_i^\beta \varphi(f)$ for all $\beta < \alpha$. So by 12.1, $\hat{\pi}_i(\varphi(f); \hat{\omega}) \geq \beta$ for all $\beta < \alpha$. So $\hat{\pi}_i(\varphi(f); \hat{\omega}) \geq \alpha$. So by 12.1, $\hat{\omega} \in P_i^\alpha \varphi(f) = \varphi(p_i^\alpha f)$. So $p_i^\alpha f \in \omega$.

Proposition 19.4. *$P_i^\alpha E_f = E_{p_i^\alpha f}$ for rational α.*

Proof. By 12.1 and 16.5, $\omega \in P_i^\alpha E_f$ iff $\alpha \leq \pi_i(E_f; \omega) := \sup(\beta : p_i^\beta f \in \omega)$; by 19.12 and 19.3, this happens iff $p_i^\alpha f \in \omega$, which in turn is iff $\omega \in E_{p_i^\alpha f}$.

Proposition 19.5. *$K_i E \subset P_i^1 E$ for all E in $\mathscr{F}_\sigma$.*

Proof. This says that $\pi_i(\cdot; \omega)$ is concentrated on $\mathbf{I}_i(\omega)$, i.e., that $\pi_i(\mathbf{I}_i(\omega); \omega) = 1$. Since $\mathbf{I}_i(\omega) = \bigcap_{k_i f \in \omega} E_{k_i f}$, and there are only denumerably many formulas in ω, it suffices to show that

$$\pi_i(E_{k_i f}; \omega) = 1 \text{ whenever } k_i f \in \omega.$$

Since $k_i f \in \omega$, 1.8 and 12.2 yield $\hat{\omega} \in \varphi(k_i f) = \hat{K}_i \varphi(f) = \hat{K}_i \hat{K}_i \varphi(f) = \hat{K}_i \varphi(k_i f) \subset \hat{P}_i^1 \varphi(k_i f)$. So by 12.1, $\hat{\pi}_i(\varphi(k_i f); \hat{\omega}) = 1$. So by 18.33, $\pi_i(E_{k_i f}; \omega) = \hat{\pi}_i(\varphi(k_i f); \hat{\omega}) = 1$.

Proposition 19.6. *$P_i^\alpha E \subset K_i P_i^\alpha E$ for all E in $\mathscr{F}_\sigma$.*

Proof. By 19.13, 19.2 and 19.4, we know that $P_i^\alpha E \subset K_i P_i^\alpha E$ when E is syntactic (i.e., of the form E_f). Now the proposition says that

$$\text{if } \kappa_i(\omega) = \kappa_i(v), \quad \text{then } \pi_i(E; \omega) = \pi_i(E; \nu).$$

Fix ω and ν such that $\kappa_i(\omega) = \kappa_i(v)$. We know that $\pi_i(E; \omega) = \pi_i(E; v)$ when E is syntactic. Since the syntactic events form a field, and this field generates $\mathscr{F}_\sigma$, it follows that any E in $\mathscr{F}_\sigma$ is approximable w.r.t. the sigma-additive measure $\pi_i(\cdot;\omega)+\pi_i(\cdot;\nu)$ by syntactic events; so $\pi_i(E;\omega)=\pi_i(E;\nu)$ for all E in $\mathscr{F}_\sigma$.

Proposition 19.7. *Then atoms of the $\mathscr{I}_i$ are $\mathscr{F}_\sigma$-measurable.*

Proof. Each atom of $\mathscr{I}_i$ is of the form $\mathbf{I}_i(\omega)$ for some ω, and $\mathbf{I}_i(\omega) = = \bigcap_{k_i f\in\omega} E_{k_i f}$.

Call a sequence $E_1, E_2, \ldots$ of events *monotone* if $E_1 \subset E_2 \subset \cdots$ or $E_1 \supset E_2 \supset \cdots$; set $\lim_{n\to\infty} E_n := \bigcup_{n=1} E_n$ in the first case and $:= \bigcap_{n=1} E_n$ in the second. Call a family $\mathscr{G}$ *monotone* if $\lim_{n\to\infty} E_n \in \mathscr{G}$ whenever $E_1, E_2, \cdots$ is a monotone sequence in $\mathscr{G}$.

Lemma 19.8. *$\mathscr{F}_\sigma$ is the smallest monotone family that includes the field $\mathscr{F}$ of all the E_f.*

Proof. This holds for all σ-fields $\mathscr{F}_\sigma$ generated by a field $\mathscr{F}$ [Halmos 1950, p. 27, Theorem B].

Proposition 19.9. *$\pi_i(E;\omega)$ is $\mathscr{F}_\sigma$-measurable in ω for each fixed E in $\mathscr{F}_\sigma$.*

Proof. We must show

$$\{\omega : \pi_i(E;\omega) \geq \alpha\} \in \mathscr{F}_\sigma \text{ for each rational } \alpha. \tag{19.91}$$

Now $\{\omega : \pi_i(E;\omega) \geq \alpha\} = P_i^\alpha E$. So when $E = E_f$, applying 19.4 yields $\{\omega : \pi_i(E;\omega) \geq \alpha\} = E_{p_i^\alpha f}$, which has the form E_g and so is indeed in $\mathscr{F}_\sigma$. Thus the family $\mathscr{G}$ of events satisfying 14.91 includes $\mathscr{F}$. It is therefore sufficient, by 19.8, to show that it is a monotone family. So let $E_1, E_2, \ldots$ be a monotone sequence in $\mathscr{G}$ with limit E. If the sequence is non-decreasing, then

$$\begin{aligned}\{\omega : \pi_i(E;\omega) \geq \alpha\} &= \{\omega : (\forall m)(\exists n)(\pi_i(E_n;\omega) \geq \alpha - (1/m))\}\\ &= \bigcap_{m=1}^{\infty}\bigcup_{n=1}^{\infty} \{\omega : \pi_i(E_n;\omega) \geq \alpha - (1/m)\} \in \mathscr{F}_\sigma,\end{aligned}$$

since $E_n \in \mathcal{G}$. If the sequence is non-increasing, then

$$\begin{aligned}\{\omega : \pi_i(E;\omega) \geq \alpha\} &= \{\omega : (\forall n)(\pi_i(E_n;\omega) \geq \alpha)\} \\ &= \bigcap_{n=1}^{\infty} \{\omega : \pi_i(E_n;\omega) \geq \alpha\} \in \mathscr{F}_\sigma,\end{aligned}$$

since $E_n \in \mathcal{G}$. So $E \in \mathcal{G}$ in both cases, so $\mathcal{G}$ is indeed monotone.

20. Discussion

20.1. *The meaning of the knowledge operators K_i*

As in the case of knowledge, the correct interpretation of the event K_iE is that "E follows logically from the syntactic events[6] that i knows." This follows from 8.51, which continues to hold — with much the same proof as before — in the context of this paper.

However, the analogue of 10.1 — that knowledge of an infinite disjunction is equivalent to knowledge of some finite subdisjunction — is *not* correct here. For example,

$$\begin{aligned}K_i(E_{p_j^{1/2}x} \cup E_{p_j^{1/3}x} \cup E_{p_j^{1/4}x} \cup \cdots) \neq K_i(E_{p_j^{1/2}x}) \cup K_i(E_{p_j^{1/3}x}) \\ \cup K_i(E_{p_j^{1/4}x}) \cup \cdots ;\end{aligned}$$

the left side equals $K_i(E_{\neg p_j^0 x})$ — i.e., it says that i knows that j's probability for x is positive — whereas the right side says that for some α that is positive, i knows that j's probability for x is at least α — a much stronger statement. Unlike that of 8.51, the proof of 10.1 involves compactness arguments, which, because of the infinitary nature of the logic, do not apply here.

20.2. *An alternative interpretation of the letters of the alphabet*

The discussion at 10(b) continues to apply here, with little or no change.

[6]Events of the form E_f.

20.3. *Knowledge-belief hierarchies*

In 10(c) we saw that the hierarchy approach to knowledge, though more cumbersome and complicated than the syntactic approach, amounts to the same thing. The situation is similar with regard to knowledge-belief hierarchies.

Historically, the hierarchy approach originated with probability systems; see Armbruster and Böge (1979), Böge and Eisele (1979) and Mertens and Zamir (1985). These systems are pure probability systems; knowledge does not enter. For simplicity, we confine attention to the case of two players. Like at 10(c), we start with a set $\mathfrak{H}$ of mutually exclusive and exhaustive "states of nature," which describe some aspect of reality (like tomorrow's temperature in Jerusalem) in terms not involving probability or knowledge. Then the hierarchy of a player i consists of the beliefs (probabilities) of i about the states of nature, i's probability distribution over the beliefs of the other player j about the states of nature, i's probability distribution over j's probability distributions over i's beliefs about the state of nature, and so on. Certain consistency conditions must be met. Moreover, j's probability distribution over i's beliefs about the states of nature may well be continuous; thus the next level of the hierarchy consists of a probability distribution over probability distributions, which requires selecting a topology on the space of probability distributions. So even without knowledge, matters quickly get rather complicated.

But knowledge *is* an intrinsic part of the picture, and should not be ignored. For example, a player necessarily *knows* his own probabilities, in the sense of absolute knowledge, not only in the sense of probability 1. The appropriate object to examine is a *knowledge-belief* hierarchy. In the case of two players, a pair of hierarchies (one for each player) looks roughly as follows: At the first level, each player i has a knowledge-belief profile over the set $\mathfrak{H}$ of states of nature; that is, he knows that the true state of nature is in a certain subset h_i of $\mathfrak{H}$, and he has a probability distribution on h_i. The knowledge of the two players must be *consistent*; one player cannot know something that the other knows to be false. At the second level of the hierarchy, each player has some knowledge and beliefs about pairs consisting of elements of $\mathfrak{H}$ and the other player's first-level knowledge and beliefs;

these second-level knowledge-belief profiles of the two players must be consistent with each other in a sense like that described for the first level, and each player's second stage profile must also be consistent with his first level profile (e.g., the first level must be the marginal of the second level when projected onto the first level). And so on, ad infinitum. A more precise description, in the spirit of 10(c), would of course be far more complicated.

All this is accomplished much more briefly and elegantly by the syntactic approach. If ω is a state of the world in the canonical knowledge-belief system Π, then $\kappa_i(\omega)$ contains *precisely* the same information as i's hierarchy in the hierarchy approach. Just list all the formulas that i knows to be true — which of course include all his probability assessments, all his probability assessments about others' probability assessments, and so on. No complicated consistency conditions, no topologies. Just a list of the formulas he knows, in no particular order.

As at 10(c), note that two states of the world ω and ω' are in the same element of i's partition of Π if and only if they correspond to the same knowledge-belief hierarchy of i. Thus i's knowledge-belief hierarchies correspond precisely to the atoms of his information partition; each can be read off from the other. In particular, it follows that the knowledge-belief hierarchy of any *one* player determines precisely the common knowledge component of the true state of the world.

References

Armbruster, W., Böge, W., 1979, Bayesian game theory. In: Möschlin O., Pallaschke D. (eds.) Game theory and related topics, North-Holland, Amsterdam.

Aumann, R. J., 1987, Correlated equilibrium as an expression of Bayesian rationality, *Econometrica* 55, 1–18. [Chapter 8]

Aumann, R. J., 1999, Interactive epistemology I: Knowledge, *International Journal of Game Theory* 28, 263–300 (denoted [A] in this paper). [Chapter 3]

Böge, W., Eisele, T., 1979, On solutions of Bayesian games, *International Journal of Game Theory* 8, 193–215.

Halmos, P. R., 1950, *Measure Theory*, Van Nostrand, Princeton.

Mertens, J. F., Zamir, S., 1985, Formulation of Bayesian analysis for games with incomplete information, *International Journal of Game Theory* 14, 1–29.

Chapter 5

Incomplete Information*

Abstract: In interactive contexts such as games and economies, it is important to take account not only of what the players believe about substantive matters (such as payoffs), but also of what they believe about the beliefs of other players. Two different but equivalent ways of dealing with this matter, the semantic and the syntactic, are set forth. Canonical and universal semantic systems are then defined and constructed, and the concepts of common knowledge and common priors formulated and characterized. The last two sections discuss relations with Bayesian games of incomplete information and their applications, and with interactive epistemology — the theory of multi-agent knowledge and belief as formulated in mathematical logic.

Journal of Economic Literature: Classification Codes: D82, C70.

Mathematics Subject Classification 2000: Primary: 03B42. Secondary: 91A10, 91A40, 91A80, 91B44.

1. Introduction

In interactive contexts such as games and economies, it is important to take account not only of what the players believe about substantive matters (such as payoffs), but also of what they believe about the

*Co-authored with A. Heifetz. Reprinted from *Handbook of Game Theory with Economic Application*, Vol. 3, chapter 43, edited by R. Aumann and S. Hart, 1665–1686, with permission from Elsevier.

beliefs of other players. This chapter sets forth several ways of dealing with this matter, all essentially equivalent.

There are two basic approaches, the syntactic and the semantic; while the former is conceptually more straightforward, the latter is more prevalent, especially in game and economic contexts. Each appears in the literature in several variations.

In the *syntactic* approach, the beliefs are set forth explicitly: One specifies what each player believes about the substantive matters in question, about the beliefs of the others about these substantive matters, about the beliefs of the others about the beliefs of the others about the substantive matters, and so on ad infinitum. This sounds — and is — cumbersome and unwieldy, and from the beginning of research into the area, a more compact, manageable way was sought to represent interactive beliefs.

Such a way was found in the *semantic* approach, which is "leaner" and less elaborate, but also less transparent. It consists of a set of *states of the world* (or simply *states*), and for each player and each state, a probability distribution on the set of all states. We will see that this provides the same information as the syntactic approach.

The subject of *common priors* is discussed in Section 9; applications to Game Theory, in Section 10; and finally, Section 11 contains a brief discussion of the theory from the viewpoint of mathematical logic.

2. The Semantic Approach

Given a set N of players, a (*finite*) *semantic belief system* consists of

(i) a finite set Ω, the *state space*, whose elements are called *states of the world*, or simply *states*, and whose subsets are called *events*; and

(ii) for each player i and state ω, a probability distribution $\pi_i(\cdot;\omega)$ on Ω; if E is an event, $\pi_i(E;\, \omega)$ is called i's *probability for E in ω*.

Conceptually, a "state of the world" is meant to encompass all aspects of reality that are relevant to the matter under consideration, including the beliefs of all players in that state. As in probability theory, an event is a set of states; thus the event "it will snow tomorrow" is represented by a set of states — those in which it snows tomorrow.

We assume that

$$\text{if } \pi_i(\{\nu\};\omega) > 0, \text{ then } \pi_i(E;\nu) = \pi_i(E;\omega) \text{ for all } E. \tag{2.1}$$

In words: If in state ω, player i considers state ν possible (in the sense of assigning to it positive probability), then his probabilities for all events are the same in state ν as in state ω. That is, he does not seriously entertain the possibility that his own probability for some event E is different from what it actually is; he is sure[1] of his own probabilities.

The restriction to finite systems in this section is for simplicity only; for a general treatment, see Section 6.

3. An Example

Here $N = \{Ann, Bob\}$, $\Omega = \{\alpha, \beta, \gamma\}$, and the probabilities $\pi_i(\{\nu\};\omega)$ are as follows:

	$\nu =$	α	β	γ
	α	1/2	1/2	0
$\omega =$	β	1/2	1/2	0
	γ	0	0	1

π_{Ann}

	$\nu =$	α	β	γ
	α	1	0	0
$\omega =$	β	0	1/2	1/2
	γ	0	1/2	1/2

π_{Bob}

[1]By "sure" we mean "assigns probability 1 to" (probabilists use "almost sure" for this, but here it would make the text unnecessarily cumbersome and opaque). Actually, in these models players "know" their own probabilities; i.e., they do not admit *any* possibility, even with probability 0, of having a different probability (see Section 7). Indeed, a person's own probability judgments would appear to be among the few things of which he can justifiably be absolutely certain.

In each of the states α and β, Ann attributes probability 1/2 to each of α and β, whereas in γ, she knows that γ is the state; and Bob, in each of the states β and γ, attributes probability 1/2 to each of β and γ, whereas in α, he knows that α is the state.

Now let $E = \{\alpha, \gamma\}$, and let us consider the probabilities of the players in state β. To start with, each player assigns probability 1/2 to E. At the next level, each player assigns probability 1/2 to the other assigning probability 1/2 to E, and probability 1/2 to the other being sure[2] of E. At the next level, Ann assigns probability 1/2 to Bob being sure that she assigns probability 1/2 to E; and probability 1/2 to Bob's assigning probability 1/2 to her being sure of E, and probability 1/2 to her assigning probability 1/2 to E. The same holds if Ann and Bob are interchanged. That's already quite a mouthful; we refrain from describing the subsequent levels explicitly.

The previous paragraph, with its explicit description of each player's probabilities for the other player's probabilities, is typical of the syntactic approach. The complexity of the description increases exponentially with the "depth" of the level, and there are infinitely many levels. Because this example is particularly symmetric, the description is relatively simple; in general, things are even more complex, by far. Note, moreover, that the syntactic treatment corresponds to just *one* of the states in the semantic model.

By contrast, the semantic model encapsulates the whole mess, simultaneously for *all* the states, in just two compact (3×3) tables.

4. The Syntactic Approach

The syntactic approach may be formalized by "belief hierarchies." One starts with an exhaustive set of mutually exclusive "states of nature" (like "snow", "rain", "cloudy", or "clear" at noon tomorrow). The first level of the hierarchy specifies, for each player, a probability

[2]Indeed, Ann assigns 1/2–1/2 probabilities to the states α and β. In β, Bob assigns probability 1/2 to E, and in α, Bob is sure of E. This demonstrates our assertion about Ann's probabilities for Bob's probabilities. The calculation of Bob's probabilities for Ann's probabilities is similar.

distribution on the states of nature. The second level specifies, for each player, a joint probability distribution on the states of nature and the others' probability distributions. The third level specifies, for each player, a joint probability distribution on the states of nature and the probability distributions of the others at the first and second levels. And so on. Certain consistency conditions are required (Mertens and Zamir 1985; see Section 8 below).

Since there is a continuum of possibilities for the probability distributions at the first level, the probability distributions at the second and higher levels may well[3] be continuous (i.e., have nonatomic components). So one needs some kind of additional structure — a topology or a measurable structure (σ-field) — on the space of probability distributions at each level. With finitely many states of nature, this offers no difficulty at the first and second levels. But already the third level consists of a probability distribution on the space of probability distributions on a continuum, which requires a topology or measurable structure on the space of probability distributions on a continuum — a nontrivial matter. Of course, this applies also to higher levels.

An alternative syntactic formalism, which avoids these complications, works with sentences[4] or assertions rather than with probability distributions.[5] Start with a set $\{x, y, \ldots\}$ of "natural sentences" (like "rain", "warm", and "humid" at noon tomorrow), which need be neither exhaustive nor mutually exclusive. One may operate on these in two ways: by logical operators and connectives, like "not" ($\neg$), "or" ($\vee$), and "and" ($\wedge$), and by belief operators p_i^α, whose interpretation is "player i attributes a probability of

[3]A discrete distribution would mean, e.g., that Ann *knows* that Bob assigns probability precisely 0, 1/2 or 1 to snow. While possible, this seems unlikely. When modelling beliefs about the beliefs of others, some fuzziness seems natural.

[4]Usually called *formulas* in the literature.

[5]Some workers reserve the term "syntactic" for this kind of system only — i.e., one using sentences and syntactic rules. We prefer a more substantive terminology, in which *syntactic* refers to any system that directly describes the actual beliefs of the players, whereas *semantic* refers to a (states-of-the-world) model from which these beliefs can be derived.

at least α to $\cdots$." The operations may be concatenated in any way one wishes; for example, $p^{1/2}_{Ann}(x \vee p^{3/4}_{Bob}(\neg p^{1/4}_{Ann} y))$ means that Ann ascribes a probability of at least 1/2 to the contingency that either x or that Bob ascribes a probability of at least 3/4 to her ascribing a probability of less than 1/4 to y. A *syntactic belief system* is a collection of such sentences that satisfies certain natural completeness, coherence, and consistency conditions (Section 8).

It may be seen that a syntactic belief system contains precisely the same substantive information as a belief hierarchy, without the topological or measure-theoretic complications.

5. From Semantics to Syntax

We now indicate how the syntactic formalism is derived from the semantic one in a general framework.

Suppose given a semantic belief system with state space Ω, and a family of "distinguished" events $X, Y, \ldots$ (corresponding[6] to the above "natural sentences" $x, y, \ldots$); such a pair is called an *augmented* semantic belief system. Let $\pi_i(E; \omega)$ be the probability of player i for event E in state ω. For numbers α between 0 and 1, let $P^\alpha_i E$ be the event that i's probability for E is at least α; i.e., the set of all states ω at which $\pi_i(E; w) \geq \alpha$. Thus the operator P^α_i in the semantic model corresponds to the operator p^α_i in the syntactic model. As usual, the set operations $\cup$ (union) and $\Omega\backslash$ (complementation) correspond to the logical operations $\vee$ (disjunction) and $\neg$ (negation). Thus each sentence in the syntactic formalism corresponds to an event in the semantic formalism. For example, the sentence $p^{1/2}_{Ann}(x \vee p^{3/4}_{Bob}(\neg p^{1/4}_{Ann} y))$ discussed above corresponds to $P^{1/2}_{Ann}(X \cup P^{3/4}_{Bob}(\Omega \backslash P^{1/4}_{Ann} Y))$, namely the event that Ann ascribes a probability of at least 1/2 to the event that either X or that Bob ascribes a probability of at least 3/4 to her ascribing a probability of less than 1/4 to Y.

[6]I.e., with the same conceptual content. Thus if in the syntactic treatment, x is the sentence "it will snow tomorrow," then in the semantic treatment, X is the event "it will snow tomorrow" (the set of all states in which it snows tomorrow).

Now fix a state ω. If e is a sentence and E the corresponding event, say that e *holds in* ω if ω is in E. If we think of ω as the "true" state of the world, then the "true" sentences are precisely those that hold in ω. These sentences constitute a syntactic belief system in the sense of the previous section.

To summarize: Starting from a pair consisting of an augmented semantic belief system and a state ω, we have constructed a syntactic belief system $\mathfrak{L}$. We call this pair (or just the state ω) a *model* for $\mathfrak{L}$.

6. Removing the Finiteness Restriction

Given a set N of players, a (*general*) *semantic belief system* consists of

(ia) a set Ω, the *state space*, whose elements are the *states*;
(ib) a σ-field $\mathcal{F}$ of subsets of Ω — the *events*; and
(ii) for each player i and state ω, a probability distribution $\pi_i(\cdot;\omega)$ on $\mathcal{F}$.

We assume that

$$\pi_i(E;\omega) \text{ is } \mathcal{F}\text{-measurable in } \omega \text{ for each fixed event } E, \text{ and} \tag{6.1}$$

$$\pi_i(\{\nu : \pi_i(E;\nu) \neq \pi_i(E;\omega)\};\omega) = 0 \text{ for each event } E \text{ and state } \omega. \tag{6.2}$$

The interpretation is as in Section 2.

7. Knowledge and Common Knowledge

In the formalism of Sections 2 and 6, the concept of knowledge — in the sense of absolute certainty[7] rather than probability 1 — plays no explicit role. However, this concept can be *derived* from that formalism. Indeed, for each state ω and player i, let $\mathbf{I}_i(\omega)$ be the set of all states in which i's probabilities (for all events) are the same

[7] I.e., with error impossible: If i "knows" an event E at a state ω, then ω *must* be in E.

as in ω; call it i's *information set in* ω. The information sets of i form a partition $\mathcal{P}_i$ of Ω, called *i's information partition.* Say that *i knows* an event E in a state ω if E includes $\mathbf{I}_i(\omega)$, and denote by K_iE the set of all states ω in which i knows E. Conceptually, this formulation of knowledge presupposes that players know their own probabilities with absolute certainty, which is not unreasonable. It may be seen that

$$K_iE \subset P_i^1 E, \tag{7.1}$$

i.e., that players ascribe probability 1 to whatever they know, and that

$$P_i^\alpha E \subset K_i P_i^\alpha E, \tag{7.2}$$

which formally expresses the principle, enunciated above, that players know their own probabilities.

Let KE be the set $\cap_i K_iE$ of all states in which all players know E, and set

$$K^\infty E := KE \cap KKE \cap KKKE \cap \cdots ;$$

thus $K^\infty E$ is the set of all states in which all players know E, all players know that, all players know *that*, and so on ad infinitum. We say that E is *commonly known in* ω if $\omega \in K^\infty E$ (Lewis 1969); for a comprehensive survey of common knowledge, see Geanakoplos (1994). If $\mathcal{P}^\infty$ is the meet (finest common coarsening) of the information partitions $\mathcal{P}_i$ of all the players i, then it may be seen (Aumann 1976, 1999a) that $K^\infty E$ is the union of all the atoms of $\mathcal{P}^\infty$ that are included in E. The atoms of $\mathcal{P}^\infty$ are called *common knowledge components* (or simply components) of Ω. In a sense, one can always restrict the discussion to such a component: The "true" state is always in some component, and then it is commonly known that it is, and all considerations relating to other components become irrelevant.

Some interactive probability formalisms (like Aumann 1999b) use a separate, exogenous, concept of knowledge, and *assume* analogues of 7.1 and 7.2 (see 7.3 and 7.4 below). In the semantic framework, such a concept is redundant: Surprisingly, *knowledge is implicit in probability.*

To see this, let $\mathcal{P}_i$, $\mathbf{I}_i$, and K_i, as above, be the knowledge concepts derived from the probabilities $\pi_i(\cdot;\omega)$, and let Q_i, $\mathbf{J}_i$, and L_i be the corresponding exogenous concepts. Assume

$$L_i E \subset P_i^1 E \text{ (players ascribe probability 1 to what they know[8])}, \quad (7.3)$$

and

$$P_i^\alpha E \subset L_i P_i^\alpha E \text{ (players know their own probabilities)}. \quad (7.4)$$

It suffices to show that $\mathbf{J}_i(\omega) = \mathbf{I}_i(\omega)$ for all ω. This follows from 7.3 and 7.4; we argue from the verbal formulations. If $\nu \in \mathbf{J}_i(\omega)$, then by 7.4, i's probabilities for all events must be the same in ν and ω, so $v \in \mathbf{I}_i(\omega)$. Conversely, i knows in ν that he is in $\mathbf{J}_i(\nu)$, so by 7.3, his probability for $\mathbf{J}_i(\nu)$ is 1. So if $\nu \notin \mathbf{J}_i(\omega)$, then $\mathbf{J}_i(\omega)$ and $\mathbf{J}_i(\nu)$ are disjoint, so in ν his probability for $\mathbf{J}_i(\omega)$ is 0, while in ω it is 1. So his probabilities are different in ω and ν, so $\nu \notin \mathbf{I}_i(\omega)$. Thus $\nu \in \mathbf{J}_i(\omega)$ if and only if $\nu \in \mathbf{I}_i(\omega)$, as claimed.

8. Canonical Semantic Systems

One may think of a semantic belief system purely technically, simply as providing the setting for a convenient, compact representation of a syntactic belief system, as in the example of Section 3. But one may also think of it substantively, as setting forth a model of interactive epistemology that reflects reality, including those states of the world that are "actually" possible,[9] and what the players know about them. This substantive viewpoint raises several questions, foremost among them being what the players know about the model itself. Does each know the space of states? Does he know the others' probabilities (in each state)? If so, from where does this knowledge derive? If not, how can the formalism indicate what each player believes about the

[8]In the remainder of this section we use "know" in the exogenous sense.

[9]Philosophers like the term "possible worlds."

others' beliefs? For example, why would the event $P^{1/2}_{Ann} P^{3/4}_{Bob} E$ then signify that Ann ascribes a probability of at least $1/2$ to Bob ascribing a probability of at least $3/4$ to E?

More generally, the whole idea of "state of the world," and of probabilities that accurately reflect the players' beliefs about other players' beliefs, is not transparent. What *are* the states? Can they be explicitly described? Where do they come from? Where do the probabilities come from? What justifies positing this kind of model, and what justifies a particular array of probabilities?

One way of overcoming these problems is by means of "canonical" or "universal" semantic belief systems. Such a system comprises a standard state space with standard probabilities for each player in each state. The system does not depend on reality; it is a framework, it fits any reality, so to speak, like the frames that one buys in photo shops, which do not depend on who is in the photo — they fit any photo with any subject, as long as the size is right. In brief, there is no substantive information in the system.

There are basically two ways of doing this. Both depend on two parameters: the set (or simply number n) of players and the set (or simply number) of "natural" eventualities. The first way (Mertens and Zamir 1985) is hierarchical. The zero'th level of the hierarchy is a (finite) set $\mathfrak{X} := \{x, y, \ldots\}$, whose members represent mutually exclusive and exhaustive "states of nature," but formally are just abstract symbols. The first level H^1 is the Cartesian product of $\mathfrak{X}$ with n copies of the $\mathfrak{X}$-simplex (the set of all probability distributions on $\mathfrak{X}$); a point in this Cartesian product describes the "true" state of nature, and also the probabilities of each player for each state of nature.

A point h^2 at the second level H^2 consists of a first-level point h^1 together with an n-tuple of probability distributions on H^1, one for each player; this describes the "true" state of nature, the probabilities of each player for the state of nature, and what each player believes about the other players' beliefs about the state of nature. There are two "consistency" conditions: First, the distribution on H^1 that h^2

assigns to i must attribute[10] probability 1 to the distribution on $\mathfrak{X}$ that h^1 assigns to i; that is, i must know what he himself believes. Second, the distribution[11] on $\mathfrak{X}$ that h^2 assigns to i must coincide with the one that h^1 assigns to i.

A third-level point consists of a second-level point h^2 together with an n-tuple of probability distributions[12] on H^2, one for each player; again, i's distribution on H^2 must assign probability 1 to the distribution on H^1 that h^2 assigns to i, and its marginal on H^1 must coincide with the distribution on H^1 that h^1 assigns to i.

And so on. Thus an $(m+1)$th-level point h^{m+1} is a pair consisting of an mth-level point h^m and a distribution on H^m; we say that h^{m+1} *elaborates* h^m. Define a state h in the canonical semantic belief system H as a sequence $h^1, h^2, \ldots$ in which each term elaborates the previous one. To define the probabilities, proceed as follows: For each subset S^m of H^m, set $\widehat{S}^m = \{h \in H : h^m \in S^m\}$; let $\mathcal{F}$ be the σ-field generated by all the $\widehat{S}^m$, where S^m is measurable; and let $\pi_i(\widehat{S}^m; h)$ be the probability that i's component of h^{m+1} assigns to S^m. In words, a state consists of a sequence of probability distributions of ever-increasing depth; to get the probability of a set of such sequences in a given state, one simply reads off the probabilities specified by that state. That this indeed yields a probability on $\mathcal{F}_\sigma$ follows from the Kolmogorov extension theorem, which requires some topological assumptions.[13]

The second construction (Heifetz and Samet 1998, Aumann 1999b) of a canonical belief system is based on sentences. It uses an

[10]Technically, h^2 assigns to i a distribution on $H^1 = \mathfrak{X} \times \Delta(\mathfrak{X})$, where Δ denotes "the set of all distributions on ...". The first consistency condition says that the marginal of this distribution on the second factor (i.e., on Δ $(\mathfrak{X})$) is a unit mass concentrated on the distribution on $\mathfrak{X}$ that h^1 assigns to i.

[11]Technically, the marginal on $\mathfrak{X}$ of the distribution on $H^1 = \mathfrak{X} \times \Delta(\mathfrak{X})$ that h^2 assigns to i. See the previous footnote.

[12]As indicated in Section 5, this involves topological issues, which we will not discuss.

[13]Without which things might not work (Heifetz and Samet 1998).

"alphabet" $x, y, \ldots$, as well as more elaborate sentences constructed from the alphabet by means of logical operations and probability operators p_i^α (as in Section 4). The letters of the alphabet represent "natural sentences," not necessarily mutually exclusive or exhaustive; but formally, as above, they are just abstract symbols. In this construction, the states γ in the canonical space Γ are simply lists of sentences; specifically, lists that are complete, coherent, and closed in a sense presently to be specified. The point is that a state is determined — or better, *defined* — by the sentences that hold there; conceptually, the state *is* simply what happens.

More precisely: A list is *complete* if for each sentence f, it contains either f itself or its negation $\neg f$; *coherent*, if for each f, it does not contain both f and $\neg f$; and *closed*, if it contains every logical consequence[14] of the sentences in it.

This defines the states γ in the canonical semantic belief system; to complete the definition of the system, we must define the σ-field $\mathcal{F}$ of events and the probabilities $\pi_i(\cdot;\gamma)$. For any sentence f, let $E_f := \{\delta \in \Gamma : f \in \delta\}$; that is, E_f is the set of all states[15] in the canonical system that contain f. We define $\mathcal{F}$ as the σ-field generated by all the events E_f for all sentences f. Then to define i's probabilities on $\mathcal{F}$ in the state γ, it suffices to define his probabilities for each E_f. Since the state is simply the list of all sentences that "hold in that state," it follows that E_f is the set of all states in which f holds — in brief, the event that f holds. The probability that i assigns to E_f in the state γ is then implicit in the specification of γ; namely, it is the supremum of all the rational α for which $p_i^\alpha f$ is in γ — the supremum α such that in γ, player i assigns a probability of at

[14]As used here, the term "logical consequence" is *defined* purely syntactically, by axioms and inference rules (Meier 2012). But it may be *characterized* semantically: A sentence g is a logical consequence of sentences $f_1, f_2, \ldots$ if and only if g holds at any state of any augmented semantic belief system at which $f_1, f_2, \ldots$ hold; i.e., if any model for $f_1, f_2, \ldots$ is also a model for g (Meier 2012). The axiomatic system is infinitary, as indeed it must be: For example, $p_i^1 f$ is a logical consequence of $p_i^{1/2} f, p_i^{3/4} f, p_i^{7/8} f, \ldots$, but of no finite subset thereof. Though written in 2001, Meier's beautiful, path-breaking paper was only published in 2012, ten years after the orginial publication of this chapter.

[15]Recall that a state is a list of sentences.

least α to f. This defines $\pi_i(E_f;\gamma)$ for each i, γ, and f; and since the E_f generate $\mathcal{F}$, it follows that it defines[16] $\pi_i(\cdot;\gamma)$. This completes the second construction, which has the advantage of requiring no topological machinery.

The canonical semantic belief system Γ is *universal* in a sense that we now describe. Let $x, y, \ldots$ be letters in an alphabet, and Ω, Ω' semantic belief systems with the same players, augmented by "distinguished" events $X, Y, \ldots$ and $X', Y', \ldots$, corresponding to the letters $x, y, \ldots$ (simply "systems" for short). A mapping M from Ω into Ω' is called a *belief morphism* if $M^{-1}(X') = X, M^{-1}(Y') = Y, \ldots$, and $\pi_i(M^{-1}(E');\omega) = \pi_i'(E';M(\omega))$ for all players i, events E' in Ω', and states ω in Ω; i.e., if it preserves the relevant aspects of the system (as usual for morphisms). A system Υ is called *universal* if for each system Ω, there is a belief morphism from Ω into Υ.

To see that Γ is universal, let Ω be a system. Then for each state ω in Ω, the family $D(\omega)$ of sentences that hold in ω (see Section 5) is a state in the canonical space Γ, and the mapping $D : \Omega \to \Gamma$ is a belief morphism — indeed the only one (Heifetz and Samet 1998). The construction of Mertens and Zamir (1985) also leads to a universal system, and the two canonical systems are isomorphic.[17]

At the end of the previous section, we noted that a separate, exogenous notion of knowledge is semantically redundant. Syntactically, it is not. To understand why, consider two two-player semantic belief systems, Ω and Ω'. The first has just one state ω, to which, of course, both players assign a probability of 1. The second has two states, ω and ω'. In ω, both players assign a probability of 1 to ω; in ω', Ann assigns a probability of 1 to ω, whereas Bob assigns a probability of 1 to ω'. Now augment both systems by assigning x to ω. Then the syntactic belief system derived from ω in Ω — the family $D(\omega)$ of all sentences that hold there — is identical to

---

[16]That is, since the E_f generate $\mathcal{F}$, there cannot be two different probability measures on $\mathcal{F}$ with the given values on the E_f. That there is *one* such measure follows from a theorem of Caratheodory on extending measures from a field to the σ-field it generates.

[17]I.e., there is a one-one belief morphism from the one onto the other.

that derived from ω in Ω'. So syntactically, the two situations are indistinguishable. But semantically, they are different: In Ω, Ann knows *for sure* in ω that Bob assigns probability 1 to x; in Ω', she does not. There is no way to capture this syntactically without explicitly introducing knowledge operators k_i for the various players i (as in Aumann 1999b; see also 1998). In particular, the canonical semantic system Γ has just one component[18] — the whole space.

9. Common Priors

Call a semantic belief system *regular*[19] if it is finite, has a single common knowledge component, and in each state, each player assigns positive probability to that state.

A *common prior* on a regular semantic belief system Ω is defined as a probability distribution π on Ω such that

$$\pi(E \cap \mathbf{I}_i(\omega)) = \pi_i(E; \omega)\pi(\mathbf{I}_i(\omega)) \tag{9.1}$$

for each event E, player i, and state ω; that is, the personal probabilities π_i in a state ω are obtained from the common prior π by conditioning on each player's private information in that state. In Section 3, for example, the distribution that assigns probability 1/3 to each of the three states is the unique common prior. Common priors can easily fail to exist; for example, if Ω has just two states, in each of which Ann assigns probabilities 1/2 – 1/2 to the two states, and Bob, probabilities 1/3 – 2/3. Conceptually, existence of a common prior signifies that differences in probability assessments are due to differences in information only (Aumann 1987, 1998); that people who have always been fed precisely the same information will not differ in their probability assessments.

[18]Except when there is only one player. This is because the probability syntax can only express beliefs of the players, not that a player knows anything about another one *for sure.*

[19]Regularity enables uncluttered statements of the definitions and results. No real loss of generality is involved.

With a common prior, players cannot "agree to disagree" about probabilities. That is, if it is commonly known in some state that for some specific α, β, and E, Ann and Bob assign probabilities α and β respectively to the event E, then $\alpha = \beta$. This is the "Agreement Theorem" (Aumann 1976).

The question arises (Gul 1998) whether the existence of a common prior can be characterized syntactically. That is, can one characterize those syntactic belief systems $\mathfrak{L}$ that are associated with common priors?[20] By a *syntactic* characterization, we mean one couched directly in terms of the sentences in $\mathfrak{L}$.

The answer is "yes." Indeed, there are two totally different characterizations. The first is based on the following, which is both a generalization of and a converse to the agreement theorem.

Proposition 9.2 (Morris 1994, Samet[21] 1998b, Feinberg 2000).[22] Let Ω be a regular semantic belief system, ω a state in Ω. Suppose first that there are just two players, Ann and Bob. Then there is *no* common prior on Ω if and only if there is a random variable[23] $\mathbf{x}$ for which it is commonly known in ω that Ann's expectation of $\mathbf{x}$ is positive and Bob's is negative.[24]

With n players, there is *no* common prior on Ω if and only if there are n random variables $\mathbf{x}_i$ identically[25] summing to 0 for whom it is commonly known in ω that each player i's expectation of $\mathbf{x}_i$ is positive.

In the two-person case, one may think of $\mathbf{x}$ as the amount of a bet between Ann and Bob, possibly with odds that depend on the

[20] More precisely, those $\mathfrak{L}$ for which there is a state ω in some finite augmented semantic belief system with a common prior such that $\mathfrak{L}$ is the collection of sentences holding at ω.

[21] Samet's proof, which uses the elementary theory of convex polyhedra, is the briefest and most elegant.

[22] For an early related result, see Nau and McCardle (1990).

[23] A real function on Ω. Although the concept of random variable may seem essentially semantic, it is not; in an augmented semantic system, random variables can in general be expressed in terms of sentences (Feinberg 2000, Heifetz 2001).

[24] Explicitly, the commonly known event in question is

$$\left\{\nu : \sum_{\xi\in\Omega} \pi_{Ann}(\{\xi\};\nu)\mathbf{x}(\xi) > 0 > \sum_{\xi\in\Omega} \pi_{Bob}(\{\xi\};\nu)\mathbf{x}(\xi)\right\}.$$

[25] At each state in Ω.

outcome. Thus the proposition says that with a common prior, it is impossible for both players to expect to gain from such a bet. The interpretation in the n-person case is similar; one may think of pari-mutuel betting in horse-racing, the track being one of the players.

In brief, common priors exist if and only if it is commonly known that you can't make something out of nothing: I.e., in a situation that is objectively zero-sum, it cannot be commonly known that all sides expect to gain.

The importance of this proposition lies in that it is formulated in terms of one single state ω only. We are talking about what Ann expects *in that state*, what she thinks *in that state* that Bob may expect, what she thinks *in that state* that Bob thinks that she may expect, and so on; and similarly for Bob. That is precisely what is needed for a syntactic characterization.[26]

Actually to derive a fully syntactic characterization from this proposition is, however, a different matter. To do so, one must provide syntactic formulations of (i) common knowledge, (ii) random variables and their expectations, and (iii) finiteness of the state space. The first is not difficult; setting $k := \wedge_i k_i$, call a sentence *e syntactically commonly known* if *e*, *ke*, *kke*, *kkke*, $\cdots$ all obtain. But (ii) and (iii), though doable — indeed elegantly (Feinberg 2000, Heifetz 2001) — are more involved; we will not discuss the matter further here.

Proposition 9.2 holds also for infinite state spaces that are "compact" in a natural sense. As before, this enables a syntactic characterization in the compact case; to do this properly one must characterize compactness syntactically. Without compactness, the proposition fails. Feinberg (2000) discusses these matters fully.

The second syntactic characterization of common priors is in terms of iterated expectations. Again, consider first the two-person

[26]Recall that we use the term *syntactic* rather broadly, as referring to anything that "actually obtains," such as the beliefs — and hence expectations — of the players. See Footnote 5.

case. If ν is a state and $\mathbf{y}$ a random variable, then Ann's and Bob's expectations of $\mathbf{y}$ in ν are

$$(\mathbf{E}_{Ann}\mathbf{y})(\nu) := \sum_{\xi\in\Omega} \pi_{Ann}(\{\xi\};\nu)\mathbf{y}(\xi) \text{ and}$$

$$(\mathbf{E}_{Bob}\mathbf{y})(\nu) := \sum_{\xi\in\Omega} \pi_{Bob}(\{\xi\};\nu)\mathbf{y}(\xi).$$

Both $\mathbf{E}_{Ann}\mathbf{y}$ and $\mathbf{E}_{Bob}\mathbf{y}$ are themselves random variables, as they are functions of the state ν. So one may form the iterated expectations

$$\mathbf{E}_{Ann}\mathbf{y}, \mathbf{E}_{Bob}\mathbf{E}_{Ann}\mathbf{y}, \mathbf{E}_{Ann}\mathbf{E}_{Bob}\mathbf{E}_{Ann}\mathbf{y}, \mathbf{E}_{Bob}\mathbf{E}_{Ann}\mathbf{E}_{Bob}\mathbf{E}_{Ann}\mathbf{y}, \ldots \text{ and} \tag{9.3}$$

$$\mathbf{E}_{Bob}\mathbf{y}, \mathbf{E}_{Ann}\mathbf{E}_{Bob}\mathbf{y}, \mathbf{E}_{Bob}\mathbf{E}_{Ann}\mathbf{E}_{Bob}\mathbf{y}, \mathbf{E}_{Ann}\mathbf{E}_{Bob}\mathbf{E}_{Ann}\mathbf{E}_{Bob}\mathbf{y}, \ldots \tag{9.4}$$

Proposition 9.5 (Samet 1998a). Each of these two sequences (9.3 and 9.4) of random variables converges to a constant (independent of the state); the system has a common prior if and only if for each random variable $\mathbf{y}$, these two constants coincide; and in that case, the common value of the two constants is the expectation of $\mathbf{y}$ over Ω w.r.t. the common prior π.

The proof uses finite state Markov chains.

Samet illustrates the proposition with a story about two stock analysts. Ann has an expectation for the price $\mathbf{y}$ of IBM in one month from today. Bob does not know Ann's expectation, but has some idea of what it might be; his expectation of her expectation is $\mathbf{E}_{Bob}\mathbf{E}_{Ann}\mathbf{y}$. And so on.

Like the previous characterization of common priors (Proposition 9.2), this one appears semantic, but in fact is syntactic: All the iterated expectations can be read off from a single syntactic belief system. As before, actually deriving a fully syntactic characterization requires formulating finiteness of the state space syntactically, which we do not do here. Unlike the previous characterization, this one has not been established for compact state spaces.

With n players, one considers arbitrary infinite sequences $\mathbf{E}_{i_1}\mathbf{y}$, $\mathbf{E}_{i_2}\mathbf{E}_{i_1}\mathbf{y}$, $\mathbf{E}_{i_3}\mathbf{E}_{i_2}\mathbf{E}_{i_1}\mathrm{y}$, $\mathbf{E}_{i_4}\mathbf{E}_{i_3}\mathbf{E}_{i_2}\mathbf{E}_{i_1}\mathbf{y}, \ldots$, where $i_1, i_2, \ldots$ is any sequence of players (with repetitions, of course), the only requirement being that each player appears in the sequence infinitely often. The result says that each such sequence converges to a constant; the system has a common prior if and only if all the constants coincide; and in that case, the common value of the constants is the expectation of $\mathbf{y}$ over Ω w.r.t. the common prior π.

10. Incomplete Information Games

The theory of incomplete information, whose general, abstract form is outlined in the foregoing sections of this chapter, has historical roots in a concrete application: games. Until the mid-sixties, game theorists did not think carefully about the informational underpinnings of their analyses. Luce and Raiffa (1957) did express some malaise on this score, but left the matter at that. The primary problem was each player's uncertainty about the payoff (or utility) functions of the others; to a lesser extent, there was also concern about the players' uncertainty about the strategies available to others, and about their own payoffs.

In path-breaking research in the mid-sixties, for which he got the Nobel Prize some thirty years later, John Harsanyi (1967–8) succeeded both in formulating the problem precisely, and in solving it. In brief, the formulation is the syntactic approach, whereas the solution is the semantic approach. Let us elaborate.

Harsanyi started by noting that though usually the players do not know the others' payoff functions, nevertheless, as good Bayesians, each has a (subjective) probability distribution over the possible payoff functions of the others. But that is not enough to analyze the situation. Each player must also take into account what the others think that he thinks about them. Even there it does not end; he must also take into account what the others think that he thinks that they think about him. And so on, ad infinitum. Harsanyi saw this infinite regress as a Gordian knot, not given to coherent, useful analysis.

To cut the knot, Harsanyi invented the notion of "type." Consider the case of two players, Ann and Bob. Each player, he said, may be one of several types. The type of a player determines his payoff function, and also a probability distribution on the other player's possible types. Since Bob's type determines his payoff function, Ann's probability distribution on his types induces a probability distribution on his payoff functions. But it also induces a probability distribution on his probability distributions on Ann's types, and so on Ann's payoff functions. And so on. Thus a "type structure" yields the whole infinite regress of payoff functions, distributions on payoff functions, distributions on distributions on payoff functions, and so on.

The reader will realize that the "infinite regress" is a syntactic belief hierarchy in the sense of Section 6, the "states of nature" being n-tuples of payoff functions; whereas a "type structure" is a semantic belief system, the "states of the world" being n-tuples of types. In modern terms, Harsanyi's insight was that a semantic system yields a syntactic system. Though this may seem obvious today (see Section 3), it was far from obvious at the time; indeed it was a major conceptual breakthrough, which enabled extending many of the fundamental concepts of game theory to the incomplete information case, and led to the opening of entirely new areas of research (see below).

The converse — that *every* syntactic system can be encapsulated in a semantic system — was not proved by Harsanyi. Harsanyi argued for the type structure on intuitive grounds. Roughly speaking, he reasoned that every player's brain must be configured in some way, and that this configuration should determine both the player's utility or payoff function and his probability distribution on the configuration of other players' brains.

The *proof* that indeed every syntactic system can be encapsulated in a semantic system is outlined in Section 8 above; the semantic system in question is simply the canonical one. This proof was developed over a number of years by several workers (Armbruster and Böge 1979, Böge and Eisele 1979), culminating in the work of Mertens and Zamir (1985) cited in Section 8 above.

Also the assumption of common priors (Section 9) was introduced by Harsanyi (1967–8), who called this the *consistent* case. He pointed out that in this case — and *only* in this case — an n-person game of incomplete information in strategic (i.e., normal) form can be represented by an n-person game of complete information in extensive form, as follows: First, "chance" chooses an n-tuple of types (i.e., a state of the world), using the common prior π for probabilities. Then, each player is informed of his type, but not of the others' types. Then the n players simultaneously choose strategies. Finally, payoffs are made in accordance with the types chosen by nature and the strategies chosen by the players.

The concept of strategic ("Nash") equilibrium generalizes to incomplete information games in a natural way. Such an equilibrium — often called a *Bayesian Nash* equilibrium — assigns to each type t_i of each player i a (mixed or pure) strategy of i that is optimal for i given t_i's assessment of the probabilities of the others' types and the strategies that the equilibrium assigns to those types. In the consistent (common prior) case, the Bayesian Nash equilibria of the incomplete information strategic game are precisely the same as the ordinary Nash equilibria of the associated complete information extensive game (described in the previous paragraph).

Since Harsanyi's seminal work, the theory of incomplete information games has been widely developed and applied. Several areas of application are of particular interest. *Repeated* games of incomplete information deal with situations where the same game is played again and again, but the players have only partial information as to what it is. This is delicate because by taking advantage of his private information, a player may implicitly reveal it, possibly to his detriment. For surveys up to 1991, see Zamir (1992) and Forges (1992). Since 1992, the literature on this subject has continued to grow; see Aumann and Maschler (1995), whose bibliography is fairly complete up to 1994. A more complete and modern treatment[27] is Mertens, Sorin, and Zamir (2015).

[27]Including also the general theory of incomplete information covered in this chapter.

Other important areas of application include auctions (see Wilson 1992), bargaining with incomplete information (Binmore, Osborne, and Rubinstein 1992 and Ausubel, Cramton, and Deneckere 2002), principal-agent problems (Dutta and Radner 1994), inspection (Avenhaus, von Stengel, and Zamir 2002), communication and signalling (Myerson 1994 and Kreps and Sobel 1994), and entry deterrence (Wilson 1992).

Not surveyed in the *Handbook* are coalitional (cooperative) games of incomplete information. Initiated by Wilson (1978) and Myerson (1984), this area is to this day fraught with unresolved conceptual difficulties. Allen (1997) and Forges, Minelli, and Vohra (2002) are surveys.

Finally, games of incomplete information are useful in understanding games of *complete* information — ordinary, garden-variety games. Here the applications are of two kinds. In one, the given complete information game is "perturbed" by adding some small element of incomplete information. For example, Harsanyi (1973) uses this technique to address the question of the significance of mixed strategies: Why would a player wish to randomize, in view of the fact that whenever a mixed strategy μ is optimal, it is also optimal to use any pure strategy in the support of μ? His answer is that indeed players never actually use mixed strategies. Rather, even in a complete information game, the payoffs should be thought of as commonly known only approximately. In fact, there are small variations in the payoff to each player that are known only to that player himself; these small variations determine which pure strategy s in the support of μ he actually plays. It turns out that the probability with which a given pure strategy s is actually played in this scenario approximates the coefficient of s in μ. Thus, a mixed strategy of a player i appears not as a deliberate randomization on i's part, but as representing the estimate of *other* players as to what i will do.

Another application of this kind comes under the heading of reputational effects. Seminal in this genre was the work of the "gang of four" (Kreps, Milgrom, Roberts, and Wilson 1982), in which a repeated prisoner's dilemma is perturbed by assuming that with some arbitrarily small exogenous probability, the players are "irrational" automata who always play "tit-for-tat." It turns out that in equilibrium, the irrationality "takes over" in some sense: Almost until the end of the game, the rational players themselves play tit-for-tat. Fudenberg and Maskin (1986) generalize this to "irrational" strategies other than tit-for-tat; as before, equilibrium play mimics the irrational perturbation, even when (unlike tit-for-tat) it is inefficient. Aumann and Sorin (1989) allow any perturbation with "bounded recall;" in this case equilibrium play "automatically" selects an efficient equilibrium.

The second kind of application of incomplete information technology to complete information games is where the object of incomplete information is not the payoffs of the players but the actual strategies they use. For example, rather than perturbing payoffs a la Harsanyi (1973 — see above), one can say that even without perturbed payoffs, players other than i simply do not know what pure strategy i will play; i's mixed strategy represents the probabilities of the other players as to what i will do. Works of this kind include Aumann (1987), in which correlated equilibrium in a complete information game is characterized in terms of common priors and common knowledge of rationality; and Aumann and Brandenburger (1995), in which Nash equilibrium in a complete information game is characterized in terms of mutual knowledge of rationality and of the strategies being played, and when there are more than two players, also of common priors and common knowledge of the strategies being played (for a more detailed account, see Hillas and Kohlberg 2002).

The key to *all* these applications is Harsanyi's "type" definition — the semantic representation — without which building a workable model for applications would be hopeless.

11. Interactive Epistemology

Historically, the theory of incomplete information outlined in this chapter has two parents: (i) incomplete information games, discussed in the previous section, and (ii) that part of mathematical logic, sometimes called *modal* logic, that treats knowledge and other epistemological issues, which we now discuss. In turn, (ii) itself has various ancestors. One is probability theory, in which the "sample space" (or "probability space") and its measurable subsets (there, like here, "events") play a role much like that of the space Ω of states of the world; whereas subfields of measurable sets, as in stochastic processes, play a role much like that of our information partitions $\mathcal{P}_i$ (Section 7). Another ancestor is the theory of extensive games, originated by von Neumann and Morgenstern (1944), whose "information sets" are closely related to our information sets $\mathbf{I}_i(\omega)$ (Section 7).

Formal epistemology, in the tradition of mathematical logic, began some forty years ago, with the work of Kripke (1959) and Hintikka (1962); these works were set in a single-person context. Lewis (1969) was the first to define common knowledge, which of course is a multi-person, interactive concept; though verbal, his treatment was entirely rigorous. Computer scientists became interested in the area in the mid-eighties; see Fagin *et al.* (1995).

Most work in formal epistemology concerns knowledge (Section 7) rather than probability. Though the two have much in common, knowledge is more elementary, in a sense that will be explained presently. Both interactive knowledge and interactive probability can be formalized in two ways: semantically, by a states-of-the-world model, or syntactically, either by a hierarchic model or by a formal language with sentences and logical inference governed by axioms and inference rules. The difference lies in the nature of logical inference. In the case of knowledge, sentences, axioms, and inference rules are all finitary (Fagin *et al.* 1995; Aumann 1999a). But probability is essentially infinitary (Footnote 14); there is no finitary syntactic model for probability.

Nevertheless, probability *does* have a finitary aspect. Heifetz and Mongin (2001) show that there is a finitary system $\mathcal{A}$ of axioms and inference rules such that if f and g are *finitary* probability sentences then g is a logical consequence[28] of f if and only if it is derivable from

[28]In the infinitary sense of Meier (2012) discussed in Section 8 (Footnote 14).

f via the *finitary* system $\mathcal{A}$. That is, though in general the notion of "logical consequence" is infinitary, for finitary sentences it *can* be embodied in a finitary framework.

Finally, we mention the matter of backward induction in perfect information games, which has been the subject of intense epistemic study, some of it based on probability 1 belief. This is a separate area.

Acknowledgement

Research partially supported under NSF grant SES-9730205.

References

Allen, B., 1997, "Cooperative Theory with Incomplete Information," in *Cooperation: Game-Theoretic Approaches,* edited by S. Hart and A. Mas-Colell, Berlin: Springer, 51–65.

Armbruster, W. and W. Böge, 1979, "Bayesian Game Theory," in *Game Theory and Related Topics,* edited by O. Moeschlin and D. Pallaschke, Amsterdam: North Holland, 17–28.

Aumann, R., 1976, "Agreeing to Disagree," *Annals of Statistics* 4, 1236–1239. [Chapter 2]

——— 1987, "Correlated Equilibrium as an Expression of Bayesian Rationality," *Econometrica* 55, 1–18. [Chapter 8]

——— 1998, "Common Priors: A Reply to Gul," *Econometrica* 66, 929–938. [Chapter 22]

——— 1999a, "Interactive Epistemology I: Knowledge," *International Journal of Game Theory* 28, 263–300. [Chapter 3]

——— 1999b, "Interactive Epistemology II: Probability," *International Journal of Game Theory* 28, 301–314. [Chapter 4]

——— and A. Brandenburger, 1995, "Epistemic Conditions for Nash Equilibrium," *Econometrica* 63, 1161–1180. [Chapter 10]

——— and M. Maschler, 1995, *Repeated Games of Incomplete Information,* Cambridge: MIT Press.

——— and S. Sorin, 1989, "Cooperation and Bounded Recall," *Games and Economic Behavior* 1, 5–39.

Aumann, R. and S. Hart, eds.: *Handbook of Game Theory with Economic Applications*, Vol. 1, 1992, Vol. 2, 1994, Vol. 3, 2002, Elsevier, Amsterdam; simply *Handbook* in the text.

Ausubel, L. M., P. Cramton, and R. J. Deneckere, 2002, "Bargaining with Incomplete Information," in *Handbook*, Volume 3, Chapter 50.

Avenhaus, R., B. von Stengel, and S. Zamir, 2002, "Inspection Games," in *Handbook*, Volume 3, Chapter 51.

Binmore, K., M. J. Osborne, and A. Rubinstein, 1992, "Noncooperative Models of Bargaining," in *Handbook*, Volume 1, Chapter 7.
Böge, W. and T. Eisele, 1979, "On Solutions of Bayesian Games," *International Journal of Game Theory* 8, 193–215.
Dutta, P. K., and R. Radner, 1994, "Moral Hazard," in *Handbook*, Volume 2, Chapter 26.
Fagin, R., J. Y. Halpern, M. Moses and M. Y. Vardi, 1995, *Reasoning about Knowledge,* Cambridge: MIT Press.
Feinberg, Y., 2000, "Characterizing Common Priors in the Form of Posteriors," *Journal of Economic Theory* 91, 127–179.
Forges, F., 1992, "Repeated Games of Incomplete Information: Non-Zero-Sum," in *Handbook*, Volume 1 , Chapter 6.
Forges, F., E. Minelli and R. Vohra, 2002, "Incentives and the Core of an Exchange Economy: A Survey," *Journal of Mathematical Economics* 38(1–2), 1–41.
Fudenberg, D. and E. Maskin, 1986, "The Folk Theorem in Repeated Games with Discounting and Incomplete Information," *Econometrica* 54, 533–554.
Geanakoplos, 1., 1994, "Common Knowledge," in *Handbook*, Volume 2, Chapter 40.
Gul, F., 1998, "A Comment on Aumann's Bayesian View," *Econometrica* 66, 923–927. [Chapter 21]
Handbook: see Aumann and Hart, above.
Harsanyi, J., 1967–8, "Games with Incomplete Information Played by 'Bayesian' Players," Parts I–III, *Management Science* 8, 159–182, 320–334, 486–502.
——— 1973, "Games with Randomly Disturbed Payoffs: A New Rationale for Mixed Strategy Equilibrium Points," *International Journal of Game Theory* 2, 1–23.
Heifetz, A., 2001, "The Positive Foundation of the Common Prior Assumption," California Institute of Technology, mimeo.
——— and P. Mongin, 2001, "Probability Logic for Type Spaces," *Games and Economic Behavior* 35, 31–53.
Heifetz, A., and D. Samet, 1998, "Topology-Free Typology of Beliefs," *Journal of Economic Theory* 82, 324–341.
Hillas, J., and E. Kohlberg, 2002, "Foundations of Strategic Equilibrium," in *Handbook*, Volume 3, Chapter 42.
Hintikka, J., 1962, *Knowledge and Belief*, Ithaca: Cornell University Press.
Kreps, D., P. Milgrom, J. Roberts and R. Wilson, 1982, "Rational Cooperation in the Finitely Repeated Prisoners' Dilemma," *Journal of Economic Theory* 27, 245–252.
Kreps, D. M., and J. Sobel, 1994, "Signalling," in *Handbook*, Volume 2, Chapter 25.
Kripke, S., 1959, "A Completeness Theorem in Modal Logic," *Journal of Symbolic Logic* 24, 1–14.
Lewis, D., 1969, *Convention*, Cambridge: Harvard University Press.
Luce, R. D., and H. Raiffa, 1957, *Games and Decisions*, New York: Wiley.
Meier, M., 2012, "An Infinitary Probability Logic for Type Spaces," *Israel Journal of Mathematics* 192(1), 1–58.

Mertens, J.-F., S. Sorin and S. Zamir, 2015, *Repeated Games*, Cambridge University Press.
Mertens, J.-F. and S. Zamir, 1985, "Formulation of Bayesian Analysis for Games with Incomplete Information," *International Journal of Game Theory* 14, 1–29.
Morris, S., 1994, "Trade with Heterogeneous Prior Beliefs and Asymmetric Information," *Econometrica* 62, 1327–1347.
Myerson, R. B., 1984, "Cooperative Games with Incomplete Information," *International Journal of Game Theory* 13, 69–96.
——— 1994, "Communication, Correlated Equilibria and Incentive Compatibility," in *Handbook*, Volume 2, Chapter 24.
Nau, R. F. and K. F. McCardle, 1990, "Coherent Behavior in Noncooperative Games," *Journal of Economic Theory* 50, 424–444.
Samet, D., 1990, "Ignoring Ignorance and Agreeing to Disagree," *Journal of Economic Theory* 52, 190–207.
——— 1998a, "Iterative Expectations and Common Priors," *Games and Economic Behavior* 24, 131–141.
——— 1998b, "Common Priors and Separation of Convex Sets," *Games and Economic Behavior* 24, 172–174.
Von Neumann, J. and O. Morgenstern, 1944, *Theory of Games and Economic Behavior*, Princeton: Princeton University Press.
Wilson, R., 1978, "Information, Efficiency, and the Core of an Economy," *Econometrica* 46, 807–816.
——— 1992, "Strategic Analysis of Auctions," in *Handbook*, Volume 1, Chapter 8.
——— 1992, "Strategic Models of Entry Deterrence," in *Handbook*, Volume 1, Chapter 10.
Zamir, S., 1992, "Repeated Games of Incomplete Information: Zero-Sum," in *Handbook*, Volume 1, Chapter 5.

Appendix: Limitations of the Syntactic Approach

Aviad Heifetz

The interpretation of the universal model of Section 8 as "canonical," with the association of beliefs to states "self-evident" by virtue of the states' inner structure, relies nevertheless on the non-trivial assumption that the players' beliefs cannot be but σ-additive. This is highlighted by the following example.

In the Mertens-Zamir (1985) construction mentioned in Section 8, we shall focus our attention on a subspace Ω whose states ω can be represented in the form

$$\omega = (s, i_1 i_2 i_3 \ldots, j_1 j_2 j_3 \ldots)$$

where each digit s, i_k, j_k may assume the value 0 or 1. The state of nature is s. The sequences $i_1 i_2 i_3 \ldots, j_1 j_2 j_3 \ldots$ encode the beliefs of the players i and j, respectively, in the following way. If the sequence starts with 1, the player assigns probability 1 to the true state of nature s in ω. Otherwise, if her sequence starts with 0, she assigns probabilities half-half to the two possible states of nature. Inductively, suppose we have already described the beliefs of the players up to level n. If $i_{n+1} = 1, i$ believes with probability 1 that the n-th digit of j equals the actual value of j_n in ω, and otherwise — if $i_{n+1} = 0$ — she assigns equal probabilities to each of the possible values of this digit, 0 or 1. This belief of i is *independent* of i's lower-level beliefs. In addition, i assigns probability 1 to her own lower-level beliefs. The $(n + 1)$th level of belief of individual j is defined symmetrically.

Notice that up to every finite level n there are finitely many events to consider, so the beliefs are trivially σ-additive. Therefore, by the Kolmogorov extension theorem, for the hierarchy of beliefs of every sequence, there is a unique σ-additive coherent extension to a probability measure[29] over Ω. When $i_n = 0$ for all n, the strong law of large numbers asserts that this limit extension assigns probability 1 to the sequences of j where

$$\lim_{n \to \infty} \frac{j_1 + j_2 + \cdots + j_n}{n} = \frac{1}{2}.$$

However, there are finitely additive coherent extensions to i's finite-level beliefs that are concentrated on the disjoint set of j's sequences where

$$\liminf_{n \to \infty} \frac{j_1 + j_2 + \cdots + j_n}{n} > \frac{1}{2} \tag{A.1}$$

[29]With the σ-field generated by the events that depend on finitely many digits.

and in fact there are finitely additive coherent extensions concentrated on any tail event of sequences $j_1 j_2 j_3 \dots$, i.e., an event where every possible initial segment $j_1 \dots j_n$ appears in some sequence.[30]

Thus, though the finite-level beliefs single out unique σ-additive limit beliefs over Ω, nothing in them can specify that these limit beliefs must be σ-additive. If finitely additive beliefs are not ruled out in the players' minds, we cannot assume that the inner structure of the states $\omega \in \Omega$ specifies uniquely the beliefs of the players.

A similar problem presents itself if we restrict our attention to knowledge. In the syntactic formalism of Section 4, replace the belief operators p_i^α with knowledge operators k_i. When associating

---

[30]To see this, observe that to any event defined by k out of j's digits, the sequence

$$i_1 i_2 i_3 \dots = 000 \dots \tag{A.2}$$

assigns the probability 2^{-k}. Therefore, the integral I w.r.t. this belief is well defined over the vector space $\mathcal{V}$ of real-valued functions which are each measurable w.r.t. finitely many of j's digits. Now, for every real-valued function g on j's sequences, define the functional

$$\bar{I}(g) = \inf\{I(f) : f \in \mathcal{V}, \mathrm{g} \le f\}.$$

Then $\bar{I}$ is clearly sub-additive, $\bar{I}(\alpha g) = \alpha \bar{I}(g)$ for $\alpha \ge 0$, and $\bar{I} = I$ on $\mathcal{V}$. Therefore, by the Hahn–Banach theorem, there is an extension (in fact, many extensions) of I as a positive linear functional to the limits of sequences of functions in $\mathcal{V}$, and further to all the real-valued functions on Ω, satisfying

$$I(g) \le \bar{I}(g).$$

Restricting our attention to characteristic functions g, we thus get a finitely additive coherent extension of (A.2) over Ω.

The proof of the Hahn–Banach theorem proceeds by consecutively considering functions g to which I is not yet extended, and defining

$$I(g) = \bar{I}(g).$$

If the first function g_1 to which I is extended is a characteristic function of a tail event (like A.1), the smallest $f \in \mathcal{F}$ majorizing g_1 is the constant function $f \equiv \mathbf{1}$, so

$$I(g) = I(\mathbf{1}) = 1,$$

and the resulting coherent extension of (A.2) assigns probability 1 to the chosen tail event.

sentences to states of an augmented semantic belief system in Section 5, say that the sentence $k_i e$ holds in state ω if $\omega \in K_i E$,[31] where E is the event that corresponds to the sentence e. The canonical *knowledge* system Γ will now consist of those lists of sentences that hold in some state of some augmented semantic belief system. The information set $\mathbf{I}_i(\gamma)$ of player i at the list $\gamma \in \Gamma$ will consist of all the lists $\gamma' \in \Gamma$ that contain exactly the same sentences of the form $k_i f$ as in γ. It now follows that

$$k_i f \in \gamma \Leftrightarrow \gamma \in K_i E_f \tag{A.3}$$

where $E_f \subseteq \Gamma$ is the event that f holds,[32] and the knowledge operator K_i is as in Section 7: $K_i E = \{\gamma \in \Gamma : \mathbf{I}_i\ (\gamma) \subseteq E\}$.

However, there are many alternative definitions for the information sets $\mathbf{I}_i(\gamma)$ for which (A.3) would still obtain.[33] Thus, by no means can we say that the information sets $\mathbf{I}_i(\gamma)$ are "self-evident" from the inner structure of the lists γ which constitute the canonical knowledge system.

To see this, consider the following example (similar to that in Fagin *et al.* 1991). Ana, Bjorn and Christina participate in a computer forum over the web. At some point Ana invites Bjorn to meet the next evening. At that stage they leave the forum to continue the chat in private. If they eventually exchange n messages back and forth regarding the meeting, there is mutual knowledge of level n between them that they will meet, but not common knowledge, which they could attain, say, by eventually talking over the phone.

Christina doesn't know how many messages were eventually exchanged between Ana and Bjorn, so she does not exclude any finite level of mutual knowledge between them about the meeting. Nevertheless, Christina could still rule out the possibility of common knowledge (say, if she could peep into Bjorn's room and see that he

---

[31] The semantic knowledge operator $K_i E$ is defined in Section 7.

[32] As in Section 8.

[33] In fact, as many as there are subsets of Γ! (Heifetz 1999.)

was glued to his computer the whole day and spoke with nobody). But if this situation is formalized by a list of sentences γ, Christina does *not* exclude the possibility of common knowledge between Ana and Bjorn *with the above definition of* $\mathbf{I}_{Christina}(\gamma)$. This is because there exists an augmented belief system Ω with a state ω' in which there is common knowledge between Ana and Bjorn, while Christina does not exclude any finite level of mutual knowledge between them, exactly as in the situation above. We then have $\gamma' \in \mathbf{I}_{Christina}(\gamma)$, where γ' is the list of sentences that hold in ω'. Thus, if we redefine $\mathbf{I}_{Christina}(\gamma)$ by omitting γ' from it, (A.3) would still obtain, because (A.3) refers only to sentences or events that describe finite levels of mutual knowledge.

At first it may seem that this problem can be mitigated by enriching the syntax with a common knowledge operator (for every subgroup of two or more players). Such an operator would be shorthand for the infinite conjunction "everybody (in the subgroup) knows, and everybody knows that everybody knows, and...". This would settle things in the above example, but create numerous new, analogous problems. *The discontinuity of knowledge is essential*: The same phenomena persist (i.e., (A.3) does not pin down the information sets $\mathbf{I}_i(\gamma)$) even if the syntax explicitly allows for infinite conjunctions and disjunctions of sentences of whatever chosen cardinality (Heifetz 1994).

References

Fagin, R., J. Y. Halpern and M. Y. Vardi, 1991, "A Model-Theoretic Analysis of Knowledge," *Journal of the Association for Computing Machinery (ACM)* 38(2), 382–428.

Heifetz, A., 1994, "Infinitary Epistemic Logic," in *Proceedings of the Fifth Conference on Theoretical Aspects of Reasoning about Knowledge (TARK 5)*, Los Altos, California: Morgan Kaufmann, 95–107. Extended version in *Mathematical Logic Quarterly* 43 (1997), 333–342.

——— 1999, "How Canonical is the Canonical Model? A Comment on Aumann's Interactive Epistemology," *International Journal of Game Theory* 28, 435–442.

Chapter 6

Musings on Information and Knowledge*

The first symposium question is, "Is there an important distinction between information and knowledge?" Of course, it depends on what is meant by these terms. An advantage (disadvantage?) of formal reasoning is that there, that kind of question does not arise. You must first define your terms, and then it's usually easy to tell whether there is or is not an important distinction. Some people might say that even informally, the question has no substance until you've said what you mean.

One could interpret the question in terms of common usage. Some of the Symposium materials (specifically, the quotations from Kenneth Boulding's *Beyond Economics* and from Paul Weiss) suggest that information is the raw material from which knowledge is manufactured; that information is purely factual, whereas knowledge is something deeper — information that has been distilled, digested, internalized, processed or somehow transformed into an idea or principle. It's an interesting thought, but doesn't reflect common usage. You can know perfectly mundane things — whether it rained yesterday, or when the train left.

A distinction in common usage is that information can be impersonal, whereas knowledge is personal. It is *people* who know things; knowledge isn't "out there," has no existence of its own that is independent of people's minds. On the other hand, information

*Reprinted from *Econ Journal Watch* (2005), 2(1), 88–96, with permission from Fraser Institute.

exists outside of people's minds; it can be gathered, so to speak. You might say to your travel agent, "Get me information on flying to New Zealand." It's quite possible that nobody in the world knows how much it costs to get from Jerusalem to Christchurch, but the information is "there," the travel agent can gather it.

Another distinction in common usage is that "knowledge" has a more precise connotation than "information." For example, a probability estimate might be considered information, but it isn't knowledge. A detective might say, I have information on who committed the murder, but I don't *know.*

Possibly neither of these distinctions is very important to economics.

There *is* an important distinction in *scientific* usage: Information can be measured, knowledge cannot. For example, the minimal number of bits needed to transmit some piece of information can be taken as a measure of the "amount" of information being transmitted. This is closely related to the idea of entropy as a measure of information. Knowledge, on the other hand, is a 0–1 affair; you either know something, or you don't.

There's also an important distinction between "knowledge *theory*" and "information *theory*." The former refers to partition models of knowledge, the syntax of knowledge, common and mutual knowledge, axiomatics, and so on. Sometimes this is called "formal epistemology," and when there are several agents, "interactive epistemology." On the other hand, "information theory" deals with information transmission, noisy channels, entropy, and so on. Though related, the two are really quite different. Both are highly relevant to economics.

Two important issues that may be relevant to a possible distinction are *awareness* and *logical omniscience.* These are worth separate treatments.

Awareness

In most formal models of knowledge — particularly, those used in economics — agents are aware of the possibilities, but do not know which obtains. But in real life, an important component of ignorance (the lack of knowledge) is ignorance of the possibilities. Columbus, when setting out westwards for India, had no idea that there might be another continent between Europe and Asia; that possibility did not enter his mind. When we do scientific research, we often have no idea what we will find. Indeed, that is the most interesting case; and it is quite different from, say, not knowing the time.

Experimental economists report that subjects in experiments tend to overestimate low probabilities; that is, they react to low probabilities as if they were higher. A possible explanation is in terms of unforeseen circumstances. The subject raises the low "official" probability because he instinctively takes unforeseen circumstances into account. Or perhaps not instinctively, but from experience; he has seen or heard of too many "safe" drugs that caused irreparable harm, "safe" ships that sank, or reputable experimenters who lied — or failed to tell the whole truth — to experimental subjects.

The basic difficulty with building a model that explicitly takes unforeseen circumstances into account is that usually (though not invariably) the agents are taken to know the model, so the unforeseen circumstances become foreseen. Though there *has* been work that addresses the problem of awareness, I know of none that has "caught on," that is truly satisfactory.

One could perhaps distinguish between "knowledge" and "information" by associating knowledge with the traditional concept — where agents are aware of all the possibilities, but do not know which obtains — and associating information with the more amorphous situation, where agents are not even aware of the possibilities. That is, one might perhaps say that one seeks "knowledge" about the time or the weather, and "information" about the results of some future exploration or scientific research.

Logical Omniscience and the Cost of Calculation

A fundamental axiom of knowledge theory is that if you know p and you know that p implies q, then you know q. That sounds perfectly harmless and even obvious. But it entails *logical omniscience*: that agents know everything that follows logically from anything that they know. It follows that they know all logical tautologies, and in particular, all theorems of mathematics. For example, that Fermat's "last theorem," which was proved only in the 1990's after remaining open for 350 years, was always known to all mathematicians (indeed to everyone) — a patently absurd proposition.

This matter is of great economic importance. A significant shortcoming of economic theory is that it fails to take the cost of calculation into account. Under logical omniscience, all results of all calculations are already known to all agents, so calculations are in effect cost-free.

In real life, obviously, computations are costly. Computation — in particular, cost calculating — is important to almost any economic activity. But there is a fundamental economic difficulty with the matter of cost calculation. Namely, in order to know how much to calculate — when doing an optimization, say — one must know *beforehand* how much *this* will cost. But this in itself involves a calculation, indeed one that is likely to be more complex than the optimization itself. One is thus led to an infinite regress of ever more complex calculations, from which there seems to be no escape. This is a very serious problem, of great economic importance, for which there exists no solution that is even remotely satisfactory.

Again, one could perhaps distinguish between "knowledge" and "information" by associating knowledge with the traditional concept — where logical omniscience does obtain — and information with the more amorphous situation, where logical omniscience is not assumed. That is, one might perhaps say that one seeks "knowledge" about the time or the weather, and "information" about some cost calculation.

Both this and the awareness distinction are in the spirit of what was said in the first section — that information is less precise, more amorphous, than knowledge.

Common Knowledge of the Model

Having responded to the first Symposium question, we skip to the last: "What other thoughts do you have on knowledge and information in economics?"

Recall that a proposition is *commonly known* if all concerned (the "players") know it, all know that all know it, all know that, all know *that*, and so on ad infinitum. In the "Game Theory" entry in the *New Palgrave Dictionary of Economics*, we wrote as follows: "The common knowledge assumption underlies all of game theory and much of economic theory. Whatever be the model under discussion, whether complete or incomplete information, consistent or inconsistent, repeated or one-shot, cooperative or noncooperative, the model itself must be assumed common knowledge; otherwise the model is insufficiently specified, and the analysis incoherent" (Aumann 1987, 473).

Today, eighteen years later, this formulation no longer seems appropriate; in a sense, it is even incorrect. For example, to get Nash equilibrium in a game G, one need assume common knowledge neither of the game nor of the players' rationality (Aumann and Brandenburger 1995). It is important that G indeed be the game, and that the players indeed be rational; but *common knowledge* of these items is *not* needed.

In another sense, though, it is correct, but unnecessary. What we were saying in 1987 is that in addition to *explicit* assumptions like zero-sum, complete information, one-shot, or whatever, it is also *implicitly* assumed that the "model" is commonly known by the players; and that this assumption — the "common knowledge assumption" — is outside the model, and cannot be, or is not, stated within the model itself. We now understand that it is not an assumption at all, but a truism, a tautology, a "theorem;" it follows from more fundamental considerations.

To understand why, we must delve a little into *interactive epistemology*, which provides tools for analyzing what the players know — about the world and about each other's knowledge. There are two parallel formalisms, the *semantic* and the *syntactic*. As a practical matter, the semantic formalism is simpler to use, so has become standard in economic applications — in spite of being conceptually roundabout and a little difficult to fathom at first. It consists of a set of possible *states of the world* (or simply *states*), and for each player, a partition of the states into *information sets*, which tells us what that player knows at each state.[1] No doubt, some readers are familiar with this formalism; for the others, it is not necessary, nor would it be useful, to describe it further here.

The syntactic formalism, on the other hand, is conceptually entirely straightforward, but in practice a little awkward. It is simply a formal language, which incorporates the basic propositions under discussion (like "Yesterday it snowed in Jerusalem"), logical connectives ("and", "or", "not", "implies"), and a way of saying "Ann knows that ...," Ann being a generic player. Fewer of our readers will be familiar with *this* formalism; but again, it is neither necessary nor useful to describe it further here.

On the face of it, there seems to be a fundamental conceptual difference between the two formalisms. The syntactic formalism is simply a language; it has no substantive content, does not say anything about the real world. It does not say that it snowed yesterday in Jerusalem, or that Ann knows that it did. It just provides a way of saying these things, *if* we want to say them.

But the semantic formalism does seem to have substantive content. Namely, that it is commonly known among the players that the states in the formalism are the only possible ones, and that the knowledge partitions really do describe the players' knowledge. In particular, each player is assumed to know the knowledge *partitions* of all the others. At the least, this *appears* to be substantive; and indeed, it isn't clear what justifies it.

There is another, related difference between the two formalisms. Given the players and the basic propositions, the syntactic formalism is *canonic*; there is only one syntax. But the semantic formalism is not; it is possible to construct the states and the information partitions in many essentially different ways.

But in fact, the semantic formalism has no substance, either; it, too, is just a language. It is, in fact, entirely equivalent to the

[1]Explicitly, two states are in different information sets of a given player if and only if in one state, the player knows that the true state is not the other.

syntactic formalism. To see this, we construct the states explicitly in terms of the syntactic formalism. Conceptually, a "state" is simply a complete specification of all (relevant) aspects of the world. Thus in each given state, *every* proposition is either definitely true or definitely false. So we may think of a state simply as a list of propositions, which contains, for each proposition, either that proposition or its negation. In addition, we must require that the list be logically consistent, i.e., that each list contain the logical consequences of the propositions in that list. Call such lists *complete* and *coherent.*

Thus we may think of a state simply as a complete coherent list of propositions. There are, of course, infinitely many such states; but the syntactic formalism is perfectly explicit and transparent, so we have a good understanding of how a state looks, and indeed of how the whole "universe" — the set of *all* states — looks.

So much for the states. How about the information partitions? Where do *they* come from? Why are *they* known to all the players, indeed commonly known?

Well, it turns out that the information partitions are implicit in — can be read off from — the states. Two states are in different information sets of Ann if and only if she knows, in one state, that the other is not the true state. That is, there must be something that Ann knows in one state, that she does not know in the other; formally, a proposition p, such that the proposition "Ann knows p" is in the list describing one state, and not in the list describing the other.

So the semantic formalism is just a different way of writing the syntactic formalism. The two are entirely equivalent, and neither has any substantive content. Both are just languages; they make no assertions — embody no assumptions — about the real world.[2]

---

[2]Other than underlying assumptions like awareness (of the basic propositions) and logical omniscience.

The semantic formalism just constructed is called the *universal* formalism. Clearly it's canonic, since it was constructed in a canonical way from the syntactic formalism. Though there also are other semantic formalisms, they're all naturally embedded in the universal formalism; the universal semantic formalism encompasses everything of epistemic interest.

So, coming back to the "assumption" of common knowledge of the model: There is nothing substantive there. The "model" may be taken to be simply the universal formalism; as we have seen, this is equivalent to the syntactic formalism, which has no substance — is just a language.

It *is* of course possible to assume that various substantive items — zero-sum, complete information, the payoffs, the players' rationality, whatever — are in fact common knowledge. But such assumptions can and should be made explicitly, *within* the model. Unlike what we thought in 1987, assumptions that are implicit — "outside the model" — are never needed.

Comments on the Symposium Materials

Binmore

In the symposium materials, Ken Binmore writes, "Game theorists usually assume that the rules of the game and the preferences of the players are common knowledge. In analyzing a game, they typically need also to assume that the fact that all the players subscribe to appropriate rationality principles is also common knowledge, although they are seldom explicit on this point." We respectfully disagree.

(1) Ever since the groundbreaking work of Harsanyi (1967, 1968) on games of incomplete information, game theorists have *not* assumed that "the rules of the game and the preferences of the players are common knowledge." To be sure, sometimes one does assume this; but for close to forty years, it has not been a part of the game-theoretic canon. Ken surely knows this; it's possible

that the quote is out of context. Anyway, we thought it important to set the record straight.

(2) The second sentence is also inaccurate. As pointed out at the beginning of the previous section, "typically" — for Nash equilibrium, say — one must assume that the players indeed "subscribe to appropriate rationality principles," but *not* that this is common knowledge.

Friedman

Jim Friedman writes, "Usually, ... games of complete information are characterized by each player knowing the entire structure of payoffs of the game, by each player knowing that all players possess this information, and by all players knowing that all players have this information. There is ... an important conceptual distinction ... between (a) a complete information game in which complete information is common knowledge and (b) a complete information game in which each player does not actually know whether the other players also have complete information." Again, we respectfully disagree. The first sentence describes *second order mutual* knowledge of the information in question, whereas what is needed is *common* knowledge. Therefore, the second sentence is also inaccurate. In a complete information game, complete information is commonly known, so option (b) is impossible; this follows from the general theorem that when something is commonly known, then it is commonly known that it is commonly known.

Rasmusen

Eric Rasmusen writes, "For clarity, models are set up so that information partitions are common knowledge. Every player knows how precise the other players' information is, however ignorant he himself may be.... Making the information partitions common knowledge is important for clear modeling.... " Here, we do not disagree, but the thrust seems misplaced. As explained in the previous section, it is *tautological* that the partitions are common knowledge.

References

Aumann, R. J., 1987, Game theory, *New Palgrave Dictionary of Economics*, vol. 2. New York: Macmillan, 473.

Aumann, R. J. and A. Brandenburger, 1995, Epistemic conditions for Nash equilibrium, *Econometrica* 63, 1161–1180. [Chapter 10]

Harsanyi, J. C., 1967, Games with incomplete information played by 'Bayesian' players, I: The basic model, *Management Science* 14(3), 159–182.

Harsanyi, J. C., 1968, Games with incomplete information played by 'Bayesian' players, II: Bayesian equilibrium points, *Management Science* 14(5), 320–334.

Harsanyi, J. C., 1968, Games with incomplete information played by 'Bayesian' players, III: Basic probability distribution of the game, *Management Science* 14(7), 486–502.

Part 2

Interactive Epistemology and Game Equilibrium

Chapter 7

Subjectivity and Correlation in Randomized Strategies*

1. Introduction

Subjectivity and correlation, though formally related, are conceptually distinct and independent issues. We start by discussing subjectivity.

A mixed strategy in a game involves the selection of a pure strategy by means of a random device. It has usually been assumed that the random device is a coin flip, the spin of a roulette wheel, or something similar; in brief, an "objective" device, one for which everybody agrees on the numerical values of the probabilities involved. Rather oddly, in spite of the long history of the theory of subjective probability, nobody seems to have examined the consequences of basing mixed strategies on "subjective" random devices, i.e. devices on the probabilities of whose outcomes people may disagree (such as horse races, elections, etc.). Even a fairly superficial such examination yields some startling results, as follows:

a. Two-person zero-sum games lose their "strictly competitive" character. It becomes worthwhile to cooperate in such games,

*Reprinted from *Journal of Mathematical Economics* (1974), 1, 67–96, with permission from Elsevier.

i.e. to enter into binding agreements.[1] The concept of the "value" of a zero-sum game loses some of its force, since *both* players can get more than the value (in the utility sense).

b. In certain n-person games with $n \geqq 3$ new equilibrium points appear, whose payoffs strictly dominate the payoffs of all other equilibrium points.[2]

Result (a) holds not just for certain selected 2-person 0-sum games, but for practically[3] all such games. Moreover, it holds if there is any area whatsoever of subjective disagreement between the players, i.e., any event in the world (possibly entirely unconnected with the game under consideration) for which Players 1 and 2 have different subjective probabilities.

The phenomenon enunciated in Result (b) shows that not only the 2-person 0-sum theory, but also the non-cooperative n-person theory is modified in an essential fashion by the introduction of this new kind of strategy. However, this phenomenon cannot occur[4] for 2-person games (zero-sum or not); for such games we will show[5] that the set of equilibrium payoff vectors is not changed by the introduction of subjectively mixed strategies.

We now turn to correlation. Correlated strategies are familiar from cooperative game theory, but their applications in non-cooperative games are less understood. It has been known for some time that by the use of correlated strategies in a non-cooperative game, one can achieve as an equilibrium any payoff vector in the convex hull of the mixed strategy (Nash) equilibrium payoff vectors. Here we will show that by appropriate methods of correlation, even points outside of this convex hull can be achieved.[6]

---

[1]Example 2.1 and sec. 6.
[2]Example 2.3.
[3]Specifically, wherever there is one payoff greater than the value and another one less than the value (for Player 1, say).
[4]Except in a very degenerate sense; see Example 2.2.
[5]Section 5.
[6]Examples 2.5 through 2.9.

In describing these phenomena, it is best to view a randomized strategy as a random variable with values in the pure strategy space, rather than as a distribution over pure strategies. In Section 3 we develop such a framework; it allows for subjectivity, correlation, and all possible combinations thereof. Thus, a side product of our study is a descriptive theory (or taxonomy) of randomized strategies.

We are very grateful to Professors M. Maschler, B. Peleg, and R. W. Rosenthal for extremely stimulating correspondence and comments on this study.

2. Examples

Example 2.1. Consider the familiar two-person zero-sum game "matching pennies," which we write in matrix form as follows:

$1, -1$	$-1, \ 1$
$-1, \ 1$	$1, -1$

.

Let D be an event to which Players 1 and 2 ascribe subjective probability 2/3 and 1/3 respectively. Suppose now that the players bindingly agree to the following pair of strategies: Player 2 will play left in any event; Player 1 will play top if D occurs, and bottom otherwise. The expectation of both players is then 1/3, whereas the value of the game is of course 0 to both players.

To make this example work, one needs an event D whose subjective probability is $>1/2$ for one player and $<1/2$ for the other. Such an event can always be constructed as long as the players disagree about something, i.e., there is some event B with $p_1(B) \neq p_2(B)$ (where p_i is the subjective probability of i). For example, if $p_1(B) = 7/8$ and $p_2(B) = 5/8$, then we can construct the desired event by tossing a fair coin twice (provided these particular coin tosses were not involved in the description of B); if C is the event "at least one head," then we have $p_1(B \cap C) = 21/32 > 1/2 > 15/32 = p_2(B \cap C)$. This kind of construction can always be carried out (see the proof of Proposition 5.1).

Example 2.2. Suppose that there is an event D to which Players 1 and 2 ascribe subjective probabilities 1 and 0 respectively and such that only Player 1 is informed before the play as to whether or not D occurs. Consider the following pair of strategies: Player 2 plays left; Player 1 plays top if D occurs, bottom otherwise. This strategy yields a payoff of $(1, 1)$; moreover, it is actually in equilibrium, in the sense that neither player has any incentive to carry out a unilateral change in strategy. However, it has a somewhat degenerate flavor, since it requires that at least one of the two players be certain of a falsehood (see Section 8). We now show that a similar phenomenon can also occur in a non-degenerate set-up; but it requires 3 players.

Example 2.3. Consider the three-person game given as follows:

$0,8,0$	$3,3,3$
$1,1,1$	$0,0,0$

$0,0,0$	$3,3,3$
$1,1,1$	$8,0,0$

.

Here Player 1 picks the row, Player 2 the column, and Player 3 the matrix. A triple of objectively mixed strategies is an equilibrium point in this game if and only if Player 1 plays bottom and Player 2 plays left; Player 3 may play any mixed strategy. All these equilibrium points have the same payoff vector, namely $(1, 1, 1)$. Suppose now that D is an event to which Players 1 and 2 ascribe subjective probabilities $3/4$ and $1/4$ respectively, and such that only Player 3 is informed as to whether or not D occurs. Consider the following strategy triple: Player 1 plays top; Player 2 plays right; Player 3 chooses the left matrix if D occurs, the right matrix if not. If Player 1 moves down he will get $1/4 \cdot 8 = 2$ rather than $1 \cdot 3 = 3$; similarly for Player 2 if he moves left; as for Player 3, he certainly cannot profit from moving, since he is getting his maximum payoff in the whole game. Therefore this is an equilibrium point; its payoff is $(3, 3, 3)$, instead of the $(1, 1, 1)$ obtained at all objective equilibrium points.

That this kind of phenomenon cannot occur with fewer than 3 players will be shown in Section 5.

An interesting feature of this example is that the higher payoff at the new, subjective, equilibrium point is not only "subjectively higher," it is "objectively higher." That is, unlike the case in Example 2.1, the payoff is higher not only because of the differing probability estimates of the players, but it is higher in any case, whether or not the event D takes place. The contribution of subjective probabilities in this case is to make the new point an equilibrium; once chosen, it is *sure* to make all the players better off than at any of the old equilibrium points.

We remark that by using different numbers we can find similar examples based on arbitrarily small probability differences.

It is essential in this example that only Player 3 be informed as to whether or not D occurs. If, say, Player 1 were also informed (before the time comes for choosing his pure strategy), he could do better by playing top or bottom according to whether D occurs on not.[7] This secrecy regarding D is quite natural. If we were to insist that all players be informed about D, it would be like insisting that in an objectively mixed strategy based on a coin toss, all players be informed as to the outcome of the toss. But much of the effectiveness of mixed strategies is based precisely on the secrecy, which would then be destroyed. In practical situations, it is of course quite common for some players to have differing subjective probabilities for events about which they are not informed, and on which other players peg their strategy choices.

Our last six examples deal with correlation.

Example 2.4. Consider the following familiar 2-person non-zero-sum game:

2, 1	0, 0
0, 0	1, 2

.

There are exactly three Nash equilibrium points: two in pure strategies, yielding $(2, 1)$ and $(1, 2)$ respectively, and one in mixed strategies, yielding $(2/3, 2/3)$. The payoff vector $(3/2, 3/2)$ is not achievable at all in (objectively) mixed strategies. It is, however, achievable in "correlated" strategies, as follows: One fair coin is tossed; if it falls heads, Players 1 and 2 play top and left respectively; otherwise, they play bottom and right.

The interesting aspect of this procedure is that it not only achieves $(3/2, 3/2)$, it is also in equilibrium; neither player can gain by a unilateral change. Any point in the convex hull of the Nash

[7] I am grateful to R. W. Rosenthal for this remark.

equilibrium payoffs of any game can be achieved in a similar fashion, and will also be in equilibrium. This is not new; it has been in the folklore of game theory for years. I believe the first to notice this phenomenon (at least in print) were Harsanyi and Selten (1972).

In the following four examples we wish to point out a phenomenon that we believe *is* new, namely that by the use of correlated strategies one can achieve a payoff vector that is in equilibrium in the same sense as above, but that is *outside* the convex hull of the Nash equilibrium payoffs. In fact, except in Example 2.7, it is better for all players than any Nash equilibrium payoff.

Example 2.5. Consider the 3-person game given as follows:

$0,0,3$	$0,0,0$
$1,0,0$	$0,0,0$

$2,2,2$	$0,0,0$
$0,0,0$	$2,2,2$

$0,0,0$	$0,0,0$
$0,1,0$	$0,0,3$

.

Here Player 1 picks the row, Player 2 the column, and Player 3 the matrix. If we restrict ourselves to pure strategies, there are only three equilibrium payoffs, namely $(0,0,0)$, $(1,0,0)$, and $(0,1,0)$. If we allow (objectively) mixed strategies, some more equilibrium payoffs are added, but none of their coordinates exceed 1. Consider now the following strategy triple: Player 3 plays the middle matrix. Players 1 and 2 get together and toss a fair coin, but do not inform Player 3 of the outcome of the toss. If the coin falls on heads, Players 1 and 2 play top and left respectively; otherwise, they play bottom and right respectively. The payoff is $(2,2,2)$. If Player 3 would know the outcome of the toss, he would be tempted to move away; for example, if it was heads, he would move left. Since he does not know, he would lose by moving. Thus the introduction of correlation among *subsets* of the players can significantly improve the payoff to everybody.

Example 2.6. Another version of Example 2.5 is the following:

$0,1,3$	$0,0,0$
$1,1,1$	$1,0,0$

$2,2,2$	$0,0,0$
$2,2,0$	$2,2,2$

$0,1,0$	$0,0,0$
$1,1,1$	$1,0,3$

.

This version has the advantage that there is only one Nash equilibrium payoff, namely $(1,1,1)$; and it can be read off from the matrices by the use of simple domination arguments, as compared to the slightly laborious computations needed in the previous example. The advantage of Example 2.5 is that the new correlated strategy equilibrium point has the property that any deviation will actually lead to a loss (not only a failure to gain).

In both examples, Player 3 will not even *want* to know the outcome of the toss; he will *want* Players 1 and 2 to perform it in secret. It is important for him that Players 1 and 2 know that he does not know the outcome of the toss; otherwise they cannot depend on him to choose the middle matrix, and will in consequence themselves play for an equilibrium point that is less advantageous for all. Thus in Example 2.6, Player 3 knows that if he can "peep," then Players 1 and 2 will necessarily play bottom and left respectively, to the mutual disadvantage of all.

Example 2.7. In Examples 2.5 and 2.6, equilibrium payoffs outside of the convex hull of the Nash equilibrium payoffs were achieved by "partial" correlation — correlation of strategy choices by two out of the three players. We now show that a similar phenomenon can occur even in 2-person games; here again a kind of partial correlation is used, but it is subtler than that appearing previously.

Consider the 2-person game given as follows:

6, 6	2, 7
7, 2	0, 0

This game has two pure strategies equilibrium points, with payoff $(2, 7)$ and $(7, 2)$ respectively, and one mixed strategy equilibrium point, with payoff $(4\frac{2}{3},\ 4\frac{2}{3})$. Consider now an objective chance mechanism that chooses one of three points A, B, C with probability $1/3$ each. After the point has been chosen, Player 1 is told whether or not A was chosen, and Player 2 is told whether or not C was chosen; nothing more is told to the players. Consider the following pair of strategies: If he is informed that A was chosen, Player 1 plays his bottom strategy; otherwise, his top strategy. Similarly, if he is informed that C was chosen, Player 2 plays his right strategy; otherwise, he goes left. It is easy to verify that this pair of strategies is indeed in equilibrium, and that it yields the players an expectation of $(5, 5)$ — a payoff that is outside the convex hull of the Nash equilibrium payoffs (listed above).

The strategies in this equilibrium point are not stochastically independent, like the mixed or pure strategies appearing in Nash equilibrium points, nor are they totally correlated, like the strategies appearing in Example 2.4. It is precisely the partial correlation that enables the phenomenon we observe here.

Example 2.8. Consider the 2-person game given as follows:

6, 6	0, 0	2, 7
0, 0	4, 4	3, 0
7, 2	0, 3	0, 0

This is obtained from the previous example by adding a middle row and a middle column, with appropriate payoffs. The strategy pairs (top, right) and (bottom, left), which previously yielded the equilibrium payoffs $(2, 7)$ and $(7, 2)$, are no longer in equilibrium; the equilibrium property has been "killed" by the addition of the new strategies. The mixed-strategy pair which previously yielded $(4\frac{2}{3},\ 4\frac{2}{3})$ remains in equilibrium here; moreover we get a new pure strategy equilibrium point yielding $(4, 4)$, and a new mixed strategy equilibrium point yielding $(2\frac{10}{23}, 2\frac{10}{23})$. These are all the Nash equilibrium payoffs. Thus we see that $4\frac{2}{3}$ is the maximum that either player can get at any Nash equilibrium point.

The equilibrium point in "partially correlated" strategies described in Example 2.7 remains in equilibrium here, and yields $(5, 5)$ — more, for both players, than that yielded by any of the Nash equilibria.

Though the random device needed in Examples 2.7 and 2.8 is conceptually somewhat more complex than the coin tosses (secret or joint) used in classical game theory and in Examples 2.4, 2.5, and 2.6, it is not at all difficult to construct. Given a roulette wheel, it is easy to attach electrical connections that will do the job. If the reader wishes, he can think of the players as jointly supervising the construction of the device, and then retiring to separate rooms to get the information and choose their strategies. It is advantageous for both players to build the device, to satisfy each other that it is working properly, and then to follow the above procedure. Once chosen, the procedure is of course self-enforcing; neither player will wish to renege at any stage.

Example 2.9. Consider again the 2-person 0-sum game "matching pennies" already treated in Example 2.1. Suppose that nature chooses one of four points A, B, C, or D, and that Players 1 and 2 ascribe to these choices subjective probabilities $(1/3, 1/6, 1/6, 1/3)$ and $(1/6, 1/3, 1/3, 1/6)$, respectively. Under no condition is either player told which point was chosen, but Player 1 is told whether the point chosen is in $\{A, B\}$ or in $\{C, D\}$, and Player 2 is told whether the point chosen is in $\{A, C\}$ or in $\{B, D\}$. Consider the following strategy pair: Player 1 chooses top or bottom according to whether he is told "$\{A, B\}$" or "$\{C, D\}$"; Player 2 chooses left or right according to whether he is told "$\{A, C\}$" or "$\{B, D\}$." Like the strategy pair in Example 2.1, this yields each player an expectation of $1/3$, whereas the value of the game is of course 0 to both players; unlike the strategy pair of Example 2.1, *this pair is in equilibrium.*

If, in a 2-person zero-sum game with value v, we permit correlation but rule out subjectivity, then the payoffs to all strategy pairs continue to sum to 0, and it is easy to see that the only equilibrium points have payoffs $(v, -v)$. If we rule out correlation (i.e. permit mixed or pure strategies only) but permit subjectivity, we still get only $(v, -v)$ as an equilibrium payoff; this follows from Proposition 5.1. But if we permit both subjectivity and correlation, then this example shows that there may exist mutually advantageous equilibrium points, even in 2-person 0-sum games.

3. The Formal Model

In this section, definitions are indicated by italics.

A *game* consists of:

1. a finite set N (the *players*); write $N = \{1, \ldots, n\}$;
2. for each $i \in N$, a finite set S_i (the *pure strategies* of i);

3. a finite set X (the *outcomes*);
4. a function g from the Cartesian product $S = \mathbf{x}_{i \in n} S_i$ onto X (*the outcome function*).

   This completes the description of the game as such; formally, however, we still need some equipment for randomizing strategies, and for defining utilities and subjective probabilities for the players. Thus to the description of the game we append the following:
5. A set Ω (the *states of the world*), together with a σ-field $\mathscr{B}$ of subsets of Ω (the *events*);
6. For each player i, a sub-σ-field $\mathscr{I}_i$ of $\mathscr{B}$ (the events in $\mathscr{I}_i$ are those *regarding which i is informed).*
7. For each player i, a relation $\succsim_i$ (the *preference order of* i) on the space of lotteries on the outcome space X, where a *lottery* on X is a $\mathscr{B}$-measurable[8] function from Ω to X.

The intuitive scenario associated with this model involves the following steps, to be thought of as occurring one after the other as follows:

i. Nature chooses a point ω in Ω.
ii. Each player i is informed as to which events in $\mathscr{I}_i$ contain ω.
iii. Each player i chooses[9] a pure strategy s_i in S_i.
iv. The outcome is determined[10] to be $g(s_1, \ldots, s_n)$.

Returning to the formal model, let us define a *randomized strategy* (or simply *strategy*) for player i to be a measurable function $\boldsymbol{s}_i$ from $(\Omega, \mathscr{I}_i)$ to S_i. Note that $\boldsymbol{s}_i$ must be measurable w.r.t. (with respect to) $\mathscr{I}_i$, not merely w.r.t. $\mathscr{B}$; this means that i can peg his strategies only on events regarding which he is informed. [In the above scenario, strategies are chosen before step (ii).]

---

[8]This means that for each $x \in X$, the set $\{\boldsymbol{x} = x\}$ [i.e. the set $\{\omega : \boldsymbol{x}(\omega) = x\}$] is in $\mathscr{B}$.

[9]Without informing the other players.

[10]Note that g does not depend on ω; see subsection (d) of Section 9.

If $\boldsymbol{s}$ is an n-tuple of strategies, then $g(\boldsymbol{s})$ is a lottery on X. An *equilibrium point* is an n-tuple $\boldsymbol{s} = (\boldsymbol{s}_1, \ldots, \boldsymbol{s}_n)$ of strategies such that for all i and all strategies $\boldsymbol{t}_i$ of i, we have

$$g(\boldsymbol{s}) \succsim_i g(\boldsymbol{s}_1, \ldots, \boldsymbol{s}_{i-1}, \boldsymbol{t}_i, \boldsymbol{s}_{i+1}, \ldots, \boldsymbol{s}_n).$$

We will assume:

Assumption I. For each i, there is a real function u_i on X (the *utility function* of i) and a probability measure[11] p_i on Ω (the *subjective probability* of i) such that for all lotteries $\boldsymbol{x}$ and $\boldsymbol{y}$ on X, we have $\boldsymbol{x} \succsim_i \boldsymbol{y}$ if and only if

$$\int_\Omega u_i(\boldsymbol{x}(\omega))\mathrm{d}p_i(\omega) \geqq \int_\Omega u_i(\boldsymbol{y}(\omega))\mathrm{d}p_i(\omega);$$

moreover, p_i is unique.[12]

This assumption says that player i's preferences between lotteries are governed by the expected utility of the outcomes of the lotteries. There are well-known systems of axioms on the preferences $\succsim_i$ that lead to utilities and subjective probabilities; see for example Savage (1954) or Anscombe and Aumann (1963).

Note that p_i is defined on all of $\mathscr{B}$, not only on $\mathscr{I}_i$; that is, i assigns a probability to all events, not only those regarding which i is informed.

Two events A and B are *i-independent* if

$$p_i(A \cap B) = p_i(A)p_i(B);$$

intuitively, this means that i can get no hint about A from information regarding B. More generally, the events $A_1, \ldots, A_k$ are

[11] σ-additive non-negative measure with $p_i(\Omega) = 1$.

[12] I.e. if (u_i', p_i') also satisfy the condition of the previous sentence, then $p_i' = p_i$. Axiom systems leading to subjective probabilities usually imply the uniqueness as well. In our case, if we had wanted to minimize our assumptions we could have avoided assuming uniqueness, at this stage. Indeed, the uniqueness of p_i follows from the *existence* of a non-atomic p_i; and this is assumed in Assumption II. It is, however, more convenient to assume uniqueness already at this stage, since it enables us to refer immediately to "the" subjective probability of player i, and this simplifies the entire discussion.

i-independent if

$$p_i(B_1 \cap \cdots \cap B_k) = p_i(B_1) \cdots p_i(B_k)$$

whenever each B_j is either A_j or Ω. Events are *independent* if they are i-independent for all i. An event is *i-secret* if it is in $\mathscr{I}_i$, and for each j other than i, it is j-independent of all events in the σ-field generated by all the $\mathscr{I}_k$ with $k \neq i$. Thus i is informed regarding each i-secret event, but players other than i can get no hint of it, even by pooling their knowledge. The family of i-secret events is denoted $\mathscr{S}_i$. We assume

Assumption II. For each i, there is a σ-field $\mathscr{R}_i$ of i-secret events such that each p_j is non-atomic on $\mathscr{R}_i$.

Intuitively, $\mathscr{R}_i$ can be constructed from a roulette spin conducted by i in secret. To obtain the non-atomicity, it is sufficient to assume that each player j assigns subjective probability 0 to each particular outcome;[13] or equivalently, that there exist finite partitions of Ω into $\mathscr{R}_i$-events whose p_j-probabilities are arbitrarily small. Such non-atomicity assumptions are familiar in treatments of subjective probability.[14] Note that the roulette wheel need not be "objective," i.e. the players may disagree about the probabilities involved.

A strategy $\boldsymbol{s}_i$ of i is *mixed* if it is $\mathscr{S}_i$-measurable, i.e. pegged on i-secret events. Strategies $\boldsymbol{s}_1, \ldots, \boldsymbol{s}_n$ are *uncorrelated* if for each $s \in S$, the n events $\{\boldsymbol{s}_j = s_j\}$ are independent. Mixed strategies are uncorrelated, but the converse is false; strategies may be uncorrelated even though they are pegged on events regarding which all players are informed.

An event A is called *objective* if all the subjective probabilities $p_i(A)$ coincide; in that case their common value is called the *probability* of A, and is denoted $p(A)$. A strategy $\boldsymbol{s}_i$ of i is called *objective* if it is pegged on objective events, i.e. if $\{\boldsymbol{s}_i = s_i\}$ is an objective event for all $s_i \in S_i$. The strategies occurring in the classical

[13] The set of outcomes is taken to be the unit interval (*not* $\{0, 1, \ldots, 36\}$).
[14] Cf. Savage (1954, pp. 38–40, especially postulates P6′ and P6).

non-cooperative theory are precisely those that are both objective and mixed.

An event or strategy is called *subjective* if it is not objective.

The preference order of i determines his utility function on X only up to a monotonic linear transformation. Given a specific choice $u_1, \ldots, u_n$ of utility functions of the players, define the *payoff function* of player i in the usual way; that is, if s is an n-tuple of pure strategies (i.e. $s \in S$), define

$$h_i(s) = u_i(g(s));$$

and if $\boldsymbol{s}$ is an n-tuple of arbitrary strategies, define

$$H_i(\boldsymbol{s}) = E_i(h_i(\boldsymbol{s})) = \int_\Omega h_i(\boldsymbol{s}(\omega))\mathrm{d}p_i(\omega), \tag{3.1}$$

E_i being the expectation operator w.r.t. the probability measure p_i on Ω. Then $g(\boldsymbol{s}) \succ_i g(\boldsymbol{t})$ if and only if $H_i(\boldsymbol{s}) > H_i(\boldsymbol{t})$. Write

$$h = (h_1, \ldots, h_n),$$
$$H = (H_1, \ldots, H_n).$$

Any vector of the form $H(\boldsymbol{s})$ is called a *feasible payoff*; if $\boldsymbol{s}$ is an equilibrium point, then $H(\boldsymbol{s})$ is called an *equilibrium payoff*; and if $\boldsymbol{s}$ is an equilibrium point in objective mixed strategies, then $H(\boldsymbol{s})$ is an *objective mixed equilibrium payoff*.

To orient the reader, we mention that Example 2.1 involves a pair of subjective strategies that is not in equilibrium; Examples 2.2 and 2.3 involve equilibrium points in mixed subjective strategies; and Examples 2.4 through 2.8 involve equilibrium points that are objective, but are not in mixed strategies (the strategies are in fact correlated, i.e. not uncorrelated).

4. Preliminaries and Generalities

This section is devoted to the *statement* of several lemmas needed in the sequel, of an existence theorem for equilibrium points (Proposition 4.3), and of a proposition concerning the nature of the sets of feasible and equilibrium payoffs. We also discuss the notion of "correlation."

Though most of the results stated in this section are intuitively unsurprising, the proofs are a little involved (because of the relatively weak assumptions we have made). *We therefore postpone these proofs to Section* 7, in order to get as quickly as possible to the conceptually more interesting results of the paper (Propositions 5.1 and 6.1). Readers who are interested only in the statements of these propositions (as opposed to the proofs) may skip this section.

The first lemma asserts that objective mixed strategies can be constructed with arbitrary probabilities, i.e. that all the "classical" mixed strategies appear in this model as well. Define a *distribution* on S_i to be a real-valued function on S_i whose values are non-negative and sum to 1.

Lemma 4.1. *Let $i \in N$, and let σ_i be a distribution on S_i. Then i has an objective mixed strategy $\boldsymbol{s}_i$ such that for all $s_i \in S_i$,*

$$p\{\boldsymbol{s}_i = s_i\} = \sigma_i(s_i).$$

Next, we have

Lemma 4.2. *For any i in N, any event B, and any α between* 0 *and* 1, *there is an objective i-secret event with probability α that is independent of B.*

Intuitively, Lemmas 4.1 and 4.2 depend on the existence of an *objective* roulette wheel that i can spin in secret. Thus they appear to go somewhat further[15] than Assumption II, and it is of some interest that in fact, they follow from it.

The next proposition asserts that the classical equilibrium points of Nash (1951) appear in this model as well. If $\sigma = (\sigma_1, \ldots, \sigma_n)$ is an n-tuple of distributions on $S_1, \ldots, S_n$ respectively, and if $i \in N$,

[15]See subsection (e) of Section 9 for a discussion of this point.

define

$$F_i(\sigma) = \sum_s h_i(s) \prod_{j \in N} \alpha_j(s_j),$$

where the sum runs over all pure strategy n-tuples $s = (s_1, \ldots, s_n)$. The *payoff to* σ is the n-tuple $F(\sigma) = (F_1(\sigma), \ldots, F_n(\sigma))$. Recall that σ is a *Nash equilibrium point* if for any i and any distribution τ_i on S_i, we have

$$F_i(\sigma) \geqq F_i(\sigma_1, \ldots, \sigma_{i-1}, \sigma_{i+1}, \ldots, \sigma_n);$$

in that case $F(\sigma)$ is called a *Nash equilibrium payoff.*

Proposition 4.3. *The set of Nash equilibrium payoffs coincides with the set of objective mixed equilibrium payoffs.*

From this proposition and Nash's theorem it follows immediately that there is an equilibrium point in every game.

We now come to the concept of correlation. Set $S_N = \bigcap_{i \in N} \mathscr{I}_i$; the members of S_N are called *public events.* A *continuous chance device*, or *roulette* for short, is a sub-σ-field $\mathscr{R}$ of Ω on which each p_j is non-atomic; if $\mathscr{R}$ consists of public events, it is called a *public roulette.*

Parallel to Lemma 4.2, we have

Lemma 4.4. *Assume that there is a public roulette. Then for any event B, and any α between* 0 *and* 1, *there is an objective public event with probability α that is independent of B.*

A public roulette can be used as a correlating device on which all players can peg their choices; this leads (cf. Example 2.4) to

Proposition 4.5. *Assume that there is a public roulette. Then the set of equilibrium payoffs and the set of feasible payoffs are both convex.*

It is not known whether the set of equilibrium — or feasible — payoffs is closed, whether or not one assumes the existence of a public roulette.

Public roulettes enable *all* players to correlate their strategies, as in Example 2.4. In Examples 2.5 through 2.9, the correlation is of a subtler kind. To describe the situation, let us call the triple consisting of the pair $(\Omega, \mathscr{B})$, the n-tuple $(\mathscr{I}_1, \ldots, \mathscr{I}_n)$, and the n-tuple $(p_1, \ldots, p_n)$ a *randomizing structure.* In Examples 2.4, 2.5, and 2.6, the randomizing structure is of a particularly simple kind, which we call *standard*, and which is described as follows:

For each $T \subset N$, let J_T be a copy of the unit interval $[0, 1]$ with the Borel sets. Let $(\Omega, \mathscr{B}) = \mathbf{x}_{T \subset N} J_T$, and let π_T be the projection of Ω on J_T. For i in N, call two members ω_1 and ω_2 of Ω *i-equivalent* if $\pi_T(\omega_1) = \pi_T(\omega_2)$ for all T containing i. Let $\mathscr{I}_i$ be the σ-field of all events in Ω that are unions of i-equivalence classes. Let all the p_i be Lebesgue measure on Ω.

Intuitively, the points of J_T are outcomes of an objective roulette spin conducted in the presence of the members of T only. Note that all the probabilities are the same, so that subjectivity does not enter the picture. Even in this relatively simple case, though, it is not clear that the set of equilibrium payoffs is closed (it is convex by Proposition 4.5). However, when $n = 2$ and the randomizing structure is standard, then it is easily verified that the set of equilibrium payoffs is precisely the convex hull of the Nash equilibrium payoffs.

In Example 2.7, the randomizing structure is not standard; but the probabilities are objective, i.e. all the p_i coincide. It is easily verified that whenever the probabilities are objective and there is a public roulette, the set of feasible payoffs is simply the convex hull of the pure strategy payoffs. In particular, this will be the case when the randomizing structure is standard.

5. Equilibrium Points in Two-Person Games

In Example 2.3 we showed that by pegging strategies on subjective events, it is possible to find a 3-person game with an equilibrium point in mixed strategies whose payoff is higher for *all* players than the payoff to any equilibrium in objective mixed strategies. In this section we show that this cannot happen in the case of 2-person games.

Proposition 5.1. *Let G be a 2-person game,*[16] *and assume that*

$$\text{for any event } B,\ p_1(B) = 0 \text{ if and only if } p_2(B) = 0. \tag{5.2}$$

Then for each equilibrium point $\boldsymbol{s}$ in mixed strategies, there is an equilibrium point $\boldsymbol{t}$ in objective mixed strategies such that $H(\boldsymbol{s}) = H(\boldsymbol{t})$.

Proof. Let $(\boldsymbol{s}_1, \boldsymbol{s}_2)$ be an equilibrium point in mixed strategies. Let $\boldsymbol{t}_1$ be an objective mixed strategy for Player 1 that mimics the way Player 2 sees $\boldsymbol{s}_1$, i.e., such that for all pure strategies s_1 of Player 1,

$$p\{\boldsymbol{t}_1 = s_1\} = p_2\{\boldsymbol{s}_1 = s_1\}; \tag{5.3}$$

such a strategy exists because of Lemma 4.1. Similarly, let $\boldsymbol{t}_2$ be an objective mixed strategy for Player 2 such that for all s_2,

$$p\{\boldsymbol{t}_2 = s_2\} = p_1\{\boldsymbol{s}_2 = s_2\}. \tag{5.4}$$

Let $s_{11}, s_{12}, \ldots$ be the pure strategies that enter actively into $\boldsymbol{s}_1$, i.e., with positive p_1-probability. Because $\boldsymbol{s}_1$ is in equilibrium,

$$E_1 h_1(s_{1j}, \boldsymbol{s}_2) = H_1(\boldsymbol{s}_1, \boldsymbol{s}_2) \tag{5.5}$$

for all j. But from (5.2) it follows that the s_{1j} are also precisely the pure strategies that enter actively into $\boldsymbol{t}_1$; hence (5.5) yields

$$H_1(\boldsymbol{t}_1, \boldsymbol{s}_2) = H_1(\boldsymbol{s}_1, \boldsymbol{s}_2). \tag{5.6}$$

Since $\boldsymbol{s}_1$ maximizes H_1 (if 2 plays $\boldsymbol{s}_2$), it follows from (5.6) that $\boldsymbol{t}_1$ also does. But by (5.4), Player 1 ascribes the same distribution to $\boldsymbol{t}_2$ as to $\boldsymbol{s}_2$; therefore

$$H_1(\boldsymbol{t}_1, \boldsymbol{t}_2) = H_1(\boldsymbol{t}_1, \boldsymbol{s}_2) = H_1(\boldsymbol{s}_1, \boldsymbol{s}_2),$$

and furthermore, $\boldsymbol{t}_1$ maximizes H_1 if 2 plays $\boldsymbol{t}_2$. Similarly,

$$H_2(\boldsymbol{t}_1, \boldsymbol{t}_2) = H_2(\boldsymbol{s}_1, \boldsymbol{t}_2) = H_2(\boldsymbol{s}_1, \boldsymbol{s}_2),$$

[16]Not necessarily 0-sum.

and $\boldsymbol{t}_2$ maximizes H_2 if 1 plays $\boldsymbol{t}_1$. Therefore $(\boldsymbol{t}_1, \boldsymbol{t}_2)$ is an objective mixed equilibrium point with the same payoff as $(\boldsymbol{s}_1, \boldsymbol{s}_2)$, and the proof of this proposition is complete.

It would have been reasonable to conjecture that this proposition remains true if both occurrences of the word "mixed" are deleted. Example 2.9 shows that this is false.

6. Two-Person Zero-Sum Games

A game is called *2-person 0-sum* if $n = 2$ and if there are utility functions u_1 and u_2 for the players such that

$$u_1(x) + u_2(x) = 0$$

for all $x \in X$. After adopting a specific such pair of utility functions, one defines the value of the game as usual. Specifically, Proposition 4.3 provides an equilibrium point in objective mixed strategies; by the minimax theorem, all such equilibrium points must have the same payoff, which is of the form $(v, -v)$. Then v is called the *value* of the game.

Proposition 6.1. *Let G be a 2-person 0-sum game with value v. Assume that*

there are outcomes x and y with $u_1(x) > v > u_1(y)$, and (6.2)

for each player i, there is a subjective event B_i regarding which i is informed. (6.3)

Then there is a pair $\boldsymbol{s}$ of strategies such that

$$H_1(\boldsymbol{s}) > v, H_2(\boldsymbol{s}) > -v. \tag{6.4}$$

Remark. The proposition is considerably easier to prove if one assumes that

there is a public subjective event B and there is a public roulette. (6.5)

To see this, assume without loss of generality that $p_1(B) > p_2(B)$ (otherwise, use the complement of B). If C is a public event and $0 \leqq \theta \leqq 1$, denote by θC a public event such that

$$p_1(\theta C) = \theta p_1(C) \quad \text{and} \quad p_2(\theta C) = \theta p_2(C);$$

the existence of such a θC follows[17] from Lemma 4.4. From (6.2) it follows that there is a β with $0 < \beta < 1$ such that

$$v = \beta u_1(x) + (1 - \beta) u_1(y).$$

For $0 < \delta < 1$, set

$$B^\delta = \Omega \backslash \delta(\Omega \backslash B).$$

Then for δ sufficiently small, we have $p_1(B^\delta) > p_2(B^\delta) > \beta$; hence if we let $A = \theta B^\delta$ for an appropriate θ, then

$$p_1(A) > \beta > p_2(A). \tag{6.6}$$

Now define $\boldsymbol{s}$ as follows: Both players choose pure strategies leading to x, or both players use pure strategies leading to y, according to whether A does or does not occur. Then (6.4) follows, and the proposition is proved under the assumption of (6.5).

Proof of Proposition 6.1. In (6.2), let $x = g(r_1, r_2)$ and $y = g(t_1, t_2)$; then $h_1(r_1, r_2) > v > h_1(t_1, t_2)$.

Suppose first that $h_1(r_1, t_2) \geqq v$. Setting

$$H^*(\varepsilon) = \varepsilon h_1(r_1, r_2) + (1 - \varepsilon) h_1(r_1, t_2)$$
$$H_*(\varepsilon) = \varepsilon h_1(t_1, r_2) + (1 - \varepsilon) h_1(t_1, t_2),$$

[17]It also follows from the theorem of Lyapunov (1940) on the range of a vector measure. We shall see in Section 8 that Proposition 4.4 is itself proved via Lyapunov's theorem; intuitively, though, Proposition 4.4 is more transparent than Lyapunov's theorem.

we find that for $\varepsilon > 0$ sufficiently small,

$$H^*(\varepsilon) > v > H_*(\varepsilon).$$

Hence there is a β in $[0, 1]$ with

$$v = \beta H^*(\varepsilon) + (1 - \beta) H_*(\varepsilon).$$

Now let A_1 be a subjective event in $\mathscr{I}_1$ with $p_1(A_1) > \beta > p_2(A_1)$. The existence of such an event may be established as in the remark [cf. (6.6)], except that now the mapping $C \to \theta C$ takes $\mathscr{I}_1$ into itself (rather than $\mathscr{I}_1 \cap \mathscr{I}_2$ into itself), Lemma 4.2 (rather than 4.4) is used to prove the existence of θC, and B_1 is substituted for B. Again using Lemma 4.2, we obtain an objective 2-secret event A_2 with probability ε that is independent of A_1. Define a strategy pair $\boldsymbol{s}$ by stipulating that $\boldsymbol{s}_i$ takes the value r_i or t_i according to whether A_i does or does not occur. Then $\boldsymbol{s}$ is uncorrelated and satisfies (6.4).

If $h_1(r_1, t_2) \leqq v$, the proof is similar, the roles of the two players being then reversed. This completes the proof of Proposition 6.1.

Proposition 6.1 fails if it is only assumed that there is a subjective event of which at least one player is informed. For example, if in the 2-person 0-sum game with matrix

1	1
2	0

there is a subjective event in $\mathscr{I}_1$ but not in $\mathscr{I}_2$, then there is no pair of strategies satisfying (6.4). In this game it is sufficient for (6.4) that there be a subjective event in $\mathscr{I}_2$. In general, the proof of Proposition 6.1 shows that in any specific game, only one player need use a subjective strategy, while the other can use an objective one; but which player it is that uses the subjective strategy may depend on the game.

It is perhaps worth noting that in Proposition 6.1, the strategies constituting $\boldsymbol{s}$ may be taken to be independent; indeed, the strategies constructed in the proof are independent.

7. Proof of the Propositions of Section 4

We start with a lemma that is basic to the proofs in this section.

Lemma 7.1. *Let $\mathscr{R}$ be a roulette, and let $B^1, \ldots, B^l$ be events. Then for any α between 0 and 1, there is an objective event in $\mathscr{R}$ with probability α that is independent of each of the B^k.*

Proof. Consider the $(1+l)n$-dimensional vector measure u on $(\Omega, \mathscr{R})$ defined by

$$\mu_i(A) = p_i(A), \quad i = 1, \ldots, n,$$

$$\mu_{kn+i}(A) = p_i(A \cap B^k), \quad i = 1, \ldots, n, \quad k = 1, \ldots, l.$$

That μ is non-atomic follows from the non-atomicity of the p_i on $\mathscr{R}$. By the theorem of Lyapunov (1940) on the range of a vector measure, the range of μ is convex. Now

$$\mu(\Omega) = (1, \ldots, 1, p_1(B^1), \ldots, p_n(B^1), \ldots, p_1(B^l), \ldots, p_n(B^l))$$

and

$$\mu(\phi) = (0, \ldots, 0).$$

Hence $\alpha\mu(\Omega)$ is in the range of μ, i.e. there is a set A in $\mathscr{R}$ such that $\mu(A) = \alpha\mu(\Omega)$. This means that $p^i(A) = \alpha$ for all i and

$$p_i(A \cap B^k) = \alpha p_i(B^k) = p_i(A)p_i(B^k)$$

for all i. The proof of the lemma is complete.

Proof of Lemma 4.1. By induction on the number m of members s_i of S_i for which $\sigma_i(s_i) > 0$. Let $\mathscr{R}_i$ be the i-secret roulette provided by Assumption II. As often in the case of inductive proofs, it is convenient to prove a somewhat stronger statement than is needed; here we show that

> a strategy $\boldsymbol{s}_1$ can be chosen obeying Proposition 4.1, so that the events $\{\boldsymbol{s}_i = s_i\}$ are in $\mathscr{R}_1$. (7.2)

If $m = 1$ there is nothing to prove. Let $m > 1$, and suppose the proposition true for $m - 1$. Let $S_i = \{s_i^1, \ldots, s_i^m, \ldots\}$, where

$\sigma_i(s_i^j) > 0$ if and only if $j \leqq m$. By the induction hypothesis, there are disjoint objective events $B^1, \ldots, B^{m-1}$ such that $p(B^j) = \sigma_i(s_i^j)/(1-\sigma_i(s_i^m))$. By Lemma 7.1 with $\mathscr{R} = \mathscr{R}_i$, there is an objective i-secret event B^m independent of each of $B^1, \ldots, B^{m-1}$, such that $p(B^m) = 1 - \sigma_i(s_i^m)$. Set $A^j = B^j \cap B^m$ for $j < m$, $A^m = \Omega \backslash B^m$, and $A^j = \phi$ for $j > m$; then $A^j \in \mathscr{R}_i$ for all j. Define $\boldsymbol{s}_i$ by $\boldsymbol{s}_i(\omega) = s_i^j$ if and only if $\omega \in A^j$. Then $\boldsymbol{s}_i$ satisfies (7.2). This completes the proof of Lemma 4.1.

Proof of Lemma 4.2. Use Assumption II, and apply Lemma 7.1 with $\mathscr{R} = \mathscr{R}_i$ and $l = 1$.

Before proving Proposition 4.3 we need a lemma.

Lemma 7.3. *Let $(\boldsymbol{s}_1, \ldots, \boldsymbol{s}_n)$ be an n-tuple of strategies, and let $s \in S$. For some $i \in N$, suppose that all the $\boldsymbol{s}_j$ except possibly $\boldsymbol{s}_i$ are mixed. Then*

$$\begin{aligned} p_i\{\boldsymbol{s} = s\} &= p_i\{\boldsymbol{s}_i = s_i\} p_i\{\boldsymbol{s}_j = s_j \quad \textit{for all } j \neq i\} \\ &= p_i\{\boldsymbol{s} = s_1\} \ldots p_i\{\boldsymbol{s}_n = s_n\}. \end{aligned}$$

Proof. W.l.o.g. let $i = 1$, and let $A_j = \{\boldsymbol{s}_j = s_j\}$ for all j; then

$$\{\boldsymbol{s} = s\} = A_1 \cap \cdots \cap A_n.$$

Moreover, $A_1 \in \mathscr{I}_1$ and $A_j \in \mathscr{S}_j$ for $j > 1$. By definition of S_j, each A_j with $j > 1$ is 1-independent of $A_{j+1} \cap \cdots \cap A_n$. Hence

$$\begin{aligned} p_1(A_2 \cap \cdots \cap A_n) &= p_1(A_2) p_1(A_3 \cap \cdots \cap A_n) \\ &= \cdots = p_1(A_2) \cdots p_1(A_n). \end{aligned}$$

Again by definition of $\mathscr{S}_j$, each A_j with $j > 1$ is 1-independent of $A_1 \cap A_2 \cap \cdots A_{j-1}$. Hence by the previous equation,

$$\begin{aligned} &p_1(A_1 \cap A_2 \cap \cdots \cap A_n) \\ &\quad = p_1(A_1 \cap A_2 \cap \cdots \cap A_{n-1}) p_1(A_n) \\ &\quad = \cdots = p_1(A_1) p_1(A_2) \cdots p_1(A_n) = p_1(A_1) p_1(A_2 \cap \cdots \cap A_n). \end{aligned}$$

This completes the proof of the lemma.

Corollary 7.4. *Let* $(\boldsymbol{s}_1, \ldots, \boldsymbol{s}_n)$ *be an n-tuple of mixed strategies. Then the* $\boldsymbol{s}_i$ *are independent.*

Proof of Proposition 4.3. If $\boldsymbol{s} = (\boldsymbol{s}_1, \ldots, \boldsymbol{s}_n)$ is an objective mixed equilibrium point, then for each strategy $\boldsymbol{t}_i$ of i,

$$H_i(\boldsymbol{s}) \geqq H_i(\boldsymbol{s}_1, \ldots, \boldsymbol{s}_{i-1}, \boldsymbol{t}_i, \boldsymbol{s}_{i+1}, \ldots, \boldsymbol{s}_n). \tag{7.5}$$

In particular, this holds when $\boldsymbol{t}_i$ is itself objective and mixed. From this it follows that $H(\boldsymbol{s})$ is a Nash equilibrium payoff.

Conversely, if $F(\sigma)$ is a Nash equilibrium payoff, then from Lemma 4.1 and Corollary 8.4 it follows that there is an n-tuple $\boldsymbol{s} = (\boldsymbol{s}_1, \ldots, \boldsymbol{s}_n)$ of objective mixed strategies with payoff $F(\sigma)$ that is in equilibrium against deviations that are restricted to objective mixed strategies; i.e. that (7.5) holds when $\boldsymbol{t}_i$ is an objective mixed strategy. In particular (7.5) holds when $\boldsymbol{t}_i$ is "pure," i.e. takes on a particular value in S_i with probability 1. To show that $\boldsymbol{s}$ is an equilibrium in our sense, we must show that (7.5) holds when $\boldsymbol{t}_i$ is *any* strategy of i, i.e. that i cannot "correlate into" the strategies of the other players. Intuitively this follows from the fact that the $\boldsymbol{s}_j$ are mixed, i.e. pegged on j-secret events; formally, though, we must show that our definition of secrecy does indeed yield this result.

W.l.o.g. let $i = 1$. Write $S' = S_2 \times \cdots \times S_n$, and $\boldsymbol{s}' = (\boldsymbol{s}_2, \ldots, \boldsymbol{s}_n)$.

For any s_1 in S_1, write

$$H_1(s_1, \boldsymbol{s}') = E_1(h_1(s_1, \boldsymbol{s}')).$$

Since (7.5) holds when $\boldsymbol{t}_i$ is "pure," it follows that for all $s_1 \in S_1$,

$$H_1(s_1, \boldsymbol{s}') \leqq H_1(\boldsymbol{s}). \tag{7.6}$$

Then for an arbitrary strategy $\boldsymbol{t}_1$ of 1, it follows from Lemma 7.3 and (7.6) that

$$\begin{aligned} H_1(\boldsymbol{t}_1, \boldsymbol{s}') &= \sum_{s \in S} p_1\{(\boldsymbol{t}_1, \boldsymbol{s}') = s\} h(s) \\ &= \sum_{s_1 \in S_1} \sum_{s' \in S'} p_1\{\boldsymbol{t}_1 = s_1\} p_1\{\boldsymbol{s}' = s'\} h_1(s) \end{aligned}$$

$$= \sum_{s_1 \in S_1} p_1\{\boldsymbol{t}_1 = s_1\} \sum_{s' \in S'} p_1\{\boldsymbol{s}' = s'\} h_1(s)$$

$$= \sum_{s_1 \in S_1} p_1\{\boldsymbol{t}_1 = s_1\} H_1(s_1, \boldsymbol{s}_2, \ldots, \boldsymbol{s}_n)$$

$$\leqq \sum_{s_1 \in S_1} p_1\{\boldsymbol{t}_1 = s_1\} H_1(\boldsymbol{s}) = H_1(\boldsymbol{s}).$$

This completes the proof of Proposition 4.3.

Proof of Lemma 4.4. Apply Lemma 7.1 with $l = 1$, taking $\mathscr{R}$ to be a public roulette.

Proof of Proposition 4.5. We first consider the equilibrium payoffs. Let $\boldsymbol{s}$ and $\boldsymbol{t}$ be equilibrium points, and let $0 \leqq \alpha \leqq 1$. Let $\mathscr{R}$ be the public roulette. By Lemma 7.1, there is an objective event A in $\mathscr{R}$ with probability α that is independent of all the events $\{\boldsymbol{s} = s\}$ and $\{\boldsymbol{t} = s\}$ for all s in S. Now let each player i play the strategy $\boldsymbol{r}_i$ defined as follows: if A occurs, play $\boldsymbol{s}_i$; if not, play $\boldsymbol{t}_i$. In other words, i plays a given pure s_i in S_i if and only if the event

$$[A \cap \{\boldsymbol{s}_i = s_i\}] \cup [(\Omega \backslash A) \cap \{\boldsymbol{t}_i = s_i\}] \tag{7.7}$$

occurs. This is indeed a strategy, since the event (7.7) is in the σ-field $\mathscr{I}_i$. It may then be verified that $\boldsymbol{r}$ is an equilibrium point and that

$$H(\boldsymbol{r}) = \alpha H(\boldsymbol{s}) + (1 - \alpha) H(\boldsymbol{t}),$$

so the set of equilibrium payoffs is convex. The proof that the set of feasible payoffs is convex is similar, so the proof of Proposition 4.5 is complete.

8. A Posteriori Equilibria

We would like to view an equilibrium point as a *self-enforcing agreement*. In the scenario described in Section 3, if the players agree on an equilibrium point $\boldsymbol{s}$ before stage (ii) (the stage at which information about ω is received), no player will want to renege [i.e. choose a pure strategy other than $\boldsymbol{s}_i(\omega)$] after stage (ii). More precisely, when making the agreement each player i assigns subjective probability 0 to the possibility that he will want to renege after receiving his information.

There is, however, a difficulty here. Though the subjective probability of wanting to renege is 0, this possibility is not entirely excluded; more important, it is quite possible that a player assigns positive probability to a *different* player's wanting to renege. In that case the equilibrium point can no longer be considered self-enforcing; the possibility of *somebody* wanting to renege is not negligible. This is exactly the phenomenon that is responsible for the equilibrium payoff of $(1, 1)$ in Example 2.2.

To legitimize the view of an equilibrium point as a self-enforcing agreement, one can either

a. make assumptions under which the possibility of some player wanting to renege is assigned probability 0 by all players; or
b. construct a model in which it is possible to define equilibrium points at which no player *ever* wants to renege.

Specifically, we may assume that though the players may have different subjective probabilities, the concept of 'impossible' or 'negligible' is the same for all. That is, if $p_i(B) = 0$ for one i then $p_i(B) = 0$ for all i; in other words, the p_i are absolutely continuous with respect to each other. [For the case of two players, this is the same as (5.2).] In that case, the possibility that any player will want to renege is negligible for all players, and so can be safely ignored.

Alternatively, one could replace the concept of equilibrium point by that of 'a posteriori equilibrium point' — a strategy n-tuple from which no player i *ever* wishes to move (unilaterally), even after receiving his information about nature's choice of ω. Formally, this can be done by adding the following to the seven items that define a game (see Section 3).

(8.) For each player i and each ω in Ω, a relation $\succsim_i^\omega$ on the space of lotteries on X (*the preference order of i given his information about ω*).

The relations $\succsim_i^\omega$ will also be called *a posteriori preferences*. An *a posteriori equilibrium point* is then defined to be an n-tuple $\boldsymbol{s}$ of strategies such that for all ω, all i, and all t_i in S_i, we have

$$g(\boldsymbol{s}) \succsim_i^{\omega} g(\boldsymbol{s}_1, \ldots, \boldsymbol{s}_{i-1}, \boldsymbol{s}_{i+1}, \ldots, \boldsymbol{s}_n).$$

Under appropriate assumptions one can then prove the following results:

(8.1) Theorem 5.1 holds without the hypothesis of mutual absolute continuity (5.2), if "equilibrium point" is replaced by "a posteriori equilibrium point."

(8.2) If all the p_i are mutually absolutely continuous, then the set of payoffs to a posteriori equilibrium points coincides with the set of payoffs to equilibrium points.

The proof of (8.1) is like the proof of Proposition 5.1, except that a pure strategy s_{ij} is now said to "enter actively" into the strategy $\boldsymbol{s}_i$ if there is *some* ω for which $\boldsymbol{s}_i(\omega) = s_{ij}$, even if i assigns probability 0 to the set of all such ω. Note that from (8.1) it follows that $(1, 1)$ is not an a posteriori equilibrium payoff in Example 2.2.

One can also prove a posteriori results that are analogous to Propositions 4.3 and 4.5.

A logically complete development of the a posteriori theory involves rewriting Assumptions I and II, redefining many of the concepts defined above (such as i-secrecy and mixed strategy), and making assumptions that relate preferences to a posteriori preferences.[18] The development therefore becomes somewhat lengthy. In view of result (8.2), it does not seem worthwhile, at least at this stage, to impose a formal description of the a posteriori theory on the reader.

9. Discussion

a. The fact that differing subjective probabilities can yield social benefit is perhaps obvious. Wagers on sporting events, stock market

[18]The a posteriori preferences of player i can be derived from his a priori preferences, but (like conditional probabilities) only for p_i-almost all ω. Of course, as we saw above, it is precisely the sets of p_i-measure 0 that cause the difficulty.

transactions, etc., though they can be explained by convexities in utility functions, can also be explained by differing subjective probabilities; and in reality, the latter explanation is probably at least as significant as the former. Correlation of strategies is basically also a fairly obvious idea. It is all the more surprising that these ideas have heretofore not been more carefully studied in game theory in general, and in the context of randomization in particular.

b. Our more substantive results can be broadly divided into two classes: Those having to do with equilibrium points (notably Examples 2.2 through 2.9, and Proposition 5.1), and those having to do with feasible points (notably Example 2.1 and Proposition 6.1). The former belong to the "non-cooperative" theory, the latter to the "cooperative" theory. An understanding of this distinction rests on an understanding of the concepts of communication, correlation, commitment, and contract. Let us examine these concepts in the context of this paper, noting in particular how they are related to "cooperative" and "non-cooperative" games.

Recall that in step (ii) of the scenario of Section 3, each player i is given his information about nature's choice of ω. By *communication* we mean communication between the players before step (ii). Strategies of the players are *correlated* if they are statistically dependent. A *commitment* is an irrevocable undertaking on the part of a player, entered into before step (ii), to play in accordance with a certain strategy.[19] A *contract* (or "binding agreement" or "enforceable agreement") is a set of commitments simultaneously undertaken by several players, each player's undertaking being in consideration of those of the others.

Of the four terms just introduced, only "correlation" has a formal meaning in the framework of our formal model (see Section 3, where

[19]One can imagine broader meanings for the word 'commitment,' in which the undertaking, though irrevocable, need not be to play in accordance with a certain strategy. For example, it could be to play in accordance with one of a certain set of strategies, or it could be contingent on the choice of ω or on other commitments. We have not found it necessary to complicate the discussion by considering these broader meanings.

"uncorrelated" is defined). The other three refer not to the model itself, but to how the model is to be interpreted.

If the players can enter into commitments and contracts, we have a *cooperative game*. If not,[20] we have a *non-cooperative game*. Formally, cooperative and non-cooperative games are described in the same way, namely by the model of Section 3. The difference between the two types of games lies not in the formal description itself, but in what we have to say about it — what kind of theorems we prove about it.

In a non-cooperative game, at each point of time, each player acts so as to maximize his utility at that point of time, without taking previous commitments into account. Therefore the only strategy n-tuples of interest are those that are in equilibrium (cf. Section 8). On the other hand, in the cooperative theory the players can enter into binding agreements before step (ii); therefore a strategy n-tuple does not have to be in equilibrium to be of interest, and one is led to study all feasible n-tuples.

In Section 8 we saw that equilibrium points can be viewed as self-enforcing agreements. This is to be contrasted with feasible points that are not in equilibrium; if the players agree before step (ii) of the scenario to play such a point, some of them will wish to renege after step (ii). Therefore a contract — and an external enforcement mechanism — are required to make such agreements stick.

Thus we see that both the non-cooperative and the cooperative theory involve agreement among the players, the difference being only in that in one case the agreement is self-enforcing, whereas in the other case it must be externally enforced. Agreement usually involves communication, so that we conclude that communication normally takes place in non-cooperative as well as cooperative games.

As for correlation, this is sometimes taken as a hallmark of cooperative games. In our view, this is a fallacy; correlation may or may not be possible in a given game, whether or not it is cooperative.

[20]These are the two extremes. In many situations, some commitments and contracts are possible, others not.

Examples 2.4 through 2.9 show that correlation may be involved in agreements that are not enforceable but are self-enforcing, so that it can be significant even in a non-cooperative game. On the other hand, even in a cooperative game it may be impossible to correlate, for example because the players are in different places and cannot observe the same random events; but nevertheless they can negotiate and even execute a contract, for example by mail.

Equilibrium points can be viewed in ways other than as self-enforcing agreements. For example, they can be viewed as strategy n-tuples with the property that if, for some extraneous reason, they "come to the fore" or are suggested to the players, there will be no tendency to move away from them. Alternatively, they can be viewed as providing only a necessary condition for a satisfactory theory of non-cooperative games: if a theory is to "recommend" a specific strategy to each player, then the n-tuple of the recommended strategies must be in equilibrium. To make sense, these points of view do not require pre-play communication. But even without communication, correlation is by no means ruled out. Thus in Example 2.4, the payoff $(3/2, 3/2)$ is no more the result of communication than the payoff $(2, 1)$. All that is needed to achieve $(3/2, 3/2)$ is that a fair coin be tossed, or a similar random device be actuated, and that the outcome be communicated to both players before the beginning of play. If that is done, the payoff $(3/2, 3/2)$ becomes a full-fledged equilibrium payoff, conceptually indistinguishable from $(2, 1)$; and that is so even in the absence of communication.

Of course, communication may be important in order to choose a particular equilibrium point from among all those whose payoff is $(3/2, 3/2)$. But the problem of choosing a particular equilibrium point has nothing to do with correlation — it exists in most non-cooperative games. Thus in Example 2.4, even without the opportunity for correlation, it is difficult to see why one equilibrium point rather than another would be chosen. This, incidentally, is one reason for preferring to view an equilibrium point as a self-enforcing agreement.

Finally, a word about the distinction between "commitment" and "contract." Unlike a contract, a commitment is an *individual* undertaking; it may, for example, consist of giving irreversible instructions to an agent or a machine to act in accordance with a given randomized strategy, or it may involve an obligation to pay a large indemnity if one does not act in accordance with this strategy. If there is no such agent or machine, or nobody to enforce collection of the indemnity, it may be impossible to undertake commitments, and we will have a non-cooperative game. Commitments are important in game theory even when contracts are impossible [see for example Aumann and Maschler (1972)]. However, when it is possible to make commitments as well as to communicate, it should usually be possible to make contracts as well. Moreover, by permitting commitments one opens the door to preemptive tactics (such as threats) in the pre-play stage, which may easily lead the outcome away from equilibrium. Thus we feel that when one has admitted commitments, one has already gone much of the way from the non-cooperative to the cooperative theory.

To sum up: The cooperative theory requires communication as well as commitment and contracting power; and it is a priori concerned with all feasible outcomes. The non-cooperative theory requires that there be neither commitment nor contracting power, but it permits communication; and it is concerned with equilibrium outcomes. Both theories can accommodate correlation, but do not require its presence.

c. It is interesting that those of our results that belong to the "cooperative" theory are concerned with 2-person 0-sum games, which have traditionally been considered the epitome of non-cooperative games; it has been asserted that such a game can only be played non-cooperatively, since it can never be worthwhile to reach an agreement concerning it. Our results show that this is incorrect. It is not true that a 2-person 0-sum game is strictly competitive, i.e. that the preferences of the players are always in direct opposition[21]; both players can gain by the use of a binding agreement. Thus 2-person 0-sum games can profitably be played cooperatively.

---

[21]Nevertheless, even after the introduction of subjective strategies, the game remains "almost strictly competitive" in the sense of Aumann (1961).

On the other hand, when correlation is ruled out, the introduction of subjective strategies creates no new equilibrium payoffs [see (5.1)]. This indicates that subjectivity alone (without correlation) at least does not affect the non-cooperative theory of 2-person 0-sum games. However, we must be careful before reaching even this modest conclusion. The arguments for the use of minimax strategies, as presented by von Neumann and Morgenstern (1953), are of two kinds: the equilibrium arguments, which they (§17.3) call "indirect," and what they (§14, §17.4–§17.8) call "direct" arguments.[22] The indirect or equilibrium arguments are of course not affected by the introduction of subjectivity. But it is the direct arguments that have traditionally been used to support the contention that the theory of 2-person 0-sum games is conceptually more satisfactory than that of more general games. To a certain extent, these direct arguments *are* affected; implicitly, they depend on the strictly competitive character of the game, which as we know is removed by subjectivity.

d. It must be stressed that the chance elements of our model — the space $(\Omega, \mathscr{B})$ and the σ-fields $\mathscr{I}_i$ — are used for purposes of randomization only. Nature's choice of a point ω in Ω does not directly affect the outcome of the game; the outcome function g does not depend on ω. This model is therefore quite different from extensive game models in which chance makes "moves" that affect the outcome; here chance is only "made available" to the players for purposes of randomization. [See also subsection (g) below.]

e. Our use of the terms "subjective" and "objective" is a little different from the usual. The term "subjective" often signifies a personalistic definition of probability, based on preferences, such as that of Savage (1954), whereas "objective" signifies a physical (i.e. frequency) definition.[23] This is not the distinction being made here. Here the distinction is based solely on whether the players in the

---

[22]These are called "guaranteed value arguments" by Aumann and Maschler (1972).

[23]Cf. Anscombe and Aumann (1963), where personalistic and frequency probabilities were called "probability" and "chance" respectively.

game do or do not agree about the numerical value of the probability in question.[24]

f. In this paper we have extended the theory of games in strategic (i.e. normal) form by the consideration of subjective events. A parallel extension is possible for the theory of games in extensive form. Basically, such an extension would consist of replacing the probabilities now appearing in the extensive form [Kuhn (1953)] on chance moves by *vectors* of probabilities, with one component for each player. The definition of "strategy" remains unchanged; the definition of "payoff" is modified only in that one uses the different probabilities on the chance moves in calculating the payoffs for the different players. It may be verified that the basic theorems [Kuhn (1953)] of extensive game theory — namely the theorem on pure strategy equilibrium points in games of perfect information, and on behavior strategies in games of perfect recall — go through in this case as well.

One immediate application of this remark is to the theory of Harsanyi (1967, 1968) of games of incomplete information. Harsanyi has shown that in what he calls the "consistent case," a game of incomplete information in strategic form corresponds to a certain game of complete information in extensive form. In the "inconsistent case," there is no such correspondence. However, if one extends the definition of extensive games in the way indicated above, then the inconsistent case can be taken care of in essentially the same way as the consistent case.

[24]The fact that they may disagree forces us to adopt a personalistic definition of probability for at least some events; but there is nothing to prevent us from adopting a physical definition for other events (e.g. roulette spins) on whose probabilities the players agree. Hybrid systems in which the two kinds of probability exist side by side, have been investigated; cf. Anscombe and Aumann (1963). On the other hand, a purely personalistic view, such as Savage's, is also perfectly satisfactory for the purposes of this paper. Incidentally, if one does adopt such a purely personalistic view, then an a priori assumption on the existence of objective roulette wheels loses its intuitive attractiveness; thus the fact that Lemmas 4.1 and 4.2 follow from Assumption II gains in significance (see the discussion after the statement of Lemma 4.2).

g. An alternative approach to that of this paper would be to introduce the possibilities for correlation and subjective randomization explicitly into the extensive form of the game. This would mean starting the game with chance's choice of a point in Ω, and then giving each player i that information which is "his" in accordance[25] with the σ-field $\mathscr{I}_i$. The strategic form of this enlarged game could be calculated as indicated under (f) above; the Nash equilibrium points of the enlarged game correspond to the equilibrium points, as defined in this paper, of the original game. Thus in the appropriate context, our equilibrium points are special cases of Nash equilibrium points. One difficulty with this approach is that it would lead to an infinite extensive game, since Ω is infinite. But this is by no means an insuperable difficulty; models have been studied that are entirely adequate to cover such a situation [Aumann (1964)]. We did not construct our model in this way for a number of reasons. First, none of the examples or propositions would have been simplified by such a procedure; on the contrary, the extensive form is clumsy to work with, and the mathematical treatment would presumably have been more complex. Second, one usually thinks of the extensive form as representing the originally given rules of the game. In that case extraneous random events, which do not directly affect the outcome of the game, do not belong in the extensive form; one does not introduce all the possibilities for objective mixing explicitly into the game either [see subsection (e) above].

h. It is nevertheless useful to point out how some of our examples involving correlation look in an extensive framework. Example 2.4 may be restated as follows: Suppose we add a move at the beginning of the game in which chance simply announces the results of a coin toss; no other change is made in the game (see Figure 1). One would have thought that this could not possibly effect an essential change in the game. But in the classical theory of Nash (1951), it does; $(3/2, 3/2)$ becomes the payoff to an equilibrium point, whereas it was

[25]The information sets of i immediately after chance's choice would be those subsets B of Ω such that for all A in $\mathscr{I}_i$, either $B \cap A = \emptyset$ or $B \subset A$.

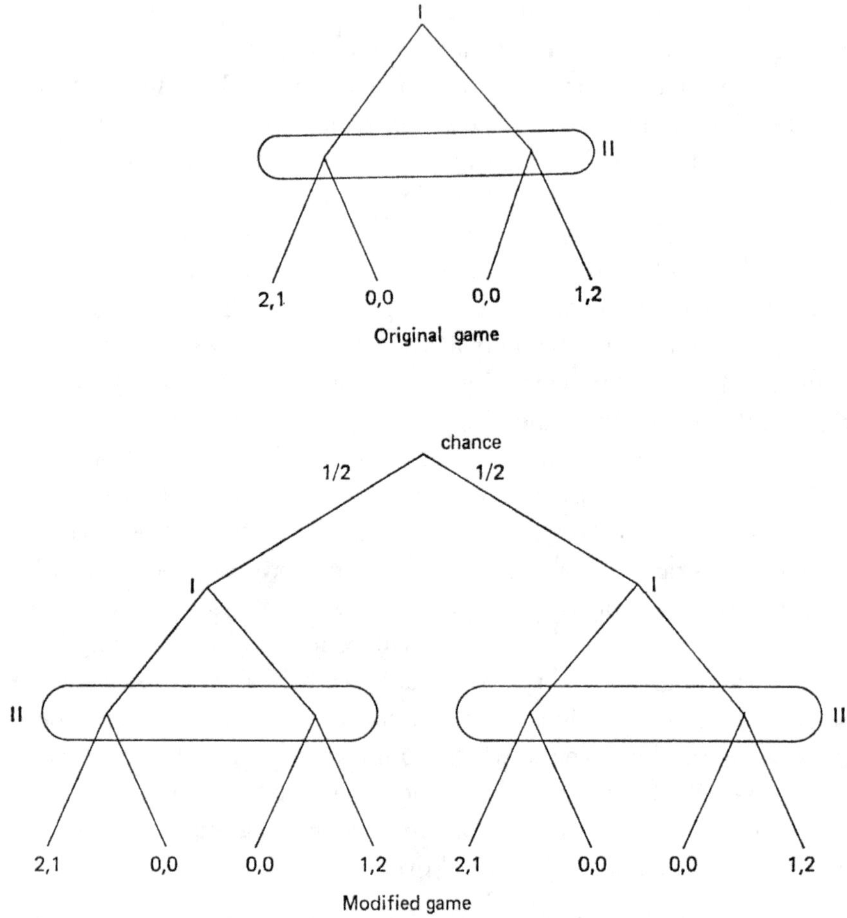

Figure 1:

not one before. Similarly if chance announces the result of a roulette spin, every point in the interval connecting $(2, 1)$ to $(1, 2)$ becomes an equilibrium payoff, whereas of these points, only the end points were equilibrium payoffs before. As we said in Section 2, all this appears already in Harsanyi and Selten (1972). But Examples 2.5 and 2.6 can be treated in a similar manner. Here one must add a move in which chance tosses a fair coin and informs Players 1 and 2 — but not Player 3 — of the outcome. Again, one would have thought that the addition of such a move could not possibly affect the game in any essential manner. But it adds a Nash equilibrium point with payoff $(2,2,2)$, whereas in the original game no player could get more than 1 at any Nash equilibrium point. Examples 2.7 and 2.8 may be treated similarly.

i. The phenomena in Examples 2.1 and 2.3, which are the basic examples regarding subjective probabilities, do not depend on each player knowing the other players' subjective probabilities *precisely.* Thus in Example 2.1, it is sufficient that both players know that Players 1 and 2 ascribe to D probabilities that are $>1/2$ and $<1/2$ respectively; in that case it will already be worthwhile to enter into a binding agreement. A similar remark holds for Example 2.3, in which it is sufficient that Players 1 and 2 ascribe to D subjective probabilities that are *approximately* 3/4 and 1/4 respectively (the precise limits of the approximation are easily calculated).

Of course there is no particular reason to treat subjective probabilities differently from utilities — if we assume that the players' utilities are known to each other, we may as well assume the same for the subjective probabilities. The above remark only points out that precise knowledge is not crucial. Situations in which the players' utilities and/or subjective probabilities are not known to each other can be treated by the methods of games of incomplete information [Harsanyi (1967, 1968)].

j. The view is sometimes held that when people have different subjective probabilities for the same event, this can only be due to differences in the information available to these people. Such a view has been eloquently set forth by John Harsanyi (1968, §16), and we will call it the *Harsanyi doctrine.* Suppose, for example, that Players 1 and 2 have subjective probabilities 2/3 and 1/3 respectively that a given horse A will run faster than another horse B in a given race. One could simply say that the subjective probabilities are different and leave it at that. But one could also imagine that both players previously had a uniform prior on the probability p that A beats B; that 1 had seen A beat B in one race, and 2 had seen B beat A in another race. Harsanyi's view is that differences in subjective probabilities can always be accounted for in such a fashion.[26]

The holders of such a view would probably consider the approach of this paper invalid. Suppose that in Example 2.1, D is the event "horse A beats horse B." Suppose further that each player knows that the other has observed exactly one previous race. Now in our context we assume that each player knows the other's probability for D. But in that case, the very knowledge of the other player's probability will cause revision of each player's own probability. The result of this revision will necessarily be $p_1(D) = p_2(D) = 1/2$, so that the previously "subjective" probabilities become "objective."

But there is also another possibility, namely that each player has made several observations, and that these observations lead the players to assign probabilities 2/3 and 1/3 respectively to D. For example, 2/3 would be the result of 3 wins for A and 1 win for B, as well as 1 win for A only. Though the players may know each other's probability, they may not know on precisely what observations it is based. Thus each player would not know if his own information is or is not more reliable than the other player's, and might be inclined to stick with his own information. Of course some revision of probabilities would certainly be called for even in such a case; but whether such a revision must always ultimately lead to equal probabilities for D is not clear.

In any event, under the Harsanyi doctrine cases of differing subjective probabilities known to all players either do not occur, or if they do occur, they should be treated by the methods of games of incomplete information. Basically, therefore, that part of this paper dealing with subjective randomization assumes that different people can have irreconcilable priors — precisely what Harsanyi calls the "inconsistent case." Most workers in the field would probably agree that the inconsistent case can occur, and we are perfectly willing to let our contribution stand or fall on this basis.

---

[26]Though Harsanyi (1968) does not state this position in such absolute terms, there is little doubt that that is his belief.

But there is also another argument for our theory, an argument based on Savage's "Small Worlds" theme (1954, §2.5 and §5.5). Suppose we are faced with a game like that in Example 2.1 or 2.3, and wish to apply the Harsanyi doctrine; this leads to an analysis by means of the theory of games of incomplete information. Now such an analysis will in general involve an enormous expansion of the formal description of the game. It may be necessary to use a population of many millions of types for each of the 2 or 3 players.[27] The resulting game will in practice be completely unanalyzable. We suggest that an equally valid practice would be to accept apparent differences in subjective probabilities at their face value, even if one adheres to the Harsanyi doctrine.

This question is not too different from the question "What is an outcome?" (cf. Savage, op. cit.). Suppose we are playing a given matrix game for money. The normal procedure would be to assign utilities to the amounts of money involved, and then solve the game using any of the standard theories. But a sum of money is not in itself valuable; it depends on how one wishes to use it. So to analyze the game properly we would have to decide on how to invest the money or what consumer article to buy with it. But even the investment or the consumer article itself is often only a means to an end; and this "end" in turn, is often again largely a means. Following through all this in a formal fashion, even if it were theoretically possible, would make the simplest of games totally unmanageable. So one isolates the given game as a "small world," using the utilities to sum up all that follows. We suggest that even if in principle one accepts the Harsanyi doctrine, one can live with differing subjective probabilities as a summation of the complex informational situation in which the players find themselves.

k. We end this paper with a discussion of two possible objections that could be raised against the idea of subjective strategies. To fix ideas, consider the situation of two politicians, Adams and Brown, running

[27]...*every* possible combination of attributes...will be represented in this population...[Harsanyi (1968, p. 176), italics in the original].

for the office of mayor of their town. Each one has a number of (pure) campaign strategies open to him. Each pair of such strategies yields a probability for the election of Adams, the complementary probability being that of the election of Brown; for simplicity, assume that these probabilities are objective. This is a classical example of a constant-sum game, since there are only two possible final outcomes; the utilities of Adams and Brown may thus be taken equal to the respective success probabilities, and the sum is therefore always constant (=1).

What is now being suggested is that Adams and Brown use randomized campaign strategies that are pegged on events for which they have different subjective probabilities. These events may be entirely disconnected with the political campaign in question; to take an extreme example, if the candidates are Americans, they may peg their choices on the outcome of a cricket match in England.

One objection that may be raised to this procedure is that whereas a prudent person might be willing to use mixed strategies based on a coin toss with known objective probabilities, he would hesitate to risk his career on the outcome of an event of which he knows little or nothing. Adams and/or Brown may know little or nothing about cricket in England; how can we suggest that they peg their decisions on it?

Though this objection has great intuitive force, it is not consistent with the theory of subjective probability. According to this theory, people have subjective probabilities for any event, no matter how well or ill they are informed about it; of course the probability will depend on the available information, but there will always *be* a probability. Once this probability is determined, it enters the decision-making process in all respects like an objective probability. A certain amount of introspection will, moreover, support the conclusions of the theory despite their apparent strangeness. Suppose Adams is asked to choose between winning the election with objective probability 1/3 and winning the election if the Manchester cricket team beats the Liverpool team. If he knows nothing at all about the cricket situation, and subscribes to the "principle of insufficient reason," he might well choose the second possibility, despite — or rather because of — his lack of information. The same point may similarly be made by considering the situation in which it is not a pre-determined coin that is tossed, but rather a biassed coin that is picked out of a hat with a wide distribution of biasses; in such a situation, the utility theory of von Neumann and Morgenstern (1953) still applies, although in a certain sense the user knows much less about the coin.

l. Another possible objection runs as follows: Both players realize that the game is basically zero-sum, since in the last analysis, only one of them can win the election. Both know it is an illusion to think that both can gain more than the value of the game; this illusion is based on what might be called a mistaken appraisal of probabilities by at least one of them (and possibly both). Would they not be more prudent, then, to guarantee to themselves the objective value of this game by the use of objectively randomized strategies, thus avoiding all possible "mistakes"?

On one level, this question can be answered simply by saying that each side is here taking advantage of what it sees as the other side's mistake, and that this is perfectly rational. On a deeper level, though, it is incorrect to speak of "mistakes" at all. Each side has well-defined systems of preferences, each perfectly consistent in itself, and these preferences are *not* directly opposed. Thus, it is incorrect to say that the situation is "basically zero-sum." This situation is analogous to a situation in which the players' preferences as between *pure* outcomes are directly opposed, though between mixtures of outcomes they may not be; such a game is not usually called zero-sum or even "strictly competitive."

Consider, for example, the game

	L	R
T	$5,0$	$2,2$
B	$1,3$	$0,5$

Preference-wise, this matrix has a saddle point at (T, R). It is, however, not constant sum, since a contract to play (T, L) and (B, R) with probability $1/2$ each is preferred by both players to the saddle point. Rather than signing the contract before tossing a coin, one could imagine that the coin has already been tossed, but that the players are not informed of the outcome. Paralleling the above argument, one could then say that both players realize that the game is "basically strictly competitive," since the preferences as between pure outcomes are directly opposed. Thus both know that it is an illusion to think that both can gain more than the 2 units assigned at the saddle point; this illusion is based on a mistaken appraisal of how the coin actually fell. Would they not be more prudent to guarantee a sure payoff of at least 2?

Certainly if they knew how the coin fell, there would be no point in using it to mix outcomes; but in the current situation, they both prefer the 1/2-1/2 combination of (T, L) and (B, R) to the saddle point (T, R). This agreement is therefore a perfectly natural one in spite of the fact that one of the players must necessarily lose out. Completely similar reasoning holds in the case of a game that is zero-sum in utilities, but that can be made non-strictly competitive by the appropriate use of subjectively randomized strategies.

Acknowledgement

Research supported in part by National Science Foundation grant GS-3269 at the Institute for Mathematical Studies in the Social Sciences, Stanford University, and in part by CORE, the Center for Operations Research and Econometrics at the Catholic University of Louvain.

References

Anscombe, F. J. and R. J. Aumann, 1963, A definition of subjective probability, *Ann. Math. Stat.* 34, 210–212.

Aumann, R. J., 1961, Almost strictly competitive games, *J. Soc. Ind. Appl. Math.* 9, 544–550.

Aumann, R. J., 1964, Mixed and behavior strategies in infinite extensive games, in: M. Dresher, L. S. Shapley and A. W. Tucker, eds., Advances in Game Theory (Princeton University Press, Princeton) 627–650.

Aumann, R. J. and M. Maschler, 1972, Some thoughts on the minimax principle, *Management Science* 18, P-54–P-63.

Harsanyi, J., 1967–68, Games of incomplete information played by Bayesian players, Parts I–III, *Management Science* 14, 159–182, 320–334, 486–502.

Harsanyi, J. and R. Selten, 1972, A generalized Nash solution for two-person bargaining games with incomplete information, *Management Science* 18, P-80–P-106.

Kuhn, H. W., 1953, Extensive games and the problem of information, in: H. W. Kuhn and A. W. Tucker, eds., Contributions to the Theory of Games II (Princeton University Press, Princeton) 193–216.

Lyapunov, A., 1940, Sur les fonctions-vecteurs completement additives, *Bull. Acad. Sci. USSR Ser. Math.* 4, 465–478.

Nash, J. F., 1951, Non-cooperative games, *Ann. of Math.* 54, 286–295.

Savage, L. J., 1954, *The Foundations of Statistics* (John Wiley, New York).

Von Neumann, J. and O. Morgenstern, 1944, *Theory of Games and Economic Behavior* (Princeton University Press, Princeton); 3rd ed., 1953.

Chapter 8

Correlated Equilibrium as an Expression of Bayesian Rationality*,†

Abstract: Correlated equilibrium is formulated in a manner that does away with the dichotomy usually perceived between the "Bayesian" and the "game-theoretic" view of the world. From the Bayesian viewpoint, probabilities should be assignable to everything, including the prospect of a player choosing a certain strategy in a certain game. The so-called "game-theoretic" viewpoint holds that probabilities can only be assigned to events not governed by rational decision makers; for the latter, one must substitute an equilibrium (or other game-theoretic) notion. The current formulation synthesizes the two viewpoints: Correlated equilibrium is viewed as the *result* of Bayesian rationality; the equilibrium condition appears as a simple maximization of utility on the part of each player, given his information.

*Reprinted from *Econometrica* (1987), 55(1), 1–18, with permission from Wiley.
†Research supported by the Institute for Mathematical Studies in the Social Sciences, Stanford University, under National Science Foundation Grant SES 83–20453; by the Institute for Mathematics and its Applications, University of Minnesota; and by the Mathematical Sciences Research Institute, Berkeley. We are grateful to Lloyd Shapley for an illuminating conversation, a decade back, that clarified for us the equivalence between the two definitions of correlated equilibrium; to Kenneth Arrow, for motivating us to write this paper; to Bob Weber, for the very apt quotation from Burns; and to Dave Kreps and two anonymous referees, for splendid editorial work.

A feature of this approach is that it does not require explicit randomization on the part of the players. Each player always chooses a definite pure strategy, with no attempt to randomize; the probabilistic nature of the strategies reflects the uncertainty of *other* players about his choice. Examples are given.

1. Introduction

O wad some pow'r the giftie gie us
To see oursels as ithers see us!
—Burns

The equilibrium concept of Nash (1951), together with its refinements,[1] is without doubt the single game-theoretic tool that is most often applied in economics. Yet, though at first the definition seems simple and natural enough, a little reflection leads to some puzzlement as to why and under what conditions the players in an n-person game might be expected to play such an equilibrium. Recall that it is defined as an n-tuple of strategies in which the component strategy of each player maximizes that player's utility given that the other players are playing their components. Now why should any player assume that the other players will play their components of such an n-tuple, and indeed why should they? This is particularly perplexing when, as often happens, there are multiple equilibria; but it has considerable force even when the equilibrium is unique. Indeed, there are games whose Nash equilibria appear quite unattractive even though they are unique (see Harsanyi, 1977, p. 125); and even without such examples, it does not seem clear why the players would play even a unique Nash equilibrium. In a two-person game, for example, Player 1 would play his component

[1]E.g., Selten (1975), Myerson (1978), Kreps and Wilson (1982), Kalai and Samet (1984), Kohlberg and Mertens (1986).

only if he believes that 2 will play his; this in turn would be justified only by 2's belief that 1 will indeed play his component; and so on. To many this will sound like a plain old circular argument: consistent, perhaps, but hardly compelling.

Nash equilibrium does make sense if one starts by assuming that, for some specified reason, each player knows which strategies the other players are using. But this assumption appears rather restrictive.

Another criticism of equilibrium that has been advanced is that it appears inconsistent with the modern subjectivist, Bayesian view of the world. According to the Bayesian view, subjective probabilities should be assignable to every prospect, including that of players choosing certain strategies in certain games. Rather than playing an equilibrium, the players should simply choose strategies that maximize their utilities given their subjective distributions over the other players' strategy choices.

It is the purpose of this paper to provide a simple rationale for equilibrium. Surprisingly, our rationale is precisely in terms of the "criticism" in the previous paragraph. We will show that, far from being inconsistent with the Bayesian view of the world, the notion of equilibrium is an unavoidable consequence of that view. It turns out, though, that the appropriate equilibrium notion is not the ordinary mixed strategy equilibrium of Nash (1951), but the more general notion of correlated equilibrium.

Specifically, we will show the following. Let us be given an n-person game G in strategic (i.e. normal) form. Assume that (i) as in Savage (1954), each player has a subjective probability distribution over the set of all states of the world; and (ii) it is common knowledge[2] that each player chooses a strategy that maximizes his expected utility given his information. Then the strategies chosen by the

[2]An event is *common knowledge* among a set of agents, if it is known to all, it is known to all that it is known to all, and so on ad infinitum. See Lewis (1969) and, for a precise mathematical formulation, Aumann (1976).

players constitute a correlated equilibrium of G. Conversely, each correlated equilibrium of G can be obtained in this way for an appropriate choice of the parameters. A precise formulation and proof will be found in Section 3.

To some readers, this may seem obvious. Once one has the formulation, it is indeed embarrassingly easy to prove, as we shall see. But it should not be confused with certain characterizations of Nash equilibrium, which look similar but are actually much more transparent. There one assumes not only that each player is a utility maximizer, but that he knows the strategies actually being used by all other players. We make no such assumption; indeed, in our treatment, the players do *not* in general know how others are playing. We assume only that it is common knowledge that all the players are Bayesian utility maximizers, that they are rational in the sense that each one conforms to the Savage theory. Such an assumption underlies most of game theory, and of economic theory as well; we show that it, by itself, is enough to assure that the outcome is a correlated equilibrium.

An important feature of our approach is that it does not require explicit randomization on the part of the players. Each player always chooses a definite pure strategy, with no attempt to randomize; the probabilistic nature of the strategies reflects the uncertainty of *other* players about his choice. This will be discussed in detail in Section 6.

The basic idea of this paper is extraordinarily simple; the main theorem is proved in less than a dozen lines. Some conceptual issues do arise, but still, we cannot grasp how such a simple idea grew into a paper of this length. A reader just interested in the main points, who knows what a correlated equilibrium is, should read Sections 3 and 6 only. Those not familiar with correlated equilibria should read Section 2 first.

2. Correlated Equilibrium

Let G be an n-person game in strategic form. For $i = 1, \ldots, n$, denote by S^i the set of pure strategies — henceforth *actions* — of Player i, and by $h^i(s)$ the payoff to i for an n-tuple $s := (s^1, \ldots, s^n)$ of actions.[3] Set $S := S^1 \cdots \times S^n$ and $h := (h^1, \ldots, h^n)$. Define a *correlated strategy n-tuple* in G as a function f from a finite[4] probability space Γ into S; that is, as a random variable whose values are n-tuples of actions.

Correlation is a more general form of strategy randomization than mixing. In both cases, the players base their choice of an action on observation of a random event; with mixed strategies, the observations are independent, whereas with correlated strategies, they need not be. To see that mixed strategies may be formally viewed as correlated strategies, take Γ to be the product probability space $\Gamma^1 \times \cdots \times \Gamma^n$, where Γ^i is the probability space by means of which i's mixed strategy is defined — the set of outcomes of his roulette spin. The simplest examples of "true" correlation (nonindependent action choices) occur when all players base their choices on observation of the *same* random variable. For example, in the prisoner's dilemma of Figure 1, the symmetric efficient outcome can be achieved if *both* players simultaneously observe a single toss of a fair coin, then play (top, right) or (bottom, left) according to whether heads or tails came up. It cannot, however, be achieved by mixed strategies.

In general, the observations of the players need be neither identical nor independent. Chance chooses an element γ of Γ, then suggests to each player i that he take the action $f^i(\gamma)(:= (f(\gamma)^i))$. If all players follow the suggestions, the correlated strategy n-tuple f results.

2, 2	0, 6
6, 0	1, 1

Figure 1

[3]The symbol := means that the expression on the left is being defined.

[4]I.e., with a finite number of points (and so also of events). The finiteness of Γ plays no role in the sequel; we assume it only to avoid complicating the model with irrelevant generality.

The function f may be identified with the n-tuple $(f^1, \ldots, f^n)$. If g^i is a different function from Γ to S^i, then as usual,

$$(f^{-i}, g^i) := (f^1, \ldots, f^{i-1}, g^i, f^{i+1}, \ldots, f^n).$$

Throughout the sequel, E denotes "expectation." If f is a correlated strategy n-tuple, note that $h^i(f)$ is a real-valued random variable.

Definition 2.1. A *correlated equilibrium* (c.e.) in G is a correlated strategy n-tuple f such that

$$Eh^i(f) \geqslant Eh^i(f^{-i}, g^i) \tag{2.2}$$

for each player i and each g^i that is a function of f^i.

In form this definition is very similar to that of Nash equilibrium. Equilibrium is achieved when no player can gain by deviating from the suggestions, given that the others obey them. The deviations g^i are restricted to be functions of f^i (i.e., compositions of some other function with f^i) because i is informed of $f^i(\gamma)$ only, and so can distinguish only between members of Γ that are distinguished by f^i.

It will be useful to define the *distribution* of a correlated strategy n-tuple f as the function that assigns to each n-tuple s of actions the number $\text{Prob}\{f^{-1}(s)\}$. Much like mixed strategies, correlated strategy n-tuples can for most practical purposes be identified with their distributions. Thus the correlated strategy n-tuple discussed above (Figure 1) can, using a familiar notation, be written $\frac{1}{2}$(top, right)+$\frac{1}{2}$(bottom, left). Another way to represent the distribution is to insert the appropriate probability in each square of the payoff matrix; for the above example, the distribution is that of Figure 2.

This distribution is not a *correlated equilibrium distribution* (c.e.d.), i.e., it does not represent a correlated equilibrium. Indeed, in the prisoner's dilemma, it is *always* worthwhile for Player 1 to play bottom, also if it is suggested that he play top. Figure 3 contains an example of a game ("the battle of the sexes") and a correlated strategy distribution that *is* in equilibrium. If top is suggested to 1, then he knows that left was suggested to 2, so he would lose

0	1/2
1/2	0

Figure 2

2, 1	0, 0
0, 0	1, 2

1/2	0
0	1/2

Figure 3

6, 6	2, 7
7, 2	0, 0

Figure 4

1/3	1/3
1/3	0

Figure 5

by deviating to bottom; similarly if bottom is suggested, and for Player 2.

By similar methods it may be seen that any convex combination of Nash equilibria is a correlated equilibrium. But there are also other kinds of correlated equilibria. For example, Figure 4 illustrates a two-person game ("chicken") with three Nash equilibria, whose payoffs are (2, 7), (7, 2), and ($4\frac{2}{3}$, $4\frac{2}{3}$). The distribution of Figure 5 may be seen to be a correlated equilibrium, whose payoff (5, 5) is outside the convex hull of the Nash equilibrium payoffs. It follows that the distribution of Figure 5 is itself outside the convex hull of the Nash equilibria. Other examples of correlated equilibria that are outside the convex hull of the Nash equilibria may be found in

Aumann (1974); for a particularly beautiful example, see Moulin and Vial (1978).

Computationally, correlated equilibria are simpler objects than Nash equilibria. The correlated equilibrium distributions of a given game G constitute a compact convex polyhedron whose defining linear inequalities can be explicitly written down. Here we treat only the two-person case, which is notationally less cumbersome; the principle, however, is no different in the general case.

Let $n = 2$; set $l := |S^1|, m := |S^2|, h_{jk} := h(j,k)$ for $j \in S^1$ and $k \in S^2$. Let $\sum_j$ and $\sum_k$ denote summation over all j in S^1 and all k in S^2 respectively. The distribution of a correlated strategy pair is an lm-tuple (p_{jk}), where j and k range over S^1 and S^2 respectively,

$$p_{jk} \geqslant 0 \text{ for all } j \text{ and } k, \quad \text{and} \quad \Sigma_j \Sigma_k p_{jk} = 1.$$

We will call such objects simply *distributions* for short.

Proposition 2.3. *A distribution (p_{jk}) is a correlated equilibrium distribution if and only if*

$$\sum_k (h^1_{jk} - h^1_{qk}) p_{jk} \geq 0 \quad \text{for all } j, q \text{ in } S^1, \quad \text{and} \tag{2.4}$$

$$\sum_j (h^2_{jk} - h^2_{jr}) p_{jk} \geq 0 \quad \text{for all } k, r \text{ in } S^2. \tag{2.5}$$

Proof. For (2.2) it is necessary and sufficient that for each i, the expectation still obeys the inequality when conditioned on each possible value of f^i, i.e. on each possible "suggestion" to Player i (a suggestion is called *possible* if it has positive probability). Suppose j is a possible suggestion to Player 1, i.e., $\Sigma_k p_{jk} > 0$. Given this suggestion, the conditional probability of 1 that k was suggested to 2 is $p_{jk}/\Sigma_k p_{jk}$; hence 1's conditional expected payoff is $\Sigma_k h^1_{jk} p_{jk}/\Sigma_k p_{jk}$, which we denote $H^1(j|j)$. If 1 were to deviate to the action q, his conditional expected payoff would be $\Sigma_k h^1_{qk} p_{jk}/\Sigma_k p_{jk}$, since the payoffs change, but 1's information remains the same; we denote this by $H^1(q|j)$. The equilibrium condition (2.2) for $i = 1$ says that deviation to q is not worthwhile, i.e., that $H^1(j|j) \geqslant H^1(q|j)$; if we multiply through by $\Sigma_j p_{jk}$, we obtain (2.4). Similarly, (2.5) is seen to express the equilibrium condition (2.2) for $i = 2$.

Definition 2.1 appears a little different from our 1974 definition of correlated equilibrium; there, the players may get more information about γ than just the suggested action $f^i(\gamma)$. It turns out, though, that practically speaking, the two definitions are equivalent. This will be discussed again below (Section 4g).

3. Bayesian Rationality in Games

We assume exogenously given an n-person game as in the previous section. Also exogenously given are the following: (i) a finite[5] set Ω, with generic element ω; (ii) for each player i in G, a probability measure p^i on Ω; (iii) for each player i in G, a partition $\mathscr{P}^i$ of Ω. The set Ω represents the set of all possible *states of the world*, and each ω denotes a specific such state. The probability measure p^i is i's *prior* on Ω. The partition $\mathscr{P}^i$ is i's *information partition*; if the true state of the world is $\omega \in P \in \mathscr{P}^i$, then i knows that some element of P is the true state of the world, but he does not know which one it is.

The term "state of the world" implies a definite specification of all parameters that may be the object of uncertainty on the part of any player of G. In particular, each ω includes a specification of which action is chosen by each player of G at that state ω. Conditional on a given ω, everybody knows everything; but in general, nobody knows which is really the true ω. Taking the "atoms" of Ω to represent complete specifications of all possible variables enables us to represent *all* aspects of uncertainty on the part of any player — including uncertainty about the uncertainty of other players — by means of the partitions $\mathscr{P}^i$. This constitutes the standard model for "differential" ("incomplete") information in multi-person contexts; its implications will be discussed in more detail in the next section.

[5]See Section 4c.

We will use the following assumption:

Common Prior Assumption: All the priors p^i are the same; that is, there is a probability measure p on Ω such that $p^1 = p^2 = \cdots = p^n = p$.

This is sometimes called the *Harsanyi Doctrine*. It does *not* imply that all players have the same subjective probability. The subjective probability of a player is his posterior given his information; these may well be different. Roughly speaking, the common prior assumption says that differences in probability estimates of distinct individuals should be explained by differences in information and experience. This, too, will be discussed further in the sequel, and we will also indicate how our results must be modified when the common prior assumption is relaxed or abandoned.

Denote by $\mathbf{s}^i(\omega)$ the action chosen by Player i in the game G at the state ω of the world. Formally, each $\mathbf{s}^i$ is simply an exogenously specified function from Ω to S^i; it may be considered item (iv) in the informational model of the world specified at the beginning of this section. We make the modest assumption that each player i knows which action he chooses, i.e., that $\mathbf{s}^i$ is measurable[6] w.r.t. (with respect to) $\mathscr{P}^i$.

Let $\mathbf{s}(\omega) := (\mathbf{s}^i(\omega), \ldots, \mathbf{s}^n(\omega))$ be the n-tuple of actions chosen at state ω. Call a player i *Bayes rational* at ω if his expected payoff given his information, $E(h^i(\mathbf{s})|\mathscr{P}^i)(\omega)$, is at least as great as the[7] amount $E(h^i(\mathbf{s}^{-i}, s^i)|\mathscr{P}^i)(\omega)$ that it would have been had he chosen an action s^i other than the action $\mathbf{s}^i(\omega)$ that he did in fact choose; in brief, if he chooses an action that maximizes his payoff given his information.

---

[6]A random variable is *measurable* w.r.t. a partition if it is constant on each element of the partition. Intuitively, this means that the r.v. contains no more information than the partition; a person who knows which event in the partition obtains, also knows the value of the r.v.

[7]Recall that if x is a random variable, then $E(\mathbf{x}|\mathscr{P}^i)$ is defined as the r.v. whose value at a specific ω is $E(\mathbf{x}|P)$, where P is the event in $\mathscr{P}^i$ that contains ω. (P represents i's knowledge, the smallest event that he knows to have occurred.)

Main Theorem. *If each player is Bayes rational at each state of the world, then the distribution of the action n-tuple* $\mathbf{s}$ *is a correlated equilibrium distribution.*

Proof. We must exhibit a probability space Γ and a function $f : \Gamma \to S$ that is a correlated equilibrium and that has the same distribution as $\mathbf{s}$. Indeed, if we set $\Gamma := (\Omega, p)$, then $\mathbf{s}$ itself is such a function. To see this, let $i \in N$, and let $g^i : \Omega \to S^i$ be any function of $\mathbf{s}^i$. Since $\mathbf{s}^i$ is $\mathscr{P}^i$-measurable, g^i also is; that is, it is constant on each P in $\mathscr{P}^i$. The Bayes rationality of i at each state implies that for each such P and each s^i in S^i,

$$E(h^i(\mathbf{s})|P) \geq E(h^i(\mathbf{s}^{-i}, s^i)|P).$$

Taking s^i to be the constant value of g^i throughout P yields

$$E(h^i(\mathbf{s})|P) \geq E(h^i(\mathbf{s}^{-i}, g^i)|P);$$

multiplying both sides by Prob P and summing over all P in $\mathscr{P}^i$ yields

$$E(h^i(\mathbf{s})) \geq Eh^i(\mathbf{s}^{-i}, g^i).$$

For $f = \mathbf{s}$, this is precisely the condition (2.2) that defines correlated equilibrium.

4. Discussion

(a) *Personal Choice as a State Variable.* The chief innovation in our model is that it does away with the dichotomy usually perceived between uncertainty about acts of nature and of personal players. Of course, a player always knows which decision he himself takes; here, this information is not treated differently from private information he may have about other aspects of the state of the world.

This point is a little subtle and is worth some discussion. In traditional Bayesian decision theory, each decision maker is permitted to make whatever decision he wishes, after getting whatever information he gets. In our model this appears not to be the case, since the decision taken by each decision maker is part of the description of the state of the world. This sounds like a restriction on the decision maker's freedom of action; at a given state ω, it is as if the model forces him to take the decision dictated by ω.

But closer examination reveals that "freedom of choice" is not an issue. The model describes the point of view of an outside observer. Such an observer has no a priori knowledge of what the players will choose; for him, the choices of the players are part of the description of the states of the world. This does not mean that the players cannot choose whatever they want, but only that the observer will not in general know what they want.

This "outside observer" perspective is common to all differential information models in economics (as well as to all extensive games that are not of perfect information). In such models, each player gets some information or "signal"; he hears only the signal sent to him, not that of others. In analyzing this situation, each player i must first look at the whole picture as if he were an outside observer; he cannot ignore the possibility of his having gotten a signal other than the one he actually got, even though he knows that he did not actually get such a signal. This is because the *other* players do not know what signal he got. Player i must take the ignorance of the other players into account when deciding on his own course of action, and he cannot do this if he does not explicitly include in the model signals other than the one he *knows* he got. The "outside observer" referred to above is thus a surrogate for the ignorance of the system as a whole — the lack of common knowledge — of the signals received by each player.

Similarly, each player is of course free to choose whatever action he wishes. That we include his action as part of the description of the state of the world is only a convenient way of expressing the fact that the other players do not know which action he wishes to choose.

The reader may still be puzzled by the fact that in deriving his posterior about other players' choices, each player conditions on his own information, which includes his own choice. How can a player's own choice help him to guess what other players will do?

But again, this paradox is illusory. The player is not really conditioning on his choice, but on the substantive information that leads him to make this choice. This substantive information leads to a posterior on the other players' choices, which in turn leads to an optimal choice, or to a set of such choices. Intuitively, the fact that a player's choice is part of his information is used not so much in deriving his own posterior about what others will do, but rather in estimating the others' posteriors about what he will do. They cannot simply make arbitrary "guesses" about this, but must take into account that he is maximizing given his own information. Since he is reasoning similarly about them, it appears that one might be led to troubling circular reasoning. This precisely is avoided by the model of the previous section.

To sum up, a game in which the players do not know what the other players do should be treated like any other model of differential information, where the possible values of the parameters about which some of the players are ignorant are used as specifications of the state of the world.

(b) *Common Knowledge of Information Partitions and Priors.* A question that often crops up when models of differential information are discussed is whether there can be uncertainty on the part of one player about the information partitions $\mathscr{P}^i$ of other players.

The answer is "no". While Player 1 may well be ignorant of what Player 2 knows — i.e., of the element of $\mathscr{P}^2$ that contains the "true" state ω of the world — 1 cannot be ignorant of the *partition* $\mathscr{P}^2$ itself. Indeed, $\mathscr{P}^2$ is part of the description of the model, and does not enter the description of any particular ω; it therefore cannot be the object of uncertainty, it must be common knowledge.

This is not an assumption, but a "theorem", a tautology; it is implicit in the model itself. Since the specification of each ω includes a complete description of the state of the world, it includes also a list of those other states ω' of the world that are, for Player 2, indistinguishable from ω. If there were uncertainty about this list on the part of Player 1 (or of any other player), then the description of ω would not be complete; one should then split ω into several states, depending on which states are, for 2, indistinguishable from ω.

Therefore the very description of the ω's implies the structure of $\mathscr{P}^2$, and similarly of all the $\mathscr{P}^i$. The description of the ω's involves no "real" knowledge; it is only a kind of code book or dictionary. The structure of the $\mathscr{P}^i$ also involves no real knowledge; it simply represents different methods of classification in the dictionary.

The situation with priors is similar. Once one accepts the Bayesian viewpoint, that each player has a prior on Ω, it follows that there cannot be any uncertainty on the part of one player about other players' priors. Each player's prior must be common knowledge among all players. (This in itself does not imply the further assumption, which we have made, that all the priors are the same; this further assumption will be discussed separately below.)

The reasoning leading to the conclusion that the priors are common knowledge is similar to that leading to the conclusion that the $\mathscr{P}^i$ are common knowledge. It is enough to convince ourselves that Player 1's prior $p^1(\omega)$ for each given state ω of the world is common knowledge. If it were not, then the description of ω would be incomplete; we would be able to split ω into several states, depending on the various possibilities for $p^1(\omega)$.

The reader may ask why we adduce verbal, informal arguments for these assertions, rather than proving them as formal theorems. The answer is that the assertions have no formal content. Within the model, knowledge refers to events, i.e., sets of states. One can ask whether at a given state ω, a player i knows an event A; this is the case if and only if A includes that element of $\mathscr{P}^i$ that contains ω. But neither a partition nor a prior is an event; formally speaking, the concepts of knowledge and common knowledge do not apply to them. In the above informal discussion, when we refer to the partitions, say, as "common knowledge", we mean that all players know them, all know that all know them, and so on, where "know" has its informal, everyday meaning.

It is important to realize that while the above assertions (that the partitions and priors are common knowledge) aid us in understanding the model, they do not affect the conclusions. Each player uses only his own prior and his own partition in reaching a decision; within the model, it does not matter that he "knows" the partitions and priors of the others. It is only in interpreting the results that these points become significant.

(c) *Finiteness of the Model.* Unlike the finiteness of Γ assumed in Section 2, the finiteness of Ω does involve some loss of generality. For example, in describing uncertainty about other people's uncertainty, it is perhaps more natural to allow a continuum of states. Models that do this in full generality and entirely explicitly are, in fact, available; e.g., Mertens and Zamir (1985).

We nevertheless chose the finite model, because the point we make is basically very simple, and has nothing to do with whether the model is finite or infinite. This simplicity might be obscured by an infinite model, with its relatively heavy apparatus of σ-fields, measures, integrals, Radon-Nikodym derivatives, and so on. Such an analysis can probably be carried out in a manner analogous to that presented here; but we have not actually done this, and the possibility of unexpected difficulties cannot be excluded.

In the last analysis, the world *is* usually considered finite; in a sense, finite models do appear more natural. An infinite model is appropriate when there is something to be gained from it, when we are dealing with a phenomenon that is not conveniently expressible in a finite framework. The choice of model is a matter of convenience; here, the finite model is the more convenient and transparent one.

(d) *The Converse.* Let us call the system consisting of Ω, p, the $\mathscr{P}^i$, and $\mathbf{s}$ an *information system.* The main theorem asserts that under Bayesian rationality, every information system corresponds to a correlated equilibrium. The converse also holds: Under Bayesian rationality, every correlated equilibrium corresponds to some information system. More precisely, for each game G and each correlated equilibrium f of G, there is an information system for which it is Bayes rational for the players to play in accordance with $\mathbf{s}$, and the resulting distribution is the same as that of f.

For the proof, note that f itself provides an example of such an information system. We need only define $(\Omega, p) := \Gamma$, $\mathbf{s} := f$, and $\mathscr{P}^i$ to be the partition of Ω generated by f^i (i.e., ω and ω' are in the same element of $\mathscr{P}^i$ iff $f^i(\omega) = f^i(\omega')$).[8] Bayesian rationality is then a restatement of (2.2). Thus under Bayesian rationality, the set of all information systems corresponds precisely to the set of all correlated equilibria.

(e) *Exogeneity and Endogeneity.* As we indicated at the beginning of the previous section, it is probably best to think of the information system as exogenous. But a case could be made for another view. While a part of each player's information is undoubtedly generated by overt signals from the outside world, another part is obtained by reasoning about how other players reason. For example, this is so for the information that a strictly dominated strategy will not be used. Some readers might prefer to call that kind of information "endogenous." In actuality, much information is a mixture of both kinds, which it is not easy to untangle.

The distinction between "exogenous" and "endogenous" is often useful in economics, but it should not be pushed too far. In the natural sciences, such a distinction is little used.[9] When discussing the motion of the planets, should the motion of Uranus be considered "exogenous" and that of Neptune "endogenous", or the other way around? Perhaps it is not so terribly important. What *is* important is the relationship between the motions.

The purpose of this paper is to record the observation that common knowledge of rationality implies correlated equilibrium. For this, it is not very important whether the information of the players — or even their actions — are considered exogenous or endogenous.

(f) *Mixed Strategies.* In view of the fact that the players may wish to use mixed strategies, the reader might question the assumption

[8]Note that the definitions of Ω, p, and $\mathbf{s}$ go in exactly the opposite direction from the corresponding ones in the proof of the main theorem, where we defined $\Gamma := (\Omega, p), f := \mathbf{s}$. But the proof of the main theorem is not simply a mirror image of this one, since there p' was not necessarily generated by f'.

[9]We are aware of the pitfalls of blindly applying the methodology of one science to another. But neither should one go to the other extreme, of blindly rejecting all parallels.

that each player knows his own action. There is no problem if, as usual, one thinks of a mixed strategy simply as a random device for helping the player make up his mind, so that in the end he does know which action he takes. But it is conceivable that a player can actually commit himself to a mixed strategy before he knows its pure outcome; in that case, the assumption in question seems formally incorrect.

The simplest way to circumvent the difficulty is to say that if indeed it is possible for a player i to commit himself irrevocably to a definite mixed strategy, then such a commitment should itself be considered an action — a member of S^i — and then, of course, there is no difficulty. It should be noted that this will not change the set of possible outcomes; adding an action whose payoffs are a convex combination of the payoffs to other actions does not change the set of correlated equilibria.

(g) *Alternative Definitions of Correlated Equilibrium.* In our 1974 definition of correlated equilibrium, each player i is endowed with an information partition $\mathscr{I}_i$ on the underlying probability space (the space of possible outcomes of the randomizing device). After finding out which element of $\mathscr{I}_i$ took place, i may take any action he wishes. Thus an equilibrium is a function from outcomes of the randomizing device to action n-tuples, whose ith component is $\mathscr{I}_i$-measurable (each player knows which action he takes). The equilibrium condition is as in Section 2 above.

At first blush, this definition appears different from that of this paper (2.1), since here a player is told *only* what action he takes, and is given no further information. For fixed $\mathscr{I}_i$, the definitions are indeed different. But if the $\mathscr{I}_i$ are allowed to vary, the set of correlated equilibrium distributions obtained under the 1974 definition is the same as that of this paper.

To see this, note that the 1974 set-up is formally identical with that of Section 3 above, with $\mathscr{I}_i$ instead of $\mathscr{P}^i$. Thus the fact that every c.e.d. in the 1974 sense is also a c.e.d. in the current sense is simply a restatement of our main theorem. The converse is immediate, since we may, if we wish, take $\mathscr{I}_i$ to consist of the coarsest partition of the underlying probability space for which i's action is measurable.

The reason that in this paper we chose the definition without the $\mathscr{I}_i$ is that it makes the explicit calculation of the set of all c.e.d.'s more transparent.

(h) *Common Knowledge and Universality.* The formulation of our result in the introduction assumes common knowledge (c.k.) of rationality. The formal treatment of Section 3 assumes *universal* rationality, i.e., rationality at each point of the state space Ω. These two formulations are equivalent. Indeed, our 1976 treatment of c.k. implies that the universal event Ω is itself c.k. (i.e., anything that is true at all possible states of the world is common knowledge). Conversely, a c.k. event can without loss of generality be assumed universal, because one can always restrict the universe to the smallest c.k. event (i.e., to that member of the meet $\wedge\, \mathscr{P}^i$ of the information partitions that contains the true state ω of the world).

5. The Common Prior Assumption

This section is devoted to a discussion of the only element of our model that is not a tautological consequence of the Bayesian approach: the common prior assumption (CPA for short; see Section 3).

Common priors are explicit or implicit in the vast majority of the differential information literature in economics and game theory. As soon as one writes, "let p (rather than p^i) be the probability of...", one has assumed common priors. The assumption is pervasive in the enormous literature on rational expectations, trading in securities, bargaining under incomplete information, auctions, repeated games, signalling, discrimination, insurance, principal-agent, moral hazard, search, entry and exit, bankruptcy, what have you. Citing the relevant papers would make our references longer than our text. Occasionally the definitions do pay lip-service to the possibility of distinct priors p^i; but usually this is quickly abandoned, and in the theorems and examples, one returns to common priors.[10]

In game theory, the standard representation of extensive games[11] involves moves of "chance" or "nature" where each alternative has a single probability, common to all players. The standard formulation of Nash equilibrium (1951) uses mixed strategies for which the probabilities are common to all players. Both these definitions have been used hundreds — perhaps thousands — of times in economic applications, almost without question.

Why is this so? Why has the economic community been unwilling, in practice, to accept and actually use the idea of truly *personal* probabilities, in much the same way that it did accept the idea of personal utility functions? After all, in the development of Savage (1954), both the utilities and the probabilities are derived separately for each decision maker. Why were utilities accepted as personal, but probabilities not?

Perhaps the most basic reason is that utilities directly express tastes, which are inherently personal. It would be silly to talk about "impersonal tastes", tastes that are "objective" or "unbiased." But it is not at all silly to talk about unbiased probability estimates, and even to strive to achieve them. On the contrary, people are often criticized for wishful thinking — for letting their preferences color their judgment. One cannot sensibly ask for expert advice on what one's tastes should be; but one may well ask for expert advice on probabilities.[12]

---

[10]A notable exception is Harrison and Kreps (1978).

[11]von Neumann and Morgenstern (1944), Kuhn (1953).

[12]That Bayesian decision theory a la Savage derives both utilities and probabilities from preferences does not imply that it does not discriminate conceptually between these two concepts. Savage used preferences to get a rigorous handle on probabilities, a coherent formulation free of inner contradictions. At the same time, he strove, to the extent possible, to rid his probabilities of personal elements, to make them fit for use not only in decision theory but also for scientific induction. He was fond of pointing out that after sufficiently many observations,

On a more pragmatic level, the CPA expresses the view that probabilities should be based on information; that people with different information may legitimately entertain different probabilities, but there is no rational basis for people who have always been fed precisely the same information to do so.

Differently put, a major message of modern economic theory is the vital importance of information in economic activity, and of differences in information. Under the CPA, differences in probabilities express differences in information *only.* Thus the CPA enables one to zero in on purely informational issues in analyzing economic (and other interactive) models with uncertainty.

If, in spite of all this, we abandon the CPA, all is not lost. One can define a *subjective correlated equilibrium* as in Section 2, replacing the single probability p on Γ by n different probabilities $p^1, \ldots, p^n$. In the main theorem, then, one must only replace "correlated equilibrium distribution" by "subjective correlated equilibrium distribution."

---

all "reasonable" priors lead to similar conclusions. His postulate P4 (roughly speaking, that the probability of an event is independent of the prize offered contingent on that event) can only be understood in terms of a probability concept that has an existence of its own in the decision maker's mind, quite apart from preferences on acts. He wrote that "... the ... view sponsored here does not leave room for optimism or pessimism ... to play any role in the person's judgment" (1954, p. 68). And again, "All views of probability are rather intimately connected with one another. For example, any necessary view can be regarded as an extreme personalistic view in which so many criteria of consistency have been invoked that there is no role left for individual judgment" (1954, p. 60).

Savage is dead — so much the worse for us — and one can only speculate as to how he would have regarded the CPA. As far as we know, he never dealt formally with more than one decision maker at a time. The CPA can be brought formally into his framework via an axiom that says that under common knowledge of rationality, risk averse agents with precisely the same information will never bet against each other (one must, in some appropriate way, exclude hedging). Contrary to the modern vogue, Savage was not a minimalist; he did not try to make his axioms as few and weak as possible, but as useful as possible. At one point he wrote that "the personalistic view incorporates all ... criteria for reasonableness in judgment known to me, and ... when any criteria that may have been overlooked are brought forward, they will be welcomed ..." (1954, p. 67). It's just possible that he would have welcomed the CPA.

While such an approach is mathematically perfectly consistent, it yields results that are far less sharp than those obtained with common priors. For example, if a 2-person 0-sum game G in strategic form has a unique pair s of optimal (maxmin and minmax) strategies, which are moreover pure, then one would certainly expect rational players to play s; the reasoning leading to this conclusion, which was spelled out in detail by von Neumann and Morgenstern (1944), is extremely compelling. And indeed, s is the only correlated equilibrium point[13] in g. But, it is far from the only subjective correlated equilibrium point. For example, in the game of Figure 6, the unique pair of optimal strategies is (top, left); it leads to the payoff $+1$ for the row player, and -1 for the column player. But the subjective distribution indicated in Figure 7 is a subjective correlated equilibrium; its payoff is $+3$ for *each* player (in spite of the game being zero sum!), and it makes no use at all of the unique optimal strategies.

This game is not a fluke. Quite generally, the concept of subjective correlated equilibrium places very few restrictions on the

1	2	2
–2	9	–9
–2	–9	9

Figure 6

0,0	0,0	0,0
0,0	1/3, 1/6	1/6, 1/3
0,0	1/6, 1/3	1/3, 1/6

Figure 7

[13]More generally, in any 2-person 0-sum game, all correlated equilibria are convex combinations of pairs of optimal strategies.

possible outcomes. To get the flavor of this, note that for *any* two-person game, not necessarily zero-sum, in which there are no weakly dominated actions, there is a subjective correlated equilibrium at which both players assign positive probability to each outcome (action pair); and there is also a subjective correlated equilibrium that gives each of the two players an expected payoff as close as you wish to his maximum possible payoff. Such results indicate that the subjective correlated equilibrium is a relatively "weak" concept, giving little information; and that while logically consistent, it involves a conceptual inconsistency between the players, which distorts and hides the conflict of interests that is the subject of game-theoretic analysis.

The case of distinct priors was considered by John Harsanyi (1967) in his path-breaking papers on games of incomplete information; he called it the "inconsistent case." The idea of subjective randomization was introduced and developed in our 1974 paper; this idea depends essentially on distinct priors. Neither idea had any considerable echo. Apparently, economists feel that this kind of analysis is too inconclusive for practical use, and side-steps the major economic issues.

6. Randomness as an Expression of Ignorance

In the traditional view of strategy randomization, the players use a randomizing device, such as a coin flip, to decide on their actions. This view has always had difficulties. Practically speaking, the idea that serious people would base important decisions on the flip of a coin is difficult to accept. Conceptually, too, there are problems. The reason a player must randomize in equilibrium is only to keep others from deviating; for himself, randomizing is unnecessary.

The first to break away from the idea of explicit randomization was J. Harsanyi (1973). He showed that if the payoffs to each player i in a game are subjected to small independent random perturbations, known to i but not to the other players, then the resulting game of incomplete information has *pure* strategy equilibria that correspond to the mixed strategy equilibria of the original game. In plain words, nobody really randomizes. The appearance of randomization is due to the payoffs not being exactly known to all; each player, who does know his own payoff exactly, has a unique optimal action against his estimate of what the others will do.

Here we take this reasoning one step further. Even without perturbed payoffs, the players simply do not know what actions the other players will take. In "matching pennies", each player knows very well what he himself will do, but ascribes $1/2 - 1/2$ probabilities to the other's actions, and knows that the other ascribes those probabilities to his own actions.

With this view, mixed strategy equilibria appear quite special and rather unnatural. They imply that the players always act as if they all had the same beliefs about what all other players will do, and as if these beliefs were common knowledge. (The actions themselves, of course, need not be common knowledge, except in the case of pure strategy equilibria.) In particular, they act as if[14] each player i always knew exactly what each other player believes about his (i's) actions.

Correlated strategy n-tuples, on the other hand, do allow for varying beliefs about the beliefs of other players. In the distribution of Figure 8, for example, Player 1 may ascribe probabilities that are either $1/2 - 1/2$ or $3/4 - 1/4$ to Player 2's actions; and 2 can never

[14]The phrase "act as if' means that we ignore irrelevant information, information that does not affect the actions of the players. Technically speaking, the corresponding assertions hold when each player conditions on his own action only. Without this caveat, they are false. For example, consider a three-person game in which each player chooses 0 or 1, and then is paid 0 or 1 according to whether the sum of the chosen numbers is even or odd. It is a Nash equilibrium for each player to play 0 or 1 with $1/2 - 1/2$ probabilities. One explicit scenario for this is that each player decides on his action in accordance with a completely private coin toss. A second scenario is like the first, except that 2 observes l's toss. In that case, 2 believes with certainty that 1 will do what he in fact will do, but this belief is not shared by 3, who still ascribes probabilities $1/2 - 1/2$ to l's actions. A third scenario is like the second, except that 2's observation of l's toss is transmitted through a noisy channel; in that case, 1 will not know what 2 believes about l's action. (In each case, the scenario is assumed common knowledge.) The point is that for practical purposes, all three scenarios are equivalent, since the additional information never causes any player to change his action.

3	3
3	1

Figure 8

0, 0, 3	0, 0, 0
1, 0, 0	0, 0, 0

2, 2, 2	0, 0, 0
0, 0, 0	2, 2, 2

0, 0, 0	0, 0, 0
0, 1, 0	0, 0, 3

Figure 9

know what 1 believes about his (2's) actions. Such phenomena are often of the essence in the analysis of real situations, but they are ruled out by the mixed strategy paradigm.

In games with more than two players, correlation may express the fact that what 3, say, thinks that 1 will do may depend on what he thinks 2 will do. This has no connection with any overt or even covert collusion between 1 and 2; they may be acting entirely independently. Thus it may be common knowledge that both 1 and 2 went to business school, or perhaps to the same business school; but 3 may not know what is taught there. In that case 3 would think it quite likely that they would take similar actions, without being able to guess what those actions might be.

For example, consider the game of Figure 9 (Aumann, 1974). Players 1, 2, and 3 pick the row, column, and matrix respectively. No mixed strategy equilibria yield any player more than 1. But there is a correlated equilibrium yielding (2, 2, 2): Player 3 picks the middle matrix with certainty, while 1 and 2 pick (top, left) with probability 1/2, and (bottom, right) with probability 1/2 . This does *not* imply collusion between 1 and 2; it simply means that it is common knowledge that 3 has no idea what they will do, but does think with certainty that they will either play (top, left) or (bottom, right). This, of course, is an extreme situation; it will perhaps be more common to find situations where in 3's estimate, the actions of 1 and of 2 are neither perfectly correlated nor independent. Again, such situations are plentiful, but cannot be described by means of mixed strategies.

7. The Literature

The idea presented here was briefly outlined in Appendix 4 of Aumann (1981). Kadane and Larkey (1982) also expressed the idea that the theory of games should be consistent with Bayesian decision theory. But they ignored the fact that a rational player must take into account how other players reason about him, and concluded that under Bayesian theory, nothing at all could be said about what each player thinks others would do. One must, they said, turn to disciplines such as psychology to gain insight into how rational agents should or would play a game.

More recently, Bernheim (1984) and Pearce (1984) have independently developed the theory of rationalizability. This is related to the notion of subjective correlated equilibrium mentioned in Section 5 above; a rationalizable outcome is much like one that occurs with positive probability in a subjective correlated equilibrium (see Tan and Werlang, 1984, and Brandenburger and Dekel, 1985). Nevertheless, there are differences; for example, rationalizability as currently defined does not permit one player to perceive the strategies of other players as correlated (see Section 6 above).

References

Aumann, R. J., 1974, "Subjectivity and Correlation in Randomized Strategies," *Journal of Mathematical Economics* 1, 67–96. [Chapter 7]

——— 1976, "Agreeing to Disagree," *Annals of Statistics* 4, 1236–1239. [Chapter 2]

——— 1981, "Survey of Repeated Games," in *Essays in Game Theory and Mathematical Economics in Honor of Oskar Morgenstern*. Mannheim, Wien, Zurich: Wissenschaftsverlag, Bibliographisches Institut, 11–42.

Bernheim, B. D., 1984, "Rationalizable Strategic Behavior," *Econometrica* 52, 1007–1028.

Brandenburger, A., and E. Dekel, 1985, "Rationalizability and Correlated Equilibria," unpublished preprint, Stanford University and Harvard University.

Harrison, J. M., and D. M. Kreps, 1978, "Speculative Investor Behavior in a Stock Market with Heterogeneous Expectations," *Quarterly Journal of Economics* 92, 323–336.

Harsanyi, J. C., 1967, "Games with Incomplete Information Played by Bayesian Players," Parts I, II, III, *Management Science* 14, 159–182, 320–334, 486–502.

——— 1973, "Games with Randomly Disturbed Payoffs: A New Rationale for Mixed Strategy Equilibrium Points," *International Journal of Game Theory* 2, 1–23.

——— 1977, *Rational Behavior and Bargaining Equilibrium in Games and Social Situations.* Cambridge: Cambridge University Press.

Kadane, J. B., and P. D. Larkey, 1982, "Subjective Probability and the Theory of Games," *Management Science* 28, 113–120.

Kalai, E., and D. Samet, 1984, "Persistent Equilibria in Strategic Games," *International Journal of Game Theory* 13, 129–144.

Kohlberg, E., and J. F. Mertens, 1986: "On the Strategic Stability of Equilibria," *Econometrica* 54, 1003–1037.

Kreps, D., and R. Wilson, 1982, "Sequential Equilibria," *Econometrica* 50, 863–894.

Kuhn, H. W., 1953, "Extensive Games and the Problem of Information," in *Contributions to the Theory of Games II.* ed. by H. W. Kuhn and A. W. Tucker. Princeton: Princeton University Press, 193–216.

Lewis, D. K., 1969, *Convention.* Cambridge: Harvard University Press.

Mertens, J. F., and S. Zamir, 1985, "Formulation of Bayesian Analysis for Games with Incomplete Information," *International Journal of Game Theory* 14, 1–29.

Moulin, H., and J. P. Vial, 1978, "Strategically Zero-Sum Games: The Class of Games Whose Completely Mixed Equilibria Cannot be Improved Upon," *International Journal of Game Theory* 7, 201–221.

Myerson, R. B., 1978, "Refinement of the Nash Equilibrium Concept," *International Journal of Game Theory* 7, 73–80.

Nash, J. F., 1951, "Non-Cooperative Games," *Annals of Mathematics* 54, 286–295.

von Neumann, J., and O. Morgenstern, 1944, *Theory of Games and Economic Behavior.* Princeton: Princeton University Press.

Pearce, D. G., 1984, "Rationalizable Strategic Behavior and the Problem of Perfection," *Econometrica* 52, 1029–1050.

Savage, L. J., 1954, *The Foundations of Statistics.* New York: Wiley.

Selten, R., 1975, "Re-examination of the Perfectness Concept for Equilibrium Points in Extensive Games," *International Journal of Game Theory* 4, 25–55.

Tan, T. C.-C., and S. R. da Costa Werlang, 1984, "The Bayesian Foundations of Rationalizable Strategic Behavior and Nash Equilibrium Behavior," unpublished preprint, University of Chicago.

Chapter 9

Rational Expectations in Games*

Abstract: A player i's actions in a game are determined by her beliefs about other players; these depend on the game's real-life context, not only its formal description. Define a *game situation* as a game together with such beliefs; call the beliefs — and i's resulting expectation — *rational* if there is *common knowledge of rationality* and a *common prior*. In two-person zero-sum games, i's only rational expectation is the game's value. In an arbitrary game G, we characterize i's rational expectations in terms of the correlated equilibria of the *doubled* game $2G$ in which each of i's strategies in G appears twice. (JEL C72, D83, D84)

Modern game theory was born in 1928, when John von Neumann published his Minimax Theorem. Inter alia, this theorem ascribes to all two-person zero-sum games a *value* — what rational players should expect to get.

Almost 80 years later, strategic game theory has not gotten beyond that initial point, insofar as the basic question of value is concerned. To be sure, we do have equilibrium theories: the initial concept of John F. Nash (1951) and its various refinements and coarsenings. But when the game is not two-person zero-sum, none of

*Co-authored with J. H. Dreze. Reprinted from American Economic Review (2008), 98, 72–86, with permission from American Economic Association.

these theories actually tells the players what to expect. Even when there is just one Nash equilibrium, it is not at all clear that the players "should" expect its payoff.[1] Can one ascribe a value to each player — what she should expect — in an arbitrary n-person game?

As stated, the question has no answer; the problem is underspecified. Formally, a game is defined by its strategy sets and payoff functions. But in real life, many other parameters are relevant; there is a lot more going on. Situations that substantively are vastly different may nevertheless correspond to precisely the same strategic game. For example, in a parliamentary democracy with three parties, the winning coalitions are the same whether the parties each hold a third of the seats in parliament, or, say, 49 percent, 39 percent, and 12 percent, respectively. But the political situations are quite different. The difference lies in the attitudes of the players, in their expectations about each other, in custom, and in history, though the rules of the game do not distinguish between the two situations. Another example revolves around the ultimatum game (Werner Güth, Rolf Schmittberger, and Bernd Schwarze 1982), which, when played in different cultures, leads to systematically different outcomes (Alvin E. Roth *et al.* 1991).

Thus, if one is given only the abstract formulation of a game, one cannot reasonably hope for an expectation. Somehow, the real-life context in which the game is played must be taken into account. We are discussing not just a game, but a "game situation," i.e., a game played in a specific context; and we should be prepared to let a player's expectation depend upon the context — the "situation."

Call the player in whose expectation we are interested the *protagonist*, and designate her[2] *Player* 1 (P1). The essential element

---

[1]For example, see Example 3.2.

[2]The protagonist is female. The other players are of indeterminate gender; to distinguish them from the protagonist, we use masculine pronouns for them. Similarly, we use masculine pronouns for players in general, who may or may not include the protagonist.

in the above notion of "context" is the protagonist's belief about the actions and beliefs of the other players. These are described by a *belief hierarchy:* her belief about what the others play, about what they believe she — and the others — play, about what they believe about *that*, and so on. Formally, therefore, we define a *game situation* Γ to consist of (a) a strategic game G as defined by its strategy sets and payoff functions, and (b) a belief hierarchy of P1 in G; we say that Γ is *based* on G and G *underlies* Γ.

To start with, each game situation has a well-defined *expectation:* the protagonist's expected payoff, as calculated from her strategy and her belief about the strategies of the others. But in itself, this doesn't get us very far: without further restrictions, even two-person zero-sum game situations may well have expectations that are very far from the value. Indeed, they may be anything at all between the protagonist's maximum and minimum payoffs.

To achieve a meaningful extension of von Neumann's value, we must take into account the interactive nature of games: that the players are rational, and reason about each other. This may be done by restricting attention to game situations with *common knowledge of rationality* (*CKR*) and *common priors (CP).*[3] The relevance of these two conditions to the value problem is brought out by

Theorem A. *The expectation of any two-person zero-sum game situation with common knowledge of rationality and common priors is the value of the underlying game.*

Both *CKR* and *CP* are needed here; without either one, the result fails (Sections 4, 4.1 and 4.2). It is thus natural to define a *rational*

[3]A player is *rational* if his strategy choice maximizes his expected payoff. *CKR* means that all players are rational, all know it, all know *that*, and so on. Roughly, *CP* means that differences in the players' probability assessments are due to differences in information *only*; for a precise definition, see Section 1. If *CKR* — or *CP* — obtain, then all players know it, so it can be read off from the protagonist's belief hierarchy.

expectation[4] in a game G as the expectation of a game situation based on G for which CKR and CP obtain. In Section 7.4, we relate this definition to the classical notion of rational economic expectations, as originally promulgated by John F. Muth (1961).

What Theorem A says is that in two-person zero-sum games, rational expectations are *not* situation-specific: any such expectation must be the value of the game. But in general, rational expectations *are* situation-specific. Here, we investigate the set of rational expectations that can arise in situations based on a given game G; i.e., the restrictions on such expectations that are implied by the formal definition of the game itself, whatever the specific situation may be.

On the face of it, the task of operationally calculating these expectations appears formidable; inter alia, because of the complexity of belief hierarchies. It is made approachable by our Theorem B, which characterizes the rational expectations in terms of the correlated equilibria (Aumann 1974) of the *doubled* game $2G$ — which is the same as G, except that each of the protagonist's strategies is listed twice.[5] To state it, recall that a *correlated equilibrium* of G is a probability distribution ρ on pure strategy profiles (a.k.a. n-tuples), such that if "chance" chooses a profile in accordance with ρ, and informs each player only of *his* strategy in the chosen profile, then it is optimal for him to play that strategy, assuming that the others play *their* strategies. The protagonist's expected payoff, after being told which strategy to play, is called a *conditional payoff to* ρ (because it is conditional on her information, namely the strategy). Correlated equilibria are described by a limited number of explicit linear inequalities;[6] so they, and the corresponding

[4]This definition is not used in Enrico Minelli (1995).

[5]Doubling a game affects its correlated equilibria in a nontrivial way; they are *not* just doubled versions of the correlated equilibria of the original game.

[6]See Aumann (1987), Proposition 2.3. With two players having k and l strategies, respectively, there are $k^2 - k + l^2 - l$ inequalities in kl variables, plus the $kl + 2$ inequalities that say that the probabilities are nonnegative and sum to one (no more and no less).

conditional payoffs, are explicitly describable in terms of G. We then have

Theorem B. *The rational expectations in a game G are precisely the conditional payoffs to correlated equilibria in the doubled game $2G$.*

The above presentation contains the gist of the paper. The remainder is organized as follows: Section 1 discusses belief hierarchies, and characterizes them in terms of our main conceptual tool — that of *belief system*. Some auxiliary propositions are stated in Section 2, and an alternative formulation of Theorem B appears in Section 5. Section 4 discusses two-person zero-sum games; in particular, it argues that the classical justifications for the value in such games (von Neumann and Morgenstern 1944) are less than convincing. Numerical examples are adduced in Sections 3 and 4. Section 6 provides intuitions for Theorems A and B. Section 7 discusses the relation of our concept to earlier work of Aumann (1987), which seems to give a different answer to the same question (7.1), and to Nash equilibrium (7.2). Section 7.3 interprets rational expectations as "benchmark" outcomes of games; Section 7.4 relates them to Muthian rational expectations. Section 8 is devoted to the background and literature, and Section 9 concludes. The Appendix provides formal proofs.

1. Belief Hierarchies and Belief Systems

Formally, a (strategic) n-person *game* G consists of n finite sets $S_1, S_2, \ldots, S_n$ (the *strategy sets* of the players) and n functions $h_1, h_2, \ldots, h_n$ from $S = S_1 \times S_2 \times \cdots \times S_n$ to $\mathbb{R}$ (the *payoff functions*). A belief hierarchy is most easily represented by means of a *belief system*[7] B for G consisting of

(i) For each player i a finite set T_i whose members t_i are called *types* of i; and

[7]Originated by John C. Harsanyi (1967–1968).

(ii) For each type t_i of each player i:

(a) A strategy[8] of i in G denoted $s_i(t_i)$; and
(b) A probability distribution on $(n-1)$-tuples of types of the other players, called t_i*'s theory.*

It may be seen that a player's type uniquely determines the whole hierarchy of his beliefs. Conversely, every belief hierarchy satisfying certain basic consistency conditions is the belief hierarchy of some type in some belief system (Jean-François Mertens and Shmuel Zamir 1985; see also Aumann and Heifetz 2002, sect. 8).

A *common prior* is a probability distribution π on $T_1 \times \cdots \times T_n$ that assigns positive probability to each type of each player, such that the theory of each type of each player is the conditional of π given that that player is of that type.[9] Less formally, such that each player's probability for a strategy profile is its probability under the common prior, conditioned on his information — i.e., on his being the type he is; examples are provided in Section 3. A type of a player is *rational* if the strategy it prescribes maximizes his expected payoff given its theory. Rationality is *commonly known* if this is so for all types of all players.[10] A belief system is *rational* if *CKR* and *CP* obtain. A *rational expectation* in G is an expected payoff of some type of the protagonist in some rational belief system for G.

2. Auxiliary Results

Our main results are Theorems A and B, stated in the introduction. The results in this section are used in analyzing the examples below, and in the proofs of Theorems A and B.

[8]Member of S_i — what is usually called a *pure* strategy. Mixed strategies play no explicit role in this treatment. If a player wishes to use a mixed strategy, say by tossing a coin, he may certainly do so; but then the type describes the situation *after* the coin toss.

[9]In symbols, $\pi_i(t^{-i}; t_i) = \pi(t)/\pi(t_i)$ for each i and each t in $T_1 \times \cdots \times T_n$ where $\pi_i(\cdot\,; t_i)$ is t_i*'s* theory and t^{-i} is the $(n-1)$-tuple of types assigned by t to players other than i.

[10]This is equivalent to the definition in terms of iterated knowledge given in the introduction.

Proposition C.

(i) *Every conditional correlated equilibrium payoff — in particular, every Nash equilibrium payoff — is a rational expectation.*
(ii) *Rational expectations are unchanged by iterated deletion of strongly dominated strategies.*
(iii) *Every rational expectation is at least the protagonist's maxmin payoff.*[11]
(iv) *The rational expectations are covariant under multiplication of a player's payoffs by a positive constant, and under addition of a constant to a player's payoffs for fixed strategies of the other players.*

Item (i) says that the notion of rational expectation is weaker than that of Nash or even correlated equilibrium. Nevertheless, it is strong enough to yield the value in two-person zero-sum games (Theorem A). Proposition C follows from Theorem B; for item (iv), we note that these transformations do not change the correlated equilibria.

To state the next proposition, recall that Roger B. Myerson (1997) called a game *elementary* if it has a correlated equilibrium that assigns positive probability to each strategy of each player, and all the inequalities associated with this equilibrium are strict.[12] We then have

Proposition D. *Every elementary game has a maximum rational expectation, namely the (protagonist's) highest payoff at any strategy pair.*

Finally, we have

Proposition E. *If all correlated equilibrium payoffs are the protagonist's minimax payoff v, then v is the only rational expectation.*

---

[11]That is, it is her security level, what she can guarantee to herself when using mixed strategies.

[12]That is, if a player is informed that the chosen strategy profile calls for him to play a certain strategy, then it is strictly *better* for him to choose that strategy than any other strategy. Myerson showed that, in a certain sense, all games may be "reduced" to elementary games.

3. Examples

In the two-person games below, the row and column players are Rowena and Colin, respectively. Rowena is the protagonist.

3.1. *Rational expectations may be mutually inconsistent*

The game G in Figure 1(a) ("Chicken") has three Nash equilibria: two pure, yielding (2, 7) and (7, 2), and one mixed, yielding $(4^2/_3, 4^2/_3)$. Consider now a belief system with four states, TL, TR, BL, and BR, with each player's probabilities *for* each state *in* each state as depicted in Figures 1(b) and 1(c). For example, in BL as well as in BR, Rowena's probabilities for BL and BR are $^7/_8$ and $^1/_8$ respectively, while for TL and TR they are 0. Rowena has the two types T and B, Colin the two types L and R.

The expectation of Rowena's type B is $6^1/_8$. She attributes probability $^1/_8$ to Colin's type being R, in which case his expectation, too, will be $6^1/_8$. So in that case, the players will each expect $6^1/_8$. These expectations are mutually inconsistent; $(6^1/_8, 6^1/_8)$ is infeasible — it is outside the convex hull of the possible payoff vectors. And this

	L	R
T	6, 6	2, 7
B	7, 2	0, 0

(a) The game G

	L	R
T	1/2	1/2
B	7/8	1/8

(b) Rowena's beliefs

	L	R
T	1/2	7/8
B	1/2	1/8

(c) Colin's beliefs

	L	R
T	7/22	7/22
B	7/22	1/22

(d) The common prior

	L	R
T	1/2	1/2
B	1	0

(e) Rowena's beliefs

	L	R
T	1/2	1
B	1/2	0

(f) Colin's beliefs

	L	R
T	1/3	1/3
B	1/3	0

(g) The common prior

Figure 1

in spite of common knowledge of rationality, which the reader may verify, and the existence of a common prior, depicted in Figure 1(d).

BR is the conflict outcome in Chicken. We see here that conflict may occur even when the players reason perfectly rationally and attribute rationality to each other; both players know about the inconsistency, and indeed it is commonly known that it may occur. Contrary to common wisdom (or rather, foolishness), the conflict is not due to any irrationality, but simply to differing assessments, which may well ensue when players are provided with different information.

To be sure, the mixed Nash equilibrium may also lead to conflict. But in that case, the players' assessments of the situation are not inconsistent. It is the inconsistency of the assessments that is noteworthy here.

The distribution in Figure 1(d) is a correlated equilibrium of G, and $6^1/_8$ is its conditional payoff given B.

Another belief system for G is depicted in Figures 1(e)–1(g). Here, it is common knowledge that the conflict outcome *BR* is impossible. In particular, a type B Rowena expects 7 and knows that Colin is of type L, so expects 4. The payoff pair (7, 4) is, however, infeasible. Thus here again, the expectations of the players are mutually inconsistent, in spite of there being no irrationality in the system.

3.2. *Different conditional correlated equilibrium payoffs in 2G and G*

The game G of Figure 2(a) (Lloyd S. Shapley 1964) has a single Nash equilibrium, namely, $((^1/_3, {}^1/_3, {}^1/_3), (^1/_3, {}^1/_3, {}^1/_3))$, yielding the payoff (3, 3). Consider now a belief system with seven states, T_1R, T_2C, T_2R, *ML, MR, BL*, and *BC*, with each player's probabilities set forth in Figures 2(b) and 2(c) (as in Section 3.1); Rowena's strategy in rows T_1 and T_2 is T. If Rowena's type is T_1, the game situation has expectation 5. She knows that Colin's type is R, so that his expectation is $4^1/_2$. Thus Rowena *knows* that the players' expectations are the infeasible[13] pair (5, $4^1/_2$) — in spite of common knowledge of

[13]The payoffs sum to $9^1/_2$, whereas the maximum sum in the matrix is 9.

	L	C	R
T	0, 0	4, 5	5, 4
M	5, 4	0, 0	4, 5
B	4, 5	5, 4	0, 0

(a)

The game G

	L	C	R
T^1	0	0	1
T^2	0	2/3	1/3
M	1/2	0	1/2
B	1/2	1/2	0

(b)

Rowena's beliefs

	L	C	R
T^1	0	0	1/4
T^2	0	1/2	1/4
M	1/2	0	1/2
B	1/2	1/2	0

(c)

Colin's beliefs

	L	C	R
T^1	0	0	1/12
T^2	0	1/6	1/12
M	1/6	0	1/6
B	1/6	1/6	0

(d)

The common prior

0,0	4,5	5,4
0,0	4,5	5,4
5,4	0,0	4,5
5,4	0,0	4,5
4,5	5,4	0,0
4,5	5,4	0,0

(e)

The doubled game $2G$

0	0	1/12
0	1/6	1/12
1/6	0	1/6
0	0	0
1/6	1/6	0
0	0	0

(f)

A correlated equilibrium in $2G$

Figure 2

rationality and a common prior (depicted in Figure 2(d)). Here, unlike in the previous example, 5 is not a conditional payoff to a correlated equilibrium of G, given any strategy of Rowena.[14]

But it *is* a conditional payoff to a correlated equilibrium of the doubled game $2G$, depicted in Figure 2(e); the correlated equilibrium in question is depicted in Figure 2(f). Note that if we eliminate the rows in which all the probabilities vanish, Figure 2(f) becomes

[14]By G's symmetry, we may suppose that Rowena's component of the strategy pair is T. The correlated equilibrium cannot then assign positive probability to TC, as Rowena's conditional payoff would then be < 5. So everything is eliminated by a sequence of strict dominations: C by L, then B by M, then L by R, then M by T, and finally R by C, leaving nothing. In fact, the highest conditional payoff to a correlated equilibrium of G, given a strategy of Rowena, is $5-(1/3126) \approx 4.99968$.

	L	R
T	1, 1	0, 0
B	0, 0	0, 0

The game G

Figure 3 The game G.

Figure 2(d). A similar relationship obtained in our first example, but with G instead of $2G$.

Alternatively, a correlated equilibrium of this game may be obtained by assigning probability 1/6 to the entries with payoffs (4, 5) or (5, 4). The associated inequalities are all strict, so the game is elementary. So by Proposition D, the maximum rational expectation is 5.

3.3. *The set of rational expectations need not be convex*[15]

In each of the previous two examples adduced up to now, the set of rational expectations is an interval. In the game G of Figure 3, this is not so; here, there are precisely two rational expectations: 1 and 0.

4. Two-Person Zero-Sum Games

Von Neumann and Morgenstern (1944) advance two arguments to support the minmax value of two-person zero-sum games. One is the *equilibrium* argument; the other is the *guaranteed value* argument, which says that the row player can guarantee getting the value v, and the column player can guarantee not paying more than v, "so" rational players must reach precisely the value.

The equilibrium argument is of a formal, mathematical nature; one *proves* that there is a unique equilibrium payoff, namely

[15]By contrast, with an ex ante viewpoint, as in Section 7.1, one gets the set of all unconditional correlated equilibrium payoffs, which is always convex.

the value. But the guaranteed value argument is more tenuous. We purposely put the word "so" in quotation marks, because there is a bit of a non sequitur there. Fully to justify this kind of argument, one needs a formal framework. In fact, though this "argument" appears to depend only on the rationality of the players, it is not true that players who are merely rational must necessarily reach the value; one needs *common knowledge* of rationality, and one also needs common priors (see Sections 4.1 and 4.2).

One may think of Theorem A as reflecting the guaranteed value argument, but in a rather subtle way. The players do *not* actually guarantee the value. In many two-person zero-sum games,[16] it is in fact impossible to do so in pure strategies; and here, we think of the players as using pure strategies only. Rather, the protagonist *expects* the value. Guarantees enter the argument in showing that what she expects cannot be less than the value, because she *could* — by using mixed strategies — attain at least the value in expectation. One needs further arguments, revolving around the common knowledge, the common prior, and the zero-sumness to show that she also cannot expect more than the value.

Indeed, the current perspective shows exactly where the "classical" argument breaks down. It is true that Players 1 and 2 can guarantee v and $-v$, respectively; so, since the sum of payoffs is 0, the only feasible "individually rational"[17] payoff pair is $(v, -v)$. It is also true that any rational expectation (of either player) must be individually rational, that is, Proposition C (iii). What is *not* generally true is that the players' expectations must constitute a feasible pair, i.e., be "consistent." Indeed, we saw in Section 3 that inconsistent expectations are the rule rather than the exception; in particular, we saw that it is possible for Rowena to *know* that Colin expects a payoff that is inconsistent with the payoff she *knows* she is getting, even though rationality is commonly known and there is a common prior. On the face of it, there is no reason to suppose that a similar situation could not arise also in two-person zero-sum games.

[16]Specifically, unless the game has a pure strategy saddle point.

[17]This means that each player gets at least what he can guarantee to himself.

But in fact, it cannot. Theorem A says that there is something special about two-person zero-sum games that makes it impossible. So this theorem goes considerably beyond the classical "guaranteed value" argument for the value.

As for the equilibrium argument, this is addressed in Section 7.2, where we discuss Nash equilibrium in general n-person games.

4.1. *Failure of Theorem A without common priors*

The game G is "matching pennies." With the depicted belief system — which has no common prior — it is common knowledge that it is optimal for each player to play that strategy with which his type is designated. In particular, Rowena's type T plays T and expects 0.8, whereas the value of the game is 0.

Careful consideration of the example leads to some discomfort. It is commonly known that Rowena believes[18] that Colin believes that Rowena does the opposite of what she really does — and vice versa,[19] i.e., that each player ascribes grave errors to the other. This is typical of situations without common priors. Common knowledge of rationality does obtain in this example.

4.2. *Failure of Theorem A without CKR*

Figure 5 depicts a common prior for a belief system in the game "matching pennies" (see Figure 4(a)). Type L_3 of Colin is irrational, but all other types of both players are rational. So, type T_1 of Rowena is rational, knows that Colin is rational, knows that he knows that she is rational, knows that he knows that she knows that he is rational, and knows that he knows that she knows that he knows that she is rational; moreover, T_1's expectation is 1, whereas the value of the game is 0. The example can be extended to an arbitrarily high level of iterated mutual knowledge of rationality; but, by Theorem A, not to common knowledge.

[18]Short for "ascribes probability 0.9 to."

[19]That is, with Rowena and Colin interchanged.

	L	R
T	1, −1	−1, 1
B	−1, 1	1, −1

(a)

The game G

	L	R
T	0.9	0.1
B	0.1	0.9

(b)

Rowena's beliefs

	L	R
T	0.1	0.9
B	0.9	0.1

(c)

Colin's beliefs

Figure 4

	L_1	L_2	R_1	R_2	L_3
T_1	0.1	0.1	0	0	0
B_1	0.1	0	0.1	0	0
B_2	0	0.1	0	0.1	0
T_2	0	0	0.1	0	0.1
T_3	0	0	0	0.1	0.1

Figure 5 The common prior.

5. An Alternative Formulation of Theorem B

Theorem B is stated in terms of the doubled game $2G$. It can also be stated in terms of a set of "augmented" games, in each of which a single strategy of the protagonist is "doubled." Thus, given a strategy r_1 of the protagonist in G, define the *augmented* game G_{2r_1} as the n-person game in which just r_1 is replaced by two copies, and the payoff does not depend on which copy is used. We then have

Theorem B′. *Rational expectations in the game G coincide with conditional correlated equilibrium payoffs in the augmented games G_{2s_1}, where s_1 ranges over the protagonist's strategies.*

Thus, α is a rational expectation in G if and only if the protagonist has a strategy s_1 such that in the augmented game G_{2s_1}, there are a correlated equilibrium ρ and a strategy such that α is the conditional payoff to ρ given that strategy.

6. Intuitions for Theorems B′, B, and A

Two intuitions underlie our results: (i) that the common prior probability of a rational belief system (henceforth RBS; see Section 1) B in a game G is essentially the same thing as a correlated equilibrium (CE) of a game G_B closely related to G — that in which each strategy of each player appears as many times as there are types that play that strategy in B; and (ii) that the conditional expectation of a strategy in a CE does not change when *other* strategies that are "identical" — i.e., have the same payoffs no matter what the other players do — are amalgamated. *Amalgamation* of identical strategies in a CE of a game means going to the corresponding CE of a game in which the amalgamated strategies are replaced by a single strategy, inheriting as prior probabilities the sums of the prior probabilities before amalgamation.

By (i), every rational expectation in G is a conditional correlated equilibrium payoff in G_B. Define a game G_{2s_1} by amalgamating in G_B all "identical" strategies other than some specified strategy s_1 of the protagonist, retained twice. Then by (ii), a conditional CE payoff in G_B for strategy s_1 is also a conditional CE payoff in G_{2s_1} for s_1. This yields Theorem B′, and Theorem B follows.

Finally, let G be a two-person zero-sum game with value v. Call Player 1 Rowena, Player 2 Colin. Let t_1 be a type of Rowena in an RBS. Rowena has a mixed strategy μ that yields $\geq v$ against any pure strategy of Colin, and so also against her belief under t_1 of how he plays. So at least one of her pure strategies must yield an expectation $\geq v$ under that belief. So by *CKR*, the strategy prescribed by t_1 must also yield $\geq v$; thus, all types of Rowena expect $\geq v$. Similarly, all types of Colin expect $\geq -v$; so the average of all of Colin's payoffs under the common prior π is $\geq -v$. If some type of Rowena would expect $> v$, then the average of all of Rowena's payoffs under π would be $> v$, contradicting the zero-sumness. So all types of Rowena expect exactly v, as Theorem A asserts.

7. Discussion

7.1. *Ex ante and interim viewpoints*

Economists distinguish three stages in differential information environments. Ex ante, no one has any private information; in the *interim*, each agent has his private information only; ex post, all information is revealed to all. In our context, ex ante the protagonist knows only the belief system B — which is commonly known by all players; in the interim, each player knows his type, but not those of the others; ex post, each player knows the types of all players.

Some readers may be curious about the relationship of the current work to Aumann (1987), which appears to make the same assumptions — *CKR* and *CP* — but reaches distinctly different conclusions.[20] Namely, the 1987 paper arrives at *unconditional* expectations of correlated equilibria (CEs) of the *given* game G; here, we arrive at *conditional* expectations of CEs of the *doubled* game $2G$.

The puzzle is solved by noting that the 1987 paper concerns the possible ex ante expectations, under which the alternative interim situations are weighted by their probabilities under the common prior. In contrast, this paper characterizes all possible rational expectations at the interim stage.

In practice, the interim viewpoint is the more important. Almost invariably, real players have differential information. What they would have expected had they not had the information that they do have may be of theoretical interest, but has little practical significance. So with all due respect to the 1987 paper, we consider the current one more significant. Needless to say, the 1987 paper was an indispensable stepping stone.

7.2. *Nash equilibrium*

A major argument for Nash equilibrium, advanced already by von Neumann and Morgenstern (1944), is that if game theory is

[20]Indeed, many who have been present at preliminary presentations of this material have expressed puzzlement on this matter.

to recommend strategies to the players in a game, then those recommendations must constitute a Nash equilibrium. When carefully examined, the argument breaks down. It assumes that the putative "recommendation of game theory" must be for each player to play some specified (mixed or pure) strategy, *known to all players.* But game theory need not make that kind of recommendation; its recommendation could be — indeed, *should* be — "respond optimally to your private information." The players are faced with a game *situation*, not just a game. Even when the *game* is commonly known, the game situation usually is not. It is, indeed, replete with private information, which the players ignore at their peril (see, e.g., Section 3.1).

Nash equilibrium is of central importance in studying *norms* of strategic behavior,[21] and we do not suggest abandoning it as a solution concept for strategic games. But for the one-shot game, rational expectations are more fundamental.

7.3. *Rational expectations as a benchmark*

Any reasonably intelligent child knows that tic-tac-toe "is" a draw — that that is the "right" outcome of the game. That is not to say that in real life she would always play for a draw; she might play for a win, and lose (or win!), even while knowing that the game "is" a draw.

The formal expression of this is that the value of tic-tac-toe is a draw. Similarly, in any two-person zero-sum game, the value is the "right" outcome. In n-person game situations, rational expectations capture this idea.

The building blocks of rational expectations — *CKR* and *CP* — are rarely literally true in real life. Nor are they in any sense normative: in a given situation, they either hold or they do not hold; it makes no sense to say that they "should" hold. Nevertheless, they constitute the appropriate benchmark — characterize the "right outcomes" — just like in tic-tac-toe.

---

[21]In his thesis, Nash (1950, 21–22) suggested the related concept of "mass action" as an interpretation of his equilibrium.

7.4. *Relation with Muthian rational expectations*

In his classic 1961 paper, John Muth characterized expectations as "rational" if they are "essentially the same as the predictions of the relevant economic theory" (316). In games, the "relevant theory," whatever it is, certainly "predicts" simple rationality — utility maximization — on the part of the players. Thus with rational expectations, each player expects all players to be rational. So the "relevant theory" predicts not only simple rationality on the part of all players (R), but also *mutual knowledge of rationality* (KR), i.e., that all players know[22] all players to be rational. But then all players "expect" — or know — KR; so the "relevant theory" predicts not only KR, but also K^2R. Continuing in this way, we get K^mR for all m, which amounts to CKR. So in games, Muth's rational expectations comprise CKR.

What about CP? One might think of the "relevant theory" as yielding a probability distribution π on the strategies and beliefs of the players — i.e., on their types. If an analyst is then informed of player i's type, his "prediction" will be the conditional of π given that type. With rational expectations, i himself, who is indeed informed of his type, will have the same expectations, or beliefs, as the prediction of the informed analyst: the conditional of π given his type. But his beliefs are his theory (in the technical sense of "theory"; see Section 1, (ii)(b)). So his theory is the same as the conditional — which is precisely CP.

8. Background and Literature

The theory presented in this paper differs from much of the strategic game literature in that it does not deal with equilibria; rather, it recommends that a player in a game, like in a one-person decision problem, should simply maximize against her subjective probabilities for the other players' actions. R. Duncan Luce and Howard Raiffa (1957, 306) were among the earliest to consider this approach. They

[22]To be sure, this glosses over the difference between "expecting" and "knowing." In any case, the discussion here is meant to be suggestive, not mathematically precise.

wrote that in a game, "one *modus operandi* for the decision maker is to generate an *a priori* probability distribution over the ... pure strategies ... of his adversary by taking into account both the strategic aspects of the game and ... 'psychological' information ... about his adversary, and to choose an act which is best against this ... distribution."

Joseph B. Kadane and Patrick D. Larkey (1982) expressed a similar view, but unlike Luce and Raiffa (1957), they eschewed the "strategic aspects." This ignores *the* fundamental insight of game theory, an insight that is captured by the idea of rational expectations introduced here: that a rational player must take into account that the players reason about each other in deciding how to play.

While the theory presented here is new, to a large extent it flows naturally from previous developments in game theory. First was von Neumann's (1928) minimax for two-person zero-sum games; this led to Nash's (1951) strategic equilibrium; this, in turn, to correlated equilibrium; and this, to the theory of rational expectations presented here. The crucial idea here is to analyze game *situations* rather than games — to view games from "inside," without common knowledge of the situation — and it is Harsanyi's (1967-1968) theory of types that enables this.

9. Conclusion

The fundamental object of study in game theory should be the game *situation* Γ rather than its underlying game G. In game situations, the recommendation of game theory is precisely that of one-person decision theory: choose your strategy to maximize your expected payoff, given your information. But unlike in one-person decisions, rational players should take account of the interactive nature of games — that all the players are rational, and reason about each other. Here, this notion is captured by restricting attention to game situations with *common knowledge of rationality* and *common priors.* We characterize, directly in terms of the underlying game G, the expectations that may result under this restriction; and show that in two-person zero-sum games, the only such expectation is von Neumann's value of the underlying game.

Appendix: Proofs

Proof of Theorem B′. Let B be an RBS for G with π the common prior, t_i^1 and t_i^2 two types of player i who play the same strategy, and B' the belief system obtained from B by *amalgamating* t_i^1 and t_i^2 into a single type u_i^0. Specifically, in B', the type space of each player j other than i is T_j; the type space U_i of i is obtained from T_i by removing t_i^1 and t_i^2 and replacing them by u_i^0, where

$$s_i(u_i^0) := s_i(t_i^1) = s_i(t_i^2); \tag{1}$$

and the common prior π' in B' is defined by

$$\pi'(u_i, t^{-i}) := \pi(u_i, t^{-i}) \text{ if } u_i \neq u_i^0, \tag{2}$$

and

$$\pi'(u_i^0, t^{-i}) := \pi(t_i^1, t^{-i}) + \pi(t_i^2, t^{-i}). \tag{3}$$

Lemma 4. *CKR obtains in B'.*

Proof. We must show that in B', the strategy of each type maximizes that type's expectation. For types of players j other than i, this is immediate, since their (conditional) expectations are the same in B' as in B, whether or not they play the strategies prescribed by their types. The same holds for types u_i of i other than u_i^0. For i's type u_i^0, one must show that i's conditional expectation

$$\frac{\sum_{t^{-i}\in T^{-i}} \pi'(u_i^0, t^{-i}) h_i(s_i(u_i^0), t^{-i})}{\sum_{t^{-i}\in T^{-i}} \pi'(u_i^0, t^{-i})}$$

if he plays the strategy $s_i(u_i^0)$ prescribed by u_i^0 is at least as great as his conditional expectation

$$\frac{\sum_{t^{-i}\in T^{-i}} \pi'(u_i^0, t^{-i}) h_i(r_i, t^{-i})}{\sum_{t^{-i}\in T^{-i}} \pi'(u_i^0, t^{-i})}$$

if he plays some other strategy r_i, i.e., since the denominators are the same in the two expressions, that

$$\sum_{t^{-i}\in T^{-i}} \pi'(u_i^0, t^{-i})h_i(s_i,(u_i^0), t^{-i}) \geqq \sum_{t^{-i}\in T^{-i}} \pi'(u_i^0, t^{-i})h_i(r_i, t^{-i}). \tag{5}$$

But by the same token, the optimality (in B) of $s_i(t_i^1)$ for t_i^1 and of $s_i(t_i^2)$ for t_i^2 yield

$$\sum_{t^{-i}\in T^{-i}} \pi(t_i^1, t^{-i})h_i(s_i,(t_i^1), t^{-i}) \geqq \sum_{t^{-i}\in T^{-i}} \pi(t_i^1, t^{-i})h_i(r_i, t^{-i}), \tag{6}$$

and

$$\sum_{t^{-i}\in T^{-i}} \pi(t_i^2, t^{-i})h_i(s_i(t_i^2), t^{-i}) \geqq \sum_{t^{-i}\in T^{-i}} \pi(t_i^2, t^{-i})h_i(r_i, t^{-i}); \tag{7}$$

and, by (1) and (3), adding (6) and (7) yields (5). This establishes Lemma 4.

Corollary 8. *Amalgamation does not affect the expectation of any type of any player, except for the types that have been amalgamated.*

Let α be a rational expectation in G; we must prove that it is a conditional correlated equilibrium payoff in one of the augmented games. By definition of "rational expectation," there is for G an RBS B, and a type u_1 of the protagonist whose expectation is α. Let $r_1 := s_1(u_1)$ be the strategy played by type u_1. Without loss of generality, there is another type — different from u_1 — who plays r_1. For if not, we may split u_1 into two identical types, with the same strategy and theory as u_1. The new common prior (after the split) is then obtained from the original one by halving the probabilities of all states affected by the split.

Repeatedly amalgamating types and using Lemma 4 and its corollary, we arrive at an RBS B'' with a common prior π'', such that (i) for each strategy of each player — other than r_1 — at most one type plays that strategy; (ii) the protagonist has a type u_1^1 that is "like" u_1, in that it plays the same strategy r_1, and has the same expectation α; and (iii) the protagonist has exactly one other type, u_1^2, that plays[23] r_1.

The game G_{2r_1} is exactly like G, except that the strategy r_1 is "doubled": call the duplicates r_1^1 and r_1^2. Each type in B'' corresponds to a strategy in G_{2r_1}; specifically, u_1^1 and u_1^2 correspond to r_1^1 and r_1^2. Hence π'' induces a probability distribution ρ on the strategy profiles in G_{2r_1}, it being understood that strategy profiles without a counterpart in B'' are assigned probability 0.

Lemma 9. *ρ is a correlated equilibrium in G_{2r_1}.*

Proof. CKR in B'' tells us that the expectation of any type is at least as great if it plays the strategy prescribed for that type, as if it plays some other strategy. Rephrasing, any strategy in G_{2r_1} with positive ρ-probability yields to its player a conditional expected payoff under ρ at least as great as any other strategy.

By Lemma 9 and Corollary 8, α is a conditional correlated equilibrium payoff in G_{2r_1}. This completes the proof of Theorem B′ in one direction.

In the other direction, let β be a conditional correlated equilibrium payoff in an augmented game G_{2r_1}, specifically, the conditional payoff to the correlated equilibrium ρ, given some strategy s_1 in G_{2r_1}. Define a belief system B for G as follows: the types of i in B are in one-one correspondence with those of his strategies in G_{2r_1} to which ρ assigns positive probability; the theory of a type is the conditional of ρ given the strategy corresponding to that type. Then ρ is a common prior for B, and that CKR holds in B is the same as saying that ρ is a correlated equilibrium in G_{2r_1}. This completes the proof of Theorem B′.

Proof of Theorem B. If α is a rational expectation in G, then by Theorem B′, it is a conditional payoff to a correlated equilibrium

[23]Obtained by amalgamating all the types of the protagonist who play r_1 other than u_1^1.

ρ' in some augmented game G_{2r_1}, given a strategy x' of the protagonist in that game. The strategy profiles in G_{2r_1} are in one-one correspondence with those strategy profiles in $2G$ whose first component either is *either one* of the two copies of r_1 in $2G$, or is the *first* copy of a strategy other than r_1. Assigning to any such profile the ρ'-probability of the corresponding profile in G_{2r_1}, and 0 to all other profiles, yields a correlated equilibrium ρ in $2G$. The strategy x' in G_{2r_1} corresponds to some strategy x in $2G$, and then α is the conditional payoff to ρ in $2G$ given x. This completes the proof of Theorem B in one direction.

In the other direction, let β be a conditional payoff to a correlated equilibrium ρ in $2G$, given a strategy x of the protagonist; let r_1 be the strategy in G of which x is a copy in $2G$. "Amalgamating" the two copies in $2G$ of all strategies other than r_1 yields a correlated equilibrium ρ' in G_{2r_1}, and turns x into a strategy x' in G_{2r_1}. Then β is a conditional payoff to ρ' in G_{2r_1}, given x'. So by Theorem B', β is a rational expectation in G. This completes the proof of Theorem B.

Proof of Proposition C.

(i) The first part follows from Theorem B, as every correlated equilibrium in G can also be viewed as a correlated equilibrium in $2G$, since one can simply assign probability 0 to one of the two duplicates of each of the protagonist's strategies. The part about Nash equilibrium follows from the fact that at a Nash equilibrium v, all "active" strategies of the protagonist (indeed, of any player) — i.e., those with positive probability at v — must get the same payoff, so that the conditional expected payoffs coincide with the total expected payoff.

(ii) Follows from the fact that a strictly dominated strategy can never appear with positive probability in a correlated equilibrium, as it is always worthwhile to switch to the dominating strategy.

(iii) Let α be a rational expectation, t_1^* a type of the protagonist with expectation α in an RBS, $s_1^* := s_1^*(t_1^*)$ the strategy played by type t_1^*, and p the probability distribution over $S_{-1} := S_2 \times \ldots \times S_n$ that t_1^*'s theory induces. Thus

$\alpha = \sum_{s_{-1} \in S_{-1}} p_{s_{-1}} h_1(s_1^*, s_{-1})$. By CKR, s_1^* maximizes t_1^*'s expectation given its theory, so by the minimax theorem,

$$\begin{aligned}\alpha &= \max_{s_1 \in S_1} \sum_{s_{-1} \in S_{-1}} p_{s_{-1}} h_1(s_1, s_{-1}) \\ &\geq \min_q \max_{s_1 \in S_1} \sum_{s_{-1} \in S_{-1}} q_{s_{-1}} h_1(s_1, s_{-1}) \\ &= \max_r \min_{s_{-1} \in S_{-1}} \sum_{s_1 \in S_1} r_{s_1} h_1(s_1, s_{-1}),\end{aligned}$$

where q and r range over all probability distributions over S_{-1} and S_1, respectively.

(iv) Follows from Theorem B, since correlated equilibria are covariant in the required manner.

Proof of Proposition E. Proposition C(iii) says that every rational expectation is $\geq v$. Suppose α is a rational expectation that is $> v$. From Theorem B it follows that α is a conditional payoff of a correlated equilibrium ρ in the doubled game $2G$. By Proposition C(iii) and Theorem B, all other conditional payoffs to ρ in $2G$ are $\geq v$. Since the unconditional payoff to ρ is the expectation of the conditional payoffs, and α appears in this expectation with positive probability, it follows that the unconditional payoff to ρ is $> v$. But an unconditional payoff to the correlated equilibrium ρ in $2G$ is also an unconditional payoff to a correlated equilibrium in G, obtained by amalgamating duplicated strategies. So we get a correlated equilibrium payoff in G that is $> v$, contrary to hypothesis.

Proof of Theorem A. Follows from Proposition E, since in two-person zero-sum games, the (unconditional) expected payoff to every correlated equilibrium is the value.[24]

Proof of Proposition D. By definition, the given game G has a correlated equilibrium μ that assigns positive probability to each

[24] Aumann (1974), last paragraph of Section 2.

strategy of each player, and in which the associated inequalities are strict. Let S be the set of strategy profiles in G. If ι assigns equal probabilities to all strategy profiles, and $\varepsilon > 0$ is sufficiently small, then $\lambda := (1-\varepsilon)\mu + \varepsilon\iota$ assigns positive probability to each strategy profile, and the associated inequalities are still strict. Let w be a strategy profile in G that yields the protagonist her highest payoff in G. For each strategy profile s in G, let s^1 and s^2 be the two copies of s in $2G$. Let $0 < \delta < \lambda_w$. Define a probability distribution ρ on the set $2S$ of strategy profiles in $2G$ by $\rho_{s^1} := \lambda_s,\ \rho_{s^2} := 0$ for $s \neq w$, and $\rho_{w^1} := \lambda_w - \delta,\ \rho_{w^2} := \delta$. We will show that ρ is a correlated equilibrium of $2G$ when δ is sufficiently small.

Indeed, the inequalities associated with ρ in $2G$ are the same as those associated with λ in G, except for those that correspond to $w_1^1$and w_1^2 in $2G$. Since δ is small, and the inequalities corresponding to w_1 in G are strict, those corresponding to w_1^1 in $2G$ still hold. As for w_1^2, if the protagonist is informed of w_1^2, she knows for sure that she will get the highest possible payoff in the whole game if she indeed plays w_1^2, so it certainly is not worthwhile for her to switch. Therefore, ρ is indeed a correlated equilibrium of $2G$.

It then follows from Theorem B that the conditional payoff corresponding to w_1^2 is a rational expectation. This conditional payoff is the protagonist's payoff in G at w, which is her highest payoff at any strategy pair.

Acknowledgment

Aumann gratefully acknowledges research support from Israel Science Foundation grant 1343105.

References

Aumann, Robert J., 1974, "Subjectivity and Correlation in Randomized Strategies." *Journal of Mathematical Economics*, 1(1): 67–96. [Chapter 7]

Aumann, Robert J., 1987, "Correlated Equilibrium as an Expression of Bayesian Rationality." *Econometrica*, 55(1): 1–18. [Chapter 8]

Aumann, Robert J., and Aviad Heifetz, 2002, "Incomplete Information." In *Handbook of Game Theory with Economic Applications, Volume 3*, ed. Robert J. Aumann and Sergiu Hart, 1665–86. Amsterdam: Elsevier. [Chapter 5]

Güth, Werner, Rolf Schmittberger, and Bernd Schwarze, 1982, "An Experimental Analysis of Ultimatum Bargaining." *Journal of Economic Behavior and Organization,* 3(4): 367–88.

Harsanyi, John C., 1967–1968, "Games of Incomplete Information Played by Bayesian Players I, II, III." *Management Science,* 14(3): 159–82, 320–34, 486–502.

Kadane, Joseph B., and Patrick D. Larkey, 1982, "Subjective Probability and the Theory of Games." *Management Science,* 28(2): 113–20.

Luce, R. Duncan, and Howard Raiffa, 1957, *Games and Decisions.* New York: John Wiley.

Mertens, Jean-François, and Shmuel Zamir, 1985, "Formulation of Bayesian Analysis for Games with Incomplete Information." *International Journal of Game Theory,* 14(1): 1–29.

Minelli, Enrico, 1995, *Rational Expectations in Games.* Unpublished.

Muth, John F., 1961, "Rational Expectations and the Theory of Price Movements." *Econometrica,* 29(6): 315–35.

Myerson, Roger B., 1997, "Dual Reduction and Elementary Games." *Games and Economic Behavior,* 21(1–2): 183–202.

Nash, John F., 1950, "Non-cooperative Games." PhD diss. Princeton University. Repr. in *The Essential John Nash,* ed. Harold W. Kuhn and Sylvia Nasar, 53–84. Princeton: Princeton University Press, 2002.

Nash, John F., 1951, "Non-cooperative Games." *Annals of Mathematics,* 54(2): 286–95.

von Neumann, John, 1928, "Zur Theorie der Gesellschaftsspiele." *Mathematische Annalen,* 100: 295–320.

von Neumann, John, and Oskar Morgenstern, 1944, *Theory of Games and Economic Behavior.* Princeton: Princeton University Press.

Roth, Alvin E., Vesna Prasnikar, Masahiro Okuno-Fujiwara, and Shmuel Zamir, 1991, "Bargaining and Market Behavior in Jerusalem, Ljubljana, Pittsburgh, and Tokyo: An Experimental Study." *American Economic Review,* 81(5): 1068–95.

Shapley, Lloyd S, 1964, "Some Topics in Two-Person Games." In *Advances in Game Theory,* ed. Melvin Dresher, Lloyd S. Shapley, and Albert W. Tucker, 1–28. Princeton: Princeton University Press.

Chapter 10

Epistemic Conditions for Nash Equilibrium*,[1]

Abstract: Sufficient conditions for Nash equilibrium in an n-person game are given in terms of what the players know and believe — about the game, and about each other's rationality, actions, knowledge, and beliefs. Mixed strategies are treated not as conscious randomizations, but as conjectures, on the part of other players, as to what a player will do. Common knowledge plays a smaller role in characterizing Nash equilibrium than had been supposed. When $n = 2$, mutual knowledge of the payoff functions, of rationality, and of the conjectures implies that the conjectures form a Nash equilibrium. When $n \geq 3$ and there is a common prior, mutual knowledge of the payoff functions and of rationality, and common knowledge of the conjectures, imply that the conjectures form a Nash equilibrium. Examples show the results to be tight.

1. Introduction

In recent years, a literature has emerged that explores noncooperative game theory from a decision-theoretic viewpoint. This literature analyzes games in terms of the rationality[2] of the players and

*Co-authored with A. Brandenburger. Reprinted from *Econometrica* (1995), 63(5), 1161–1180, with permission from Wiley.

[1]We are grateful to Kenneth Arrow, John Geanakoplos, and Ben Polak for important discussions, and to a co-editor and the referees for very helpful editorial suggestions.

[2]We call a player *rational* if he maximizes his utility given his beliefs.

their *epistemic* state: what they know or believe about the game and about each other's rationality, actions, knowledge, and beliefs. As far as Nash's fundamental notion of strategic equilibrium is concerned, the picture remains incomplete;[3] it is not clear just what epistemic conditions lead to Nash equilibrium. Here we aim to fill that gap. Specifically, we seek sufficient epistemic conditions for Nash equilibrium that are in a sense as "spare" as possible.

The stage is set by the following *Preliminary Observation: Suppose that each player is rational, knows his own payoff function, and knows the strategy choices of the others. Then the players' choices constitute a Nash equilibrium in the game being played.*[4]

Indeed, since each player knows the choices of the others, and is rational, his choice must be optimal given theirs; so by definition,[5] we are at a Nash equilibrium.

Though simple, the observation is not without interest. Note that it calls for *mutual* knowledge of the strategy choices — that each player know the choices of the others, with no need for the others to know that he knows (or for any higher order knowledge). It does *not* call for *common* knowledge, which requires that all know, all know that all know, and so on ad infinitum (Lewis (1969)). For rationality and for the payoff functions, not even mutual knowledge is needed; only that the players are in fact rational, and that each knows his own payoff function.[6]

The observation applies to pure strategies — henceforth called *actions*. It applies also to mixed actions, under the traditional view of mixtures as conscious randomizations; in that case it is the mixtures that must be mutually known, not their pure realizations.

---

[3]See Section 7.9.

[4]For a formal statement, see Section 4.

[5]Recall that a Nash equilibrium is a profile of strategies in which each player's strategy is optimal for him, given the strategies of the others.

[6]Knowledge of one's own payoff function may be considered tautologous. See Section 2.

In recent years, a different view of mixing has emerged.[7] According to this view, players do not randomize; each player chooses some definite action. But other players need not know which one, and the mixture represents their uncertainty, their conjecture about his choice. This is the context of our main results, which provide sufficient conditions for a profile of conjectures to constitute a Nash equilibrium.[8]

Consider first the case of two players. Here the conjecture of each is a probability distribution on the other's actions — formally, a mixed action of the other. We then have the following (Theorem A): *Suppose that the game being played (i.e., both payoff functions), the rationality of the players, and their conjectures are all mutually known. Then the conjectures constitute a Nash equilibrium.*[9]

In Theorem A, as in the preliminary observation, common knowledge plays no role. This is worth noting, in view of suggestions that have been made that there is a close relation between Nash equilibrium and common knowledge — of the game, the players' rationality, their beliefs, and/or their choices.[10] On the face of it,

---

[7]Harsanyi (1973), Armbruster and Boege (1979), Aumann (1987a), Tan and Werlang (1988), Brandenburger and Dekel (1989), among others.

[8]The preliminary observation, too, may be interpreted as referring to an equilibrium in conjectures rather than actions. When each player knows the actions of the others, then conjectures coincide with actions: what people do is the same as what others believe them to do. Therefore, the conjectures as well as the actions are in equilibrium.

[9]The idea of the proof is not difficult. Call the players "Rowena" and "Colin"; let their conjectures and payoff functions be ϕ, g and ψ, h respectively. Let a be an action of Rowena to which Colin's conjecture ψ assigns positive probability. Since Colin knows that Rowena is rational, he knows that a is optimal against her conjecture, which he knows to be ϕ, given her payoff function, which he knows to be g. Similarly any action b to which ϕ assigns positive probability is optimal against ψ given Colin's payoff function h. So (ψ, ϕ) is a Nash equilibrium in the game defined by (g, h).

[10]Thus Kreps and Wilson (1982, p. 885): "An equilibrium in Nash's sense supposes that strategies are 'common knowledge' among the players." Or Geanakoplos, Pearce, and Stacchetti (1989, p. 62): "In traditional equilibrium analysis, the

such a relation sounds not implausible. One might have reasoned that each player plays his part of the equilibrium "because" the other does so; he, in turn, also does so "because" the first does so; and so on ad infinitum. This infinite regress does sound related to common knowledge; but the connection, if any, is murky.[11] Be that as it may, Theorem A shows that in two-person games, epistemic conditions not involving common knowledge in any way already imply Nash equilibrium.

When the number n of players exceeds 2, the conjecture of a player i is not a mixed action of another player, but a probability distribution on $(n-1)$-tuples of actions of all the other players. Though not itself a mixed action, i's conjecture does induce a mixed action[12] for each player j other than i; we call this i's *conjecture about* j. However, different players other than j may have different conjectures about j. Since j's component of the putative equilibrium is meant to represent the conjectures of other players i about j, and these may be different for different i, it is not clear how j's component should be defined.

To proceed, we need another definition. The players are said to have a *common prior*[13] if all differences between their probability

---

equilibrium strategy profile is taken to be common knowledge." Or Milgrom and Roberts (1991, p. 82): "Equilibrium analysis dominates the study of games of strategy, but ... many ... are troubled by its assumption that players ... identify and play a particular vector of equilibrium strategies, that is, ... that the equilibrium is common knowledge." See also, inter alia, Arrow (1986, p. S392), Binmore and Dasgupta (1986, pp. 2–5), Fudenberg and Kreps (1988, p. 2), Tan and Werlang (1988, pp. 381–385), Fudenberg and Tirole (1989, p. 267), Werlang (1989, p. 82), Binmore (1990, pp. 51, 61, 210), Rubinstein (1991, p. 915), Binmore (1992, p. 484), and Reny (1992, p. 628).

We ourselves have written in this vein (Aumann (1987b, p. 473) and Binmore and Brandenburger (1990, p. 119)); see Section 7.6.

[11] Brandenburger and Dekel (1989) do state a relation between common knowledge and Nash equilibrium in the two-person case, but it is quite different from the simple sufficient conditions established here. See Section 7.9.

[12] The marginal on j's actions of i's overall conjecture.

[13] Aumann (1987a); for a formal definition, see Section 2. Harsanyi (1967–68) uses the term "consistency" to describe this situation.

assessments are due only to differences in their information; more precisely, if one can think of the situation as arising from one in which the players had the same information and probability assessments, and then got different information.

Theorem B, our n-person result, is now as follows: *In an n-player game, suppose that the players have a common prior, that their payoff functions and their rationality are mutually known, and that their conjectures are commonly known. Then for each player j, all the other players i agree on the same conjecture σ_j about j; and the resulting profile $(\sigma_1, \ldots, \sigma_n)$ of mixed actions is a Nash equilibrium.*

So common knowledge enters the picture after all, but in an unexpected way, and only when there are at least three players. Even then, what is needed is common knowledge of the players' conjectures, not of the game or of the players' rationality.

Theorems A and B are formally stated and proved in Section 4.

In the observation as well as the two results, the conditions are sufficient, not necessary. It is always possible for the players to blunder into a Nash equilibrium "by accident," so to speak, without anybody knowing much of anything. Nevertheless, the statements are "tight," in the sense that they cannot be improved upon; none of the conditions can be left out, or even significantly weakened. This is shown by a series of examples in Section 5, which, in addition, provide insight into the role played by the epistemic conditions.

One might suppose that one needs stronger hypotheses in Theorem B than in Theorem A only because when $n \geq 3$, the conjectures of two players about a third one may disagree. But that is not so. One of the examples in Section 5 shows that even when the necessary agreement is assumed outright, conditions similar to those of Theorem A do not suffice for Nash equilibrium when $n \geq 3$.

Summing up: With two players, mutual knowledge of the game, of the players' rationality, and of their conjectures implies that the conjectures constitute a Nash equilibrium. To reach the same conclusion when there are at least three players, one must also assume a common prior and common knowledge of the conjectures.

The above presentation, while correct, has been informal, and sometimes slightly ambiguous. For an unambiguous presentation, one needs a formal framework for discussing epistemic matters in game contexts; in which, for example, one can describe a situation where each player maximizes against the choices of the others, all know this, but not all know that all know this. In Section 2 we describe such a framework, called an *interactive belief system*; it is illustrated in Section 3. Section 6 defines infinite belief systems, and shows that our results apply to this case as well.

The paper concludes with Section 7, where we discuss conceptual matters and related work.

The reader wishing to understand just the main ideas should read Sections 1 and 5, and skim Sections 2 and 3.

2. Interactive Belief Systems

Let us be given a strategic *game form*; that is, a finite set $\{1, \ldots, n\}$ (the *players*), together with an *action set* A_i for each player i. Set $A := A_1 \times \cdots \times A_n$. An *interactive belief system* (or simply *belief system*) for this game form is defined to consist of:

$$\text{for each player } i, \text{ a set } S_i \text{ (}i\text{'s } \textit{types}\text{)}, \tag{2.1}$$

and for each type s_i of i,

a probability distribution on the set S^{-i} of $(n-1)$-tuples

of types of the other players (s_i's *theory*), (2.2)

an action a_i of i (s_i's *action*), and (2.3)

a function $g_i : A \to \mathbf{R}$ (s_i's *payoff function*). (2.4)

The action sets A_i are assumed finite. One may also think of the type spaces S_i as finite throughout the paper; the ideas are then more transparent. For a general definition, where the S_i are measurable spaces and the theories are probability measures, see Section 6.

Set $S := S_1 \times \cdots \times S_n$. Call the members $s = (s_1, \ldots, s_n)$ of S *states of the world*, or simply *states*. An *event* is a subset

E of S. By (2.2), s_i's theory has domain S^{-i}; define an extension $p(\cdot; s_i)$ of the theory to S, called i's *probability distribution on S at s_i*, as follows: If E is an event, define $p(E; s_i)$ as the probability that s_i's theory assigns to $\{s^{-i} \in S^{-i} : (s_i, s^{-i}) \in E\}$. Abusing our terminology a little, we will use "belief system" to refer also to the system consisting of S and the $p(\cdot; s_i)$; no confusion should result.[14]

A state is a formal description of the players' actions, payoff functions, and beliefs — about each other's actions and payoff functions, about these beliefs, and so on. Specifically, the theory of a type s_i represents the probabilities that s_i ascribes to the types of the other players, and so to their actions, their payoff functions, and their theories. It follows that a player's type determines his beliefs about the actions and payoff functions of the others, about their beliefs about these matters, about their beliefs about others' beliefs about these matters, and so on ad infinitum. The whole infinite hierarchy of beliefs about beliefs about beliefs ... about the relevant variables is thus encoded in the belief system.[15]

A function $g : A \to \mathbf{R}^n$ (an n-tuple of payoff functions) is called a *game*.

Set $A^{-i} := A_1 \times \cdots \times A_{i-1} \times A_{i+1} \times \cdots \times A_n$; for a in A, set $a^{-i} := (a_1, \ldots, a_{i-1}, a_{i+1}, \ldots, a_n)$. When referring to a player i, the phrase "at s" means "at s_i." Thus "i's action at s" means s_i's action (see (2.3)); we denote it $\mathbf{a}_i(s)$, and write $\mathbf{a}(s)$ for the n-tuple $(\mathbf{a}_1(s), \ldots, \mathbf{a}_n(s))$ of actions at s. Similarly, "i's payoff function at s" means s_i's payoff function (see (2.4)); we denote it $\mathbf{g}_i(s)$, and

---

[14]The extension $p(\cdot; s_i)$ is uniquely determined by two conditions: first, that its marginal on S^{-i} be s_i's theory; second, that it assign probability 1 to i being of type s_i. We are thus implicitly assuming that a player of type s_i assigns probability 1 to being of type s_i. For a discussion, see Section 7.3.

[15]Conversely, it may be shown that any such hierarchy satisfying certain minimal coherency requirements may be encoded in some belief system (Mertens and Zamir (1985); also Armbruster and Boege (1979), Boege and Eisele (1979), and Brandenburger and Dekel (1993)).

write $\mathbf{g}(s)$ for the n-tuple $(\mathbf{g}_1(s), \ldots, \mathbf{g}_n(s))$ of payoff functions[16] at s. Viewed as a function of a, we call $\mathbf{g}(s)$ "the game being played at s," or simply "the game at s."

Functions defined on S (like $\mathbf{a}_i$, $\mathbf{a}$, $\mathbf{g}_i$, and $\mathbf{g}$) may be viewed like random variables in probability theory. Thus if $\mathbf{x}$ is such a function and x is one of its values, then $[\mathbf{x} = x]$, or simply $[x]$, denotes the event $\{s \in S : \mathbf{x}(s) = x\}$. For example, $[a_i]$ denotes the event that i chooses the action a_i, $[g]$ denotes the event that the game g is being played; and $[s_i]$ denotes the event that i's type is s_i.

A *conjecture* ϕ^i of i is a probability distribution on A^{-i}. For $j \neq i$, the marginal of ϕ^i on A_j is called the *conjecture of i about j induced by ϕ^i*. The theory of i at a state s yields a conjecture $\boldsymbol{\phi}^i(s)$ called *i's conjecture at s*, given by $\boldsymbol{\phi}^i(s)(a^{-i}) := p([a^{-i}]; s_i)$. We denote the n-tuple $(\boldsymbol{\phi}^1(s), \ldots, \boldsymbol{\phi}^n(s))$ of conjectures at s by $\boldsymbol{\phi}(s)$.

Player i is called *rational at s* if his action at s maximizes his expected payoff given his information (i.e., his type s_i); formally, letting $g_i := \mathbf{g}_i(s)$ and $a_i := \mathbf{a}_i(s)$, this means that $\exp(g_i(a_i, \mathbf{a}^{-i}); s_i) \geq \exp(g_i(b_i, \mathbf{a}^{-i}); s_i)$ for all b_i in A_i. Another way of saying this is that i's actual choice a_i maximizes the expectation of his actual payoff g_i when the other players' actions are distributed according to his actual conjecture $\boldsymbol{\phi}^i(s)$.

Player i is said to *know* an event E *at* s if at s, he ascribes probability 1 to E. Define K_iE as the set of all those s at which i knows E. Set $K^1E := K_1E \cap \cdots \cap K_nE$; thus K^1E is the event that all players know E. If $s \in K^1E$, call E *mutually known at s*. Set $CKE := K^1E \cap K^1K^1E \cap K^1K^1K^1E \cap \cdots$; if $s \in CKE$, call E *commonly known at s*.

A probability distribution P on S is called a *common prior* if for all players i and all of their types s_i, the conditional distribution of P given s_i is $p(\cdot; s_i)$; this implies that for all i, all events E and F, and all numbers π,

$$\text{if } p(E; s_i) = \pi p(F; s_i) \text{ for all } s_i \in S_i, \text{ then } P(E) = \pi P(F). \quad (2.5)$$

[16]Thus i's actual payoff at the state s is $\mathbf{g}_i(s)(\mathbf{a}(s))$.

In words, (2.5) says that for each player i, if two events have proportional probabilities given any s_i, then they have proportional prior probabilities.[17]

Belief systems provide a formal language for stating epistemic conditions. When we say that a player knows some event E, or is rational, or has a certain conjecture ϕ^i or payoff function g_i, we mean that that is the case at some specific state s of the world. Some of these ideas are illustrated in Section 3.

We end this section with a lemma that is needed in the sequel.

Lemma 2.6. *Player i knows that he attributes probability π to an event E if and only if he indeed attributes probability π to E.*

Proof. *If*: Let F be the event that i attributes probability π to E; that is, $F := \{t \in S : p(E; t_i) = \pi\}$. Thus $s \in F$ if and only if $p(E; s_i) = \pi$. Therefore if $s \in F$, then all states u with $u_i = s_i$ are in F, and so $p(F; s_i) = 1$; that is, i knows F at s.

Only if: Suppose that i attributes probability $p \neq \pi$ to E. By the "if" part of the proof, he must know this, contrary to his knowing that he attributes probability π to E. Q.E.D.

3. An Illustration

Consider a belief system in which all types of each player i have the same payoff function g_i, namely that depicted in Figure 1. Thus the game being played is commonly known. Call the row and column players (Players 1 and 2) "Rowena" and "Colin" respectively. The theories are depicted in Figure 2; here C_1 denotes a type of Rowena whose action is C, whereas D_1 and D_2 denote two different types of Rowena whose actions are D. Similarly for Colin. Each square

	c	d
C	2, 2	0, 0
D	0, 0	1, 1

Figure 1

[17] Note for specialists: We do not use "mutual absolute continuity."

	c_1	d_1	d_2
C_1	1/2, 1/2	1/2, 1/2	0, 0
D_1	1/2, 1/2	0, 0	1/2, 1/2
D_2	0, 0	1/2, 1/2	1/2, 1/2

Figure 2

denotes a state, i.e., a pair of types. The two entries in each square denote the probabilities that the corresponding types of Rowena and Colin ascribe to that state. For example, Colin's type d_2 attributes $\frac{1}{2}-\frac{1}{2}$ probabilities to Rowena's type being D_1 or D_2. So at the state (D_2, d_2), he knows that Rowena will choose the action D. Similarly, Rowena knows at (D_2, d_2) that Colin will choose d. Since d and D are optimal against each other, both players are rational at (D_2, d_2) and (D, d) is a Nash equilibrium.

We have here a typical instance of the preliminary observation. At (D_2, d_2), there is mutual knowledge of the actions D and d, and both players are in fact rational. But the actions are not common knowledge. Though Colin knows that Rowena will play D, she doesn't know that he knows this; indeed, she attributes probability $\frac{1}{2}$ to his attributing probability $\frac{1}{2}$ to her playing C. Moreover, though both players are rational at (D_2, d_2), there isn't even mutual knowledge of rationality there. For example, Colin's type d_1 chooses d, with an expected payoff of $\frac{1}{2}$, rather than c, with an expected payoff of 1; thus this type is irrational. At (D_2, d_2), Rowena attributes probability $\frac{1}{2}$ to Colin being of this irrational type.

Note that the players have a common prior, which assigns probability 1/6 to each of the six boxes not containing 0's. This, however, is not relevant to the above discussion.

4. Formal Statements and Proofs of the Results

We now state and prove Theorems A and B formally. For more transparent formulations, see Section 1. We also supply, for the record, a precise, unambiguous formulation of the preliminary observation.

Preliminary Observation: *Let a be an n-tuple of actions. Suppose that at some state s, all players are rational, and it is mutually known that $\mathbf{a} = a$. Then a is a Nash equilibrium.*

Theorem A. *With $n = 2$ (two players), let g be a game, ϕ a pair of conjectures. Suppose that at some state, it is mutually known that $\mathbf{g} = g$, that the players are rational, and that $\boldsymbol{\phi} = \phi$. Then (ϕ^2, ϕ^1) is a Nash equilibrium of g.*

The proof of Theorem A uses two lemmas.

Lemma 4.1. *Let ϕ be an n-tuple of conjectures. Suppose that at some state s, it is mutually known that $\boldsymbol{\phi} = \phi$. Then $\boldsymbol{\phi}(s) = \phi$. (In words: if it is mutually known that the conjectures are ϕ, then they are indeed ϕ.)*

Proof. Follows from Lemma 2.6. Q.E.D.

Lemma 4.2. *Let g be a game, ϕ an n-tuple of conjectures. Suppose that at some state s, it is mutually known that $\mathbf{g} = g$, that the players are rational, and that $\boldsymbol{\phi} = \phi$. Let a_j be an action of a player j to which the conjecture ϕ^i of some other player i assigns positive probability. Then a_j maximizes g_j against*[18] *ϕ^j.*

Proof. By Lemma 4.1, the conjecture of i at s is ϕ^i. So i attributes positive probability at s to $[a_j]$. Also, i attributes probability 1 at s to each of the three events [j is rational], $[\phi^j]$, and $[g_j]$. When one of four events has positive probability, and the other three each have probability 1, then their intersection is nonempty. So there is a state t at which all four events obtain: j is rational, he chooses a_j, his conjecture is ϕ^j, and his payoff function is g_j. So a_j maximizes g_j against ϕ^j. Q.E.D.

Proof of Theorem A: By Lemma 4.2, every action a_1 with positive probability in ϕ^2 is optimal against ϕ^1 in g, and every action a_2 with

[18]That is, $\exp g_j(a_j, a^{-j}) \geq \exp g_j(b_j, a^{-j})$ for all b_j in A_j, when a^{-j} is distributed according to ϕ^j.

positive probability in ϕ^1 is optimal against ϕ^2 in g. This implies that (ϕ^2, ϕ^1) is a Nash equilibrium of g. Q.E.D.

Theorem B. *Let g be a game, ϕ an n-tuple of conjectures. Suppose that the players have a common prior, which assigns positive probability to it being mutually known that $\mathbf{g} = g$, mutually known that all players are rational, and commonly known that $\boldsymbol{\phi} = \phi$. Then for each j, all the conjectures ϕ^i of players i other than j induce the same conjecture σ_j about j, and $(\sigma_1, \ldots, \sigma_n)$ is a Nash equilibrium of g.*

The proof requires several more lemmas. Some of these are standard when "knowledge" means absolute certainty, but not quite as well known when it means probability 1 belief, as here.

Lemma 4.3. $K_i(E_1 \cap E_2 \cap \ldots) = K_iE_1 \cap K_iE_2 \cap \ldots$ *(a player knows each of several events if and only if he knows that they all obtain).*

Proof. At s, player i ascribes probability 1 to $E_1 \cap E_2 \cap \ldots$ if and only if he ascribes probability 1 to each of $E_1, E_2, \ldots$. Q.E.D.

Lemma 4.4. $CKE \subset K_iCKE$ *(if something is commonly known, then each player knows that it is commonly known).*

Proof. Since $K_iK^1F \supset K^1K^1F$ for all F, Lemma 4.3 yields $K_iCKE = K_i(K^1E \cap K^1K^1E \cap \ldots) = K_iK^1E \cap K_iK^1K^1E \cap \ldots \supset K^1K^1E \cap K^1K^1K^1E \cap \ldots \supset CKE$. Q.E.D.

Lemma 4.5. *Suppose P is a common prior, $K_iH \supset H$, and $p(E; s_i) = \pi$ for all $s \in H$. Then $P(E \cap H) = \pi P(H)$.*

Proof. Let H_i be the projection of H on S_i. From $K_iH \supset H$ it follows that $p(H; s_i) = 1$ or 0 according to whether s_i is or is not[19] in H_i. So when $s_i \in H_i$, then $p(E \cap H; s_i) = p(E; s_i) = \pi = \pi p(H; s_i)$; and when $s_i \notin H_i$, then $p(E \cap H; s_i) = 0 = \pi p(H; s_i)$. The lemma now follows from (2.5). Q.E.D.

[19]In particular, i always knows whether or not H obtains.

Lemma 4.6. *Let Q be a probability distribution on A with*[20] $Q(a) = Q(a_i)Q(a^{-i})$ *for all a in A and all i. Then* $Q(a) = Q(a_1)\ldots Q(a_n)$ *for all a.*

Proof. By induction. For $n = 1$ and 2 the result is immediate. Suppose it is true for $n-1$. From $Q(a) = Q(a_1)Q(a^{-1})$ we obtain, by summing over a_n, that $Q(a^{-n}) = Q(a_1)Q(a_2, \ldots, a_{n-1})$. Similarly $Q(a^{-n}) = Q(a_i)Q(a_1, \ldots, a_{i-1}, a_{i+1}, \ldots, a_{n-1})$ whenever $i < n$. So the induction hypothesis yields $Q(a^{-n}) = Q(a_1)Q(a_2)\cdots Q(a_{n-1})$. Hence $Q(a) = Q(a^{-n})Q(a_n) = Q(a_1)Q(a_2)\cdots Q(a_n)$. Q.E.D.

Proof of Theorem B: Set $F := CK[\phi]$, and let P be the common prior. By assumption, $P(F) > 0$. Set $Q(a) := P([a]|F)$. We show that for all a and i,

$$Q(a) = Q(a_i)Q(a^{-i}). \tag{4.7}$$

Set $H := [a_i] \cap F$. By Lemmas 4.3 and 4.4, $K_i H \supset H$, since i knows his own action. If $s \in H$, it is commonly, and so mutually, known at s that $\boldsymbol{\phi} = \phi$; so by Lemma 4.1, $\boldsymbol{\phi}(s) = \phi$; that is, $p([a^{-i}];\ s_i) = \phi^i(a^{-i})$. So Lemma 4.5 (with $E = [a^{-i}]$) yields $P([a] \cap F) = P([a^{-i}] \cap H) = \phi^i(a^{-i})P(H) = \phi^i(a^{-i})P([a_i] \cap F)$. Dividing by $P(F)$ yields $Q(a) = \phi^i(a^{-i})Q(a_i)$; then summing over a_i, we get

$$Q(a^{-i}) = \phi^i(a^{-i}). \tag{4.8}$$

Thus $Q(a) = Q(a^{-i})Q(a_i)$, which is (4.7).

For each j, define a probability distribution σ_j on A_j by $\sigma_j(a_j) := Q(a_j)$. Then (4.8) yields $\phi^i(a_j) = Q(a_j) = \sigma_j(a_j)$ for $j \neq i$. Thus for all i, the conjecture about j induced by ϕ^i is σ_j, which does not depend on i. Lemma 4.6, (4.7), and (4.8) then yield

$$\phi^i(a^{-i}) = \sigma_1(a_1)\cdots\sigma_{i-1}(a_{i-1})\sigma_{i+1}(a_{i+1})\cdots\sigma_n(a_n); \tag{4.9}$$

that is, the distribution ϕ^i is the product of the distributions σ_j with $j \neq i$.

---

[20] We denote $Q(a^{-i}) := Q(A_i \times \{a^{-i}\}), Q(a_i) := Q(A^{-i} \times \{a_i\})$, and so on.

Since common knowledge implies mutual knowledge, the hypothesis of the theorem implies that there is a state at which it is mutually known that $\mathbf{g} = g$, that the players are rational, and that $\boldsymbol{\phi} = \phi$. So by Lemma 4.2, each action a_j with $\phi^i(a_j) > 0$ for some $i \neq j$ maximizes g_j against ϕ^j. By (4.9), these a_j are precisely the ones that appear with positive probability in σ_j. Again using (4.9), we conclude that each action appearing with positive probability in σ_j maximizes g_j against the product of the distributions σ_k with $k \neq j$. This implies that $(\sigma_1, \ldots, \sigma_n)$ is a Nash equilibrium of g. Q.E.D.

5. Tightness of the Results

This section explores possible variations on Theorem B. For simplicity, let $n = 3$ (three players). Each player's "overall" conjecture is then a distribution on pairs of actions of the other two players; so the three conjectures form a triple of probability mixtures of action pairs. On the other hand, an equilibrium is a triple of mixed actions. Our discussion hinges on the relation between these two kinds of objects.

First, since our real concern is with mixtures of *actions* rather than of action *pairs*, could we not formulate conditions that deal directly with each player's "individual" conjectures — his conjectures about each of the other players — rather than with his overall conjecture? For example, one might hope that it would be sufficient to assume common knowledge of each player's individual conjectures.

Example 5.1 shows that this hope is vain, even when there is a common prior, and rationality and payoff functions are commonly known. Overall conjectures do play an essential role.

Nevertheless, *common* knowledge of the overall conjectures seems a rather strong assumption. Couldn't we get away with less — say, with mutual knowledge of the overall conjectures, or with mutual knowledge to a high order?[21]

[21]Set $K^2E := K^1K^1E$, $K^3E := K^1K^2E$, and so on. If $s \in K^mE$, call E *mutually known to order* m at s.

Again, the answer is no. Recall that people with a common prior but with different information may disagree on their posterior probabilities for some event E, even though these posteriors are mutually known to an arbitrarily high order (Geanakoplos and Polemarchakis (1982)). Using this, one may construct an example with arbitrarily high order mutual knowledge of the overall conjectures, common knowledge of rationality and payoff functions, and a common prior, where different players have different individual conjectures about some particular player j. Thus there isn't even a clear *candidate* for a Nash equilibrium.[22]

The question remains whether (sufficiently high order) mutual knowledge of the overall conjectures implies Nash equilibrium of the individual conjectures when the players do happen to agree on them. Do we then get Nash equilibrium? Again, the answer is no; this is shown in Example 5.2.

Finally, Example 5.3 shows that the common prior assumption is really needed: Rationality, payoff functions, and the overall conjectures are commonly known, and the individual conjectures agree; but there is no common prior, and the agreed-upon individual conjectures do *not* form a Nash equilibrium.

Summing up, one *must* consider the overall conjectures; and nothing less than common knowledge of these conjectures, together with a common prior, will do.

Also, one may construct examples showing that in Theorems A and B, mutual knowledge of rationality cannot be replaced by the simple fact of rationality, and that knowing one's own payoff function does not suffice — all payoff functions must be mutually known.

Except in Example 5.3, the belief systems in this section have common priors, and these are used to describe them. In all the examples, the game being played is (as in Section 3) fixed throughout the belief system, and so is commonly known. Each example has

[22]This is *not* what drives Example 5.1; since the individual conjectures are commonly known there, they must agree (Aumann (1976)).

three players, Rowena, Colin, and Matt, who choose the row, column, and matrix (west or east) respectively. As in Section 3, each type is denoted by the same letter as its action, and a subscript is added.

Example 5.1. Here the individual conjectures are commonly known and agreed upon, rationality is commonly known, and there is a common prior, and yet we don't get Nash equilibrium.[23] Consider the game of Figure 3, with theories induced by the common prior in Figure 4. At each state, Colin and Matt agree on the conjecture $\frac{1}{2}U + \frac{1}{2}D$ about Rowena, and this is commonly known. Similarly, it is commonly known that Rowena and Matt agree on the conjecture $\frac{1}{2}L + \frac{1}{2}R$ about Colin, and that Rowena and Colin agree on $\frac{1}{2}W + \frac{1}{2}E$ about Matt. All players are rational at all states, so rationality is common knowledge at all states. But $(\frac{1}{2}U + \frac{1}{2}D,\ \frac{1}{2}L + \frac{1}{2}R,\ \frac{1}{2}W + \frac{1}{2}E)$ is not a Nash equilibrium, because if these were independent mixed strategies, Rowena could gain by moving to D.

Note that the overall conjectures are not commonly (nor even mutually) known at any state. For example, at (U_1, L_1, W_1), Rowena's conjecture is $(\frac{1}{2}LW + \frac{1}{2}RE)$, but nobody else knows that that is her conjecture.

	L	R
U	1, 1, 1	0, 0, 0
D	1, 0, 0	1, 1, 1

W

	L	R
U	0, 0, 0	1, 1, 1
D	1, 1, 1	0, 0, 0

E

Figure 3

[23] Examples 2.5, 2.6, and 2.7 of Aumann (1974) display correlated equilibria that are not Nash, but they are quite different from Example 5.1. First, the context there is *global*, as opposed to the *local* context considered here (Section 7.9). Second, even if we do adapt those examples to the local context, we find that the individual conjectures are not even mutually known, to say nothing of being commonly known; and when there are more than two players (Examples 2.5 and 2.6), the individual conjectures are not agreed upon either.

	L_1	R_1
U_1	1/4	0
D_1	0	1/4

W_1

	L_1	R_1
U_1	0	1/4
D_1	1/4	0

E_1

Figure 4

	h	t
H	1, 0, 3	0, 1, 0
T	0, 1, 0	1, 0, 3

W

	h	t
H	1, 0, 2	0, 1, 2
T	0, 1, 2	1, 0, 2

E

Figure 5

Example 5.2. Here we have mutual knowledge of the overall conjectures, agreement of individual conjectures, common knowledge of rationality, and a common prior, and yet the individual conjectures do not form a Nash equilibrium. Consider the game of Figure 5. For Rowena and Colin, this is simply "matching pennies;" their payoffs are not affected by Matt's choice. So at a Nash equilibrium, they must play $\frac{1}{2}H+\frac{1}{2}T$ and $\frac{1}{2}h+\frac{1}{2}t$ respectively. Thus Matt's expected payoff is $\frac{3}{2}$ for W, and 2 for E; so he must play E. Hence $(\frac{1}{2}H+\frac{1}{2}T, \frac{1}{2}h+\frac{1}{2}t, E)$ is the unique Nash equilibrium of this game.

Consider now the theories induced by the common prior in Figure 6. Rowena and Colin know which of the three large boxes contains the true state, and in fact this is commonly known between the two of them. In each box, Rowena and Colin "play matching pennies optimally;" their conjectures about each other are $\frac{1}{2}H + \frac{1}{2}T$ and $\frac{1}{2}h + \frac{1}{2}t$. Since these conjectures obtain at each state, they are commonly known (among all three players); so it is also commonly known that Rowena and Colin are rational.

	h_1	t_1	h_2	t_2	h_3	t_3
H_1	$9x$ W_1	$9x$ E_1				
T_1	$9x$ E_1	$9x$ W_1				
H_2			$3x$ W_2	$3x$ W_1		
T_2			$3x$ W_1	$3x$ W_2		
H_3					x W_3	x W_2
T_3					x W_2	x W_3

$(x = 1/52)$

Figure 6

As for Matt, suppose first that he is of type W_1 or W_2. Each of these types intersects two adjacent boxes in Figure 6; it consists of the diagonal states in the left box and the off-diagonal ones in the right box. The diagonal states on the left have equal probability, as do the off-diagonal ones on the right; but on the left it is three times higher than on the right. So Matt assigns the diagonal states three times the probability of the off-diagonal states; i.e., his conjecture is $\frac{3}{8}Hh+\frac{3}{8}Tt+\frac{1}{8}Th+\frac{1}{8}Ht$. Therefore his expected payoff from choosing W is $\frac{3}{8}\cdot 3+\frac{3}{8}\cdot 3+\frac{1}{8}\cdot 0+\frac{1}{8}\cdot 0 = 2\frac{1}{4}$, whereas from E it is only 2 (as all his payoffs in the eastern matrix are 2). So W is indeed the optimal action of these types; so they are rational. It may be checked that also E_1 and W_3 are rational. Thus the rationality of all players is commonly known at all states.

Consider now the state $s := (H_2, h_2, W_2)$ (the top left state in the middle box). Rowena and Colin know at s that they are in the middle box, so they know that Matt's type is W_1 or W_2. We have just seen that these two types have the same conjecture, so it follows that Matt's conjecture is mutually known at s. Also Rowena's and Colin's conjectures are mutually known at s (Rowena's is $\frac{1}{2}hW + \frac{1}{2}tW$, Colin's is $\frac{1}{2}HW + \frac{1}{2}TW$).

Finally, the individual conjectures derived from Matt's overall conjecture $\frac{3}{8}Hh+\frac{3}{8}Tt+\frac{1}{8}Th+\frac{1}{8}Ht$ are $\frac{1}{2}H+\frac{1}{2}T$ for Rowena and $\frac{1}{2}h+\frac{1}{2}t$ for Colin. These are the same as Rowena's and Colin's conjectures about each other. Since Matt plays W throughout the middle box, both Rowena and Colin conjecture W for Colin there. Thus throughout the middle box, individual conjectures are agreed upon.

	h_1	t_1
H_1	1/2, 1/2, 3/8	1/2, 1/2, 1/8
T_1	1/2, 1/2, 1/8	1/2, 1/2, 3/8

W_1

Figure 7

To sum up: There is a common prior; at all states, the game is commonly known and all players are commonly known to be rational. At the top left state in the middle box, the overall conjectures of all players are mutually known, and the individual conjectures are agreed: $\sigma_R = \frac{1}{2}H + \frac{1}{2}T$, $\sigma_C = \frac{1}{2}h + \frac{1}{2}t$, $\sigma_M = W$. But $(\sigma_R, \sigma_C, \sigma_M)$ is not a Nash equilibrium.

One can construct similar examples in which the mutual knowledge of the conjectures is of arbitrarily high order, simply by using more boxes; the result follows as before.

Example 5.3. Here we show that one cannot dispense with common priors in Theorem B. Consider again the game of Figure 5, with the theories depicted in Figure 7 (presented in the style of Figure 2). At each state there is common knowledge of rationality, of the overall conjectures (which are the same as in the previous example), and of the game. As before, individual conjectures are in agreement. And as before, the individual conjectures $(\frac{1}{2}H + \frac{1}{2}T, \frac{1}{2}h + \frac{1}{2}t, W)$ do not constitute a Nash equilibrium.

6. General (Infinite) Belief Systems

For a general definition of a belief system, which allows it to be infinite,[24] we specify that the type spaces S_i be measurable spaces. As before, a *theory* is a probability measure on $S^{-i} = \mathsf{X}_{j \neq i} S_j$, which is

[24]Infinite belief systems are essential for a complete treatment: The belief system required to encode a given coherent hierarchy of beliefs (see footnote 15) is often uncountably infinite.

now endowed with the standard product structure.[25] The state space $S = \times_j S_j$, too, is endowed with the product structure. An *event* is now a measurable subset of S. The "action functions" $\mathbf{a}_i$ ((2.3)) are assumed measurable; so are the payoff functions $\mathbf{g}_i$ ((2.4)), as functions of s_i, for each action n-tuple a separately. Also the "theory functions" (2.2) are assumed measurable, in the sense that for each event E and player i, the probability $p(E; s_i)$ is measurable as a function of the type s_i. It follows that the conjectures ϕ^i are also measurable functions of s_i.

With these definitions, the statements of the results make sense, and the proofs remain correct, without any change.

7. Discussion

7.1. *Belief systems*

An interactive belief system is not a prescriptive model; it does not suggest actions to the players. Rather, it is a formal framework — a language — for *talking* about actions, payoffs, and beliefs. For example, it enables us to say whether a given player is behaving rationally at a given state, whether this is known to another player, and so on. But it does not prescribe or even suggest rationality; the players do whatever they do. Like the disk operating system of a personal computer, the belief system simply organizes things, so that we can coherently discuss what they do.

Though entirely apt, use of the term "state of the world" to include the actions of the players has perhaps caused confusion. In Savage (1954), the decision maker cannot affect the state; he can only react to it. While convenient in Savage's one-person context, this is not appropriate in the interactive, many-person world under study here. To describe the state of such a world, it is fitting to consider all the players simultaneously; and then since each player must take into account the actions of the others, the actions should be included in the description of the state. Also the plain, everyday meaning of

[25]The σ-field of measurable sets is the smallest σ-field containing all the "rectangles" $\times_{j \neq i} T_j$, where T_j is measurable in S_j.

the term "state of the world" includes one's actions: Our world is shaped by what we do.

It has been objected that since the players' actions are determined by the state, they have no freedom of choice. But this is a misunderstanding. Each player may do whatever he wants. It is simply that whatever he does do is part of the description of the state. If he wishes to do something else, he is heartily welcome to it; but then the state is different.

Though including one's own action in the state is not a new idea,[26] it may still leave some readers uncomfortable. Perhaps this discomfort stems from a notion that actions should be part of the solution, whereas including them in the state might suggest that they are part of the problem.

The "problem-solution" viewpoint is the older, classical approach of game theory. The viewpoint adopted here is different — it is *descriptive*. Not *why* the players do what they do, not what *should* they do; just what *do* they do, what *do* they believe. Are they rational, are they irrational, are their actions — or beliefs — in equilibrium? Not "why," not "should," just *what*. Not that i does a *because* he believes b; simply that he does a, and believes b.

The idea of belief systems is due to John Harsanyi (1967–68), who introduced the concept of *I-game* to enable a coherent formulation of games in which the players needn't know each other's payoff functions. I-games are just like belief systems, except that in I-games a player's type does not determine his action (only his payoff function).

As indicated above, belief systems are primarily a convenient framework to enable *us* — the analysts — to discuss the things we want to discuss: actions, payoffs, beliefs, rationality, equilibrium, and so on. As for the players themselves, it's not clear that they need concern themselves with the structure of the model. But if they, too, want to talk about the things that we want to talk about, that's OK; it's just as convenient a framework for them as it is for us. In this connection, we note that the belief system itself may always be considered common knowledge among the players. Formally, this

[26]See, e.g., Aumann (1987a).

follows from the work of Mertens and Zamir (1985); for an informal discussion, see Aumann (1987a, p. 9 ff.).

7.2. *Knowledge and belief*

In this paper, "know" means "ascribe probability 1 to." This is sometimes called "believe," while "know" is reserved for absolute certainty with no possibility at all for error. Since our conditions are sufficient, the results are stronger with probability 1 than with absolute certainty. If probability 1 knowledge of certain events implies that σ is a Nash equilibrium, then a fortiori, so does absolute certainty of those events.

7.3. *Knowledge of one's own type*

It is implicit in our set-up that each player i knows his own type s_i — that is, he knows his theory, his payoff function g_i, and his action a_i.

Knowledge of one's theory is not a substantive restriction; the theory consists of beliefs, and it is tautologous that one knows what one's beliefs are (a formal expression of this is Lemma 2.6).

Knowledge of one's payoff function is a more subtle matter. On the face of it, it would seem quite possible for a player's payoff to depend on circumstances known to others but not to himself. In our set-up, this could be expressed by saying that a player's payoff might depend on the types of other players as well as his own. To avoid this, one may interpret $g_i(a)$ as expressing the payoff that i *expects* when a is played, rather than what he actually gets. And since one always knows one's own expectation, one may as well construct the system so that knowledge of one's own payoff is tautological.

We come finally to knowledge of one's own action. If one thinks of actions as conscious choices, as we do here, this is very natural — one might almost say tautologous. That players are aware of — "know" — their own conscious choices is implicit in the word "conscious."

Of course, if explicit randomization is allowed, then the players need *not* be aware of their own pure actions. But even then, they *are* aware of the mixtures they choose; so *mutatis mutandis*, our analysis applies to the mixtures. See Section 1 for a brief discussion of this case; it is not our main concern here, where we think of i's mixed actions as representing the beliefs of other players about what i will do.

7.4. *Knowledge of conjectures*

Both our theorems assume some form of knowledge (mutual or common) of the players' *conjectures*. Though knowledge of what others will *do* is undoubtedly a strong assumption, one can imagine circumstances in which it would obtain. But can one know what others *think*? And if so, can this happen in contexts of economic interest?

In fact, it might happen in several ways. One has to do with players who are members of well-defined economic populations, like insurance companies and customers, or sellers and buyers in general. For example, someone is buying a car. She knows that the salesman has statistical information about customers' bargaining behavior, and she even knows what that statistical information is. So she knows the salesman's conjecture about her. The conjecture may even be commonly known by the two players. But it is more likely that though the customer knows the salesman's conjecture about her, she does not know that he knows that she knows, and indeed perhaps he doesn't; then the knowledge of the salesman's conjecture is only mutual.

No doubt, this story has its pros and cons; we don't want to make too much of it. It is meant only to show that a player may well know another's conjecture in situations of economic interest.

7.5. *Knowledge of equilibrium*

Our results state that a specified (mixed) strategy n-tuple σ is an equilibrium; they do not state that the players know it to be an equilibrium, or that this is commonly known. In Theorems A and B, though, it is in fact mutual knowledge to order 1 — but not necessarily to any higher order — that σ is a Nash equilibrium. In the preliminary observation, it need not even be mutual knowledge to order 1 that σ is a Nash equilibrium; but this does follow if, in addition to the stated assumptions, one assumes mutual knowledge of the payoff functions.

7.6. *Common knowledge of the model*

Binmore and Brandenburger (1990, p. 119) have written that "in game theory, it is typically understood that the structure of the game ... is common knowledge." In the same vein, Aumann (1987b, p. 473) has written that "the common knowledge assumption underlies all of game theory and much of economic theory. Whatever be the model under discussion, ... the model itself must be common knowledge; otherwise the model is insufficiently specified, and the analysis incoherent." This seemed sound when written, but in the light of recent developments — including the present work[27] — it no longer does. Admittedly, we do use a belief system, which is, in fact, commonly known. But the belief system is not a "model" in the sense of being exogenously given; it is merely a language for discussing the situation (see Section 7.1). There is nothing about the real world that must be commonly known among the players. When writing the above, we thought that some real exogenous framework must be commonly known; this no longer seems appropriate.

7.7. *Independent conjectures*

The proof of Theorem B implies that the individual conjectures of each player i about the other players j are independent. Alternatively, one could *assume* independence, as in the following:

Remark 7.1. Let σ be an n-tuple of mixed strategies. Suppose that at some state, it is mutually known that the players are rational, that the game g is being played, that the conjecture of each player i about each other player j is σ_j, and that it is independent of i's conjecture about all other players. Then σ is a Nash equilibrium in g.

[27]Specifically, that common knowledge of the payoff functions plays no role in our theorems.

Here we assume mutual rather than common knowledge of conjectures and do not assume a common prior. On the other hand, we assume outright that the individual conjectures are agreed upon, and that each player's conjectures about the others are independent. We consider this result of limited interest in the context of this paper; neither assumption has the epistemic flavor that we are seeking. Moreover, in the current subjectivist context, we find independence dubious as an assumption (though not necessarily as a conclusion). See Aumann (1987a, p. 16).

7.8. *Converses*

We have already mentioned (at the end of Section 1) that our conditions are not necessary, in the sense that it is quite possible to have a Nash equilibrium even when they are not fulfilled. Nevertheless, there is a sense in which the converses hold: Given a Nash equilibrium in a game g, one can construct a belief system in which the conditions are fulfilled. For the preliminary observation, this is immediate: Choose a belief system where each player i has just one type, whose action is i's component of the equilibrium and whose payoff function is g_i. For Theorems A and B, we may suppose that as in the traditional interpretation of mixed strategies, each player chooses an action by an independent conscious randomization according to his component σ_i of the given equilibrium σ. The types of each player correspond to the different possible outcomes of the randomization; each type chooses a different action. All types of player i have the same theory, namely, the product of the mixed strategies of the other $n-1$ players appearing in σ, and the same payoff function, namely g_i. It may then be verified that the conditions of Theorems A and B are met.

These "converses" show that the sufficient conditions for Nash equilibrium in our theorems are not too strong, in the sense that they do not imply more than Nash equilibrium; every Nash equilibrium is attainable with these conditions. Another sense in which they are not too strong — that the conditions cannot be dispensed with or even appreciably weakened — was discussed in Section 5.

7.9. *Related work*

This paper joins a growing epistemic literature in noncooperative game theory. For two-person games, Tan and Werlang (1988) show that if the players' payoff functions, conjectures, and rationality are all commonly known, then the conjectures constitute a Nash equilibrium.[28] Brandenburger and Dekel (1989) take this further. They ask, "when is Nash equilibrium equivalent to common knowledge of rationality? When do these two basic ideas, one from game theory and the other from decision theory, coincide?" The answer they provide is that in two-person games, a sufficient condition for this is that the payoff functions and conjectures be commonly known.[29] That is, *if* the payoff functions and the conjectures are commonly known, *then* rationality is commonly known if and only if the conjectures constitute a Nash equilibrium. The "only if" part of this is precisely the above result of Tan-Werlang.[30, 31]

---

[28]This is a restatement of their result in our formalism and terminology, which differ substantially from theirs. In particular, two players' "knowing each other" in the sense of Tan and Werlang implies that in our sense, their conjectures are common knowledge.

[29]For example, if there is an accepted convention as to how to act in a certain situation (like driving on the right), then that convention constitutes a Nash equilibrium if and only if it is commonly known that everyone is acting rationally.

[30]We may add that Armbruster and Boege (1979) also treat two-person games in this spirit.

[31]One may ask whether our theorems can be extended to equivalence results in the style of Brandenburger-Dekel. The answer is yes. For two-person games, it can be shown that if the payoff functions and the conjectures are mutually known, then rationality is mutually known if and only if the conjectures constitute a Nash equilibrium; this extends Theorem A. Theorem B may be extended in a similar fashion, as may the preliminary observation. The "only if" parts of these extensions coincide with the theorems established in the body of this paper.

The "if" parts of these extensions are interesting, but perhaps not as much as the "if" part of the Brandenburger-Dekel result: Mutual knowledge of rationality is weaker than common knowledge, and so it is less appealing as a conclusion. That is one reason that we have not made more of these extensions.

Our Theorem A improves on the Tan-Werlang result in that it assumes only mutual knowledge where they assume common knowledge.

Aumann (1987a) is also part of the epistemic literature, but the question it addresses is quite different from that of this paper. It asks about the distribution of action profiles over the entire state space when all players are assumed rational at all states of the world and there is a common prior. The answer is that it represents a correlated (not Nash!) equilibrium. Conceptually, that paper takes a *global* point of view; its result concerns the distribution of action profiles as a whole. Correlated equilibrium itself is an essentially global concept; it has no natural local formulation. In contrast, the viewpoint of the current paper is *local.* It concerns the information of the players, at some specific state of the world; and it asks whether the players' actions or conjectures *at that state* constitute a Nash equilibrium. Matters like knowledge that is mutual but not common, or players who are rational but may ascribe irrationality to one another, do not come under the purview of Aumann (1987a).

Brandenburger and Dekel (1987, Proposition 4.1) derive Nash equilibrium in n-person games from independence assumptions, as we do[32] in Proposition 7.1. As we have already noted (Section 7.7), such assumptions lack the epistemic flavor that interests us here.

In brief: The aim of this paper has been to identify sufficient epistemic conditions for Nash equilibrium that are as spare as possible; to isolate just what the players themselves must know in order for their conjectures about each other to constitute a Nash equilibrium. For two-person games, our Theorem A goes significantly

[32]Though their result (henceforth B&D4) differs from our Proposition 7.1 (hereforth P7) in several ways. First, B&D4 makes an assumption tantamount to common knowledge of conjectures, while P7 asks only for mutual knowledge. Second, P7 directly assumes agreement among the individual conjectures, which B&D4 does not. Finally, B&D4 requires "concordant" priors (a weaker form of common priors), while P7 does not.

beyond that done previously in the literature on this issue. For n-person games, little had been done before.

References

Armbruster, W. and W. Boege, 1979, "Bayesian Game Theory," in *Game Theory and Related Topics*, ed. by O. Moeschlin and D. Pallaschke. Amsterdam: North-Holland.

Arrow, K., 1986, "Rationality of Self and Others in an Economic System," *Journal of Business* 59, S385–S399.

Aumann, R., 1974, "Subjectivity and Correlation in Randomized Strategies," *Journal of Mathematical Economics* 1, 67–96. [Chapter 7]

—— 1976, "Agreeing to Disagree," *Annals of Statistics* 4, 1236–1239. [Chapter 2]

—— 1987a, "Correlated Equilibrium as an Expression of Bayesian Rationality," *Econometrica* 55, 1–18. [Chapter 8]

—— 1987b, "Game Theory," in *The New Palgrave:A Dictionary of Economics*, ed. by J. Eatwell, M. Milgate, and P. Newman. London: The MacMillan Press Ltd.

Binmore, K. 1990, *Essays on the Foundations of Game Theory.* Oxford: Basil Blackwell.

—— 1992, *Fun and Games.* Lexington: D.C. Heath and Company.

Binmore, K. and A. Brandenburger, 1990, "Common Knowledge and Game Theory," in *Essays on the Foundation of Game Theory*, ed. by K. Binmore. Oxford: Basil Blackwell, 105–150.

Binmore, K. and P. Dasgupta, 1986, "Game Theory: A Survey," in *Economic Organizations as Games*, ed. by K. Binmore and P. Dasgupta. Oxford: Basil Blackwell, 1–45.

Boege, W. and T. Eisele, 1979, "On Solutions of Bayesian Games," *International Journal of Game Theory* 8, 193–215.

Brandenburger, A. and E. Dekel, 1987, "Rationalizability and Correlated Equilibria," *Econometrica* 55, 1391–1402.

—— 1989, "The Role of Common Knowledge Assumptions in Game Theory," in *The Economics of Missing Markets, Information, and Games*, ed. by F. Hahn. Oxford: Oxford University Press, 46–61.

—— 1993, "Hierarchies of Beliefs and Common Knowledge," *Journal of Economic Theory* 59, 189–198.

Fudenberg, D. and D. Kreps, 1988, "A Theory of Learning, Experimentation, and Equilibrium in Games," unpublished, Graduate School of Business, Stanford University.

Fudenberg, D. and J. Tirole, 1989, "Noncooperative Game Theory for Industrial Organization: An Introduction and Overview," in *Handbook of Industrial Organization*, Vol. 1, ed. by R. Schmalensee and R. Willig. Amsterdam: North-Holland, 259–327.

Geanakoplos, J., D. Pearce, and E. Stacchetti, 1989, "Psychological Games and Sequential Rationality," *Games and Economic Behavior* 1, 60–79.

Geanakoplos, J. and H. Polemarchakis, 1982, "We Can't Disagree Forever," *Journal of Economic Theory* 28, 192–200.

Harsanyi, J., 1967–68, "Games with Incomplete Information Played by 'Bayesian' Players," Parts I–III, *Management Science* 8, 159–182, 320–334, 486–502.

——— 1973, "Games with Randomly Disturbed Payoffs: A New Rationale for Mixed Strategy Equilibrium Points," *International Journal of Game Theory* 2, 1–23.

Kreps, D. and R. Wilson, 1982, "Sequential Equilibria," *Econometrica* 50, 863–894.

Lewis, D., 1969, *Convention: A Philosophical Study*. Cambridge: Harvard University Press.

Mertens, J.-F. and S. Zamir, 1985, "Formulation of Bayesian Analysis for Games with Incomplete Information," *International Journal of Game Theory* 14, 1–29.

Milgrom, P. and J. Roberts, 1991, "Adaptive and Sophisticated Learning in Normal Form Games," *Games and Economic Behavior* 3, 82–100.

Nash, J., 1951, "Non-Cooperative Games," *Annals of Mathematics* 54, 286–295.

Reny, P., 1992, "Backward Induction, Normal Form Perfection and Explicable Equilibria," *Econometrica* 60, 627–649.

Rubinstein, A., 1991, "Comments on the Interpretation of Game Theory," *Econometrica* 59, 909–924.

Savage, L., 1954, *The Foundations of Statistics*. New York: Wiley.

Tan, T. and S. Werlang, 1988, "The Bayesian Foundations of Solution Concepts of Games," *Journal of Economic Theory* 45, 370–391.

Werlang, S., 1989, "Common Knowledge," in *The New Palgrave: Game Theory*, ed. by J. Eatwell, M. Milgate, and P. Newman. New York: W. W. Norton, 74–85.

Part 3

Interactive Epistemology and Backward Induction

Chapter 11

Backward Induction and Common Knowledge of Rationality*,†

1. Introduction

Backward induction, the oldest idea in game theory, has maintained its centrality to this day. Cornerstone of Zermelo's (1913) proof that chess has optimal pure strategies, it subsequently played a vital role in the development of perfect equilibrium (Selten, 1965, 1975). In turn, this led to the modern "refinement" literature, which seeks to identify particularly "significant" equilibria in a game.

*Reprinted from *Games and Economic Behavior* (1995), 8, 6–19, with permission from Elsevier.

†Research support under NSF grant SES-9209277 at the Economics Department, Stanford University, is gratefully acknowledged. Also gratefully acknowledged are numerous discussions with the participants of the following conferences, at which earlier versions of this paper were presented: the Nobel Symposium on Game Theory, Bjorkborn, June 1993; the First Summer Workshop on Game Theory, Valencia, June 1993; the Fourth International Conference on Game Theory, Stony Brook, July 1993; and the annual summer workshop of the Stanford Institute for Theoretical Economics, Stanford, August 1993. The individuals whose comments materially affected the current form of the paper are too numerous to mention here, but three who were especially helpful should be singled out. Long conversations with Dov Samet enabled the author to sort out many of the conceptual problems raised by the analysis herein; Phil Reny kept the author on his toes by shooting down countless previous attempts to get this thing right; and a long correspondence with Ken Binmore helped us to focus our presentation.

Quite apart from its relation to Zermelo's theorem and to refinements, backward induction has a compelling logic of its own, especially in perfect information (PI) games (like chess). The last player, who must choose between leaves of the game tree, makes a choice that maximizes his payoff; taking this as given, the previous player makes a choice maximizing *his* payoff; and so on, until the beginning of the game is reached. Nothing seems simpler or more natural.

Yet it is precisely this logic that has come under increasing recent scrutiny (e.g., Basu, 1990; Ben Porath, 1997; Bicchieri, 1989, 1992; Bicchieri and Antonelli, 1995; Binmore, 1987; Binmore and Brandenburger, 1990; Bonanno, 1991; Pettit and Sugden, 1989; Reny, 1992). Indeed, it is not obvious just what assumptions on the rationality of the players would justify it. Simple rationality on the part of each player — each player's being a utility maximizer — is certainly not enough; in some sense, the players must also ascribe rationality to each other. It has been suggested that one assume "common knowledge of rationality": that all players know that all are rational, all know this, all know *this,* and so on ad infinitum (or at least, for a number of levels no less than the maximum duration of the game). But as the works cited above show, in extensive games there are serious difficulties in formulating the relevant concepts (knowledge, rationality, etc.).

The aim of this paper is to present a coherent formulation and proof of the principle that "in PI games, common knowledge of rationality implies backward induction." Some of its features are as follows:

(i) Each player chooses a *strategy,* in the usual game theoretic sense of the term (Kuhn, 1953, say); that is, he decides what to do at each of his vertices v in the game tree, whether or not v is reached.

(ii) When deciding what to do at v, the player considers the situation *from that point on:* he acts *as if* v is reached. It is this feature that distinguishes the current analysis from a strategic form analysis.

(iii) *Rationality* of a player means that he is a habitual payoff maximizer: that no matter where he finds himself — at which vertex — he will not knowingly continue with a strategy that yields him less than he could have gotten with a different strategy.

(iv) The result is not empty; common knowledge of rationality is possible in every PI game.

(v) Knowledge means absolute certainty, not probability 1 belief. Probability plays no role in the model.[1] However, probability may easily be introduced, and then the results hold with the usual expected-utility-maximizing definition of rationality.

(vi) The *time* of the players' knowledge is the start of play, before any actions are taken.

The plan of the paper is as follows: Section 2 contains the formal statements of our results, Section 3, the proofs. The formalism is interpreted in Section 4. Finally, Section 5 is devoted to discussion.

2. The Results

Let a PI (perfect information) game (Kuhn, 1953) with n players be given. Assume that it is in "general position," i.e., that the payoffs to each player at different leaves of the game tree are different. Say that vertex w comes *after* vertex v (written $w > v$) if each play through w also goes through v.

To define the concept of inductive (short for backward inductive) choice, let v be a vertex of Player i, and suppose that the inductive choice is defined at all vertices w after v. Then the *inductive choice* b^v at v is defined as the action that maximizes i's payoff when all players make the inductive choices at all vertices after v. In particular, when there are no vertices after v — when the action at v directly determines the outcome — then the inductive choice is simply the action maximizing i's payoff. When the inductive choices

[1]Thus one does not need Savage's (1954) axioms or any similar axioms.

are made at all vertices, the resulting outcome is called the *inductive outcome.*

To formalize knowledge, we use the standard partition model. A *strategy* of Player i is a function s_i that assigns to each vertex v of i an action at that vertex. Denote the set of i's strategies by S_i. A *knowledge system* (for the given game) consists of

a set Ω (the *states of the world*, or simply *states*),

a function $\mathbf{s}$ from Ω to $\times_i S_i$,

and for each player i,

a partition $\mathscr{K}_i$ of Ω (i's *information partition*).

Intuitively, i can distinguish between two states if and only if they are in different atoms of $\mathscr{K}_i$, and $\mathbf{s}(\omega)$ represents the n-tuple of the players' strategies at the state ω. We assume that

$\mathbf{s}_i$ is measurable with respect to $\mathscr{K}_i$,

which means that $\mathbf{s}_i(\omega) = \mathbf{s}_i(\nu)$ whenever ω and ν are in the same element of $\mathscr{K}_i$. Intuitively, measurability of $\mathbf{s}_i$, says that i knows his own strategy.

An *event* is a set of states. If E is an event, K_iE denotes the union of those elements of the information partition $\mathscr{K}_i$ that are included in E; in words, K_iE is the event that i *knows* E. Set $KE := \cap_i K_iE$ and

$$CKE := KE \cap KKE \cap KKKE \cap \cdots .$$

In words, *CKE* is the event that E is *commonly known.*

Let s be an n-tuple of strategies, one for each player, and let v be a vertex of Player i. Define i's *conditional payoff* $h_i^v(s)$ *for* s *at* v as his payoff at the leaf to which the players are led if starting at v, they play[2] s. In a given state ω of the world, call i *rational at* v if there is no strategy that i knows would have yielded him a

[2]When v is not reached, i's conditional payoff is different from his actual payoff.

conditional payoff at v larger than that which in fact he gets.[3] Call *i rational* if he is rational at each of his vertices. Denote by R_i the event[4] "i is rational." The event "all players are rational," denoted R, is the intersection of all the R_i.

In each state ω, there is a unique outcome: that determined by $\mathbf{s}(\omega)$. Denote by I the event that this is the inductive outcome.

The first result states that if rationality is commonly known, the inductive outcome results. The formal statement is

Theorem A. $CKR \subset I$.

The second result is that common knowledge of rationality is indeed possible in every PI game; i.e., for every PI game there is a knowledge system with a state of the world at which it is commonly known that all players are rational. This distinguishes the present model from certain others, in which common knowledge of rationality is in many games unachievable. The formal statement is

Theorem B. *For every PI game, there is a knowledge system with* $\emptyset \neq CKR$.

3. Proofs

It is convenient to develop some notation, and recall some facts from the theory of knowledge, before coming to the proofs themselves.

If s is a strategy profile and v a vertex, denote by s^v the action that s prescribes at v; if a^v is another action at v, denote by $(s; a^v)$ the profile obtained from s by replacing s^v by a^v. If t_i is a strategy of i, denote by $(s; t_i)$ the profile obtained from s by replacing s_i by t_i. Thus if b is the strategy profile that assigns the inductive choice

[3] I.e., larger than i's conditional payoff at v for $\mathbf{s}(\omega)$. This is weaker than (i.e., implied by) expected utility maximization; if an agent is maximizing expected utility, surely he cannot have an option that he knows, with certainty, will yield a preferred outcome. Thus our result remains true if we substitute expected utility maximization for the above definition of rationality. See Section 4c.

[4] For a characterization of R_i in symbols, see (3) in Section 3.

to each vertex v, then for each vertex v of each player i,

$$h_i^v(b) \geq h_i^v(b; a^v) \quad \text{for all actions } a^v \text{at } v. \tag{1}$$

Functions defined on Ω (like $\mathbf{s}$ or $\mathbf{s}_i$), which appear in bold face, may be viewed like random variables in probability theory. An assertion about such a function corresponds to an event, which we denote by putting square brackets around the assertion. For example, $[\mathbf{s}_i = s_i]$ is the event that i chooses the strategy s_i (i.e., the set of all states ω for which $\mathbf{s}_i(\omega) = s_i$); and $[h_i^v(\mathbf{s}; t_i) > h_i^v(\mathbf{s})]$ is the event that i's conditional payoff would have been higher if he had chosen the strategy t_i rather than what he did choose. With this notation, the measurability requirement for $\mathbf{s}_i$ translates to

$$[\mathbf{s}_i = s_i] \subset K_i[\mathbf{s}_i = s_i] \quad \text{for all } s_i \in S_i \tag{2}$$

(if i chooses the strategy s_i, then he knows that he chooses it); the event "i is rational" is given by

$$R_i = \bigcap_{v \in V_i} \bigcap_{t_i \in S_i} (\sim K_i[h_i^v(\mathbf{s}; t_i) > h_i^v(\mathbf{s})]), \tag{3}$$

where $\sim$ denotes complementation (for each of his vertices v and strategies t_i, it is not the case that i knows that t_i would yield him a higher conditional payoff at v than the strategy he chooses); and the event "the inductive choice is made at v" is

$$I^v := [\mathbf{s}^v = b^v].$$

The proof uses seven lemmas; Lemmas 4 through 9 are standard in knowledge theory, and also easily proved directly.

Lemma 4. $CKE = K_i CKE$.

Lemma 5. *If* $E \subset F$, *then* $K_i E \subset K_i F$.

Lemma 6. $K_i E \cap K_i F = K_i(E \cap F)$.

Lemma 7. $CKE \cap E$.

Lemma 8. $K_i \sim K_i E = \sim K_i E$.

Lemma 9. $K_i E \subset E$.

Lemma 10. *$I^v \subset K_i I^v$ for each vertex v of Player i (if i chooses b^v at v, then he knows this).*

Proof. Let B_i^v denote the set of those strategies s_i of i for which $s_i^v = b^v$. Then by (2) and Lemma 5, $I^v = [\mathbf{s}_i^v = b^v] = \cup_{s_i \in B_i^v}[\mathbf{s}_i = s_i] \subset \cup_{s_i \in B_i^v} K_i[\mathbf{s}_i = s_i] \subset \cup_{s_i \in B_i^v} K_i[\mathbf{s}_i^v = b^v] \subset \cup_{s_i \in B_i^v} K_i I^v = K_i I^v$.

This completes the preliminaries, and brings us to the

Proof of Theorem A. It suffices to show that

$$CKR \subset I^v$$

for each vertex v. Proceeding inductively, assume

$$CKR \subset I^w$$

for all $w > v$. Let v be a vertex of Player i. By Lemmas 4 and 5, $CKR = K_i CKR \subset K_i I^w$ for all such w, so by Lemma 6,

$$CKR \subset \bigcap_{w>v} K_i I^w = K_i \bigcap_{w>v} [\mathbf{s}^w = b^w] = K_i[\mathbf{s}^{>v} = b^{>v}], \tag{11}$$

where $s^{>v}$ denotes the profile of actions prescribed by s at vertices after v. Using Lemma 7, and setting $t_i = b_i$ in (3), we get

$$CKR \subset R \subset R_i \subset {\sim}K_i[h_i^v(\mathbf{s}; b_i) > h_i^v(\mathbf{s})]. \tag{12}$$

Now since $h_i^v(s)$ depends only on s^v and $s^{>v}$, Lemma 6 yields

$$\begin{aligned} K_i[\mathbf{s}^{>v} = b^{>v}] &\cap K_i[h_i^v(\mathbf{s}; b_i) > h_i^v(\mathbf{s})] \\ &= K_i[\mathbf{s}^{>v} = b^{>v} \wedge h_i^v(\mathbf{s}; b_i) > h_i^v(\mathbf{s})] \\ &= K_i[\mathbf{s}^{>v} = b^{>v} \wedge h_i^v(b) > h_i^v(b; \mathbf{s}^v)] \\ &= K_i[\mathbf{s}^{>v} = b^{>v}] \cap K_i[h_i^v(b) > h_i^v(b; \mathbf{s}^v)], \end{aligned}$$

so by complementation w.r.t. $K_i[\mathbf{s}^{>v} = b^{>v}]$,

$$\begin{aligned} K_i[\mathbf{s}^{>v} = b^{>v}] &\cap {\sim}K_i[h_i^v(\mathbf{s}; b_i) > h_i^v(\mathbf{s})] \\ &= K_i[\mathbf{s}^{>v} = b^{>v}] \cap {\sim}K_i[h_i^v(b) > h_i^v(b; \mathbf{s}^v)] \\ &\subset {\sim}K_i[h_i^v(b) > h_i^v(b; \mathbf{s}^v)]. \end{aligned} \tag{13}$$

Finally, (11–13, 1, 2), and Lemmas 8–10 yield

$$\begin{aligned} CKR &\subset K_i[\mathbf{s}^v = b^{>v}] \cap {\sim}K_i[h_i^v(\mathbf{s}; b_i) > h_i^v(\mathbf{s})] \\ &\subset {\sim}K_i[h_i^v(b) > h_i^v(b; \mathbf{s}^v)] \\ &= {\sim}K_i[\mathbf{s}^v \neq b^v] = {\sim}K_i \sim I^v = {\sim}K_i \sim K_i I^v \\ &= \sim\sim K_i I^v = K_i I^v \subset I^v, \end{aligned}$$

as was to be proved.

Proof of Theorem B. Define a knowledge system by stipulating that Ω consists of a single state ω, in which each player makes his inductive choice at each of his vertices. Then $\omega \in CKR$.

4. Interpretation

4.1. *Strategies*

A player's strategy specifies what he does at each of his vertices, *if* reached. To clarify and fix the ideas, it may be useful to think of the players as attaching automata to their vertices before play starts. They program the automata to take a unique action at each vertex; if play reaches a vertex v, the attached automaton is triggered, and the programmed action is played. Each player knows how he programs his own automata; also, he may — but need not — know something about how the other players' automata are programmed, and about what they know about each other's knowledge. It is this knowledge that is represented by the knowledge system.

4.2. *Rationality*

Rationality of a player at a vertex v is defined in terms of what happens at vertices *after*[5] v; his payoff *if* v is reached. The idea is that when programming his automaton at v, the player does so as if

[5]This should not be misunderstood; see Section 5d.

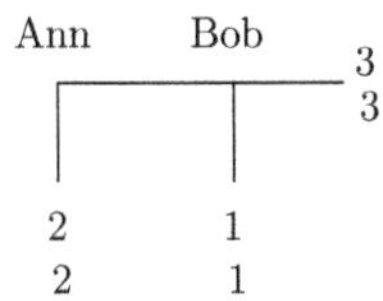

Game 1

v will be reached — even when he knows that it will not be! Each choice must be rational "in its own right" — a player may not rely on what happened previously to get him "off the hook."

This point is crucial. If we demand rationality only at vertices that are actually reached, the theorem fails already in the simplest cases. In Game 1, for example, if it is commonly known that both Ann and Bob go down, then it is commonly known that both are rational at reached vertices, since Bob's vertex is not reached. Nevertheless, the outcome is not that of backward induction, and indeed seems inconsistent with the plain meaning of the words "Ann is rational and knows that Bob is." The point is that to decide what to do, Ann must ask herself what Bob would do if she went across. The subjunctive mood — what he "would" do, even when not given the opportunity — is of the essence here.

Please see Sections 5b and 5c for further discussion of this point.

4.3. *Probability*

Though our model uses no probabilities, one can, if one wishes, introduce them. Thus for each state ω and player i, one may specify a probability distribution over i's information set,[6] signifying his probabilities over the state space Ω, given his information. In that case rationality in the traditional sense of utility maximization (i.e., that a player's action maximizes the expectation of his conditional payoff) implies rationality in the sense of Sections 2 and 3; so it follows from our theorem that common knowledge of rationality in

[6]The element of $\mathcal{K}_i$ containing ω.

the sense of utility maximization implies that the outcome is that of backward induction.

4.4. *Time*

Already in the introduction, we touched on the question of the time at which the knowledge obtains. When we say that a player knows something, it is appropriate to ask, when? To what time are we referring? Clearly, a player may learn something — e.g., about actions of other players — during the course of play, so it is important to specify the time of the knowledge.

The formalism, which does not refer explicitly to this matter, is subject to different interpretations. We adopt the most straightforward, that all knowledge refers to the start of play: For a player to "know" something means that he knows it before any actions are taken.

5. Discussion

5.1. *The literature*

Most of the recent literature on the subject of this paper (see Section 1) takes one of two positions (and sometimes both): that common knowledge of rationality (*CKR*) is impossible in most perfect information (PI) games; or, that it is possible, but need not lead to backward induction (BI). We do not take issue with this literature here. Whether or not *CKR* is possible and implies BI depends crucially on the precise model; the models in the cited literature are substantially different from ours, and our results do not formally contradict anything in this literature.

Nevertheless, there is a very clear, compelling intuition that *CKR* both implies BI and is possible. The model presented here is designed to capture this intuition. Moreover, we feel that it faithfully reflects the usual meanings of the key concepts: knowledge and rationality.

In another direction, a number of recent papers have been devoted to the program of formulating the fundamental notions of noncooperative game theory directly in terms of one person decision theory — i.e., in terms of the rationality of each player and what he knows about the game and about the other players. These include Aumann (1987), which treats correlated equilibrium in the strategic ("normal") form; Brandenburger and Dekel (1989) and Aumann and Brandenburger (1995), which treat Nash equilibrium in the strategic form; and others (e.g., Tan and Werlang, 1988). The current work extends this literature in two directions: First, it treats PI games — a particular class of extensive games — rather than the strategic form games treated in the previous literature; second, it treats backward induction, which is a refinement of Nash equilibrium. It remains to be seen whether our methods will shed light on the question of refinements in more general extensive games.

5.2. *Conditionals*

A crucial role in this paper is played by conditionals — statements of the form "if p, then q." In mathematics, this means simply "q or not p;" such conditionals are called *material.* But in everyday discourse, a conditional usually expresses a substantive relation between the antecedent p and the consequent q. We call such conditionals *substantive.*[7]

A *counterfactual* is a substantive conditional with a false antecedent. Thus a substantive conditional may be viewed as the disjunction of a material conditional and a counterfactual.

Consider, for example, the statement "If White pushes his pawn, Black's queen is trapped." For this to hold in the material sense, it is sufficient that White does not, in fact, push his pawn. For the substantive sense, we ignore White's actual move, and *imagine* that

[7]This term was coined by us. Philosophers have various names for different kinds of substantive conditional, but there is no consensus on a general term. Some use "strict," but apparently this is reserved for a special kind of nonmaterial conditional. Some use "subjunctive"; the subjunctive mood does indeed have the flavor we are trying to express (see Section 4b), but sounds like a grammatical technicality. In plain English, moreover, the subjunctive is widely used with a false antecedent only, which is not what we want here.

he pushes his pawn. If Black's queen is then trapped, the substantive conditional is true; if not, then not.

If White did not push his pawn, we may still say "If he *had* pushed his pawn, Black's Queen *would* have been trapped." This is a counterfactual. To determine whether it holds, we proceed as above: imagine that the pawn was pushed, and see whether the Queen was trapped.

Philosophers have long grappled with the task of assigning precise meaning to counterfactuals like "If Hitler had crossed the Channel after Dunkirk, he would have won the war." Such statements are indeed problematic, because the hypothesis is not completely specified. If Hitler had crossed the Channel, the world would have been different in a myriad of ways. To assign meaning to such a conditional, one must be more specific about the hypothetical world created by the crossing. That is a nontrivial task, even in principle, and there is no consensus among philosophers on how to approach it.

But there is no such problem with the chess example above; the conditional has a clear, precise, natural meaning. Similarly, the substantive conditionals we shall encounter below have unambiguous meanings.

Though they do not occur in pure mathematics, one really cannot discuss rationality, or indeed decision making, without substantive conditionals and counterfactuals. Making a decision means choosing among alternatives. Thus one *must* consider hypothetical situations — what would happen if one did something different from what one actually does. In Game 2 (actually a one-person decision problem), Bob's only rational choice is "across." That means that if he were to go down, he would get less — a counterfactual. In interactive decision making — games — you must consider what other people would do if you did something different from what you actually do.

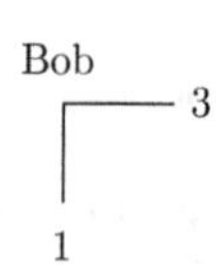

Game 2

5.3. *Rationality and substantive conditionals*

Substantive conditionals are not part of our formal[8] apparatus, but they are important in interpreting four key concepts that were formally defined in Section 2: strategy, conditional payoff, rationality at a vertex, and rationality. Briefly, the interpretations are as follows:

A player's strategy specifies what he does at each of his vertices, *if* reached. His conditional payoff (Section 2) at a vertex v signifies what he gets *if* v is reached. For him to be rational at v means that he cannot knowingly increase his payoff *if* v is reached. And for him to be rational means that for each of his vertices v, he cannot knowingly increase his payoff *if* v is reached. All these "if"s are substantive.

One may consider substituting a material "if" for the substantive "if" in the interpretation of rationality. Formally, this amounts to demanding rationality at reached vertices only (rather than at all vertices, as in the definition of rationality). Let us call this *material rationality;* it is clearly weaker — less demanding — than rationality as defined.[9] Game 1 (Section 4b) shows that common knowledge of material rationality does *not* imply backward induction.

It may be useful to think of (substantive) rationality as an attribute of *players,* and of material rationality as an attribute of *play.* A rational player is a habitual maximizer. Since he can be depended on always to choose rationally, one may say that if an unreached vertex v *were* reached, he *would* choose rationally there. On the other hand, "play" may reasonably be understood to refer to reached vertices only. For Ann to go down in Game 1 is, as we said above, inconsistent with the plain meaning of the words "Ann is rational and knows that Bob is." But it is not inconsistent with common knowledge of rational play; Bob does not get to play, so if Ann expects him to go down, all actual play is rational.

---

[8]A formal theory of substantive conditionals has recently been devised by Samet (1996).

[9]Which might also be called *substantive* rationality.

5.4. *Taking account of past play*

In Section 4b, we said that "rationality of a player i at a vertex v is defined in terms of what happens at vertices *after* v." What this means is that when evaluating his conditional payoff at v, the player must assume that v is reached, even when he knows that it is not; he cannot say "Since I know that v is not reached, whatever I do there is rational." It does *not* mean that i should ignore what happened before v in forming his opinions about what will happen afterwards. He can base his opinions as to what happens after v on whatever he wants; it's just that he cannot say "let's ignore v, it's irrelevant."

For example, consider Game 3, which is one of Rosenthal's (1982) "centipede" games. At each vertex, the inductive choice is to go down. If Bob finds himself at his first vertex, then it is clear to him that Ann did not make her inductive choice at her first vertex. It's quite possible, then, that he will consider it likely that she will not make her inductive choice at her second vertex either. In that case it is entirely rational for him to go "across" at his first vertex.

To be sure, *common knowledge* of rationality does imply that the strategies of both players call for them to go down at each vertex; that follows from our Theorem A. But rationality itself does not. Rationality permits the players to take account of past play in any way they want when forming estimates as to what will happen in the future. In fact, it places no restrictions at all on what they think others will do.

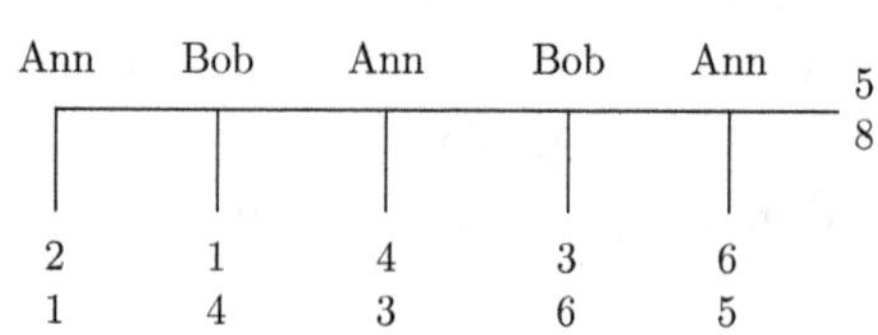

Game 3

5.5. *Ex post rationality*

As noted in Section 4d, it is best to think of knowledge in our model as obtaining at the start of play. Thus for a player to be rational at a vertex v means that he has no choice at v that he knows *already at the start of play* would yield him a conditional payoff larger than that which in fact he gets. To underscore this point, we shall in this subsection refer to what we have called "rationality" as "ex ante rationality."

There is another kind of rationality that might seem more relevant. Call a player "ex post rational" at v if he has no choice at v that he knows *at the time of his move* would yield him a conditional payoff larger than that which in fact he gets. One may ask whether our results remain valid when we substitute ex post for ex ante rationality.

The answer is "yes." When the time comes for a player to move, he certainly knows at least as much as he did when play started. So if he knew when play started that his choice is suboptimal — i.e., that a different choice would yield him a larger conditional payoff — then a fortiori he knows this at the time of his move. So if he does not know at the time of his move that his choice is suboptimal, then a fortiori he did not know this at the start of play. Thus ex post rationality implies ex ante rationality. Therefore common knowledge of ex post rationality implies common knowledge of ex ante rationality. By Theorem A, common knowledge of ex ante rationality implies backward induction (BI); so common knowledge of ex post rationality also implies BI. In the other direction, it may be seen as in the proof of Theorem B that common knowledge of ex post rationality is possible in every PI game.

In brief, ex ante rationality is weaker — less demanding — than ex post rationality, and so more desirable in a hypothesis.

The reader may ask why we do not formalize the definitions of ex post and ex ante and make formal theorems out of the verbal discussion here. The reason is that to do this, we would have had to assign several knowledge operators to each player, one for each of his vertices, and we wanted to keep the formal model as transparent and simple as possible.

5.6. *Off-path behavior*

The results of this paper say nothing about the behavior of players at vertices that are off the backward induction path and are actually reached. Under common knowledge of rationality (*CKR*), vertices off the backward induction path *cannot* be reached; and when *CKR* does not obtain, the results do not apply.

5.7. *Belief with probability 1*

Our approach views knowledge as absolute certainty. It does not work with probability 1 belief. Probabilistic approaches to backward induction present their own problems[10] — having to do mainly with off-path behavior — which are not easy to sort out. We have nothing to report on this matter here.

5.8. *Backward induction and rationality: A disclaimer*

We have shown that common knowledge of rationality (*CKR*) implies backward induction. Does that mean that in perfect information games, only the inductive choices are appropriate or wise? Would we always recommend the inductive choice?

Certainly not. *CKR* is an ideal[11] condition that is rarely met in practice; when it is not met, the inductive choice may be not only unreasonable and unwise, but quite simply irrational. In Rosenthal's (1982) centipede games, for example, even minute departures from

[10]One difficulty is that the reasoning in Section 5e breaks down; ex post rationality need not imply ex ante rationality. If you knew something at the beginning of play, then you certainly know it later; but if you ascribe probability 1 to it at the beginning of play, you need not do so at a later vertex, if that vertex initially had probability 0. One can try to fix this, but then something else unravels. Perhaps it can be done, but we have not succeeded.

[11]This is not a value judgment; "ideal" is meant as in "ideal gas."

CKR may make it incumbent on rational players to "stay in" until quite late in the game (Aumann, 1992); the resulting outcome is very far from that of backward induction. What we have shown is that *if* there is *CKR, then* one gets the backward induction outcome; we do not claim that *CKR* obtains or "should" obtain, and we make no recommendations.

References

Aumann, R. J., 1987, "Correlated Equilibrium as an Expression of Bayesian Rationality," *Econometrica* 55, 1–18 [Chapter 8].

Aumann, R. J., 1992, "Irrationality in Game Theory," in *Economic Analysis of Markets and Games*, Essays in Honor of Frank Hahn (P. Dasgupta, D. Gale, O. Hart, and E. Maskin, Eds.), 214–227. Cambridge: MIT Press [Chapter 14].

Aumann, R. J. and Brandenburger, A., 1995, "Epistemic Conditions for Nash Equilibrium," *Econometrica* 63, 1161–1180 [Chapter 10].

Basu, K., 1990, "On the Non-Existence of a Rationality Definition for Extensive Games," *Int. J. Game Theory* 19, 33–44.

Ben Porath, E., 1997, "Rationality, Nash Equilibrium, and Backward Induction in Perfect Information Games," *Rev. Econ. Studies* 64, 23–46.

Bicchieri, C., 1989, "Self-Refuting Theories of Strategic Interaction: A Paradox of Common Knowledge," *Erkenntniss* 30, 69–85.

Bicchieri, C., 1992, "Knowledge-Dependent Games: Backward Induction," in *Knowledge, Belief and Strategic Interaction* (C. Bicchieri and M. L. Dalla Chiara, Eds.), Cambridge: Cambridge Univ. Press.

Bicchieri, C. and Antonelli, G. A., 1995, "Game-Theoretic Axioms for Local Rationality and Bounded Knowledge," *J. Logic Lang. Info.* 4, 145–167.

Binmore, K., 1987, "Modelling Rational Players I," *Econ. Philos.* 3, 179–214.

Binmore, K. and Brandenburger, A., 1990, "Common Knowledge and Game Theory," in *Essays on the Foundations of Game Theory,* 105–150. Oxford: Basil Blackwell.

Bonanno, G., 1991, "The Logic of Rational Play in Games with Perfect Information," *Econ. Philos.* 7, 37–65.

Brandenburger, A. and Dekel, E., 1989, "The Role of Common Knowledge Assumptions in Game Theory," in *The Economics of Missing Markets, Information, and Games* (F. Hahn, Ed.), 46–61. Oxford: Oxford Univ. Press.

Kuhn, H. W., 1953, "Extensive Games and the Problem of Information," in *Contributions to the Theory of Games II* (H. W. Kuhn and A. W. Tucker, Eds.), Annals of Mathematics Studies, 28, 193–216, Princeton: Princeton Univ. Press.

Pettit, P. and Sugden, R., 1989, "The Backwards Induction Paradox," *J. Philos.* 4, 1–14.

Reny, P., 1992, "Rationality in Extensive Form Games," *J. Econ. Perspect.* 6, 103–118.

Rosenthal, R., 1982, "Games of Perfect Information, Predatory Pricing, and the Chain Store Paradox," *J. Econ. Theory* 25, 92–100.

Samet, D., 1996, "Hypothetical Knowledge and Games with Perfect Information," *Games Econ. Behav.* 17, 230–251.

Savage, L. J., 1954, *The Foundations of Statistics.* New York: John Wiley.

Selten, R., 1965, "Spieltheoretische Behandlung eines Oligopolmodells mit Nachfrage trägheit," *Z. Ges. Staatswiss.* 121, 301–324.

Selten, R., 1975, "Reexamination of the Perfectness Concept for Equilibrium Points in Extensive Games," *Int. J. Game Theory* 4, 25–55.

Tan, T. and Werlang, S., 1988, "The Bayesian Foundations of Solution Concepts of Games," *J. Econ. Theory* 45, 370–391.

Zermelo, E., 1913, "Üeber eine Anwendung der Mengenlehre auf die Theorie des Schachspiels," in *Proceedings of the Fifth International Congress of Mathematicians, Cambridge, 1912*, Vol. II, 501–504. Cambridge: Cambridge Univ. Press.

Chapter 12

The Logic of Backward Induction*,†,††

Dedicated to Moshe Arieli on the occasion of his 70th birthday

Abstract: Call a perfect information (PI) game *simple* if each player moves just once. Call a player *rational* if he never takes an action while believing, with probability 1, that a different action would yield him a higher payoff. Using syntactic logic, we show that an outcome of a simple PI game is consistent with common strong belief of rationality iff it is a backward induction outcome. The result also applies to general PI games in which a player's agents act independently, rendering forward inferences invalid.

JEL classification: C72; D83

*Co-authored with I. Arieli. Reprinted from *Journal of Economic Theory* (2015), 159, 443–464, with permission from Elsevier.

†The authors wish to express their deep gratitude to Adam Brandenburger; in the nineties of the last century, he was instrumental in formulating the underlying concepts, and he also contributed importantly to shaping the current presentation. We also thank Joe Halpern, who referred us to the work cited in Footnote 22. Finally, we are much indebted to the editor and the referees, whose comments brought about a very significant improvement of the paper. Needless to say, none of the above are responsible for errors, misstatements, or expressions of opinion herein.

††Aumann thanks the Israel Science Foundation (Grant number 1216/10) for research support.

1. Introduction

The backward induction (BI) algorithm for perfect information (PI) games is based on the following reasoning: The last player, who must choose between outcomes of the game, chooses an action that maximizes his payoff; taking this as given, the previous player maximizes *his* payoff; and so on, until the beginning of the game is reached.

Though on its face convincing enough, this reasoning has for the past quarter century been discussed, scrutinized, analyzed intensely, and even rejected. Our goal here is to clarify the assumptions on the players' knowledge and rationality on which it rests.

Two preliminary observations: First, the above reasoning, and indeed the BI algorithm, is unchanged if each player i is split into several independent "agents," one for each of i's decision nodes, each with the same payoff as i. So[1] we restrict attention to *simple* PI games — those in which each player moves at just one node. Call a player *rational* if he has no action that he believes (with probability 1) yields him a higher payoff than the action he took.

Second, for the reasoning to work, more than just rationality is needed; roughly, the players must also ascribe rationality to each other. More precisely, we may take the players' rationality (r) to be *common knowledge* (ck); i.e., all players know that all are rational, all know that all know it, all know *that*, and so on. This implies that players at preterminal nodes[2] choose rationally; knowing that, players at prepreterminal[3] nodes choose rationally — i.e., the BI action; and so on. Formally, that *ckr* entails BI follows from a theorem of Aumann (1995).

Aumann's work was criticized because *ckr* involves a conceptual conundrum. A player i on the BI path must either continue on the BI

[1]Please see Section 9.1 for an explanation of this point.

[2]Those all of whose sons are outcomes.

[3]Those all of whose sons are terminal or preterminal.

path or go off. If he goes off, the player j who is reached is unreachable under *ckr*; and j knows this, as commonly known propositions are a fortiori known by all players. Since j bases his choice on what he thinks subsequent players will do, and his "knowledge" has been contradicted, it is not clear what he (j) will do. But i must base *his* choice on what *he* thinks j will do, so it is not clear what i should do, either. Specifically, it is not clear that the BI action is indeed rational for i — that he could not do better by leaving the BI path.

To avoid grappling with this conundrum,[4] we replace "knowledge" by "strong belief", where a player *strongly believes* a proposition p if he believes it unless it is logically inconsistent with his node being reached. *Common* strong belief of p signifies that p holds, all players strongly believe p, all strongly believe the foregoing, all strongly believe the foregoing, and so on. We then have our

Main Theorem. *An outcome of a simple PI game is consistent with common strong belief of rationality* (*csbr*) *iff it is a BI outcome.*

With *csbr*, the conundrum disappears. As before, suppose a player i on the BI path considers going off, say to j. When *ckr* obtains, j knows that he cannot be reached, as he knows *ckr*; so if he *is* reached, then his knowledge is contradicted, and we get the conundrum. Also when *csbr* obtains, j cannot be reached, by our theorem. But j does *not know* that he cannot be reached, as he does not know[5] *csbr*. He knows only those components of *csbr* that pertain to his beliefs and actions if reached,[6] and these are consistent.[7] Also i has beliefs about the actions of other players, including j; our

[4]As have Binmore (1996) and Aumann (1996), inter alia.

[5]We (the analysts) know *csbr*; the players do not.

[6]Spelled out in Remark 2.1. We don't mean that j doesn't know anything else, but only that *csbr* does not call for him to know anything else.

[7]As *csbr* is consistent, which follows from our theorem.

theorem implies that with these beliefs, it is rational for him to stay on the BI path.

The theorem has both substantive and methodological interest. Substantively, it characterizes the BI outcome in simple PI games by *csbr*, which means that in general PI games, BI is characterized by common strong belief (*csb*) of the rationality of the *agents*. Previously, Battigalli and Siniscalchi (2002) (henceforth BS), who introduced the fundamental notion of strong belief, had characterized the BI outcome by *csb* of the rationality of the *players*. Ascribing rationality to *players* renders forward inferences relevant (Section 9.1.1). Thus what BS show is that reasoning with forward as well as backward inferences leads to the BI outcome; whereas we show that the BI outcome results when reasoning with backward inferences only (Section 9.1.2) — a task that, while not straightforward, is intrinsically simpler than BS's.

Methodologically, the theorem is formulated and proved in syntactic rather than semantic terms (Section 5). The notion of strong belief depends on that of logical impossibility. In the more widely used semantic methodology, formulating the notion of logical impossibility involves defining and constructing "complete" state spaces (Section 9.2). In the syntactic methodology, "logical impossibility" has its ordinary, everyday meaning.[8]

Several other features of our treatment are worth noting:

(1) **Belief:** Rather than expected payoff maximization, we use probability 1 belief only; easily formulated properties of this concept suffice, obviating the need for the logical apparatus required by numerical probabilities.
(2) **Genericity:** Much of the BI literature makes essential use of various genericity conditions (Section 10.3). Our treatment, too, is more transparent with genericity, but the result holds for all PI games, generic or not.
(3) **Strategies:** In simple PI games, *csbr* is always consistent not only with the BI outcome, but also with the BI *strategies*.

[8]That is, a "logically impossible" proposition is one that involves a logical contradiction.

There may also be other strategies with which it is consistent (Section 10.2).

The plan of the paper is as follows: Section 2 formulates the result, and Section 3 demonstrates it, carefully but still informally, assuming genericity; this may already satisfy some readers, who may skip any or all of the remainder. Section 4 removes the genericity condition. Sections 5–8 comprise the formal development: Section 5 discusses syntactic and semantic formalisms, the advantages of each, and the reasons for choosing the syntactic one here; Section 6 lays out the basic logical apparatus, which is used in Section 7 to formulate the result precisely, and in Section 8 to prove it rigorously. Section 9 is devoted to discussion: Section 9.1, of substance, and Section 9.2, of methodology. Finally, Section 10 reviews some of the literature, concentrating on BS. Appendix A proves a needed technical result outside the paper's mainstream.

2. Informal Formulation

A simple PI game is defined by a *rooted tree* T. Terminal nodes are called *outcomes*, nonterminal nodes — *players*. Each player h chooses (or *plays*) an *action* a_h — an edge at h that does not lead back to the root. At each outcome, each player has a *payoff*.

Parts of this and the next section[9] assume *genericity* — that each player has different payoffs at different outcomes; this renders the treatment significantly more transparent. In particular, BI then determines a unique outcome. The genericity assumption is removed in Section 4.

2.1. *Actions, beliefs, rationality, and csbr*

Assume that each player has beliefs concerning actions played, and beliefs held, by other players. Call an action a_h of player h *belief-dominated* if he has an action a'_h that he believes yields him a higher

[9]Specifically, Sections 2.2, 2.3, and 3.2.

payoff than a_h. Call it *rational* if it is not belief-dominated. Say that *csbr* obtains if

r: only rational actions are played,[10]
and
r^1: each player believes r, unless it precludes reaching him,
and
r^2: each player believes the foregoing, unless it[11] precludes reaching him,
and
...
and
r^n: each player believes the foregoing,[12] unless it precludes reaching him,
and so on ad infinitum.

In terms of the actions and beliefs of the individual players, we have

Remark 2.1. *csbr* obtains iff each player plays a rational action, and for each n, believes[13] $r \wedge r^1 \wedge \cdots \wedge r^n$ when it does not preclude reaching him.

2.2. *Backward induction (generic)*

Label the nodes of the game tree T as follows: Label each outcome z by z. Proceeding by (backward) induction, label each player h by that one of his sons' labels that yields him the most. Denote the root's label by $BI(T)$, and call it the *BI outcome.*

2.3. *The Main Theorem (generic)*

Say that a node v is *reachable under* an assertion f if reaching v is consistent with f.

[10]The play and beliefs of a player are those that apply if he is reached.
[11]The foregoing.
[12]*All* the foregoing; i.e., r and r^1 and r^2 and $\cdots$ and r^{n-1}.
[13]$\wedge$ means "and."

Generic Main Theorem. *An outcome of a generic simple PI game is reachable under csbr iff it is the BI outcome.*

3. Informal Demonstration

The demonstration has two parts. The first describes a process of successively "pruning" branches of the game tree, and shows that only the BI outcome survives that process. The second identifies *csbr* with the pruning process.

3.1. *The pruning process*

Say that action a'_h *(strictly) dominates* action a_h if a'_h yields a higher payoff to h, no matter what is done by subsequent players. The *pruning process* (*PP*) proceeds by eliminating each dominated action of each player, and the entire subsequent branch, and then iterating until no dominated actions remain.

3.2. *Pruning process → BI outcome (generic)*

Lemma 3.1. *Pruning a dominated action a_h does not change h's label.*

Proof.[14] Label each action by the label of the node to which it leads. The label of an action depends only on the labels of nodes after that action, so the labels of actions other than a_h do not change when a_h is pruned. Since a_h is dominated, h's label is one of those other labels, so it does not change.

Corollary 3.2. *Simultaneously pruning several dominated actions does not change the remaining players' labels.*

Theorem A. *Generically, BI(T) is the unique outcome of the fully pruned tree T_P.*

[14]The argument here is fully rigorous, so the word "proof' (rather than "demonstration") is in place.

Proof. Repeated use of Corollary 3.2 shows that $BI(T)$ is an outcome of T_P. If T_P had more outcomes, one could first eliminate players who have only one action, then prune some action of a preterminal player.

3.3. *Pruning process* $\leftrightarrow$ *csbr*

This part does *not* assume genericity; it is completely general.

Theorem B. *For all* n*, a node survives stage* $n+1$ *of the pruning process if and only if it is reachable under* $r \wedge r^1 \wedge \cdots \wedge r^n$.

Demonstration.[15] Formally, this is proved in Section 8. Informally, denote the result of stage n of the PP by T^n. Note first that r excludes precisely the dominated actions, no more and no less.

"No less" follows from a dominated action being a fortiori belief-dominated; "no more," from r allowing a player to believe that *all* players subsequent to his action could be reached. So T^1 comprises precisely what is reachable under r. This is case $n = 0$ of the theorem.

Next, we examine reachability under $r \wedge r^1$. As we have seen, r implies that only nodes in T^1 can be reached. So by r^1, all players in T^1 believe that only nodes in T^1 can be reached. Since by r, all players are also rational, it follows that actions in T^1 that are dominated in T^1 are excluded by $r \wedge r^1$. So $r \wedge r^1$ implies that only nodes in T^2 are reached. But under r, every node in T^1 is possible; so under r^1, each player h in T^1 may consider all subsequent nodes in T^1 possible. So $r \wedge r^1$ excludes *only* actions at nodes in T^1 that are dominated in T^1; so in T^1, that leaves precisely the nodes in T^2. The nodes outside of T^1 are already excluded by r, so T^2 is precisely what is reachable under $r \wedge r^1$. This is case $n = 1$ of the theorem.

---

[15]This is not an outline of the formal proof in Section 8, but a relatively brief argument showing informally "why" the theorem holds.

For general n, we proceed by induction. Assume that the result T^n of stage n of the PP comprises precisely what is reachable under $r \wedge r^1 \wedge \cdots \wedge r^{n-1}$; we examine what is reachable under $r \wedge r^1 \wedge \cdots \wedge r^n$. By r^n, every player believes $r \wedge r^1 \wedge \cdots \wedge r^{n-1}$, unless it precludes reaching him; by the induction hypothesis, this means that every player in T^n believes that only players in T^n — and all[16] such players — can be reached. So as with $n = 1$, but with T^n instead of T^1, we conclude that the result T^{n+1} of stage $n+1$ of the PP comprises precisely what is reachable under $r \wedge r^1 \wedge \cdots \wedge r^n$, as asserted.

Corollary 3.3. *An outcome survives the PP iff it is reachable under csbr.*

Demonstration. By Theorem B, an outcome is consistent with $r \wedge r^1 \wedge \cdots \wedge r^n$ iff it survives stage $n+1$ of the PP. So it is consistent with r and *all* the r^n — i.e., with *csbr* — iff it survives *all* stages of the PP.

Demonstration of the Generic Main Theorem. Combine Corollary 3.3 with Theorem A.

4. Dispensing with Genericity

Without the genericity restriction, the BI process — as specified above (Section 2.2) — does not apply, since a player may have several sons whose labels are best for him. We here generalize the definition of BI to the unrestricted case (Section 4.1), show that BI and the PP still have the same result (Section 4.2), and finally, state and demonstrate the unrestricted Main Theorem (Section 4.3).

4.1. *Backward induction*

As in the generic case, we use an inductive labeling process, but now each node h of the tree T is labeled with a *set* Z_h of outcomes.[17]

[16] Justifying the word "all" is the main burden of the rigorous proof (Section 8).
[17] The idea is that if h is reached, any outcome in Z_h may occur.

Among the outcomes in Z_h, denote the maximum and minimum payoffs to h's *father* by $\max h$ and $\min h$ respectively. Call a node h *inferior* if it has a brother h' with $\min h' > \max h$.

Start the process by labeling each outcome z by $\{z\}$. Then, inductively label each player by the union of the labels of his non-inferior sons. Denote the root's label by $BI(T)$, and call its members *BI outcomes*.[18]

The idea is that if all the sons of a player h are outcomes, then he chooses an action that maximizes his payoff; the resulting outcomes constitute the set Z_h. If h's father $\hat{h}$ chooses h, then $\hat{h}$ can count on h choosing *some* member of Z_h, but not *which* one. So if h is inferior — has a brother who is necessarily better for $\hat{h}$ than h — then $\hat{h}$ would certainly rather choose the brother, so his choosing h may be excluded. But $\hat{h}$ might well choose any non-inferior son; this defines the label $Z_{\hat{h}}$. The process continues similarly to $\hat{h}$'s ancestors, until the root is reached.

4.2. *Backward induction ↔ pruning process*

Theorem C. *$BI(T)$ is the set of outcomes of the fully pruned tree T_P.*

Proof. Let $O(T_P)$ be the set of outcomes of T_P. That $BI(T) \subset O(T_P)$ follows as in Theorem A. Suppose $BI(T) \underset{\neq}{\subset} O(T_P)$. Let T' be a minimal subtree of T with $BI(T') \underset{\neq}{\subset} O(T_P)$; i.e., $O(T''_P) = BI(T'')$ for any proper subtree T'' of T'. Let $z \in O(T'_P) \backslash BI(T')$, let h' be the root of T', let $a_{h'}$ be the action leading to z, and let h'' be the son of h' to which $a_{h'}$ leads. Since z is not in $BI(T')$, it is eliminated by the BI process at h'; so h'' is inferior. So letting T'' be the tree with root h'', we conclude from $O(T''_P) = BI(T'')$ that $a_{h'}$ is dominated in T'_P, which contradicts T'_P being fully pruned.

[18] In generic games, this process reduces to that of Section 2.2, except that there $BI(T)$ is the unique BI outcome, and here it is the singleton consisting of that outcome.

4.3. *The Main Theorem*

Main Theorem.[19] *An outcome of a PI game is reachable under csbr iff it is a BI outcome.*

Demonstration. Like that of the Generic Main Theorem, with Theorem C instead of Theorem A.

5. Syntax and Semantics

The Main Theorem belongs to an area of mathematical game theory called *interactive epistemology.* There are two parallel kinds of formalism in that area: the *semantic* and the *syntactic*. Semantic formalisms employ *state spaces*; each such space consists of a set of *states of the world* (or simply *states*), together with a structure representing the players' knowledge and beliefs (partitions, probability distributions, and the like). A particular state space represents a particular realization of epistemic principles, just as a particular group represents a particular realization of the axioms of group theory. To use the semantic formalism to prove a general assertion, one establishes the assertion at each state in an arbitrary state space.

Syntactic formalisms are different; they work directly with sentences, rather than with states. There is a formal language, and there are axioms, inference rules, and formal proofs using the axioms and rules. In many contexts (see Chellas, 1980, Chapter 1), a sentence "holds" at each state in an arbitrary state space iff in the corresponding syntactic formalism, it is a *tautology*,[20] by which we mean that it follows logically from the axioms and inference rules.

[19]This differs from the Generic Main Theorem (Section 2.3) only in that the word "generic" is removed, and "a BI outcome" replaces "the BI outcome."

[20]In formal logic, this is usually called a "theorem;" the word "tautology" is reserved for theorems of the propositional calculus. We prefer to reserve the term "theorem" for the more usual kind of theorem — the kind that appears in mathematical papers like this.

Each kind of formalism has advantages. The main advantages of semantic formalisms are practical: they are easier to fathom, and easier to work with. They are also more widely used, especially in the economic literature, and so are more familiar. The main advantage of a syntactic formalism is conceptual: basically it says in plain words what it is that one wants to prove, and then proves it, logically, from explicit assumptions. To prove something in a semantic formalism, one must first restate it in the language of sets, and then establish it in an arbitrary state space. As Professor Dov Samet has put it (private communication), if you want to explain it to your barber, say it syntactically; there's no way he'll understand the semantic formulation.

There is, however, one important respect in which semantic formalisms are superior — one kind of task they can perform, that most syntactic formalisms cannot. Namely, they can prove consistency. In most[21] syntactic formalisms, one cannot show directly from the axioms that a sentence is consistent — that its negation is not a tautology. For that, one needs a *model* of the sentence — a state in a semantic state space at which the sentence in question "holds." Indeed, throughout mathematics, consistency proofs have traditionally used models, starting with the Bolyai–Lobachevsky proof that Euclid's parallel postulate does not follow from his other axioms — i.e., that its negation is consistent with those axioms.

In particular, the proof of our main theorem — that *csbr* is consistent and entails a BI outcome — intertwines syntactic with semantic methods. But, whereas the *proof* uses semantics, the *formulation* is purely syntactic. Indeed, the consistency of an assertion is intrinsically a syntactic notion: it means that the negation of the assertion is not a tautology.

In the present context, there is an additional aspect of the syntactic formalism that bears mentioning. This concerns the fundamental notion of "strong belief," which calls for the notion of "tautology" to play an important formal role *within* the statement of the result. Of

[21]See the next footnote.

course this paper, like all others in mathematics, is about tautologies; all theorems are tautologies — what mathematics does is to establish tautologies. But usually, the notion of "tautology" is not part of the statement of the result; the result is stated without involving the notion of tautology, and then one simply asserts and proves the statement.

Here the situation is different. Assertions that some specific statements are or are not tautologies are elements in more complex assertions; these, in turn, are elements in still more complex assertions, and so on. Specifically, strong belief of a statement means that it is believed unless it is logically impossible; i.e., unless its negation is a *tautology. Common* strong belief iterates this assertion, indeed unboundedly often. Thus, in addition to the usual logical operators and connectives like "not," "or," and "and," we use an additional operator, t, which signifies that the sentence following it is a tautology; and whereas this operator is familiar in the metalanguage of logic, it is unusual[22] that it becomes part of the object language — the formal syntax — from which new assertions can be formed.

With additional machinery, the tautology operator can be treated also within the semantic formalism, as we shall see in Section 9.2 below.

6. Framework

6.1. *Syntax*

Given a finite PI game, we construct a formal language. The building blocks are as follows:

- *Atomic sentences.* These have the form "player h chooses action a_h," denoted simply a_h.

[22]Halpern and Lakemeyer (2001) have published a model of this kind; they use an operator called *Val*, which is t in our language. With this operator and a few more axioms, they construct a formalism in which consistency can be proved syntactically.

- *Left parentheses* and *right parentheses.*
- *Connectives and operators of the propositional calculus.* As is known, it is sufficient to take "or" ($\vee$) and "not" ($\neg$) as primitives, and in terms of them to define "and" ($\wedge$) and "implies" ($\rightarrow$).
- *Belief modalities.* For each player h, there is a belief modality b_h. Informally, if g is a sentence (see below), then $b_h(g)$ means that if reached, h ascribes probability 1 to g. Verbally, we say "h believes g."
- A *tautology modality,* denoted t. Informally, if f is a sentence, $t(f)$ signifies that f is a tautology.

Define a *sentence*[23] as a finite string obtained by applying the following two rules, in some order, finitely often:

- Every atomic sentence is a sentence.
- If f and g are sentences, so are $(f) \vee (g), \neg(f), t(f)$, and $b_h(f)$, for every player h.

Henceforth, we may omit parentheses when the intended meaning is clear.

The set of all sentences for the game under consideration is called the *syntax* of that game, denoted χ'. Call a sentence f in χ' *basic* if it does not involve the modality t. The set of all basic sentences is called the *basic syntax*, denoted χ.

If h is a player and g a node, then $g \succ h$ (or $h \prec g$) means that g follows h in the game tree. The sentence "h is reached" is denoted simply h; i.e., $h := \bigwedge_g a_g^h$, where the conjunction is over all players g that precede h, and a_g^h is the action at g that leads to h. The set of all actions of h is denoted A_h, and the set of all players H.

[23] A.k.a. "formula" in the logic literature. The term "sentence," which, too, is used in the logic literature, seems conceptually more apt and indicative of this object's role.

6.2. *Basic logic*

We now present the axioms and inference rules that govern the internal logic of our language. The axioms are as follows:

(1) The axioms of the propositional calculus.
And, for all sentences f and g, and all players h,
(2) $\bigvee a_h$, the disjunction being over all actions a_h at h.
(3) $\neg(a_h \wedge a'_h)$, where a_h and a'_h are different actions at h.
(4) $b_h(f \to g) \to (b_h f \to b_h g)$.
(5) $b_h f \to \neg b_h \neg f$.
(6) $\neg b_h f \to b_h \neg b_h f$.
(7) $a_h \leftrightarrow b_h a_h$ for all actions a_h at h.
(8) $b_h h$.

Axioms (2) and (3) say that each player chooses exactly one action. (4) and (5) represent classical modal belief axioms (see, e.g., Chellas, 1980), with clear conceptual content. (6) is "negative introspection:" that if you do not believe something, then you believe that you do not believe it; it is known to entail "positive introspection," that if you believe something, then you believe that you believe it. (7) and (8) say that h believes that he chooses the action that he indeed chooses, and that he is reached.

A *list* $\mathfrak{L}$ is a set of sentences in χ'. It is *logically closed* if it satisfies *modus ponens*:

(9) $f \in \mathfrak{L}$ and $f \to g \in \mathfrak{L}$ implies $g \in \mathfrak{L}$;

epistemically closed if it satisfies *generalization*:

(10) $f \in \mathfrak{L}$ implies $b_h f \in \mathfrak{L}$ for all players h;

tautologically closed if

(11) $f \in \mathfrak{L}$ implies $tf \in \mathfrak{L}$;

closed if it satisfies (9) and (10); and *strongly closed* if it satisfies (9), (10) and (11). The (*strong*) *closure* of $\mathfrak{L}$ is the smallest (strongly) closed list that includes $\mathfrak{L}$. Conditions (9–11) are often called *inference rules.*

A sentence f is called a *basic tautology* if it is in the closure of the list of all basic sentences having one of the forms (1–8). The set of all basic tautologies is denoted $\mathfrak{B}$.

6.3. *The logic of tautologies*

In ordinary usage, a "tautology" is a statement that is necessarily true — simply by the laws of logic and grammar — and does not make a substantive assertion about the real world. A tautology in the syntax χ — i.e., a basic tautology — is a basic sentence that follows from the axioms: i.e., holds no matter what the players actually do and believe. Similarly in the full syntax χ', tautologies should hold no matter what the players actually do and believe. Formally, we define a *tautology* as a sentence in the strong closure of the following list:

(1) Axioms[24] (6.2.1)–(6.2.8);
(2) $\neg tf$, when f is a basic sentence that is not a basic tautology;
(3) $t(f \to g) \to (tf \to tg)$, for all sentences f and g.

Denote the set of all tautologies by $\mathfrak{T}$. Write $\vdash f$ if $f \in \mathfrak{T}$. Call a list $\mathfrak{L}$ *coherent* if there is no f for which both f and $\neg f$ are in $\mathfrak{L}$.

Theorem D.

(4) *$\mathfrak{T}$ is coherent,*
(5) *a basic sentence is a tautology iff it is a basic tautology; and*
(6) *for every sentence f there is a basic sentence f' with* $\vdash f \leftrightarrow f'$;

Proof. See Appendix A.

There is an important conceptual difference between tautologies, as just defined, and basic tautologies, defined in Section 6.2. A basic

[24](6.2.1) stands for Axiom 1 in Section 6.2. A similar convention is used throughout, also for numbered formulas, definitions and assertions.

tautology f is *provable* from the axioms: it is possible to write a finite string of sentences ending with f, in which each sentence is either an axiom or follows from the previous sentences using the rules of modus ponens (9) and generalization (10). In contrast, a tautology as just defined need not be provable in this sense. The reason lies in (2) above, which says that if a basic sentence f is not a tautology, then it is a tautology that it is not a tautology. But proving $\neg tf$ would seem to require examining all the basic tautologies to see that f is not among them; and that is not a finite process. So while our concept of tautology is perfectly well-defined, it is not equivalent to provability.

We end this section by setting forth some terminology. A sentence f is *inconsistent* if its negation is a tautology; otherwise it is *consistent.* It *entails* g if $f \to g$ is a tautology. It is *consistent with* g if $f \wedge g$ is consistent. The sentences $f_1, f_2, \dots$ are *inconsistent* if the conjunction of some finite subset of them is inconsistent; otherwise they are *consistent.* They *entail* g if the conjunction of some finite subset of them entails g.

6.4. *Semantics*

The notion of strong belief, which plays a central role in our theorem, depends crucially on that of consistency. Proving consistency of a sentence f — i.e., proving $\neg t(\neg f)$ — is a tricky matter. As noted above, it would seem to require writing down all tautologies and checking that $\neg f$ is not among them — which seems impossible. To cope with this difficulty, we construct a semantic formalism for our syntax.

For each player h, denote by $\mathbf{A}_{\not\leq h}$ the set of profiles of actions of players other than h and not preceding him. Define a *simple model*[25] of the syntax χ as a mapping $\mathbf{C}$ that assigns to each action a_h of each player h, a non-empty subset $\mathbf{C}(a_h)$ of $\mathbf{A}_{\not\leq h}$.

[25]We use the term "simple model" because in the literature, the term "model" has a wider meaning, of which our simple models constitute instances. See Footnote 27.

Conceptually, a profile $\mathbf{a} := (a_h)_{h \in H}$ of actions constitutes a *state of the world*; the set $\mathbf{A} := \mathsf{X}_{h \in H} A_h$ of all such profiles is the *state space,* and subsets of $\mathbf{A}$ are *events.* A player h playing an action a_h has beliefs about the possible states. In each state $\mathbf{b}$ that he considers possible, the action b_h must be a_h, since he knows what he plays; moreover, the action b_g of each player g preceding h must be the action a_g^h leading to h. There are no other a priori restrictions on h's beliefs; so we may describe them as a subset $\mathbf{C}(a_h) \times \mathbf{D}(a_h)$ of $\mathbf{A}$, where $\mathbf{D}(a_h) := \{a_h\} \times \mathsf{X}_{g:g \prec h}\{a_g^h\}$, and $\mathbf{C}(a_h)$ is a non-empty subset[26] of $\mathbf{A}_{\not\preceq h}$.

Example 6.1. $\mathbf{C}(a_h) := \mathsf{X}_{g:g \not\preceq h} A_g$. Here each player believes only that he has been reached; for players off the path to him, he considers any action possible.

Given a model $\mathbf{C}$ and a sentence f, denote by $\|f\|$ the *realization* of f in the model $\mathbf{C}$, i.e., the event that f *holds.* Formally, when f is basic, define $\|f\|$ inductively by:

(1) $\| a_h \| := \{\mathbf{b} \in \mathbf{A} : b_h = a_h\}$,
(2) $\| \neg f \| := \mathbf{A} \backslash \| f \|$,
(3) $\| f \vee g \| := \| f \| \cup \| g \|$, and
(4) $\| b_h(f) \| := \{\mathbf{a} \in \mathbf{A} : \mathbf{C}(a_h) \times \mathbf{D}(a_h) \subset \| f \|\}$;

it follows from Lemma 6.2 below that

(5) $\| f \| = \| g \|$ *whenever* $f \leftrightarrow g$ *is a basic tautology.*

When f is not basic, define

(6) $\| f \| := \| f' \|$, where f' is a basic sentence with $\vdash f \leftrightarrow f'$

(see (6.3.6)); by (5) and (6.3.5), $\| f \|$ does not depend on the choice of f'.

[26]Though h believes that only nodes following a_h are possible, we must nevertheless consider beliefs regarding actions at nodes that follow other actions, in order to assess the rationality of choosing a_h. As for actions at nodes that do not follow h, these really play no substantive role; they are there for notational convenience only.

Lemma 6.2. *Every basic tautology holds in every state of every simple model.*

Proof. It suffices to show that each of the axioms (6.2.1–8) holds in every state of every simple model, and that the list of sentences holding in a given state of a given simple model is closed. These checks are standard.

Corollary 6.3. *Every sentence that holds in some state of some simple model is consistent.*[27]

7. The Main Theorem: Formal Formulation

7.1. *Rationality*

Call an action of a player *rational* if he has no action that he believes would yield him a higher payoff. In symbols, if a_h and a'_h are actions, denote by $p(a'_h, a_h)$ the statement that it is better[28] for h to play a'_h than a_h. Define

(1) $r(a_h) := \bigwedge_{a'_h \in A_h} \neg b_h p(a'_h, a_h)$;

$r(a_h)$ says that the action a_h is rational. Next, define

(2) $r_h := \bigwedge_{a_h \in A_h} (a_h \to r(a_h))$;

r_h says that h is *rational* — that he plays only rational actions. Finally, define

(3) $r := \bigwedge_{h \in H} r_h$;

r says that action rationality obtains — i.e., that all players are rational.

[27]In the language of formal logic, Corollary 6.3 says that the class of simple models is *sound.* We do *not* assert that it is *complete,* which is the converse of soundness — that every consistent sentence holds in some state of some simple model. Indeed, we don't need completeness, as what interests us is proving consistency. So to keep our formalism as simple as possible, we use a restricted class of models (see Footnote 25).

[28]I.e., better for h, given the actions of players after h.

On its face, it is not clear that $p(a'_h, a_h)$ is a sentence in the syntax. To see that it is, let $\mathbf{a}_{\succ h}$ be a profile of actions of players after h, and $\mathbf{a}^{\wedge}_{\succ h}$ their conjunction. Together with an action a'_h, the profile $\mathbf{a}_{\succ h}$ determines an outcome $z(\mathbf{a}_{\succ h}, a'_h)$, and so a payoff $u_h(z(\mathbf{a}_{\succ h}, a'_h))$ to h. Then $p(a'_h, a_h)$ is the disjunction of all those conjunctions $\mathbf{a}^{\wedge}_{\succ h}$ for which $u_h(z(\mathbf{a}_{\succ h}, a'_h)) > u_h(z(\mathbf{a}_{\succ h}, a_h))$; so it is indeed in the syntax, so r_h and r are also in the syntax.

7.2. *Common strong belief and the Main Theorem*

Say that a sentence g is *strongly believed* (written sbg) if each player h believes g whenever g is consistent with h being reached; i.e.,

(1) $sbg := \bigwedge_{h \in H}[b_h g \vee t \neg(h \wedge g)]$.

Mutual strong belief of g of order $n \geq 0$ (written $sb^n g$) is defined inductively by

(2) $sb^n g := g^0 \wedge g^1 \wedge \cdots \wedge g^n$,

where $g^0 := g$ and[29] $g^{m+1} = sb(g^0 \wedge g^1 \wedge \cdots \wedge g^m)$ for all m. So, for $n \geq 1$,

(3) $sb^n g = sb^{n-1} g \wedge sb(sb^{n-1} g)$;

thus each iteration provides for the previous iteration and strong belief thereof. *Common strong belief* of g (written[30] $csbg$) comprises all[31] $sb^n g$ for all n.

The Main Theorem is stated in Section 1, and restated in Section 4.2.

---

[29] So $sb^n g = sb^{n-1} g \wedge sb(g \wedge sb^{n-1} g)$ for $n > 1$, which in turn yields, by induction, that all $sb^n g$ are consistent with all h. For $n = 1$, if g is consistent with h, then so is $b_h g$.

[30] $csbg$ is not a sentence, but an infinite conjunction of sentences.

[31] Note that $csbg$ asserts, inter alia, that g itself is actually true.

8. The Main Theorem: Formal Proof

One part of the demonstration of the Main Theorem — that the Pruning Process (PP) yields the BI outcomes (Theorem C) — is rigorous. But the other, which identifies stages of the PP with iterated strong belief of rationality (Theorem B), while sounding convincing, is not entirely rigorous. We now complete the proof of the Main Theorem by proving Theorem B rigorously.

Let T be the tree of an unrestricted[32] PI game, T^n the subtree[33] that survives stage n of the PP. By (7.2.2), $r \wedge r^1 \wedge \cdots \wedge r^n = sb^n r$; thus Theorem B asserts that a node h is in T^{n+1} iff it is reachable under $sb^n r$ — i.e., iff the sentence $h \wedge sb^n r$ is consistent. Consistency proofs use semantic models (Section 6.4). So, we define a simple model $\mathbf{C}$ of the syntax $\mathcal{X}$; in it, a player h playing an action a_h believes in the maximum degree of iterated elimination of dominated actions (of all players) that allows h and for which a_h is rational. We will show that in this model, the nodes that may be reached when $sb^n r$ holds are precisely those in T^{n+1}.

Let T' be a subtree of T; think of it as comprising actions as well as nodes. Say that an action a_h in T' is *dominated in* T' if there is an action a'_h in T' that is better for h than a_h no matter what is done subsequently, as long as all subsequent actions are in T'. For each positive integer n and player h, let m be the largest integer $\leq n-1$ with $h \in T^m$, and let A_h^n be the set of all actions of player h in T^m that are undominated in T^m. Then define

$$\mathbf{A}^n := \mathop{\times}_{h \in H} A_h^n;$$

note that the $\mathbf{A}^n$ are nested. For each undominated action a_h, let $n(a_h)$ be the greatest[34] m for which a_h is in T^m and is undominated

[32]Not necessarily generic.

[33]A *subtree* T' of a tree T is obtained from T by eliminating one or more branches. Thus T and T' have the same root.

[34]There always is a greatest such m, since there are only finitely many T^n, as the PP is a finite process.

in T^m. Define a simple model **C** by

$$\mathbf{C}(a_h) := \bigtimes_{g \not\preceq h} A_g^{n(a_h)}.$$

Given an action a_h and a profile $\mathbf{a}_{\succ h}$ of actions after h, say that h, *when playing* a_h, *believes in* **C** *that* $\mathbf{a}_{\succ h}$ *is possible*, if $\mathbf{a}_{\succ h}$ is the restriction to the players after h of a profile $\mathbf{a}_{\not\preceq h}$ in $\mathbf{C}(a_h)$.

Call a_h *belief-dominated in* **C** if h has an action a'_h that yields him a better payoff[35] than a_h, for all $\mathbf{a}_{\succ h}$ that he believes in **C** are possible when playing a_h. Denote by $\|f\|$ the realization of f in the model **C**. It may be verified that

Remark 8.1. A state **a** in the model **C** is in $\|r\|$ iff no action a_h is belief-dominated in **C**.

Lemma 8.2. *No action is belief-dominated in* **C***, unless it is dominated in* T.

Proof. For brevity and clarity, in this proof the term "belief" will mean "belief in **C**."

Let a_h be undominated in T. Thus the first line in the definition of $n(a_h)$ applies; so setting $n := n(a_h)$, we have (i) a_h is in T^n and is undominated in T^n, and (ii) $\mathbf{C}(a_h) := \bigtimes_{g \not\preceq h} A_g^n$. So if h plays a_h, he believes that players g after h play actions in A_g^n. We shall show (iii) a_h is not belief-dominated by any action b_h at h in T.

First we show (iv) a_h is not belief-dominated by any action b_h in T^n. Suppose it is. Then the player g immediately following b_h is also in T^n. Player h believes that if he would play b_h, then g would[36] play an action b_g in A_g^n, i.e., one that is undominated in T^{n-1}. So since $g \in T^n$, also $b_g \in T^n$. Applying the same argument repeatedly, we conclude that h believes that b_h would lead to an outcome in T^n. Conversely, it may be seen that if h would play b_h, then he believes that any outcome in T^n after b_h would be possible.

[35] I.e., $u_h(z(\mathbf{a}_{\succ h}, a'_h)) > u_h(z(\mathbf{a}_{\succ h}, a_h))$.
[36] Please see Footnote 26.

Since a_h is in T^n, it may be seen similarly that h believes that an outcome following a_h is possible iff it is in T^n. So by (i), b_h cannot belief-dominate a_h.

Next, we show that (v) a_h is not belief-dominated by any action b_h in T^m, for any $m \leq n$; this yields (iii). The proof is by (backward) induction on m. For $m = n$, we have just proved it. Assume it true for a given m, and let b_h be in T^{m-1}. If b_h is in T^m, then (v) is the induction hypothesis. So let b_h be in $T^{m-1} \backslash T^m$. Since $b_h \notin T^m$, it is dominated in T^{m-1}, say by c_h. If $c_h \notin T^m$, then it is dominated in T^{m-1} by an action c'_h; by the transitivity of domination, c'_h dominates b_h in T^{m-1}. Continuing in this way, we eventually reach an action d_h in T^m that dominates b_h in T^{m-1}. But h believes that players after b_h play actions in T^{m-1}; so since d_h dominates b_h in T^{m-1}, and b_h belief-dominates a_h, it follows that d_h belief-dominates a_h. But by (iv), that cannot be.

If $\mathbf{a} \in \mathbf{A}$, denote by $\mathbf{a}^\wedge$ the conjunction $\bigwedge_{h \in H} a_h$ of the actions in $\mathbf{a}$.

Proposition 8.3. *For each $n \geq 0$,*

(1_n) *If $\mathbf{a}^\wedge$ is consistent with $sb^n r$, then $\mathbf{a} \in \mathbf{A}^{n+1}$; and*
(2_n) $\mathbf{A}^{n+1} = ||sb^n r||$.

Together, (1_n) *and* (2_n) *yield*

(3_n) *a player is in T^{n+1} iff reaching that player is consistent with $sb^n r$.*

Remark 8.4. That (3_n) obtains for all n is precisely Theorem B, which is what is needed to complete the proof of the Main Theorem.

Proof. We first show that (1_n) and (2_n) yield (3_n). To show "if," let h be consistent[37] with $sb^n r$. Then there is a profile $\mathbf{a}$ in $\mathbf{A}$, with

[37]Recall that in the syntax, h means that the player h is reached (Section 6.1).

the actions a_g of players g before h leading to h, such that $\mathbf{a}^\wedge$ is consistent with $sb^n r$. So from (1_n) we get $\mathbf{a} \in \mathbf{A}^{n+1}$, and it follows that $h \in T^{n+1}$.

To show "only if," let $h \in T^{n+1}$. Define a profile $\mathbf{a}$ in $\mathbf{A}$ by letting a_g lead to h for players g before h; and for other players g, letting a_g be an arbitrary member of A_g^{n+1}. Then $\mathbf{a} \in \mathbf{A}^{n+1}$, so (2_n) yields $\mathbf{a} \in ||sb^n r||$. So $\mathbf{a}^\wedge \wedge sb^n r$ holds in state $\mathbf{a}$ of the model $\mathbf{C}$, so is consistent. But $\mathbf{a}^\wedge$ entails h, so also $h \wedge sb^n r$ is consistent.

We prove (1_n) and (2_n) — and so also (3_n) — by induction on n.

$\mathbf{(1_0)}$. Let $\mathbf{c} \notin \mathbf{A}^1$; we prove that $\mathbf{c}^\wedge$ is inconsistent with $sb^0 r$. Since $\mathbf{c} \notin \mathbf{A}^1$, there is an h for which $c_h \notin A_h^1$. So c_h is dominated, say by d_h. So $u_h(z(\mathbf{a}_{\succ h}, d_h)) > u_h(z(\mathbf{a}_{\succ h}, c_h))$ for all $\mathbf{a}_{\succ h}$, so $p(d_h, c_h)$ is a tautology. So by generalization (6.2.10), $b_h p(d_h, c_h)$ is a tautology. So $\bigwedge_{a'_h \in A_h} \neg b_h p(a'_h, c_h)$ is inconsistent. Now r_h entails $c_h \to (\bigwedge_{a'_h \in A_h} \neg b_h p(a'_h, c_h))$, so $c_h \wedge r_h$ entails $\bigwedge_{a'_h \in A_h} \neg b_h p(a'_h, c_h)$. So $c_h \wedge r_h$ is inconsistent. But $\mathbf{c}^\wedge$ entails c_h, so $\mathbf{c}^\wedge \wedge r$ entails $c_h \wedge r_h$, which is inconsistent. So $\mathbf{c}^\wedge \wedge sb^0 r = \mathbf{c}^\wedge \wedge r$ is inconsistent.

$\mathbf{(2_0)}$. Let $\mathbf{a} \in \mathbf{A}^1$; thus no a_h is dominated in T. So by Lemma 8.2, no a_h is belief-dominated in $\mathbf{C}$. So by Remark 8.1, $\mathbf{a}$ is in $||r||$, which by (7.2.2), $= ||sb^0 r||$. So $\mathbf{A}^1 \subset ||sb^0 r||$. For the opposite inclusion, let $\mathbf{a} \in ||sb^0 r|| = ||r||$. Then $\mathbf{a}^\wedge \wedge sb^0 r$ holds in the model $\mathbf{C}$, so is consistent; so 1_0 yields $\mathbf{a} \in \mathbf{A}^1$.

Now let $n > 0$, and assume (1_{n-1}) and (2_{n-1}) (and so also (3_{n-1})).

$\mathbf{(1_n)}$. Let $\mathbf{c} \notin \mathbf{A}^{n+1}$; we will prove that $\mathbf{c}^\wedge$ is inconsistent with $sb^n r$. If $\mathbf{c} \notin \mathbf{A}^n$, then by $(\mathbf{1}_{n-1})$, $\mathbf{c}^\wedge$ is inconsistent with $sb^{n-1} r$, so a fortiori with $sb^n r$, which by definition entails $sb^{n-1} r$. So we may assume $\mathbf{c} \in \mathbf{A}^n \backslash \mathbf{A}^{n+1}$. So $c_h \in A_h^n \backslash A_h^{n+1}$ for some h in T^n. So some action d_h in T^n dominates c_h in T^n; that is, d_h is better than c_h, no matter what the subsequent actions are, as long as they are in T^n. So

(4) $\vdash \bigvee_{T^n} \mathbf{a}_{\succ h}^\wedge \to p(d_h, c_h)$,

the disjunction being over all profiles $\mathbf{a}_{\succ h}$ of actions after h all of which are in T^n. By (3_{n-1}), reaching a player h is consistent with $sb^{n-1}r$ iff h is in T^n. So by (7.2.1),

(5) $sb(sb^{n-1}r) = \bigwedge_{h\in T^n} b_h(sb^{n-1}r)$.

So by (7.2.3), $\vdash sb^n r \to b_h(sb^{n-1}r)$ for all h in T^n. By (1_{n-1}), $\vdash sb^{n-1}r \to \bigvee_{\mathbf{a}\in\mathbf{A}^n} \mathbf{a}^{\wedge}_{\succ h}$; so by generalization (6.2.10) and (6.2.4),

(6) $\vdash sb^n r \to b_h(\bigvee_{\mathbf{a}\in\mathbf{A}^n} \mathbf{a}^{\wedge})$.

It may be seen that $\vdash (b_h f \wedge b_h g) \to b_h(f \wedge g)$; so by (6), (4), and (6.2.4),

$$\vdash sb^n r \to b_h(\bigvee_{T^n} \mathbf{a}^{\wedge}_{\succ h}) \to b_h p(d_h, c_h).$$

But by (7.2.2) and (7.1.1–3), $\vdash sb^n r \wedge \mathbf{c} \to r \wedge c_h \to \neg b_h p(d_h, c_h)$, so $sb^n r \wedge c_h$ entails a contradiction; i.e., $\mathbf{c}$ is inconsistent with $sb^n r$.

(2_n). Let $\mathbf{c} \in \mathbf{A}^{n+1}$. By (7.2.3) and (5), $\vdash sb^{n-1}r \wedge \bigwedge_{h\in T^n} b_h(sb^{n-1}r) \leftrightarrow sb^n r$; so by $(\mathbf{2}_{n-1})$,

(7) $\mathbf{A}^n \cap \bigcap_{h\in T^n} ||(b_h(sb^{n-1}r))|| = ||sb^n(r)||$.

First note that since $\mathbf{A}^{n+1} \subset \mathbf{A}^n$, it follows that

(8) $\mathbf{c} \in \mathbf{A}^n$.

Next, let $h \in T^n$. From $\mathbf{c} \in \mathbf{A}^{n+1}$ we get $c_h \in A_h^{n+1}$, so c_h is in T^n and is undominated in T^n. So $n(c_h) \geq n$. So $\mathbf{C}(c_h) \subset \mathsf{X}_{g\not\preceq h} A_g^n$, since the $\mathbf{A}^n$ are nested. Next, we show that $\mathbf{D}(c_h)$, which $:= \{c_h\} \times \mathsf{X}_{g:g\prec h}\{c_g^h\}$, is included in $\mathsf{X}_{g\preceq h} A_g^n$. The action c_h itself is in A_h^n; indeed it is in A_h^{n+1}, which A_h^n includes. When g precedes h, the action c_g^h leading to h is in T^n, and leads to a player in T^n; so $c_g^h \in A_g^n$. So indeed, $\mathbf{D}(c_h) \subset \mathsf{X}_{g\preceq h} A_g^n$. So $\mathbf{C}(a_h) \times \mathbf{D}(a_h) \subset \mathsf{X}_{g\in H} A_g^n = \mathbf{A}^n$.

So $(\mathbf{2}_{n-1})$ and (6.4.4) yield

$$\mathbf{c} \in \{\mathbf{a} \in \mathbf{A} : \mathbf{C}(a_h) \times \mathbf{D}(a_h) \subset \mathbf{A}^n\}$$
$$= \{\mathbf{a} \in \mathbf{A} : \mathbf{C}(a_h) \times \mathbf{D}(a_h) \subset ||sb^{n-1}r||\} = ||b_h(sb^{n-1}r)||;$$

together with (7) and (8), this yields $\mathbf{c} \in ||sb^n(r)||$. So $\mathbf{A}^{n+1} \subset ||sb^n r||$.

For the opposite inclusion, let $\mathbf{a} \in ||sb^n r||$. Then $\mathbf{a}^\wedge \wedge sb^n r$ holds in the model $\mathbf{C}$, so is consistent; so 1_n yields $\mathbf{a} \in \mathbf{A}^{n+1}$.

9. Discussion

9.1. *Players and agents*

9.1.1. *Forward inferences*

To understand the substantive contribution of this work, it is useful to relate it to the seminal work of BS (Battigalli and Siniscalchi, 2002). Like us, BS show that common strong belief (*csb*) of rationality yields the BI outcome.[38] Unlike us, they refer to general PI games, in which players may have several decision nodes; whereas we refer to *simple* PI games, in which each player has just one node. Equivalently, one may say that both BS and we consider general PI games G; but we assume *csb* of the *agents*' rationality,[39] whereas BS assume *csb* of the *players*' rationality.[40]

The game G of Figure 1 (Reny, 1992) illustrates the distinction. First assume *csb* of the agents' rationality (r). By Remark 2.1, Bob_1 is rational and believes that all agents — in particular Ann_1 — are rational; there are no further restrictions on his beliefs.[41] So he may well believe that Ann_2 exits, in which case he, too, should exit.

[38] We do not formulate their definition or result precisely here.

[39] I.e., *csbr* in the simple game G' that is like G, except that the players in G' are the agents in G.

[40] Their definition of rationality is based on utility maximization rather than probability 1 belief.

[41] He can't believe $r \wedge r^1$, as Ann_1's rationality and her belief in Bob_2's rationality would require her to exit, which would preclude reaching him.

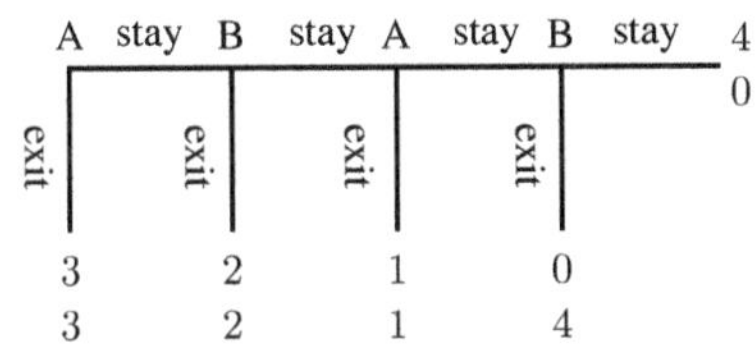

Figure 1: Reny's game.

Now assume *csb* of the *players'* rationality. If Bob's first node is reached, he *can* impute rationality to Ann; but only if he believes that she believes that he will stay at his second node. In that case, his only rational strategy is to stay at his first node and exit at his second. Thus, if he is rational and imputes rationality to Ann, he should *stay* at his first node.[42]

That is a *forward* inference. At his first node, Bob asks, what can I infer from the past about the future? What did Ann think when she did what she did, and what can I infer about what she *will* do? So we're presuming that the player Ann chooses a strategy that dictates what both her agents do. Forward inferences depend on *players* choosing *strategies* rationally; they are impossible in simple games, where each player has just one node.

Note that *csb* of player rationality uses backward as well as forward inferences. After using a forward inference to decide what Ann$_2$ will do, Bob$_1$ reasons *backward* from Ann$_2$'s inferred action to decide what he should do. Non-simple games involve both kinds of inference.

9.1.2. *Backward inferences*

Recall the BI reasoning, as set forth at the start of the paper: The last player, who must choose between outcomes, chooses an action that maximizes his payoff; taking this as given, the previous player maximizes *his* payoff; and so on, until the beginning of the game is reached.

[42]We are reasoning here with pure strategies. Similar, but more complicated, considerations apply to mixed strategies.

These are backward inferences. Starting from the outcomes, we infer *back* to the actions of preterminal players; then *back* to prepreterminal players; and so on. No forward inferences are involved; indeed, the concept of "player" plays no role in BI — the agents act independently, as if the game were simple and they the players. Nothing in the BI reasoning connects the agents of a player to each other; *strategies* — as opposed to actions — play no role.

Basically, therefore, the BI reasoning applies only to simple games. By extension, it applies also to general PI games G in which the agents act independently. So to clarify the epistemic assumptions underlying BI, one replaces G by a simple game G' whose players are the agents in G; this rules out forward inferences. And then, *csbr* yields the BI outcome.

9.2. *Consistency and completeness*

To understand the methodological contribution of this work, it is, as with its substantive contribution, useful to relate it to BS (Battigalli and Siniscalchi, 2002).

Our result is formulated syntactically; BS's, semantically. In most applications, semantic results may also be formulated syntactically, and vice versa. In the present application, the matter is less straightforward.

To explain, we start by describing the usual relationship between semantic and syntactic formalisms more carefully. Each sentence in a syntactic formalism corresponds to a set in each semantic state space — conceptually, the set of states in that space at which that sentence "holds." Moreover, each logical operator corresponds to a set operation: "and" to intersection, "or" to union, and "not" to complementation (w.r.t. that particular space); and a tautology in the syntax corresponds to the entire state space, since it must hold at each state. Conversely, if a sentence in the syntax corresponds in each arbitrary state space to the entire state space, then it is a tautology.

All that is well and good as long as the tautology operator t (Section 5) is not in the formal object language, but only in the metalanguage. As soon as t becomes part of the object language, the elegant one–one correspondence between syntax and semantics breaks down. Indeed, the operator t does not correspond to any set operation within a particular state space, since it refers simultaneously to *all* state spaces. For a sentence to be a tautology means that in *each* state space, the sentence corresponds to the entire space; and there is no way of saying that within a particular space.

BS work with semantics, so that is an obstacle for them. They overcome it by working not with arbitrary state spaces, as is usual in the semantic approach, but with one particular one, called the *complete type space*; this has the property that if in the complete type space, a sentence corresponds to the entire space, then in every semantic state space, that sentence corresponds to the entire space. Constructing the complete type space, and proving that it has the basic property just enunciated, is not elementary; see Battigalli and Siniscalchi (1999). But such an object does exist; indeed, has by now become familiar in epistemic game theory.

Now, this complete type space enables a valid semantic representation of sentences involving the tautology operator t. Namely, the tautology operator corresponds to a set operator that takes the entire complete type space to itself, and all its proper subsets to the empty set. Formally, then, BS prove that the BI outcome is reached at any element of the complete type space at which there is *csb* of player rationality.[43]

A reader has remarked that completeness of the type space requires all possible types to be present; this, he says, is an assumption on the players' reasoning that the syntactic analysis "hides," and that should be made explicit. But that is precisely the beauty of the syntactic analysis! With it, completeness shows up as nothing but plain logical reasoning. On the contrary, it is incomplete type spaces that make hidden implicit assumptions — namely, that certain types are *absent* — that go beyond plain logical reasoning.

[43]See Footnote 40.

10. Literature

10.1. *Battigalli–Siniscalchi and related literature*

The literature on the foundations of BI is far too large to survey here, so we will review only the most directly relevant work. Foremost is BS (Battigalli and Siniscalchi, 2002). Though in substance, their result is utterly different from ours — theirs deals with forward and backward inferences, ours with backward inferences only — there are interesting parallels in form. For one thing, the notion of strong belief, originated by BS, plays a central role also in our theorem. For another, the *formulations* of the results are roughly parallel: Our result characterizes *csb* of the agents' rationality (r); theirs, of the players' rationality[44] (pr). Finally, the proofs are analogous in grand structure, though BS's proof lies far deeper than ours — as indeed the result itself does.

Like ours, BS's proof has two parts. In one — analogous to our Theorem B — they show that *csbpr* is equivalent to extensive form rationalizability (EFR) a la Pearce (1984) or Battigalli (1997). In the other — analogous to our Theorem A — they recall that EFR entails the BI outcome, as proved by Reny (1992), who used tools from algebraic topology developed by Kohlberg and Mertens (1986) (see also Battigalli, 1997).[45] An "elementary" proof[46] of this result is obtained by applying to PI games a theorem of Chen and Micali (2013) about general extensive games. Looking at PI games only, Heifetz and Perea (2015) obtained an alternative elementary proof that EFR entails the BI outcome.

Battigalli and Friedenberg (2012) show that completeness is indispensable for the BS result. As already mentioned, completeness is implicit in the syntactic approach.

---

[44]See Footnote 40.

[45]Professor Marciano Siniscalchi has pointed out that in simple PI games, EFR is in fact equivalent to the Pruning Process. The proof is not entirely straightforward.

[46]One not using algebraic topology.

10.2. *Other literature*

Perhaps the first to provide an epistemic foundation for BI based on action rationality was Stalnaker (1998). Like us, he treats simple games only. But unlike our players, whose beliefs are predicated on being reached, his players have prior beliefs at the beginning of play, which are updated as play proceeds. He assumes common prior belief of rationality (*cbr*), and that the prior beliefs of each player about other players are in a sense independent. This implies that at each node v, there is *cbr* among the players at and after v; together with rationality, this yields BI.

In broad outline, our paper is conceptually similar. One would like to assume *cbr*; like with *ckr*, this leads to difficulties off the BI path. So at off-path nodes, one somehow weakens *cbr*. *Stalnaker's* players do so by saying, well, I see that the players before me did not conform to *cbr*. But by independence, that says nothing about the players after me; so among *them*, I retain *cbr*.

Our players say, for me, any deviation from *cbr* by some players indicates that others may be similar.[47] So I abandon *cbr*, maintaining only as much mutual belief of rationality as is possible at my node.

Note that Stalnaker gets not only the BI outcome, but also the BI *strategies*, and them *only*. In contrast, *csbr* allows the BI strategies, but not *only* them.[48] And *csbpr* may exclude the BI strategies altogether (Section 9.1.1).

Other approaches that determine the BI strategies include Aumann (1995), Asheim and Perea (2005), and Perea (2008).

Halpern and Pass (2009) define a semantic operator $\Diamond$ that may be interpreted as consistency w.r.t. a given class of models; from it, one may derive a tautology operator w.r.t. that class. Though it is not a priori clear, it might be possible to base a semantic treatment

[47]This is, after all, a forward inference of sorts. Lessons from the past are applied to the future, if only to abandon previously held beliefs. In contrast, Stalnaker's agents learn nothing from the past.

[48]Thus in Reny's game (Figure 1), BI calls for Bob_1 to exit, whereas *csbr* allows him either to stay or to exit.

parallel to our syntactic treatment on this operator, rather than on the complete type space.

10.3. *Genericity*

Though the conceptual insights of this paper are most easily seen under genericity, we in fact require no genericity at all. In contrast, BS require the game to have "no relevant ties" (NRT) (see also Battigalli, 1997); i.e., that the last common ancestor of any two outcomes have different payoffs at those outcomes. NRT ensures a unique BI outcome. The requirement has teeth; e.g., it excludes chess. Heifetz and Perea (2015) also use NRT.

Without any genericity condition, EFR still implies a BI outcome. But there are BI outcomes that are inconsistent with EFR; see Chen and Micali (2013), p. 149, Example 7.

Appendix A. Proof of Theorem D

Lemma A.1. *The list $\mathfrak{B}$ of all basic tautologies is coherent.*

Proof. Follows from Lemma 6.2 and Example 6.1.

Let 1 denote an arbitrary but fixed basic tautology (like $a_h \vee \neg a_h$), and set $0 := \neg 1$. Define a mapping from sentences $f \in \chi'$ to basic sentences $f' \in \chi$ inductively as follows:

(1) $(a_h)' := a_h$ for every action a_h.
(2) $(f \vee g)' := f' \vee g'$.
(3) $(\neg f)' := \neg f'$.
(4) $(b_h f)' := b_h(f')$.
(5) $(tf)' := 1$ if $f' \in \mathfrak{B}$ and $(tf)' = 0$ if $f' \notin \mathfrak{B}$.

It may be seen that $f' = f$ for every basic sentence f. Now let

(6) $\mathfrak{L} = \{f : f' \in \mathfrak{B}\}$.

Lemma A.2. *$\mathfrak{L}$ is coherent, strongly closed, and includes all tautologies.*

Proof. We first prove coherence. Suppose f and $\neg f$ are in $\mathfrak{L}$. Then by definition, f' and $(\neg f)'$ are basic tautologies. But $(\neg f)' = \neg f'$, so the list of basic tautologies is incoherent, contradicting Lemma A.1.

To see that $\mathfrak{L}$ is logically closed, assume $f \in \mathfrak{L}$ and $(f \to g) \in \mathfrak{L}$. Then by definition, $f' \in \mathfrak{B}$ and $(f \to g)' \in \mathfrak{B}$. But $(f \to g)' = f' \to g'$; so $g' \in \mathfrak{B}$, which entails $g \in \mathfrak{L}$. That $\mathfrak{L}$ is epistemically closed follows similarly from $\mathfrak{B}$ being epistemically closed. To see that $\mathfrak{L}$ is tautologically closed, let $f \in \mathfrak{L}$; then by definition, $f' \in \mathfrak{B}$, so $(t(f))' = 1$, so $t(f) \in \mathfrak{L}$.

That $\mathfrak{L}$ contains all sentences in (6.3.1) follows from k' being an axiom if k is.

That $\mathfrak{L}$ contains all sentences in (6.3.2) follows from the definition of $\mathfrak{L}$.

To see that $\mathfrak{L}$ contains all sentences in (6.3.3), let $k = t(f \to g) \to (t(f) \to t(g))$. If $(t(f \to g))' = 0$ then clearly k' is in $\mathfrak{B}$. If $(t(f \to g))' = 1$, then $f' \to g' \in \mathfrak{B}$; so since $\mathfrak{B}$ is logically closed, g' is in $\mathfrak{B}$ whenever f' is in $\mathfrak{B}$; so $(tf \to tg)'$ is in $\mathfrak{B}$.

Lemma A.3. *$\vdash f \leftrightarrow f'$ for every sentence f.*

Proof. By induction. For basic f it is clear, since $f' = f$. Next, let $f = b_h(g)$ for some g. By the induction hypothesis, $\vdash g \leftrightarrow g'$, so since $\mathfrak{T}$ is epistemically closed, $\vdash b_h(g \leftrightarrow g')$. Now by axiom (6.2.4), $\vdash b_h(g \leftrightarrow g') \to (b_h g \leftrightarrow b_h(g'))$. So since $\mathfrak{T}$ is logically closed, $\vdash b_h(g) \leftrightarrow b_h(g')$; i.e., $\vdash f \leftrightarrow f'$.

If $f = tg$, then by the induction hypothesis,

(7) $\vdash g \leftrightarrow g'$.

So since $\mathfrak{T}$ is tautologically closed, $\vdash t(g \leftrightarrow g')$. But $\vdash t(g \leftrightarrow g') \to (tg \leftrightarrow t(g'))$, by (6.3.3). So since $\mathfrak{T}$ is logically closed,

(8) $\vdash tg \leftrightarrow t(g')$.

If $g' \in \mathfrak{B}$, then $\vdash g$, by (7); so $\vdash tg$, since $\mathfrak{T}$ is tautologically closed; by (5), $(tg)' = 1$, so $\vdash (tg)'$; so

(9) $\vdash tg \to (tg)'$.

If $g' \notin \mathfrak{B}$, then $\vdash \neg t(g')$, by (6.3.2); by (5), $(tg)' = 0$, so $\vdash \neg(tg)'$; so $\vdash t(g') \leftrightarrow (tg)'$; so by (8), we again get (9). So (9) holds in either case; i.e., $\vdash f \leftrightarrow f'$.

If $f = \neg g$ or $f = g \vee k$, the induction hypothesis easily yields $\vdash f \leftrightarrow f'$.

Lemma A.4. $\mathfrak{T} \cap \chi = \mathfrak{B}$.

Proof. Since $\mathfrak{T}$ is closed and contains the basic axioms (6.2.1–8), it follows that $\mathfrak{B} \subset \mathfrak{T}$. But $\mathfrak{T} \subset \mathfrak{L}$ by Lemma A.1, and $\mathfrak{L} \cap \chi = \mathfrak{B}$; so $\mathfrak{T} \cap \chi = \mathfrak{B}$.

Lemma A.5. $\mathfrak{T} = \mathfrak{L}$.

Proof. By Lemma A.3, a sentence f is in $\mathfrak{T}$ iff f' is in $\mathfrak{T}$. But f' is basic and $\mathfrak{T} \cap \chi = \mathfrak{B}$ by Lemma A.4, so $\mathfrak{T} = \{f | f' \in \mathfrak{B}\} = \mathfrak{L}$.

(6.3.4) now follows from Lemmas A.2 and A.4, (6.3.5) from Lemma A.4, and (6.3.6) from Lemma A.3.

References

Asheim, G. and Perea, A., 2005, Sequential and quasi-perfect rationalizability in extensive games, *Games Econ. Behav.* 53, 15–42.

Aumann, R. J., 1995, Backward induction and common knowledge of rationality, *Games Econ. Behav.* 8, 6–19 [Chapter 11].

Aumann, R. J., 1996, Reply to Binmore, *Games Econ. Behav.* 17, 138–146 [Chapter 16].

Battigalli, P., 1997, On rationalizability in extensive games, *J. Econ. Theory* 74, 40–61.

Battigalli, P., Friedenberg, A., 2012, Forward induction reasoning revisited, *Theor. Econ.* 7, 57–98.

Battigalli, P. and Siniscalchi, M., 1999, Hierarchies of conditional beliefs and interactive epistemology in dynamic games, *J. Econ. Theory* 88, 188–230.

Battigalli, P. and Siniscalchi, M., 2002, Strong belief and forward induction reasoning, *J. Econ. Theory* 106, 356–391 (BS).

Binmore, K., 1996, A note on backward induction, *Games Econ. Behav.* 17, 135–137 [Chapter 15].

Chellas, B. F., 1980, Modal Logic: An Introduction. Cambridge University Press, Cambridge–New York.

Chen, J. and Micali, S., 2013, The order independence of iterated dominance in extensive games, *Theor. Econ.* 8, 125–163.

Halpern, J. Y. and Lakemeyer, G., 2001, Multi-agent only knowing, *J. Log. Comput.* 11, 41–70.

Halpern, J. Y. and Pass, R., 2009, A logical characterization of iterated admissibility. In: Theoretical Aspects of Rationality and Knowledge: Proc. Twelfth Conference. TARK 2009, 146–155.

Heifetz, A. and Perea, A., 2015, On the outcome equivalence of backward induction and extensive form rationalizability, *Int. J. Game Theory* 44, 37–59.

Kohlberg, E. and Mertens, J. F., 1986, On strategic stability of equilibria, *Econometrica* 54, 1003–1037.

Pearce, D., 1984, Rationalizable strategic behavior and the problem of perfection, *Econometrica* 52, 1029–1050.

Perea, A., 2008, Minimal belief revision leads to backward induction, *Math. Soc. Sci.* 56, 1–26.

Reny, P., 1992, Backward induction, normal form perfection and explicable equilibria, *Econometrica* 60, 627–649.

Stalnaker, R., 1998, Belief revision in games: forward and backward induction, *Math. Soc. Sci.* 36, 31–56.

Chapter 13

On the Centipede Game*,†

Abstract: In Rosenthal's Centipede Game, if at the start of play it is commonly known that the players will choose rationally at vertices that are actually reached, then the backward induction outcome results; that is, the first player "goes out" at the first move. *Journal of Economic Literature* Classification Numbers: C72, C73, D82. ©1998 Academic Press, Inc.

1. Introduction

In perfect information (PI) games, common knowledge of rationality implies that the backward induction outcome is reached (Aumann, 1995; henceforth [A]). Conceptually, this result depends on the notion of *counterfactual conditional.* It is assumed common knowledge that each player i would act rationally at each of his vertices v, even when i *knows* that v will *not* be reached; in [A], we called this condition *substantive* rationality. Though it is generally acknowledged that counterfactual reasoning is inescapable in game theory, much of

*Reprinted from *Games and Economic Behavior* (1998), 23, 97–105, with permission from Elsevier.

†Dov Samet has become an indispensable sounding board for our work in this area. Once again, we thank him heartily for his generous input. We also gratefully acknowledge research support from the Game Theory Program at SUNY–Stony Brook.

the discussion of [A] (e.g., Binmore, 1996) has revolved around the counterfactual nature of substantive rationality.

An alternative condition, called *material* rationality in [A], stipulates that i act rationally at those of his vertices that are actually reached. The counterfactual component of this condition is much smaller than in substantive rationality. Though the players must still consider what actions might be taken at unreached vertices, nothing is *a priori* assumed about these actions; in particular, they are not required to be rational. Unfortunately, common knowledge of material rationality does *not* in general lead to the backward induction outcome; see, e.g., Game 1 in [A].

In recent years, Rosenthal's (1982) centipede game has become a touchstone of the theory of PI games. Almost every paper on the subject mentions it, and in many it is the chief object of analysis.[1] Much of this discussion revolves around the counterfactual aspect of substantive rationality. It is therefore of some interest that in the particular case of the centipede game, common knowledge of material rationality *is* sufficient to ensure backward induction; one need *not* assume rationality at unreached vertices. The stronger, more subtle condition of substantive rationality is not needed in the centipede game.

As in [A], time plays an important role. Here, like there, "common knowledge" refers to the start of play. "Rationality" means that *when choosing,* the chooser does not know of a choice that yields him more; in [A], we called this *ex post rationality.*[2] Thus, what we show here is that *in Rosenthal's centipede game, if at the start of play there is common knowledge of ex post material rationality, then the backward induction outcome results: the first player "goes out" immediately.*

[1]Most recently, Binmore has used it as a prime witness in his (1996) critique of [A].

[2]Please see Sections 4b and 5 for further discussion of these concepts.

2. Formal Statement of the Result and Outline of the Proof

We freely use the terminology and notation of [A]. At first, we work with general PI games, specializing to the centipede game only afterward.

Let v be a vertex of Player i. Denote by Ω^v the event "v is reached," i.e., the set of all states ω for which the branch of the game tree determined by the strategy profile $\mathbf{s}(\omega)$ goes through v. Recall that the partition $\mathscr{K}_i$ of Ω represents i's information at the start of play. Let $\mathscr{K}_i^v$ be the join (coarsest common refinement) of $\mathscr{K}_i$ and the partition $\{\Omega^v, \sim \Omega^v\}$. Conceptually, $\mathscr{K}_i^v$ represents i's information when he learns whether v is reached; that is, the information he had at the start of play, updated by the information that v is (or isn't) reached.[3] If E is an event, $\mathscr{K}_i^v E$ denotes the union of those elements of the partition $\mathscr{K}_i^v$ that are included in E. In words, $K_i^v E$ is the event that *i will know E when learning whether v is reached*; or for short, *i knows E at v*. The operators K_i continue to refer to the start of play; thus $K_i E$ is the event that i knows E at the start of play, and CKE is the event that at the start of play, E is commonly known.

In a given state ω, call *i ex post rational at v* if there is no strategy that i knows at v would have yielded him a conditional payoff at v larger than that which in fact he gets; call *i ex post materially rational* if he is ex post rational at each of his reached vertices. Denote by R_i^v the event[4] "i is ex post rational at v;" then the event "i is ex post materially rational," denoted R_i^M, is given by

$$R_i^M = \bigcap_{v \in V_i} (\sim\Omega^v \cup R_i^v), \tag{1}$$

where V_i is the set of i's vertices (for each of i's vertices v, either v is not reached, or i is ex post rational at v). The event "all players

[3] If i gets other information between starting play and reaching v, then his information "at v" is finer than $\mathscr{K}_i^v$. It may be seen that our result remains true in that case (cf. [A, Section 5e]).

[4] For a characterization of R_i^v in symbols, see (3) in Section 3.

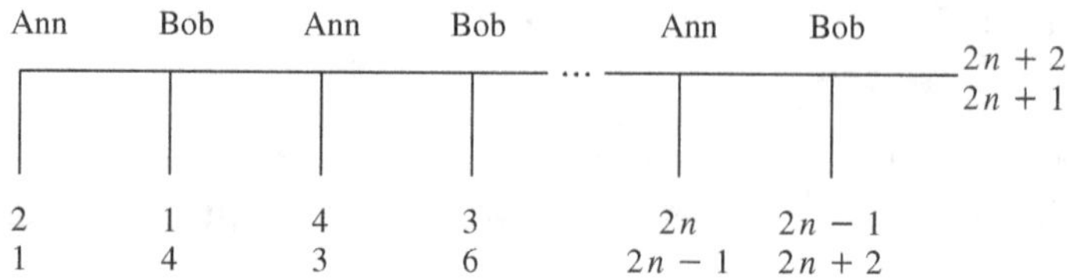

Figure 1: The game Γ_{2n}.

are ex post materially rational," denoted R^M, is the intersection of all the R_i^M.

Denote by Γ_{2n} the game in Figure 1; this is one of Rosenthal's (1982) "centipede" games. Another centipede game, denoted Γ_{2n-1}, is obtained by denying Bob the option of choosing *across* at his last move.

Theorem. *$CKR^M \subset I$ in the game Γ_r.*

In words: In Rosenthal's centipede game, if it is commonly known at the start of play that all players choose rationally at all *reached* vertices, then the first player "goes out" at the first move. Needless to say, this result holds also for any game ordinally equivalent to Γ_r.

The idea of the proof is as follows: Let m be the last vertex that is reached at any state in CKR^M; thus in some state ω in R^M, the vertex m is reached, and it is commonly known that no vertex beyond m is reached. If m is the first move in the game, we are finished. Otherwise, suppose w.l.o.g. that m belongs to Ann. Then when the vertex just before m is reached in ω, Bob knows that he can improve his payoff by going *down* rather than *across*; this contradicts his ex post material rationality.

A formal proof is given in the next section.

3. Proof

We begin with some preliminaries. Recall that $h_i^v(s)$ denotes i's conditional payoff at the vertex v for the strategy profile s. Denoting the initial vertex of the game tree by v^1, define $h_i := h_i^{v^1}$; that is,

$h_i(s)$ is i's actual payoff if the strategy profile s is played. Recall that $\mathbf{s}_i(\omega)$ is i's strategy in state ω, and $\mathbf{s}(\omega) := (\mathbf{s}_1(\omega), \ldots, \mathbf{s}_n(\omega))$ is the profile of all the players' strategies in that state. Functions defined on Ω (like $\mathbf{s}$ or $\mathbf{s}_i$), which appear in boldface, may be viewed like random variables in probability theory. An assertion about such a function corresponds to an event, which we denote by putting square brackets around the assertion. For example, $[\mathbf{s}_i = s_i]$ is the event that i chooses the strategy s_i (i.e., the set of all states ω for which $\mathbf{s}_i(\omega) = s_i$ holds); $[h_i^v(\mathbf{s}; t_i) > h_i^v(\mathbf{s})]$ is the event that i's conditional payoff at v would have been higher if he had chosen the strategy t_i rather than what he did choose; and $[h_i(\mathbf{s}) = 3]$ is the event that i's actual payoff is 3. As in [A], we assume that if i chooses the strategy s_i, then he knows that he chooses it; in symbols,

$$[\mathbf{s}_i = s_i] \subset K_i[\mathbf{s}_i = s_i] \quad \text{for all strategies } s_i \text{ of } i. \tag{2}$$

The event "i is ex post rational at v" is given by

$$R_i^v = \bigcap_{t_i \in S_i} (\sim K_i^v[h_i^v(\mathbf{s}; t_i) > h_i^v(\mathbf{s})]), \tag{3}$$

where S_i is the set of i's strategies (for each of his strategies t_i, it is not the case that i knows at v that t_i would yield him a higher conditional payoff at v than the strategy he chose).

The following four lemmas from [A] will be needed:

Lemma 4. *$CKE = K_i CKE$.*

Lemma 5. *If $E \subset F$, then $K_i E \subset K_i F$.*

Lemma 6. *$K_i E \cap K_i F = K_i(E \cap F)$.*

Lemma 7. *$CKE \subset E$.*

These lemmas are standard in knowledge theory, and also easily proved directly. They yield:

Lemma 8. *If a^v is an action of i at v, then $[\mathbf{s}^v = a^v] \subset K_i[\mathbf{s}^v = a^v]$ (if i chooses a^v at v, then he knows that he does).*

Proof. Let A_i^v be the set of those strategies s_i of i for which $s_i^v = a^v$. Then by (2) and Lemma 5,

$$[\mathbf{s}_i^v = a^v] = \bigcup_{s_i \in A_i^v} [\mathbf{s}_i = s_i] \subset \bigcup_{s_i \in A_i^v} K_i[\mathbf{s}_i = s_i]$$

$$\subset \bigcup_{s_i \in A_i^v} K_i[\mathbf{s}_i^v = a^v] = K_i[\mathbf{s}_i^v = a^v].$$

Finally, note that if v is a vertex of i, then

$$K_i(E) \cap \Omega^v \subset K_i^v(E \cap \Omega^v). \tag{9}$$

Formally, this follows without difficulty from the definitions. Intuitively, if v is reached, then at v, Player i knows this, as well as what he knew at the beginning of play.

So much for the preliminaries, which apply to all PI games. We come now to the proof itself, which, of course, refers to the centipede game only. Denote the vertices $1, 2, \ldots, r$, and let m be the last vertex that is reached in any state in CKR^M; thus

$$CKR^M \subset {\sim}\Omega^{m+1}, \tag{10}$$

and there is a state ω with

$$\omega \in \Omega^m \tag{11}$$

and

$$\omega \in CKR^M. \tag{12}$$

If $m = 1$, we are finished. Assume therefore that $m > 1$. Let m belong to Ann, say $m = 2k - 1 \geq 3$. From (12), Lemma 4, (10), and Lemma 5 we get

$$\omega \in CKR^M = K_B CKR^M \subset K_B \sim \Omega^{m+1}, \tag{13}$$

where B stands for Bob. By the definition of Ω^j, we have $\Omega^m \subset \Omega^{m-1}$, so by (11),

$$\omega \subset \Omega^{m-1}. \tag{14}$$

By (11) and Lemma 8, $\omega \in [\mathbf{s}_B^{m-1} = \mathit{across}] = K_B[\mathbf{s}_B^{m-1} = \mathit{across}]$; from this, (13), and Lemma 6, we get $\omega \in K_B([\mathbf{s}_B^{m-1} = \mathit{across}]\backslash\Omega^{m+1})$. So by (14), (9), and the rules of the game,

$$\begin{aligned}\omega \in K_B^{m-1}([\mathbf{s}_B^{m-1} = \mathit{across}] \cap (\Omega^{m-1}\backslash\Omega^{m+1})) &= K_B^{m-1}(\Omega^m\backslash\Omega^{m+1}) \\ &= K_B^{m-1}[h_B(\mathbf{s}) = 2k-1]. \end{aligned} \tag{15}$$

In particular, applying Lemma 5 to K_B^{m-1},

$$\omega \in K_B^{m-1}[\mathbf{s}_A^j = \mathit{across} \text{ when } j = 1, 3, \ldots, m-2], \tag{16}$$

where A stands for Ann. Now let t_B be a strategy of Bob that chooses *across* at all vertices of Bob before $m-1$, and chooses *down* at $m-1$. Then

$$[\mathbf{s}_A^j = \mathit{across} \, \text{for} \, j = 1, 3, \ldots, m-2] \subset [h_B(\mathbf{s}; t_B) = 2k];$$

so from (16), $\omega \in K_B^{m-1}[h_B(\mathbf{s}; t_B) = 2k]$; so from (15) and Lemmas 6 and 5 applied to K_B^{m-1},

$$\begin{aligned}\omega &\in K_B^{m-1}([h_B(\mathbf{s}; t_B) = 2k] \cap [h_B(\mathbf{s}) = 2k-1]) \\ &\subset K_B^{m-1}[h_B(\mathbf{s}; t_B) > h_B(\mathbf{s})]. \end{aligned} \tag{17}$$

By (12), Lemma 7, (1), $K_i^v\Omega^v = \Omega^v$, (3), and Lemma 6,

$$\begin{aligned}\omega &\in CKR^M \subset R^M \subset R_B^M \subset {\sim}\Omega^{m-1} \cup R_B^{m-1} \\ &\subset {\sim}K_B^{m-1}\Omega^{m-1} \cup {\sim}K_B^{m-1}[h_B^{m-1}(\mathbf{s}; t_B) > h_B^{m-1}(\mathbf{s})] \\ &= {\sim}K_B^{m-1}(\Omega^{m-1} \cap [h_B^{m-1}(\mathbf{s}; t_B) > h_B^{m-1}(\mathbf{s})]). \end{aligned} \tag{18}$$

Since $m-1$ is reached in each state in Ω^{m-1}, it follows from the definition of h_B that

$$h_B^{m-1}(\mathbf{s}(v); t_B) = h_B(\mathbf{s}(v); t_B) \text{ and } h_B^{m-1}(\mathbf{s}(v)) = h_B(\mathbf{s}(v))$$

for each v in Ω^{m-1}. Therefore

$$\Omega^{m-1} \cap [h_B^{m-1}(\mathbf{s}; t_B) > h_B^{m-1}(\mathbf{s})] = \Omega^{m-1} \cap [h_B(\mathbf{s}; t_B) > h_B(\mathbf{s})];$$

so (18), Lemma 6, and $K_i^v \Omega^v = \Omega^v$ yield

$$\begin{aligned}\omega &\in {\sim}K_B^{m-1}(\Omega^{m-1} \cap [h_B(\mathbf{s}; t_B) > h_B(\mathbf{s})]) \\ &= {\sim}K_B^{m-1}(\Omega^{m-1}) \cup {\sim}K_B^{m-1}[h_B(\mathbf{s}; t_B) > h_B(\mathbf{s})] \\ &= {\sim}\Omega^{m-1} \cup {\sim}K_B^{m-1}[h_B(\mathbf{s}; t_B) > h_B(\mathbf{s})],\end{aligned}$$

which is inconsistent with (14) and (17). This completes the proof when m belongs to Ann; when it belongs to Bob, the proof is similar.

4. Discussion

4.1. *Subjunctives*

Much of the discussion of the centipede game has centered around the following argument: On the one hand, we are told that under common knowledge of rationality (*CKR*), Ann *must* go out at her first move. On the other hand, the backward induction argument for this is based on what the players *would* do if Ann stayed in. But, if she did stay in, then *CKR* is violated, so the argument that she will go out no longer has a basis.

We have argued elsewhere ([A]; Aumann, 1996) that the above argument is unsound. Be that as it may, this note shows that the whole issue may be circumvented. It is not necessary to use the subjunctive mood; the proof in this note refers only to rationality at vertices that are actually reached, not to whether players "would" play rationally if their vertices "were" reached. Rather than reasoning from what happens after a given vertex, it reasons from what happens *before*: If some vertex is the last that can possibly be reached, then already the one before it should have been the last. This is quite different from the backward induction proof in [A].

4.2. *Time*

The formal contrast between the ex post notion of rationality and the ex ante notion of common knowledge may disturb some readers, but closer examination reveals no awkwardness. Rationality is *inherently* ex post: Whether or not a given choice is rational necessarily depends on the information available at the time of the choice. This has nothing to do with the *knowledge* — or common knowledge — of such rationality, which may well refer to an entirely different time. It makes perfect sense to speak of common knowledge at the *start of play* that the players will choose rationally if and when one of their vertices is actually reached. That, precisely, is the hypothesis of this note.

4.3. *Probability*

Our theorem carries over without change to probabilistic models, in which play is defined as rational if and only if it maximizes expected utility (caution: this applies to rationality only; *knowledge* — and common knowledge — must still be defined in terms of absolute certainty, not probability 1 belief). As above, the expectations must be ex post. Compare Aumann (1996), Sections 1 and 9.

4.4. *The proof*

The reader may wonder why we adduce such a lengthy formal proof for an argument that while not immediate, seems simple enough once one has found it. The reason is that this area is *very* tricky, and unless one is extremely careful and formal, it is easy to go astray — as we have found, to our dismay, on more than one occasion. (The same remark applies to [A].)

5. Previous Work

This section, which discusses technical relations between the current note and [A], may be omitted without affecting the understanding of the rest of the note.

"Common knowledge" (CK) here is precisely the same as in [A]. "Ex post rationality" here is the same as "rationality" in [A], except that the ex post knowledge operators K_i^v appearing in the definition (3) of ex post rationality replace the ex ante knowledge operators K_i appearing in the definition [A, (3)] of rationality. Thus the terminology here is fully coordinated with that of [A]. To avoid confusion, we henceforth call the rationality concept of [A] by the name "ex ante rationality."

Ex post rationality is stronger than (i.e., implies) ex ante rationality [A, Section 5e], so *CK* of ex post rationality implies *CK* of ex ante rationality. [A] shows that *CK* of ex ante substantive rationality implies backward induction; therefore, *CK* of ex post substantive rationality also does. Thus, though [A] formally uses the less intuitive ex ante version of rationality, the same result with the more intuitive ex post version follows easily.

The reason that [A] uses the less intuitive ex ante version is that it is simpler than the ex post version — that it requires less baggage, both formal and conceptual. Specifically, the ex ante version works directly with the same partitions $\mathscr{K}_i$ that are used to define *CK*, rather than with the ex post partitions $\mathscr{K}_i^v$. Since the ex ante result is logically stronger, nothing is lost.

Why, then, don't we use the simpler ex ante version here too? The reason is that here, unlike in [A], the ex ante version won't do; *CK* of ex ante material rationality does *not* yield backward induction in the centipede game. To show this, we now adduce an example of a centipede game in which there is common knowledge of material rationality — in the ex ante sense of [A], but not the ex post sense used here — and the first player does *not* "go out" at the first vertex.

Recall that a player is *ex ante materially rational* if he is ex ante rational at each of his reached vertices. Denote by R^{AM} the event "all players are ex ante materially rational;" in symbols,

$$R^{AM} = \bigcap_i \left(\bigcap_{v \in V_i} \left(\sim\Omega^v \cup \bigcap_{t_i \in S_i} (\sim K_i[h_i^v(\mathbf{s}; t_i) > h_i^v(\mathbf{s})]) \right) \right).$$

Consider now the game Γ_3, with a state space Ω consisting of three states, α, β, γ. Ann's partition at the beginning of play is $(\alpha, \beta\gamma)$, whereas Bob's is $(\alpha\beta, \gamma)$. Ann's strategy is (*across, down*) in state α, (*down, across*) in states β and γ. Bob's strategy is *across* in states α and β, *down* in state γ. It may be seen that both players are (ex ante) materially rational at all three states, so all states are in CKR^{AM}, but in state α, the players play *across* at the first two moves.

Bob's behavior in state α may seem strange, since he knows that if his vertex is reached, Ann will go *down* at her next vertex, so it would be advantageous for him to go *down* rather than *across*. But, at the start of play, Bob does not know whether the state is α or β. If it is α, he can improve his conditional payoff at his vertex by switching to *down*; this translates to a gain in actual payoff, because in state α, his vertex is actually reached. If the state is β, his conditional payoff is larger if he goes *across* than if he goes *down*, so he "loses" by switching. But, this "loss" is only in the conditional payoff, not the actual payoff, because in state β, his vertex is not reached. And he knows this, already at the start of play! Nevertheless, the fact remains that at the start of play he is not sure that he can improve his conditional payoff at his vertex, so by our definition, he is rational. This quirk in the definition of ex ante material rationality provides additional motivation for the ex post notion used here.

References

Aumann, R. J., 1995, "Backward Induction and Common Knowledge of Rationality," *Games Econ. Behav.* 8, 6–19 (**[A] in the text**) [Chapter 11].

Aumann, R. J., 1996, "Reply to Binmore," *Games Econ. Behav.* 17, 138–146 [Chapter 16].

Binmore, K., 1996, "A Note on Backward Induction," *Games Econ. Behav.* 17, 135–137 [Chapter 15].

Rosenthal, R., 1982, "Games of Perfect Information, Predatory Pricing, and the Chain Store Paradox," *J. Econ. Theory* 25, 92–100.

Chapter 14

Irrationality in Game Theory*

The history of game theory has been evolutionary rather than revolutionary. Over the years, the fundamental concepts of the theory have been used in an ever-increasing circle of contexts; some of the most important developments consisted of innovative ways of recasting the theory so as to apply to problems that previously appeared not to fit in. A prime example is Harsanyi's historic work (1967–68) on games of incomplete information. Before this work, it had been universally thought that for game theory to be applicable, the payoff matrix of the game must be commonly known. Harsanyi's achievement consisted of formulating games of incomplete information so that they could be seen and analyzed as games of complete information; by this achievement, he opened the door to the development of the enormous fields of informational game theory and economics as we know them today. Similarly, the theory was extended from perfect information (Zermelo) to imperfect information (Borel and von Neumann); from strategic (normal) form to extensive; from two-person to n-person; from zero-sum to non-zero-sum; and from TU (transferable utility) to NTU (non-transferable utility).

*Reprinted from *Economic Analysis of Markets and Games: Essays in Honor of Frank Hahn* (1992), edited by P. Dasgupta, D. Gale, O. Hart, and E. Maskin, 214–227, The MIT Press, Cambridge and London, with permission from MIT Press.

The current frontier — the one discussed here — is that of rationality. Briefly, it is suggested that game theory need not assume that the players must be rational (i.e., utility maximizers).

This may sound paradoxical to the reader. After all, rationality is what game theory is all about; game theory without rationality sounds like geology without rocks or biology without life. Yet some of the most challenging problems facing the theory concern the interface between rationality and irrationality; they are about situations that cannot be dealt with on a purely rational basis, much like geological phenomena that depend on living organisms (such as cracking of rocks by plants) or biological phenomena that are the result of the nonliving environment.

1. Approach

The underlying game model from which we take off is that presented in Aumann (1987). It starts by considering the set of all "states of the world," where the specification of a state includes all relevant factors, including the (pure) strategy that each player uses in the given game, and what he knows when he decides to do so. It then asks, *suppose* that each player is rational at each state of the world that occurs with positive probability; i.e., that the strategy that that state specifies for each player happens to be one that maximizes his utility given his information. Can we then say anything about the distribution of strategy n-tuples? Does the assumption of rationality imply any specific form for this distribution?'

The point of view of this model is not normative; it is not meant to advise the players what to do. The players do whatever they do; their strategies are taken as given. Neither is it meant as a description of what human beings actually do in interactive situations. The most appropriate term is perhaps "analytic"; it asks, what are the *implications* of rationality in interactive situations? Where does it lead? This question may be as important as, or even more important than, more direct "tests" of the relevance of the rationality hypothesis.

The answer given in Aumann (1987) was that it leads to correlated equilibrium — not that the players consciously choose a correlated equilibrium according to which they play, but that, to an outside observer with no information, the distribution of action n-tuples appears as if they had.

What is proposed here is to take this framework, remove the rationality hypothesis, and see where we are led.

Needless to say, I do not simply drop the rationality hypothesis and leave it at that. Rather, I propose to use the epistemic model of Aumann (1987) — whose roots extend back to Radner (1968, 1972), to Harsanyi (1967–68), to von Neumann and Morgenstern, to formal epistemologists such as Kripke and Hintikka, and to probabilists such as Kolmogorov — as a very general kind of framework for studying limited rationality; a unified framework for considering rationality in environments that may include irrationality, indeed where irrationality may be of the essence.

2. Formal Description of the Model

Formally, define an *information system* to consist of the following:

(i) a strategic (normal) form n-person game G;
(ii) for each player i, a set whose members, s_i, are called *information states* of i; and
(iii) a function that associates with each information state of each player i
  (a) a pure strategy of i in G; and
  (b) a probability distribution on $(n-1)$-tuples of information states of the other players.

An information system is a simultaneous representation of all the players' uncertainties. Each player makes some definite choice of a pure strategy, based on whatever he knows or believes about customs, history, personalities of the other players, and so on — in brief, based on the state of his information. He knows his own choice; that is what (iiia) says. But he does not know what the others choose, though he has some belief about this. Moreover, he does not know their information states — what information is available to them when they make their choices, what they believe about his choice, and so on.

For simplicity, we confine ourselves to information systems that are finite, i.e., in which each player has finitely many information states.

Let us use the term *surmise* for a probability distribution maintained by a player, *theory* for his surmise on the $(n-1)$-tuple of information states of the other players, and *belief* for his surmise on the $(n-1)$-tuple of pure strategies that the other players choose. Thus, (iiib) associates a theory with each information state of each player i, from which we may derive i's belief. From i's theory we may also derive a surmise on the theories of the others, and hence about *their* beliefs. This is called a *second-order* belief; it may be computed explicitly from the information system. Similarly, we may define and compute beliefs of any order. Note that the resulting "belief hierarchy" is derived from the information system, not given exogenously.

We call a player *rational* at a given information state if the pure strategy he chooses at that state maximizes his expected payoff when calculated according to his belief at that state. (See Section 7 for a discussion of this definition.)

Let us use the term *state of the world*, or simply *world*, for an n-tuple of information states; it is a complete specification of all relevant parameters. A widely used regularity condition on information systems is that there exists a single probability distribution p on the states w of the world, called a "common prior," such that the theory of each player i at each w is the conditional of p given i's information state at w (see Harsanyi 1967–68, p. 493ff., and Aumann 1987, Section 5). Intuitively, p represents the surmise about the state of the world held by an outside observer with no information at all; it is assumed that if the observer had the same information as a player he would make the same surmises. When it exists, a common prior allows a particularly concise description of the information system.

For an illustration, let G be the game with the following matrix:

	L	**R**
T	1,1	0,0
B	0,0	2,2

(as usual, the first and second coordinates of each entry represent payoffs to the row and column players — say, Alice and Bob — respectively). Consider the information system depicted by

	L	**L**	**R**
T	1,1*	1,1*	0,0
T	1,1*	1,1	0,0*
B	0,0	0,0*	2,2*

The first two rows represent two different information states of Alice, both corresponding to her pure strategy T; the last row represents a third information state, corresponding to her pure strategy B. Similarly, the columns represent Bob's information states. There are nine states of the world. Each star represents a probability of 1/6; the other probabilities vanish. Alice's first information state differs from her second in her belief; in the first, she knows that Bob plays his pure strategy L, whereas in the second, she attributes half-half probabilities to Bob's two pure strategies. Similarly for Bob.

Thus, in the world w represented by the top left comer of the 3×3 matrix, Alice plays T, and Bob knows this. But she does not know that he knows it; indeed, she ascribes a probability of only 1/2 to this event. Similarly for Bob. Finally, each player is rational in w, but neither knows that the other is; indeed, each ascribes a probability of only 1/2 to the rationality of the other.

(Throughout this paper, the term *know* is used to mean "believe with a probability of 1." In the current framework one cannot even formulate the stronger meaning of *know*, which allows no exceptions at all, even with a probability of 0.)

The above definition of an information system is analogous to Harsanyi's (1967–68) definition of a game of incomplete information. There each player may be one of several "types," where a type determines his utility function and a distribution over $(n-1)$-tuples of types of the others. Here we replace the utility functions by actions; the information states here play the same role as the types there.

Information systems are essentially equivalent to the standard partition models of information in games (as in Aumann 1987). There the primitives are the set of worlds, and n partitions of this set, one for each player. An information state of i is then defined as an atom of i's partition. Formally, information systems are slightly more parsimonious than partition models, and are better suited to our current purposes.

The purpose of this essay is to consider information systems where some players are irrational at some states of the world, and the implications this has for behavior at other states of the world, where all players *are* rational. In particular, we will see how such considerations can resolve certain "paradoxes of rationality" arising from backward induction in "centipede games."

3. High-Order Mutual Knowledge

Recall that an event is called *common* knowledge if all players know it, all know that all know it, and so on *ad infinitum*. Call an event *mutual* knowledge if all players simply know it; *second-order* mutual knowledge if it is mutual knowledge that it is mutual knowledge; and so on for any finite order. Thus, common knowledge is the same as mutual knowledge for all finite orders simultaneously.

In a conversation at Stanford during the summer of 1987, Jay Kadane of Carnegie-Mellon University suggested that it might be worthwhile to investigate the consequences of relaxing the assumption of common knowledge of rationality that underlies Aumann (1987) (see Section 1 above). At the time, the framework for carrying out such an investigation was not clear. I suggest that the framework of the previous section is appropriate for this purpose.

Indeed, in such a framework it is quite easy formally to describe a situation in which there is iterated mutual knowledge of rationality up to any given order, but not common knowledge. Thus, consider a variant of the example in the previous section, with the same game G as there, but with the information system

	L	**L**	**L**	**L**	**R**
T	1,1*	1,1*	1,1	1,1	0,0
T	1,1*	1,1	1,1*	1,1	0,0
T	1,1	1,1*	1,1	1,1*	0,0
T	1,1	1,1	1,1*	1,1	0,0*
B	0,0	0,0	0,0	0,0*	2,2*

where each star represents a probability of 1/10, and the other probabilities vanish. Then in the state of the world represented by the top left corner there is second-order — but not third-order — mutual knowledge of rationality.

Common knowledge of rationality seems a very strong assumption. Even mutual knowledge of rationality is quite strong. A player may be rational himself, but how can he know for sure that another person is? Even if he does, it seems highly unlikely that he will know for sure, without the slightest doubt, that the other player knows that he is rational. Yet this would only be second-order mutual knowledge of rationality; common knowledge of rationality is far stronger.

The question therefore arises as to what happens when we relax this requirement just a little, e.g. by allowing a small measure of doubt to enter at a high level of mutual knowledge. Suppose, for example, that both players are rational, both know for sure that both are rational, and both impute very high probability to this being so (i.e., to both knowing for sure that both are rational); but they do not know it for *sure*. Can this make a big difference in the outcome of a game?

We will see that it can make a very big difference indeed.

4. Paradoxes of Backward Induction

Among the most disturbing counterintuitive examples of rational interactive decision theory are the paradoxes of "backward induction." The best known example is the finitely repeated prisoner's dilemma, in which all Nash equilibria (and also all correlated equilibria) dictate playing "greedy" ("defect") at each stage, no matter how often play is repeated. Rosenthal (1982) constructed a particularly simple class of backward-induction paradoxes — the "centipede games" — a striking instance of which, due to Megiddo (1986), is as follows: \$10.50 is lying on a table. Alice has the option of taking \$10, leaving 50 cents for Bob. If she does, the game is over. If not, the amount on the table is increased tenfold, to \$105, and it is Bob's turn to play: he can take \$100, leaving \$5 to Alice. If he does, the game is over. If not, the amount on the table is again increased tenfold. This continues for a total of at most three rounds, and then ends. If play has not terminated before, then at the last stage Bob has the opportunity of taking \$1,000,000, leaving \$50,000 for Alice; after that, play is over, whether or not Bob takes the opportunity.

At all Nash equilibria of this game, Alice "goes out" immediately — i.e., she takes the \$10 at her first move, leaving 50 cents for Bob. This is also so for all correlated equilibria.

Some readers may feel that, upon consideration, Megiddo's example is not so terribly counterintuitive; that although Alice may feel quite frustrated, a considered analysis will nevertheless lead her in the end to pick up the money at the first opportunity. After all, there is a difference between frustration and paradoxicality; the players of a one-shot prisoner's dilemma will certainly feel frustrated, but the logic of that situation *does* inexorably point to playing "greedy," and the time has long passed since this was considered paradoxical. One might even say that properly digesting Megiddo's example makes it easier to accept the equilibrium outcome of, say, the 100-times-repeated prisoner's dilemma.

But others will feel that if this is rationality they want none of it — or, more to the point, that it represents an approach that is of little practical interest, at least in this example.

5. A Resolution of the Backward-Induction Paradoxes

What is proposed here is to apply the new kind of bounded rationality suggested in Section 3, in which all agents are in fact perfectly rational but there is some breakdown in the commonality of the knowledge that they are. Typically, we will be interested in situations where there is iterated knowledge ("Alice knows that Bob knows that Alice knows$\cdots$ ") of rationality up to a specified level, but no further. We will find that an extremely small breakdown in the commonality of the knowledge of rationality is enough to justify the kind of behavior that most of us would consider intuitively "reasonable."

The Megiddo example appears in matrix form as follows:

			Bob		
		a	b	c	d
	A	10	10	10	10
		.50	.50	.50	.50
	B	5 v	1,000 w	1,000	1,000
Alice		100	50	50	50
	C	5	500 x	100,000 y	100,000
		100	10,000	5,000	5,000
	D	5	500	50,000 z	0
		100	10,000	1,000,000	0

The rows and columns represent pure strategies of Alice and Bob, respectively. They are arranged in the order in which they prescribe "going out;" thus, Alice's third row represents the strategy in which she takes the money — "goes out" — when (and if) it is offered to her for the third time, but not before. In each entry, the upper number represents Alice's payoff, the lower one Bob's.

Consider now the information system depicted in the above matrix. Each player has just one information state for each of his pure strategies. There is a common prior, with non-negative probabilities v, w, x, y, and z; all other probabilities vanish. Note that with probability 1 Alice "stays in" on her first move.

(When one is discussing an example, as here, common priors are a desideratum, not a restriction. In theorems one strives for generality; in examples, for "regularity," for an absence of pathology. The point is that the backward-induction paradoxes can be resolved even if we restrict ourselves to common priors; *a fortiori* if we don't.)

For simplicity, consider first the case where $x = 0.99447, y = 0.0055, z = 0.00003$, and $v = w = 0$. Note that Bob is rational at all three states of the world that occur with positive probability; as for Alice, she is rational at x and at y, but not at z. Thus, Bob is rational with probability 1, and Alice with a probability very close to 1; the probability that she is irrational is only 3 in 100,000.

Suppose now that the true state of the world happens to be the one that has the overwhelming probability, namely x. Then both Alice and Bob are rational; moreover, each of them knows that both are rational. Indeed, it is common knowledge that Bob is rational. And he still gets \$10,000, which is surely the most he could reasonably hope for.

One can ring the changes on this in many ways. The underlying point is that for Bob to be rational everywhere, and Alice everywhere except at z, it suffices that, of the ratios v/w, w/x, x/y, and y/z that are not $0/0$, none exceeds 198. The probability is then 1 that Bob is rational and gets at least \$50; and at the state of the world corresponding to v, both players are rational, both know this (with certainty), both know that they know this, and both know that they know that they know this, and yet Bob collects \$100. And though Alice is irrational with positive probability, that probability may be tiny: when all the above ratios are 198, the probability z that Alice is irrational (as estimated by an outside observer) is 0.000000000648 — less than one in a billion. Multiplying this probability by the size of Alice's "loss" (or rather forgone profit) at z, namely \$50,000, we get an "expected irrationality" of less than 1/300 of a cent, an utterly insignificant sum.

Similar considerations hold for the finitely repeated prisoner's dilemma. With extremely small — practically speaking, negligible — overall probabilities of irrationality, one can, in the 100-fold repetition, justify "cooperating" until at least the 85th or the 90th stage, and even beyond. This kind of result jibes well with observed experimental behavior, in which subjects start "defecting" more and more as the game approaches its end.

This attractive resolution for these paradoxes gives a rigorous justification to the elusive idea that, whereas one should certainly play rationally at the end, it seems somehow foolish to act from the very beginning in the most pathologically pessimistic, "play it safe" way. The above analysis shows that, contrary to what had been thought, one may act in a way that is rational — even with a high degree of mutual knowledge of rationality — and yet is quite profitable. And it reflects the fact that in real interactive situations there is a great deal of uncertainty about what others will do, to what extent they are rational, what they think about what you think and about your rationality, and so on.

6. Measuring Irrationality

In this section we confine our attention to information systems with a common prior, to which the term *probability* will refer.

The methodology of Section 5 lends itself well to the task of measuring irrationality. We have already used one such measure: "expected irrationality." Formally, this is defined for each player i separately, as follows: At each of i's information states, one multiplies the probability of that state by the difference between i's expected payoff there and the maximum expected payoff that he could have gotten by changing his strategy; then one sums over all of i's information states. This measure of irrationality should be useful in comparing various approaches to approximate rationality, including the ε-rationality of Radner (1980, 1986), the "perturbations" of Kreps, Milgrom, Roberts, and Wilson (1982), and the approach of this paper. What is being suggested is that, in evaluating a specified solution in a specified context, one should take into account both the amount of irrationality (as does Radner) and its probability (as do Kreps *et al.*). There is an obvious tradeoff between the two that is not captured by either one separately: a player may be willing to tolerate a higher probability of an irrationality that results in the loss of \$1 than one costing \$1 million.

The information systems of Section 5 involve "correlated" strategies: each player's choice of a pure strategy depends on his belief, with different beliefs corresponding to different choices. Effects that are similar insofar as expected irrationality is concerned can be obtained in the independent case — with "mixed" strategies, so to speak. Thus, suppose that at each of his information states

Bob has the same belief about Alice's choice, represented by the probabilities $A, B, \ldots$ (see the matrix in Section 5). Similarly, let $a, b, \ldots$ represent Alice's belief at each of her information states. Let $B/C = C/D = a/b = b/c = 198$, and let $A = d = 0$. Then, as in the second example in Section 5, Bob's expected irrationality is 0, and Alice's is less than 1/300 of a cent. (Alice is irrational only when choosing row D.) The *probability* of irrationality is greater than in Section 5; it is $D = 0.0000253$, rather than $z = 0.000000000648$. But the *size* of the irrationality (the loss in expected payoff from making that choice rather than maximizing) is smaller; not \$50,000, but $\$50,000 \times c$. Hence, the expected irrationality is $\$50,000 \times cD$. Since $c = D$, this works out to \$0.0000320, as compared with \$0.0000324 in the second example of Section 5.

Thus, there is no appreciable difference in expected irrationality between the two systems; it is negligibly small in both (in fact, slightly smaller in the independent case). What makes the example of Section 5 more attractive is that at v, say, it displays a much higher level of mutual knowledge of rationality. By contrast, in the independent case there is no mutual knowledge of rationality at all; at v (indeed, at all states), Bob ascribes positive probability to Alice's being irrational.

We may define the *degree* of irrationality of a player i at state w of the world as minus the maximum level of mutual knowledge of i's rationality at w. This is to be distinguished from expected irrationality as defined above, which measures the "amount" of irrationality in the system. Thus, whereas the example of Section 5 has a slightly higher "amount" of irrationality than the "independent" example, it has a far lower degree.

Expected irrationality is a global measure; it applies to the information system as a whole. Degree of irrationality is a local measure; it applies to a specific state of the world. It would be desirable also to develop a local measure of expected irrationality, conditional on a specific state of the world and on the information of the players at that state. This would enable us to refer to the "amount of irrationality" that is needed in the system to justify the choice of a certain strategy pair by the players (like x in Megiddo's game), even though under the circumstances both players' choices are completely rational.

7. A Difficulty with the Definition of Irrationality

The framework of Section 2 requires each player, at each state of the world, to have well-defined probabilities for the other players' information states, pure strategies, and so on. Yet it permits him sometimes to be irrational, i.e., to fail to maximize expected utility. This raises a difficulty, since personal probabilities are usually *defined* via utility maximization (Savage 1954); nonmaximizers of utility don't have probabilities.

Consider first the case when there is a common prior, as in Sections 5 and 6. The underlying idea of common priors is that reasonable probability assessments are or should be based on information, so that people with exactly the same information "should" have the same probabilities. Thus, one can think of a common prior as representing the assessment of a rational outside observer who has no personal interest in the outcome of the game and no private information. If he then gets the same private information as a player who is rational, he will entertain the same probabilities as that player; and if the player is not rational, it is natural to think of the observer's probabilities as the "right" ones.

In the general case, when there need not be a common prior, the difficulty may be resolved by revising the definition of an information system (Section 2). Item iiib of the definition specifies a "theory" (a complete system of probability assessments) for each player at each of his information states. The revised definition specifies whether or not that player is rational at that information state, and specifies a theory for him only when he is rational. This enables us to formulate and prove general theorems, and to define the *degree* of irrationality (see Section 6); its disadvantage is that it does not enable us to measure the expected *amount* of irrationality, as in Sections 5 and 6.

8. Relations with "Crazy Perturbations"

In the "crazy perturbation" literature (e.g., Kreps *et al.* 1982; Kreps and Wilson 1982; Milgrom and Roberts 1982; Fudenberg and Maskin 1986; Aumann and Sorin 1989; Fudenberg and Levine 1989), one looks for Nash equilibria of a repeated game in which there is a small exogenous probability that a player plays irrationally but in such a way as to motivate the other player to play in some specific way — e.g., a mutually beneficial way. Most of the results say that, in one sense or another, the rational types tend to mimic those irrational types that are in some sense "best" for the player who does the mimicking. Intuitively, one might say that the rational types "disguise" themselves as irrational; they make believe they are crazy, thus "forcing" the other player to play accordingly (i.e., to maximize against the selected irrational type).

In general, this kind of theorem gives rather sharp results; it says that *all* Nash equilibria of the perturbed game have payoffs in a sharply defined class. They thus go in the opposite direction from many of the theorems on repeated games, in which results akin to the folk theorem lead to very diffuse sets of equilibrium payoffs.

Consider now a situation in which there is mutual knowledge of some given order that all players are rational, but not common knowledge; and that if the players are not rational, then they play some specified strategy, or a strategy in some specified set (such as bounded recall strategies, as in Aumann and Sorin 1989). Can theorems of the above type still be proved in this more general context? The model outlined in Section 2 provides an appropriate general framework in which to investigate this question.

For the finitely repeated prisoner's dilemma, this question was treated by Kreps *et al.* (1982). Suppose that it is first-order mutual knowledge that the players are rational: each player is rational and knows that the other is, but does not know that the other knows that he is. In particular, he thinks that the other may think that, with some fixed small probability, he is a tit-for-tat (TFT) automaton. In this situation, it would appear that each player will still be motivated to pretend that he is TFT, since he doesn't know that the other knows that he isn't. Once he plays TFT, the other is motivated to go along, to the mutual benefit of both.

Now what happens when mutual knowledge of rationality is taken one step further — i.e., when not only does each player know that the other is rational, but each also knows that the other knows that he is? Then the reasoning appears to break down; each player might feel that there is no sense in pretending to be crazy, since he knows that the other knows that he is rational.

But further analysis indicates that the reasoning survives this step as well. A player playing TFT indeed knows that the other knows that he is pretending; but she (the other) needn't know this. He therefore figures that she may well go along, in order to make him think that she believes that he is indeed crazy, and so encourage him to continue with the mutually beneficial TFT. So he tries, and she indeed goes along, for precisely that reason.

Indeed, it appears that one can carry mutual knowledge of rationality to any finite level short of common knowledge, and still get the same effect: that the players will be motivated to play mutually beneficial but seemingly irrational strategies.

Most of us have experienced situations where some harmful fact is perfectly well known but is studiously overlooked by everybody. In this case, the harmful fact is the players' rationality (!). More precisely, the fact itself need not be harmful, but common knowledge of it would be. The above approach enables us to understand this phenomenon within the context of the theory.

This reasoning presupposes the kind of setting where the perturbation is mutually beneficial. In other settings where the "crazy perturbation" methodology has been applied, such as the chain-store paradox, we do not know whether the results extend.

Dedication

Lovingly dedicated to Frank Hahn, who has always had a penchant for the irrational.

Acknowledgments

Research partially supported by NSF grant IRI-8814953 at the Institute for Mathematical Studies in the Social Sciences, Stanford University. I am grateful to Adam Brandenburger for some important input, and, in particular, for pointing out a serious error in a previous version.

References

Aumann, R. J., 1987, "Correlated equilibrium as an expression of Bayesian rationality." *Econometrica* 55, 1–18 [Chapter 8].

Aumann, R. J. and S. Sorin, 1989, "Cooperation and bounded recall." *Games and Economic Behavior* 1, 5–39.

Fudenberg, D. and D. Levine, 1989, "Reputation and equilibrium selection in games with a single patient player." *Econometrica* 57, 759–778.

Fudenberg, D. and E. Maskin, 1986, "The Folk Theorem in repeated games with discounting and with incomplete information." *Econometrica* 54, 533–554.

Harsanyi, J. C., 1967–68, "Games of incomplete information played by Bayesian players" (parts I, II, III). *Management Science* 14, 159–182, 320–334, 486–502.

Kreps, D., P. Milgrom, J. Roberts, and R. Wilson, 1982, "Rational cooperation in the finitely repeated prisoner's dilemma." *Journal of Economic Theory* 27, 245–252.

Kreps, D. and R. Wilson, 1982, "Reputation and imperfect information." *Journal of Economic Theory* 27, 253–279.

Megiddo, N., 1986, Remarks on Bounded Rationality. IBM Research Report RJ 54310.

Milgrom, P. and J. Roberts, 1982, "Predation, reputation and entry deterrence." *Journal of Economic Theory* 27, 280–312.

Radner, R., 1968, "Competitive equilibrium under uncertainty." *Econometrica* 36, 31–58.

Radner. R., 1972, "Existence of equilibrium plans, prices, and price expectations in a sequence of markets." *Econometrica* 40, 289–303.

Radner, R., 1980, "Collusive behavior in non-cooperative epsilon-equilibria in oligopolies with long but finite lives." *Journal of Economic Theory* 22, 136–154.

Radner, R., 1986, "Can bounded rationality resolve the prisoners' dilemma." In *Essays in Honor of Gerard Debreu*, ed. A. Mas-Colell and W. Hildenbrand. North-Holland, 387–400.

Rosenthal, R., 1982, "Games of perfect information, predatory pricing, and the chain store paradox." *Journal of Economic Theory* 25, 92–100.

Savage, L. J., 1954, *The Foundations of Statistics.* Wiley.

Part 4

Comments and Replies

Chapter 15

A Note on Backward Induction*,†

Ken Binmore

This note argues that the rationality of backward induction necessarily involves the study of counterfactuals.

It now seems to be generally accepted that rational players would not necessarily use their backward-induction strategies if there were to be a deviation from the backward-induction path (Binmore, 1987). But Aumann (1995) has recently offered a formal defense of the proposition that prior common knowledge of rationality implies that play will nevertheless necessarily follow the backward-induction path. This brief note, extracted from a longer philosophical paper (Binmore, 1996), questions the definition of rationality that he employs.

What keeps a rational player on the equilibrium path is his evaluation of what would happen if he were to deviate. But, if he were to deviate, he would behave irrationally. Other players would then be foolish if they were not to take this evidence of irrationality into account in planning their responses to the deviation. A formal model that neglects what *would* happen if a rational player *were* to deviate from rational play must therefore be missing something important, no matter how elaborately it is analyzed. However, Aumann (1995,

*Reprinted from *Games and Economic Behavior* (1996), 17, 135–137, with permission from Elsevier.
†The support of the ESRC Centre for Economic Learning and Social Evolution and the Leverhulme Trust is gratefully acknowledged.

Section 5f) is insistent that his conclusions say nothing whatever about what players would do if vertices of the game tree off the backward induction path were to be reached.[1] But, if nothing can be said about what would happen *off* the backward-induction path, then it seems obvious that nothing can be said about the rationality of remaining *on* the backward-induction path. How else do we assess the cleverness of taking an action than by considering what would have happened if one of the alternative actions had been taken? But this is precisely what Aumann's (1995) definition of rationality fails to do.

In Binmore (1987), I used Rosenthal's (1981) Centipede Game of Fig. 1 as an example when criticizing the defense of the backward-induction principle that was then current. The same example will also suffice here.

According to Aumann (1995), common knowledge of rationality in the Centipede makes it irrational for Player I to choose *across* at his opening move. Aumann supports this conclusion by denying that the rationality of choosing *down* need involve any knowledge at all of what would happen if *across* were played. Instead of saying that it is rational for Player I to choose *down* if he knows or believes that choosing *across* would not result in a higher payoff, Aumann says that it is rational for Player I to choose *down* if he does not know

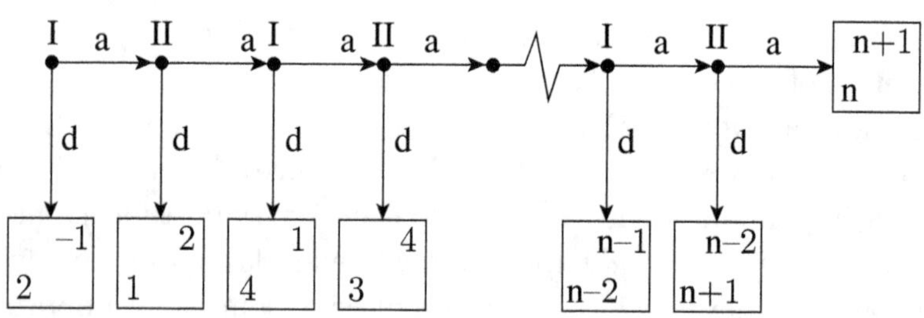

Figure 1

[1]Although he avoids the subjunctive mood, I take this to be the meaning of the apparently oxymoronic sentence, "The results of this paper say nothing about the behaviour of the players at vertices that are off the backward induction path and are actually reached."

that choosing *across* would result in a higher payoff. That is to say, Aumann moves the word "not" from one place to another.

But do we really want to deny the standard Bayesian assumption that Player I can quantify his ignorance about what would happen if he were to play *across*?[2] If not, then Player I must assign a probability p to the event that the result of his playing *across* would be a payoff of at least 4, rather than the payoff of 2 he gets by playing *down*. The latter eventuality would result, for example, if Player II were to deduce from Player I's choosing *across* at the first node that Player I would also choose *across* if the third node were reached.

If *down* is the only Bayesian-rational action at the opening, then $p < \frac{1}{2}$. But why is $p < \frac{1}{2}$?[3] We seem to be stuck with the implication that $p < \frac{1}{2}$ is somehow built into the assumption that there is common knowledge of rationality. But what would be the source of this knowledge? Surely we should not be arguing that Player I must know or believe something because the action we attribute to him is rational. The causal chain should run from knowledge to action rather than the reverse.

In denying Aumann's (1995) claim that common knowledge of rationality necessarily implies backward induction, I do not want to argue that backward induction is irrelevant to game-theoretic analyses. For example, one may use induction to demonstrate that all Nash equilibria in the Centipede require Player I to choose *down* with probability one at the opening move. Personally, I think that the Nash equilibria of interest for the issues that Rosenthal (1981) invented the Centipede to explore are those in which Player I is actually indifferent between playing *down* and *across* at the opening move — but this is another story told elsewhere (Binmore, 1996).

[2]Aumann's (1995, Section 4c) comments on how his approach can be framed in Bayesian terms are irrelevant to this point, since his formalism does not allow counterfactuals to be expressed.

[3]One cannot argue that common knowledge of rationality implies that $p = 0$ because, according to Aumann, the play of *across* at the opening move would refute the hypothesis that Player I is rational — and anything whatever follows from a contradiction.

References

Aumann, R. 1995, Backward induction and common knowledge of rationality, *Games and Econ. Behav.* 8, 6–19. [Chapter 11]

Binmore, K. 1987, Modeling rational players, I, *Econ. Philos.* 3, 9–55.

Binmore, K. 1996, Rationality and backward induction, Centre for Economic Learning and Social Evolution at University College London. (http://ada.econ.ucl.ac.uk).

Rosenthal, R. 1981, Games of perfect information, predatory pricing, and chain-store paradox, *J. Econ. Theory* 25, 92–100.

Chapter 16

Reply to Binmore*

"Go to Father," she said,
When he asked her to wed,
For she knew that he knew that her father was dead,
And she knew that he knew what a life he had led,
So she knew that he knew what she meant when she said,
"Go to Father."

—*Folk ditty*

Though we found it difficult to follow Binmore's (1996) critique (henceforth [B]) of Aumann (1995) (henceforth [A]), we acknowledge that [A] is not transparent. Here we reply to [B], and also explain the analysis of [A] in verbal, conceptual terms, covering some points not covered in [A].

Section 1 responds to Binmore's criticism of our definition of rationality. Sections 2 and 3 clear up two fundamental misunderstandings in [B]. Sections 4 through 7 discuss the proof of our Theorem A; Section 6 makes a point of general methodological interest; Section 8 discusses the proof of Theorem B. Section 9 reformulates our results in terms of ordinary Bayesian rationality (rather than the weaker form of rationality used in [A]).

*Reprinted from *Games and Economic Behavior* (1996), 17, 138–146, with permission from Elsevier.

1. [B]'s primary point concerns our definition of "rationality". Roughly, this specifies that a player i is rational if and only if it is not the case that he knows that he would be able to do better (for the precise definition, please see [A], p. 9).

Binmore questions the ordering of the words in this definition. He suggests two different emendations. In the first, i is rational if and only if he knows that he would not be able to do better. The second calls for a standard Bayesian framework, with utilities and probabilities; this enables us to apply the standard definition, according to which a player is rational if and only if he would be unable to increase his expected utility.

Leaving aside the merits of these two definitions, let us say at once that *with either one, both theorems of* [A] *remain true without any change.*

To see why, call the three forms of rationality, respectively, [A]-rationality, [B]-rationality, and Bayes rationality. Of the three, [A]-rationality is the weakest (easiest to achieve) and [B]-rationality the strongest, while Bayes rationality is between the two. That is to say, every [B]-rational choice is Bayes rational, and every Bayes rational choice is [A]-rational. Therefore, common knowledge (*CK*) of [B]-rationality implies *CK* of [A]-rationality; and, also, *CK* of Bayes rationality implies *CK* of [A]-rationality. But by Theorem A of [A], *CK* of [A]-rationality implies backward induction. Therefore *CK* of either of the other two forms of rationality implies backward induction (BI). In the other direction, one may verify directly, as in [A], that *CK* of [B]-rationality (and a fortiori of Bayes rationality) is possible in every perfect information game.

We agree with Binmore that Bayes rationality is the most natural and straightforward of the three. We nevertheless favored [A]-rationality, for several reasons. One is that it yields a stronger result; that is, the result with [A]-rationality implies that with Bayes rationality, but not the other way around. Another is that this strength is obtained at no extra cost. In fact it is cheaper, because working with Bayes rationality requires the explicit introduction of probabilities, which just complicate the system without serving any essential purpose. Finally, justifying the standard Bayesian framework requires an axiom system such as that of Savage (1954). While we ourselves have no problem with this, there are others who do; so we felt it preferable to avoid implicitly assuming axioms that really have nothing to do with the matter at hand.

In brief, our result says that *CK* of an extremely weak form of rationality already implies BI; a fortiori this is so for stronger forms of rationality, including the standard Bayesian form.

The gist of this discussion appears already[1] in [A, 4c and Footnote 4]. To avoid future misunderstandings, we present a formal treatment in Section 9 below.

2. On a more conceptual level: [B] opens with the sentence, "It now seems to be generally accepted that rational players would not necessarily use their backward induction strategies if there were to be a deviation from the backward induction path." Apparently, Binmore sees some kind of inconsistency or contradiction between this and the results of [A].

In fact, there is no inconsistency. We agree wholeheartedly with [B]'s first sentence. Indeed, we go further: even if there has been *no* deviation from the backward induction path up to some point, a rational player may well deviate at that point. A rational player may even deviate from the backward induction path at the very first move of the game. We have said this repeatedly. Thus [A, p. 18]: "... the inductive choice may be not only unreasonable and unwise, but quite simply irrational;" and Aumann (1992) shows that in the centipede game adduced in [B], it may be *incumbent* on rational players to "stay in" until quite late in the game.

Our results concern a situation with *CK* of rationality, *not* just rationality. Binmore continuously confounds these concepts, using them almost interchangeably. Here and there he pays lip service to *CK* of rationality (*CKR*); but substantively he argues as if only simple rationality were assumed. Needless to say, our argument will not work in such an environment. We do make essential use of *CKR*.

[1]Footnote 3 of [B] acknowledges this, but dismisses it for reasons that we do not understand.

3. Another error of Binmore is his failure to distinguish between the subjunctive and indicative moods. In [A, 5f], we wrote

> "The results of this paper ([A]) say nothing about the behavior of players at vertices that are off the backward induction path and are actually reached." (*)

[B] takes this to mean that nothing can be said about what players *would* do if off-path vertices *were* to be reached; he concludes that we "deny ... that the rationality of choosing *down* need involve any knowledge at all of what would happen if *across* were played." But we neither meant nor said that.[2] Indeed [A] heavily stresses the precise opposite: "The subjunctive mood — what (a player) *would* do, even when not given the opportunity — is of the essence" [A, 4b]; or, "Making a decision means choosing among alternatives. Thus one *must* consider hypothetical situations — what would happen if one did something different from what one actually does ... In ... games, you must consider what other people would do if you did something different from what you actually do" [A, 5b].

These are not just empty words; they lie at the heart not only of [A]'s conceptual approach, but also of its formal treatment. A strategy of a player is defined as a function that assigns an action to *each* of his vertices, reached or not; the rationality of a player is defined in terms of his rationality at each of his vertices; and this, in turn, is defined in terms of what he knows about the other

---

[2]Our intention could not have been made clearer. The indicative mood is heavily stressed: "are actually reached." "*Are*"; not "would", not "were to be". For the case that somebody might still misunderstand, the word "*actually*" is thrown in. And if, by some stretch of the imagination, *somebody* might *still* misunderstand, our very next sentence (not cited by Binmore) would surely clear things up: "Under *CKR*, vertices off the backward induction path *cannot* be reached; and when *CKR* does not obtain, the results do not apply."

Binmore calls (*) oxymoronic. That is beyond our comprehension. Why can't vertices off the BI path actually be reached? To be sure, they can't be reached under *CKR*, as we say explicitly in the very next sentence. But why can't they be reached when *CKR* does not obtain? And if Binmore had somehow understood that we were implicitly assuming *CKR* in (*), surely the very next sentence should have disabused him.

players' strategies. Thus in deciding whether a player i is rational when choosing *down* in the centipede game, we do explicitly take into account what i knows or thinks about what the other player would have done if i had gone across. Binmore is 180° off the mark.

4. Though Binmore makes an unconvincing case, the malaise that he evinces is not totally groundless. We believe our analysis to be both conceptually and formally sound; but it is not straightforward, and we are grateful for this opportunity to elucidate it. This and the next section discuss Theorem A of [A], according to which *CKR* implies BI; Theorem B is treated in Section 6.

To start with, one really must differentiate very sharply between rationality and *CKR* (see Section 2 above). That a player is rational at a vertex v means that his choices at v and at his subsequent vertices maximize his expected payoff given his beliefs[3] at v. In forming his beliefs at v, the player may take into account whatever he wishes. In particular, he may take into account the actions of other players at previous moves [A, 5d]. Thus in [B]'s centipede game, Player II (P2) may, at his first vertex, play *across* for precisely the reason that Binmore adduces: that noting that Player I (P1) played *across* at *her* first vertex, he estimates that she will play *across* again. P1, in turn, may take this into account when making *her* first move, so that she may well wish to play *across* at *her* first move. In fact, it makes no difference how the players form their beliefs; as long as their actions maximize their expected payoffs, they are rational. As a result, rational players may well play *across* for a very long time in the centipede game. We have said this again and again, both here and in [A], but apparently one cannot say it often enough.

But Theorem A of [A] assumes not only that the players are rational; it assumes also that this is common knowledge. In particular, P1 knows that if P2's last vertex *were* reached, he *would* play down (subjunctive!). She knows this for *sure*, without a shadow of a doubt, because she *knows* that P2 is rational. Therefore, if P1's

[3]The presentation here is in terms of Bayes rationality, in accordance with Sections 1 above and 9 below.

last vertex were reached, *she* would play down. Now P2 *knows* that P1 is rational, and he knows that she knows that he is rational. So he knows what we just concluded: that if her last vertex were reached, she would play down. He knows this for sure, without a shadow of a doubt. Therefore, if his next-to-last vertex were reached, he, being rational, would play down. And so on, until we conclude that P1 plays down at her first vertex.

The point is that while the beliefs of a rational player *might* motivate him to play *across*, they don't *have* to. The assumption of *CKR* gives us — and the players — additional information, information that enables us to conclude that each player would go down at each of his vertices v, if that vertex were reached.

5. "But," the reader may ask, "something still bothers me. You have proved that under *CKR*, P1 must go *down* at the first vertex. You did this by working your way backward from the last vertex, showing that at each vertex v, the player at v would have to go *down* if v were reached. Very good. Having proved this, you know it, I know it, and the players know it. Now let's reexamine the proof. P1 must go *down* at her first vertex. In deciding on this, she must take the alternatives into account. You yourself stressed this, both in [A] and above (Section 3). So P1 must ask herself, what would happen if she went *across*? Well, we know that under *CKR*, she *can't* go *across*; we've proved that. So if she *did* go *across*, she would be demonstrating that *CKR* does not obtain. It would then be illegitimate to use the conclusions of *CKR* also insofar as they apply to the second vertex; that is, it would be illegitimate to conclude that P2 would necessarily go *down* at the second vertex. So, he might go *across*. In that case, P1 would prefer to go *across* at the first vertex. So the proof that *CKR* implies *down* at the first vertex, which looked good at first, breaks down on reexamination. It carries within it the seeds of its own destruction."

6. Before responding to this substantively, we make a methodological point. It is difficult to evaluate the validity of this kind of contorted reasoning using verbal tools only. That is a function of mathematical formalisms. In a formal model the conclusions are derived from definitions and assumptions. Once one is satisfied that the derivation is mathematically correct, it remains only to examine the appropriateness of the definitions and assumptions. But with informal, verbal reasoning as complex as the above, one never knows for sure whether the argument is sound. One can argue until one is blue in the face, without convincing one another, because there is no criterion for deciding the soundness of an informal argument.

So we say, gentle reader, it is indeed possible that the conclusions of [A] are unsound; but if so, that can only be for one of two reasons: either there is a mathematical error in our proof, or one of our definitions or assumptions is conceptually inappropriate. No one has challenged the correctness of our mathematics. [B] does challenge the appropriateness of our definition of rationality; we respond in Sections 1 above and 9 below. We welcome other challenges to our definitions or assumptions. But the kind of verbal argument typified by most of [B], and by Section 5 above, concerns the reasoning process, the process of drawing conclusions from assumptions; and in a matter of this complexity, that is better left to the mathematics.

7. Nevertheless, we now respond to the question in Section 5 within the same informal genre. The error in the argument is that it mixes the conclusion of the proof[4] into the proof itself. That is not legitimate. Suppose we have proved a theorem of the form "p implies q." But our hypothetical reader is skeptical. "The proof sounds right," he says, "but let's look again. Assume p. Perhaps, after all, this could jibe with 'not q.' So suppose that it does — i.e., that q does not obtain. But then, since we have proved that p implies q, it cannot be that p obtains. So we conclude that after all, p doesn't obtain. But if p doesn't obtain, we no longer have grounds for concluding q. So your proof doesn't hold up under examination — you'll have to abandon it."

Clearly, this argument is absurd.

But that is exactly the argument in Section 5. Starting with *CKR*, we prove that P1 goes down at the first vertex. Now, we say, let's try

[4]That vertices off the backward induction path cannot be reached under *CKR*.

it again. Must P1 *really* go down at the first vertex? Let's suppose not — i.e., that she goes across. But then we have a contradiction to *CKR*, and anything whatever follows from a contradiction! So we must abandon *CKR*. But then there is no longer any reason to go down at the first vertex.

Just as clearly, *this* argument is absurd.

8. We come now to Theorem B, which says that *CKR* is possible in every perfect information game. Here we do *not* assume *CKR*; we want to prove that it is possible, for appropriate choices of moves and information. The proof is simple: just let each player make his inductive choice at each of his vertices v, if v is reached, and stipulate that this be commonly known. It is easily verified that *CKR* then indeed obtains.

In the centipede game, for example, we stipulate that each player play *down* at each vertex, if reached, and that this be commonly known. *CKR* then *follows*.

9. As promised in Section 1, we now provide a formal account of the results of [A] using Bayes rationality rather than the very weak version of rationality used in [A] (called [A]-rationality in Section 1). We freely use the terminology, notation, and results of [A].

Start with a knowledge system $\{\Omega, \mathbf{s}, \{\mathscr{K}_i\}_i\}$ as in [A,2], where i ranges over the players. For each vertex v and strategy n-tuple s, set $s^{\geq v} := (s^v, s^{>v})$; thus $s^{\geq v}$ is the profile of actions prescribed by s at v and at subsequent vertices. Denote by $\mathscr{F}^v$ the field of events generated by the "random variable"[5] $\mathbf{s}^{\geq v}$; that is, the smallest field with respect to which the function $\mathbf{s}^{\geq v}$ is measurable (note that this field is finite). In words, an event is in $\mathscr{F}^v$ if and only if it is describable in terms of the actions taken at v and at subsequent vertices; the events in $\mathscr{F}^v$ describe what might happen if v would be reached.

Now define a *knowledge-belief system* to consist of a knowledge system as above, and for each player i, each of i's vertices v, and each

[5]Recall that $\mathbf{s}(\omega)$ is the n-tuple of the players' strategies in the state ω.

state ω, a probability measure $\pi_i^v(\cdot;\omega)$ on $\mathscr{F}^v$; $\pi_i^v(E;\omega)$ signifies i's probability for E at v in the state ω. Set $B_i^v E := \{\omega : \pi_i^v(E;\omega) = 1\}$; in words, $B_i^v E$ is the event that i believes E — that is, ascribes probability 1 to E — at v. Assume that

$$K_i E \subset B_i^v E \tag{1}$$

for all E in $\mathscr{F}^v$ and all vertices v of i; this says that if before the beginning of play, i knows something about the actions that would be taken if v were reached, then he assigns it probability 1 at v. In a given state ω of the world, call i *Bayes rational* if

$$\mathrm{Exp}_{i,v,w} h_i^v(\mathbf{s}) \geq \mathrm{Exp}_{i,v,w} h_i^v(\mathbf{s}; t_i) \tag{2}$$

for each of i's vertices v and strategies t_i, where $\mathrm{Exp}_{i,v,w}$ denotes the expectation with respect to the probability measure $\pi_i^v(\cdot;\omega)$; since h_i^v is defined in terms of what happens starting at v only, $h_i^v(\mathbf{s})$ and $h_i^v(\mathbf{s}; t_i)$ are $\mathscr{F}^v$-measurable, so the expectations are defined.

In words, (2) says that i's strategy at ω maximizes his expected conditional payoff at v. Denote by R^B the event that all players are Bayes rational.[6]

Theorem A. $CKR^B \subset I$.

Theorem B. *For every PI game, there is a knowledge-belief system with* $\emptyset \neq CKR^B$.

In words, Theorem A says that if Bayes rationality is commonly known, the inductive outcome results; Theorem B, that common knowledge of Bayes rationality is indeed possible in every PI game.

Denote by R_i^B the event "i is Bayes rational;" thus R^B is the intersection of the R_i^B. Recall that R_i is the event "i is rational" in the sense of [A], and that the intersection of the R_i — i.e., the event that all players are rational — is denoted R.

Lemma. $R_i^B \subset R_i$.

[6]I.e., the set of all ω such that all players are Bayes rational in the state ω.

In words, if a player is Bayes rational, then he is rational in the sense of [A],

Proof. Let $\omega \in R_i^B$. Then for each vertex v and strategy t_i of i, we have (2); that is, in ω, i's expectation at v of $h_i^v(\mathbf{s}; t_i)$ is not greater than his expectation at v of $h_i^v(\mathbf{s})$. So it cannot be that in ω, Player i assigns probability 1 to the event $[h_i^v(\mathbf{s}; t_i) > h_i^v(\mathbf{s})]$; in symbols, $\omega \in {\sim}B_i^v[h_i^v(\mathbf{s}; t_i) > h_i^v(\mathbf{s})]$. So by (1), $\omega \in {\sim}K_i[h_i^v(\mathbf{s}; t_i) > h_i^v(\mathbf{s})]$. Since this holds for all v and t_i, it follows that $\omega \in \bigcap_{v \in V_i} \bigcap_{t_i \in S_i} {\sim}K_i[h_i^v(\mathbf{s}; t_i) > h_i^v(\mathbf{s})] = R_i$, by (3) of [A].

Proof of Theorem A. From the lemma and the definitions of R and R^B, we get $R^B \subset R$. Now it is known that for any events E and F, if $E \subset F$, then $CKE \subset CKF$. So $CKR^B \subset CKR$. But $CKR \subset I$, by Theorem A of [A]. So $CKR^B \subset I$.

Proof of Theorem B. Define a knowledge-belief system by letting Ω consist of a single state ω, in which each player makes his inductive choice at each of his vertices. Then $\omega \in CKR^B$.

A final note[7]: Bayes rationality is here defined in "ex-post" terms — what i would think[8] if v were reached, rather than in "ex ante" terms — what he thinks at the beginning of the game. The formal development in [A] uses the ex ante definition, because in the context of [A], it is weaker,[9] and so yields a stronger version[10] of Theorem A; see [A, 5e]. But in the current Bayesian context, ex ante rationality is neither weaker nor stronger than (nor equivalent to) ex post rationality. As explained in [A, 5e], ex post rationality seems more relevant than ex ante rationality. Therefore, since in the current context, the ex post result does *not* follow from the ex ante one, use of the ex post definition is indicated here. We stress, though, that

[7]This is a technical note, which may be ignored without affecting the understanding of the rest of the paper.

[8]The term "think" is meant to encompass both "know" and "attribute probability."

[9]That is, ex post [A]-rationality implies ex ante [A]-rationality.

[10]A weaker hypothesis means a stronger result.

this applies to rationality as such only; "knowledge" and "common knowledge" remain ex ante, i.e., refer to the beginning of the game.

Acknowledgment

Research support from the Game Theory Program at SUNY-Stony Brook is gratefully acknowledged. Also, we thank Dov Samet for many helpful conversations about this work. The folk ditty was communicated to us by Miriam Aumann (1892–1961).

References

Aumann, R. J., 1995, "Backward Induction and Common Knowledge of Rationality," *Games and Econ. Behav.* 8, 6–19 **([A] in the text)** [Chapter 11].

Aumann, R. J., 1992, "Irrationality in Game Theory," in *Economic Analysis of Markets and Games*, Essays in Honor of Frank Hahn (P. Dasgupta, D. Gale, O. Hart, and E. Maskin, Eds.), 214–227. Cambridge, MA: MIT Press [Chapter 14].

Binmore, K., 1996, "A Note on Backward Induction," *Games and Econ. Behav.* 17, 135–137 **([B] in the text)** [Chapter 15].

Savage, L. J., 1954, *The Foundations of Statistics*. New York: Wiley.

Chapter 17

Rationalizing Backward Induction?[*,†]

Ken Binmore and Larry Samuelson

'One must imagine Sisyphus happy' (Albert Camus)

1. The Myth of Sisyphus

Binmore (1987) explains why backward induction in games cannot be justified by assuming only that there is common knowledge of rationality before the game begins. In writing once more on the myth that it can, we feel like Sisyphus rolling his rock to the top of the hill again. However, it is necessary to respond to Aumann's (1995) attempt to revitalize a fallacy which game theorists must abandon if their discipline is to continue to be taken seriously.[1]

For example, backward induction calls for both players always to play *down* in Rosenthal's Centipede Game of Figure 1. It similarly requires that both players always defect in the finitely repeated

*Reprinted from *The Rational Foundations of Economic Behavior* (1996), edited by K. J. Arrow, E. Colombatto, M. Perlman and C. Schmidt, Chapter 5, 111–124, with permission from Palgrave Macmillan.

†The support of National Science Foundation grant SES 9122176 is gratefully acknowledged.

[1]Since this paper was written, a new version of Aumann's (1995) paper has been circulated. In addition to the argument criticized here, the new paper contains a different argument for backward induction which Aumann attributes to Samet. Samet's argument fails for much the same reason as Aumann's.

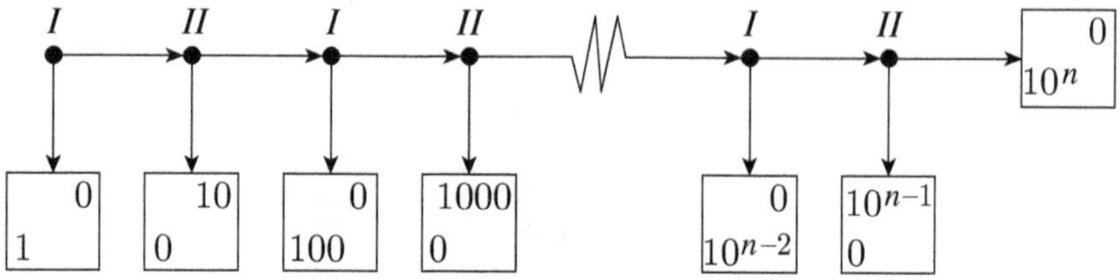

Figure 1: Rosenthal's Centipede

Prisoners' Dilemma. It also calls for an established retail chain never to resist an entrant in Selten's Chain-Store Paradox. These conclusions are not only counterintuitive. As prescriptions to be followed for purely rational reasons, they are *unsound*, as explained at length in Binmore (1987).

If our response to Aumann's (1995) argument is to be understood, it is essential to be clear from the outset that the issue is not mathematical. In presenting his paper at the recent Nobel Symposium on game theory, he predicted that his audience would find his argument either wrong or trivial. But we think the mathematical part of his argument is neither trivial nor wrong. But the character of Aumann's mathematics is beside the point. We focus on the wrong question if we look for an error in how Aumann deduces his conclusion from his hypotheses.[2] An axiom-definition-theorem-proof format is designed to close the mind to irrelevancies so that attention can be concentrated on the issues that really matter. But if an inappropriate formalism is chosen, one necessarily closes one's mind to issues that it is perilous to neglect. The proverb warns us against closing the stable door after the horse has bolted. But an even worse mistake is to bolt the stable door while the horse is still in the yard.

Similar considerations bring into question the relevance to actual human behaviour of the whole literature on refinements of Nash equilibrium. Even when the arguments given in favour of the concepts are sound, such an *eductive* approach is worthy of widespread study

[2]Or for errors in the mathematics of Bicchieri (1988), Reny (1985) and others who come to different conclusions from Aumann.

by economists only to the extent that its prognostications about ideally rational play can serve as approximations to the outcomes that would result if equilibrium were achieved using an appropriate *evolutive* process (Binmore, 1987). For example, in casting doubt on backward induction, one simultaneously casts doubt on the iterated deletion of weakly dominated strategies — one of three principles that Kohlberg and Mertens (1986) list as being fundamental to a sound eductive theory.[3] However, from an *evolutive* standpoint, even *one* round of deleting weakly dominated strategies cannot be justified (Binmore, 1990, p. 75; Samuelson, 1993).

Section 5 follows Binmore, Gale and Samuelson (1993) in using Selten's (1978) Chain-Store Game as a counterexample to the notion that deleting weakly dominated strategies is harmless. The Chain-Store Game is a particularly telling arena in which to set the debate since orthodox game theorists are stuck with predicting that the only rational outcome is the unique subgame-perfect equilibrium, whereas the experimental evidence persistently shows that real people do not play this way in the strategically similar Ultimatum Game — even for high stakes after much experience.

2. Backward Induction

Aumann's formal defence of backward induction in finite games of perfect information[4] is preceded by six statements about the formal ground-rules to which his mathematics applies. The first and second statements are:

(1) Rationality is attributed to 'agents' rather than players, where each vertex of the game tree belongs to a different agent.
(2) All agents choose actions, whether or not their vertices are reached; the action of an agent signifies what he will do *if* his vertex is reached.

[3]Binmore (1987) argues that all three principles are mistaken.
[4]With this restriction, a whole class of more general criticisms (Binmore, 1987) about the concept of common knowledge of rationality can be left on the sidelines.

If the pun may be excused, the first statement immediately gives Aumann's game away. Critics like myself express doubts about backward induction in games like Rosenthal's Centipede because it requires players to continue to believe that their opponents are rational whatever evidence to the contrary may be forthcoming. For example, if common knowledge of rationality before the game begins justifies backward induction in the Centipede, then Player II knows that she and her opponent will always play *down*. So what conclusion should she draw on finding herself at the fiftieth node of the tree after repeatedly observing the refutation of the hypothesis that her opponent is rational? Proponents of backward induction tell us that 'common knowledge of rationality before the game begins' implies that she should nevertheless continue to act as though she and her opponent were rational. We do not argue that such behaviour should be excluded as a possible recommendation that a game theorist might make — only that one cannot *deduce* that all other behaviour is irrational from the given hypotheses.

Aumann evades this difficulty by following Selten (1975) in pretending that a player in the Centipede is a collection of separate and independent agents. It then becomes possible for the rationality of twenty-five of these agents to be refuted without the need to draw any inference about the irrationality of the remaining twenty-five. However, further comment on this piece of legerdemain will need to be delayed until his second statement has been discussed.

It is significant that Aumann eschews the subjunctive mood in this second statement. Properly, we should therefore interpret its second clause as a *material implication* '$P \Rightarrow Q$' in which P is the statement that a particular vertex is reached, and Q is the statement that the agent who decides at that vertex chooses 'rationally' given his information. But, if Aumann were right, 'common knowledge of rationality before the game begins' would imply that only the first vertex can be reached. The statement P is therefore false in the case of the fiftieth vertex. The corresponding implication '$P \Rightarrow Q$' is therefore true — however one interprets the meaning of Q.[5] It is as though Alekhine were asked how he would play a game of chess on an 8×8 board with 63 squares. *Any* answer would then be rational, because *anything* follows from a contradiction.

The point of being pedantic about material implication is that the final clause of Aumann's second statement needs to be interpreted as a *subjunctive conditional* for the statement to be meaningful in the intended sense. The clause should be restated as, 'The action of an agent signifies what he *would* do, if his vertex *were* reached.' As explained for example by Sandford (1989), a subjunctive conditional 'If P, then Q' is not necessarily true when P is counterfactual. It is not true that, 'If Binmore's Dean were a man, then his salary would be doubled' even though his Dean is actually a woman.

It is idle to pretend that counterfactual reasoning can be evaded in analyzing games. A rational player stays on the equilibrium path because of what he believes *would* happen if he *were* to deviate. C.I. Lewis (1946) revived Leibniz's notion of a 'possible world' in seeking to make sense of such counterfactual assertions. More recently, his namesake, David Lewis[6] (1976) has put together a full-blown theory in which sense is made of a subjunctive conditional 'If P, then Q' in which P is counterfactual, by considering all possible worlds in which P does not hold. The subjunctive conditional is then interpreted as applying to whichever of these possible worlds is 'closest' to the actual world in which we live.

Aumann (1995) is implicitly appealing to some such theory when he tells us that a particular action is rational for Player II's

[5]Samet made the same point at the Nobel Symposium where Aumann presented his paper. When the entirely rational Samet becomes King of Sweden, his avowed plan is to swap his kingdom for a cup of coffee.

[6]The same David Lewis (1969) anticipated Aumann (1976) in saying that an event E is common knowledge if and only if everybody knows E, everybody knows that everybody knows E, and so on. However, David Lewis did not anticipate Aumann's mathematical machinery, which converted a philosophical curiosity into a practical tool.

twenty-fifth agent *if* the fiftieth vertex is reached. After observing the counterfactual event that all agents at vertices preceding the fiftieth are irrational, Aumann's story makes it overwhelmingly tempting that we assume that the possible world within which his second statement is to be interpreted is that in which agents 1 to 49 are irrational and agents 50 to 100 are rational. But this is just a piece of *interpretation*. We cannot *deduce* that *only* such an interpretation is viable merely from 'common knowledge of rationality before the game begins'. If this hypothesis is refuted in play, we have a *contradiction* from which *anything* can be deduced.

Although we invoke the authority of David Lewis, we do not think that his theory of counterfactuals helps very much with game-theory problems. Everything that matters in addressing practical problems hinges on the topology used to interpret the word 'close', and this is not a subject that it makes much sense to discuss in the abstract. Before returning to Aumann's argument, let us therefore say something about our own (not very profound) attitude to counterfactuals in games.

3. Interpreting Counterfactuals

Consider a husband who explains to his wife that he would not have lost this month's mortgage repayment if he had been dealt the Ace of Diamonds rather than the Queen of Spades in last night's poker game. His wife has no difficulty in interpreting this counterfactual assertion, because the story tells her how Nature chose an actual world from a set of possible worlds that might have been. The actual world in which she is without a roof over her head was realized as a consequence of the shuffle and deal that proceeded the disastrous hand at the poker game. If a different card *had* been dealt, she *would* have retained her home.

To make sense of counterfactuals in games, we think one always needs to find an equivalent of the deal at last night's poker game. Such an equivalent cannot be found by contemplating abstract definitions of rationality, any more than the wife could make sense of her husband's counterfactual by minutely examining the card that he actually was dealt. Just as the Queen of Spades has to be seen as having been drawn from a deck of cards, so a rational player has to be seen as having been drawn from a set of possible players — some of whom are irrational.

Selten's (1975) notion of a trembling-hand equilibrium treats counterfactuals in precisely this manner. No player ever thinks an irrational thought in Selten's story, but irrational actions are taken with some small probability δ by mistake. In the limit as $\delta \to 0$, irrational moves are counterfactual. But if they were observed they would be interpreted as having taken place in a nearby possible world in which $\delta > 0$.

Selten's trembling-hand story provides a means of interpreting subjunctive conditionals that preserves backward induction. With this story, players will always defect in the finitely repeated Prisoners' Dilemma. However, in the well-known Gang of Four paper, Kreps, Milgrom, Roberts and Wilson (1982) offer an alternative story. If irrational play is observed, it is attributed to an irrational type of player who occurs with probability $\delta > 0$ and always plays *tit-for-tat* no matter what. It is shown that rational players will then cooperate for long periods in the finitely repeated Prisoners' Dilemma even though δ may be very small.

Who is right, Selten or the Gang of Four? We hope that it is now evident that this is a badly posed question. The 'rightness' of the interpretation of counterfactuals is not a matter for the propositional calculus. Nor can counterfactuals be evaded in game theory. A rational player stays on the equilibrium path because of what *would* happen if he *were* to deviate. But it is counterfactual that he will deviate. One cannot interpret such a counterfactual without having a view on the kind of mistake that a rational player *would* make, if a rational player *were* to make a mistake. To have a view on this question, it is necessary to follow the advice of Selten and Leopold (1982) in having available a model of a player which is sufficiently rich that it includes both rational and irrational variants. In the limiting case, when irrational types occur with probability zero, certain actions will be impossible. However, in the counterfactual event that such an event occurs, one has a mechanism available for dealing with a possible world in which events that are impossible in the actual world can be realized. But there is obviously no 'right' way to construct the necessary models of irrational behaviour. One needs to look at the *context* in which the game is played for inspiration on this score. But this context is precisely what is abstracted away when one adopts the conventional mathematical formalism.

Consider, for example, the context in which chess is normally played. In such a context, it is quite extraordinarily obtuse to propose a trembling-hand interpretation of the counterfactuals that arise during play. If Black repeatedly makes bad moves, is White really to assume that she always thought everything through correctly, but that Nature kept jogging her elbow at the moment of making a move so that she somehow repeatedly found herself lifting her hand having set the wrong piece down on the wrong square? Is White also to explain his *own* mistakes with the same story — even when introspection tells him that the true explanation is that he reasoned badly? When put so baldly, the suggestion is laughable. If a player makes stupid moves in chess, the explanation of first resort must surely be that he or she reasoned badly and therefore will perhaps reason badly in the future.

Aumann (1995) mentions Zermelo's celebrated use of backward induction in 1912 to show that chess has a 'solution'. But Zermelo's argument does *not* say that common knowledge of rationality implies that a player should necessarily use a subgame-perfect strategy. It tells White what to do in order to guarantee his maximin value in every subgame — but such behaviour is not necessarily optimal. Suppose, for example, that Black has missed many opportunities to win in reaching the current position,[7] and White now faces a subgame in which the best he can do against good play by Black is to force a draw. However, White sees a move that will win unless Black

[7]It is not a valid objection to say that common knowledge of rationality before the game begins precludes such an event. Although the event cannot occur given the prior information, we still have to say what White *would* do if the event *were* to occur.

responds much more cleverly than she has in the past. However, if she does see the clever response, then White will lose for sure. What should White do? The answer depends on his estimate of the probability that Black will see her clever response. Given her past behaviour, he would be stupid to assign a probability of one to this eventuality. But this is what a trembling-hand story would require him to do.

Notice that we do not deny that Zermelo's use of backward induction demonstrates that common knowledge of rationality before the game begins will indeed result in each player getting his maximin value in chess.[8] What Zermelo claimed is indeed true. Nor do we deny that it would usually be appropriate to use backward induction to analyze the Centipede, if this were *actually* played by Aumann's 100 independent agents.[9] Nor do we deny that evolution will tend to eliminate certain types of irrationality and hence open up the prospect of convergence on a subgame-perfect equilibrium in the long run. We deny only that backward induction is a *necessary consequence* of common knowledge of rationality before the game begins.

4. Chain-Store Paradox

In this section, Selten's (1978) Chain-Store Paradox will now be used as an example while discussing assumptions under which backward

[8]To compute a maximin value, one always takes the most pessimistic view of the plans of the other players. In a two-person, zero-sum game, a player who employs backward induction as recommended by Aumann will therefore come up with a strategy that guarantees his maximin value. But, for the reasons given by von Neumann and Morgenstern (1944), with common knowledge of rationality at time zero in a two-person, zero-sum game, neither player can hope for more than his maximin value.

[9]But not always. It may be, as in the Horse Game studied in Binmore (1987), that there are grounds for supposing that some type of irrationality in one player will be correlated with the same type of irrationality in another. (After all, the number of business schools is not so very large and so different agents might well have been taught game theory by the same instructor.)

induction can be justified. Figure 2(a) shows a version of the Chain-Store Game. Player II is a chain-store and Player I is a potential rival thinking of setting up a single store that will compete with the chain in one particular town. Player I must stay out of the market by playing H or enter by playing L. In the latter case, Player II may acquiesce to the new situation by playing Y or she may initiate a price war by playing N.

A backward induction analysis results in the subgame-perfect equilibrium in which Player II chooses Y and Player I chooses L, as indicated by the doubled lines in Figure 2(a). Traditional game theory therefore predicts that the potential rival will enter and that the chain-store will acquiesce. The chain-store paradox arises when the Chain-Store Game is repeated 100 times with a new potential entrant at each repetition. Backward induction again leads to a subgame-perfect equilibrium in which all potential entrants enter the market and the chain-store always acquiesces to their entry. The doubled lines in Figure 2(b) show the subgame-perfect choices at each

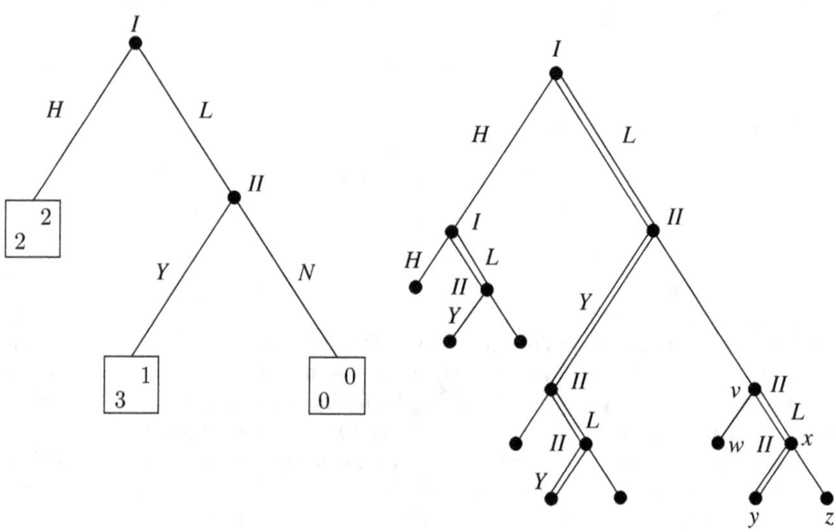

(a) Extensive form

(b) Twice-repeated game

Figure 2: The Chain-Store Game

node in the case when the Chain-Store Game is repeated only twice. Selten (1978) regarded such an outcome as paradoxical, because the chain-store has the alternative strategy of fighting the first few entrants with a view to establishing a reputation for toughness that will deter the entry of later potential entrants.

As with the repeated Prisoners' Dilemma, it is not hard to find variants of the repeated Chain-Store Game in which a traditional analysis does not eliminate the use of a tough strategy by the chain-store. One may allow the number of repetitions to be indefinite. Or one may stick with the finitely repeated case and follow Kreps, Milgrom, Roberts and Wilson (1982) by introducing a small amount of incomplete information about the type of the chain-store. Even a small prior probability that the chain-store may be an 'irrational' type who always fights is enough to overturn the subgame-perfect prediction of the original game. However, this chapter is about the validity of backward induction rather than the realism of various models. We shall therefore stick with the finitely repeated case with perfect information.

Even in this case, we argue that no paradox exists, because there are flaws in the reasoning by means of which Aumann (1995) and others with less formal arguments deduce the backward induction principle from the assumption that there is common knowledge of rationality before the game begins. In fact, the next section offers evolutive reasons why we should not exclude Nash equilibria that fail to be subgame-perfect even when the Chain-Store Game is played *once and once only*.

Nevertheless, we do not deny that there are eductive assumptions that do justify backward induction. And we agree very much with Aumann (1995) that, although the reasoning that deduces backward induction from such assumptions may be criticized as trivial, it is still worthwhile being explicit about what assumptions are necessary. However, the two alternative assumptions considered here will not be nearly as attractive to applied workers as Aumann's suggestion that it suffices to assume that there is common knowledge of rationality before the game begins.

Assumption 1. The first assumption we consider is that it is not only common knowledge before the game begins that all players are rational, but that it would always remain common knowledge that the players would act rationally in the future — regardless of what might have happened in the past. This assumption need not be discussed further since it merely makes explicit the missing assumptions in Aumann's argument.

Assumption 2. The second assumption we consider follows Binmore (1993) in appealing to a very strong form of revealed preference theory. The purpose of the argument is to show that various fallacies that purport to show that it is rational to 'make commitments' cannot possibly demonstrate that backward induction is *necessarily* irrational in certain games. The trivial argument in fact shows that *any* behaviour in a finite game of perfect information can be rationalized as being subgame-perfect if one is free to make whatever assumptions seem convenient about what is going on inside the heads of the players.

Consider, for example, the pattern of behaviour indicated in the twice-repeated, Chain-Store Game of Figure 2(b). Let us focus on the node x reached after the history *LNL*. Since the action Y at this node is doubled, assign a payoff to Player II at the node y that is reached after the history *LNLY* a higher payoff than at the terminal node z reached after the history *LNLN*. Now focus on the terminal node v reached after the history *LN*. Since the action L is doubled at this node, assign a higher payoff to Player III at the terminal node y than at the terminal node w reached after the history *LNH*. The interpretation that goes with such an assignment of payoffs is the following. It is taken to be common knowledge that Player II would choose Y if node x were reached. It is also taken to be common knowledge that Player III would choose H if node v were reached. Notice that, in the latter case, Player III has available information about the nature of Player II that will be part of what determines his knowledge about what Player II would do if Player III were to play L. The information is that Player II played N in the past. This is a counterfactual event before the game begins.

Such an extreme use of the theory of revealed preference clarifies certain logical matters. It is even more useful in exposing the fallacies of those who argue that cooperation in the one-shot Prisoners' Dilemma is necessarily rational. However, it should be emphasized that its interpretation of the payoffs in the repeated Chain-Store Game differs markedly from that normally taken for granted in game theory (although not in the one-shot Prisoners' Dilemma). In Figure 2(a), for example, the standard assumption is that the payoffs 0, 2 and 3 attributed to Player I are von Neumann and Morgenstern utilities that can be elicited by asking Player I hypothetical questions about his preferences amongst lotteries in which the prizes are the outcomes represented by the terminal nodes. But such hypothetical questions can be answered without any reference to what Player I knows about what Player II would choose if Player I were to play L.

5. Ultimatum Game

In this section, we abandon the extreme version of revealed preference theory discussed in the previous section. In the Ultimatum Game to be studied next, the payoffs can be taken to be sums of money. Our plan is to use the game as an example in which backward induction goes spectacularly awry in an evolutive context.

The Ultimatum Game involves two players who must divide a dollar. The rules specify that Player I begins by making an offer of $x \in [0, 1]$ to Player II, who then accepts or refuses. If Player II accepts, Player I gets $1 - x$ and Player II gets x. If Player II refuses, both get nothing. Traditional game theory predicts that the play of this game will result in the unique subgame-perfect equilibrium in which Player II plans to accept whatever she is offered and Player I offers Player II nothing.[10]

Although subgame-perfect predictions sometimes perform well in laboratory tests, this is not true of the Ultimatum Game. In the first of many experiments by numerous authors on this and related

[10] If offers must be made in whole number of cents, other subgame-perfect equilibria also exist, but Player II never gets more than one cent in any of these.

games, Güth *et al.* (1982) found that the modal offer was one-half and that Player I had roughly half a chance of being rejected if he offered about one-third of the sum of money available. Results of this general character have been repeatedly observed under increasingly more challenging conditions, as reported in the surveys of Bolton and Zwick (1993), Güth and Tietz (1990), Roth (1991) and Thaler (1988).

Orthodox game theorists tend to ignore these experimental results, or else express doubts about the validity of the experimental data. However, we suggest that a more realistic attitude is to question a theory whose relevance to actual behaviour is being so firmly refuted. To explore the possibility that the eductive arguments which lead to the subgame-perfect prediction in the Ultimatum Game are irrelevant to behaviour generated by an evolutive process, Binmore, Gale and Samuelson (1993) have run extensive simulations of noisy versions of the replicator dynamics for the Ultimatum Game. Even if the absolute noise levels are very small, they find that, when the responding population is noisier than the proposing population, a Nash equilibrium that is not subgame-perfect survives as an asymptotic attractor. At this Nash equilibrium, Player I offers about 20 per cent of the dollar to Player II. Player II refuses all smaller offers with some positive probability.[11]

Space does not allow a discussion of these simulations. Instead, we shall study the version of the Chain-Store Game given in Figure 2(a). This can be regarded as a simplified form of the Ultimatum Game. For this interpretation, Player I is seen as having the opportunity to make a high offer (H) or a low offer (L). If he makes a high offer, it is assumed that Player II accepts. If he makes a low offer,

[11]It is natural to object that Player II should realize that it is irrational to choose nothing when something is available without waiting to be taught by evolution. On this subject, it is perhaps instructive to follow Frank (1988) in considering how most of us behave in restaurants that we never expect to visit again. After the waiter gives your change, you can either take it all or return the customary amount. Of course, we tell ourselves little stories about why we do the latter that do not involve irrationality. This section discusses why such stories and the emotional attitudes that accompany them manage to survive.

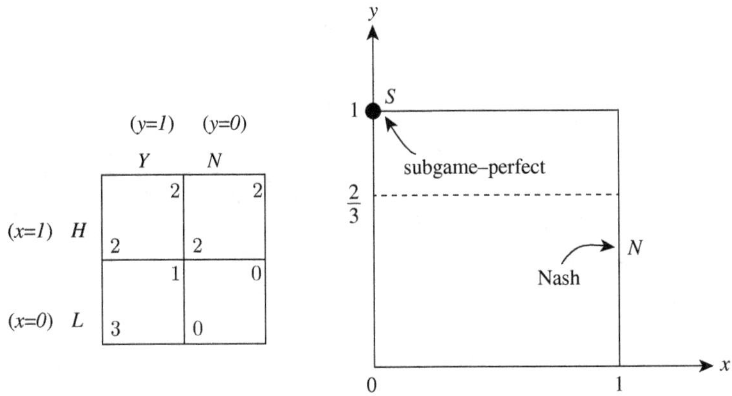

(a) (b)

Figure 3: The Chain-Store Game again

Player II may accept (Y) or refuse (N). Figure 3(b) shows the pairs (x, y) that represent equilibria in the game, where x and y are the probabilities with which H and Y are played. There is a unique subgame-perfect equilibrium S at (0, 1) in Figure 3(b), and a component N of Nash equilibria occupying the closed line segment joining (1, 2/3) and (1, 0).

Figure 4(a) shows the trajectories of the standard replicator dynamics in the Chain-Store Game:

$$\dot{x} = x(1 - x)(2 - 3y) \tag{1}$$

$$\dot{y} = y(1 - y)(1 - x) \tag{2}$$

Notice that the subgame-perfect equilibrium S is an asymptotic attractor. But there are Nash equilibria which are local attractors without being subgame-perfect. This is true of all the points in the relative interior of N.

One may reasonably respond to the observation that Nash equilibria other than the subgame-perfect equilibrium may be attractors of the replicator dynamics by observing that the model artificially excludes the evolutionary pressure against weakly dominated strategies that would otherwise eliminate them. It is therefore necessary to consider models in which small fractions of all possible strategies

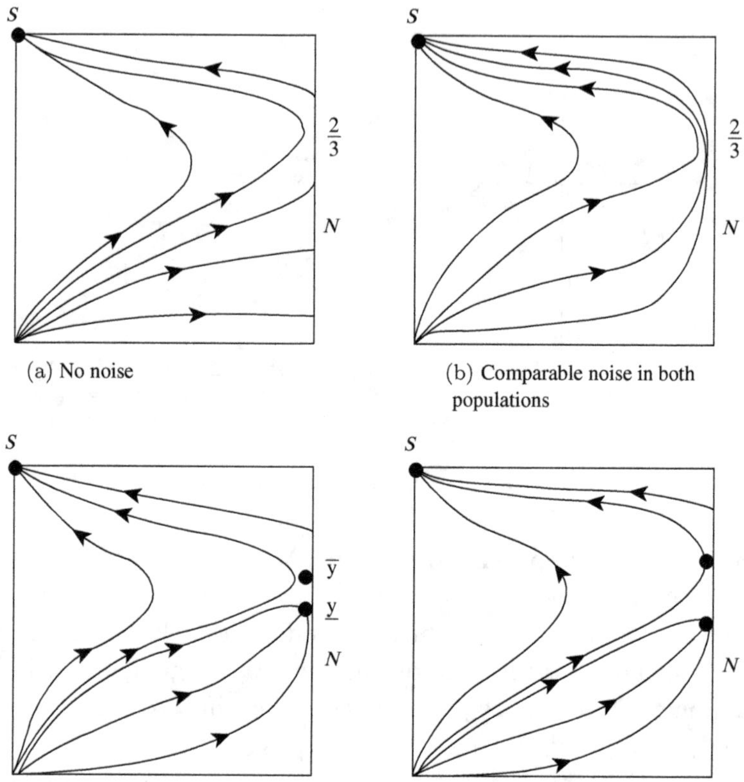

(a) No noise

(b) Comparable noise in both populations

(c) More noise in population II

(d) Endogenous noise

Figure 4: Phase diagrams

are continually injected into the population — including those that test the 'rationality' of responders who refuse positive offers. Only if the survival of Nash equilibria that are not subgame-perfect is robust in the presence of such noise can we realistically argue against the subgame-perfect prediction.

It is natural to see such a noisy model as an evolutionary gloss on Selten's (1975) trembling-hand story. However, caution is necessary before pressing the analogy too far. Samuelson and Zhang (1992) show that adding noise to the replicator and other evolutionary dynamics does not necessarily lead to the elimination of weakly dominated strategies. The question of whether only subgame-perfect equilibria can survive in a noisy evolutionary environment therefore remains open.

To investigate the robustness of the conclusion that a Nash equilibrium which is not subgame-perfect can survive as an asymptotic attractor, Binmore, Gale and Samuelson (1993) study the perturbed replicator equations:

$$\dot{x} = \Delta_1 x(1-x)(2-3y) + \delta_1 \left(\frac{1}{2} - x\right) \tag{3}$$

$$\dot{y} = \Delta_2 y(1-y)(1-x) + \delta_2 \left(\frac{1}{2} - y\right) \tag{4}$$

The case $\Delta_j = 1$ is of special interest, since it represents a situation in which agents in population j die or leave the game at rate δ_j to be replaced by novices who play strategy i with an exogenously determined probability θ_i.

Figures 4(b) and 4(c) show the trajectories for the perturbed replicator dynamics. Take $\phi = \delta_1\Delta_2/\delta_2\Delta_1$. In Figure 4(b), $\phi < 3 + 2\sqrt{2}$. In Figure 4(c), $3 + 2\sqrt{2} < \phi$. Since $3 + 2\sqrt{2} \sim 5.8$, responders are therefore appreciably noisier than proposers in the second case.

The striking difference between Figures 4(b) and 4(c) is that the second has an asymptotic attractor in the set N, whereas only the subgame-perfect equilibrium is an asymptotic attractor in the first. In the case when the responding population is significantly more noisy than the proposing population, we therefore have a substantive argument in favour of retaining a Nash equilibrium that is not subgame-perfect. But when should we expect the responding population to be noisier than the proposing population?

Some intuition on this subject can be obtained by reverting to the full Ultimatum Game. Suppose that noise in this game is caused by players misreading the strategic situation and so acting in a manner that is appropriate to some other game. For example, the Ultimatum Game might be confused with a more commonly occurring type of take-it-or-leave-it game in which the reputation for toughness matters, or with the take-it-or-leave-it game played by retail outlets, which leave a responder free to try her luck at a similar game down the street. A reasonable hypothesis would seem to be that players will be more prone to misreading games the smaller are the payoffs at stake. But, close to the subgame-perfect equilibrium, responders will have very little at stake in the Ultimatum Game. We should therefore anticipate that their behaviour will tend to be much noisier than the behaviour of proposers, for whom an inappropriate choice can be very costly. In the Ultimatum Game, this consideration creates an evolutionary pressure *against* the subgame-perfect equilibrium.

In the Chain-Store Game, matters are not so clear-cut because the subgame-perfect equilibrium always has a substantial basin of attraction even in Figure 4(c). However, a natural avenue of investigation is to endogenize the noise. For example, consider the case when $\Delta_j = 1 - \delta_j$ and δ_j is related to the current payoff levels at the time t by the formula

$$\delta_i(t) = \frac{\alpha\beta}{\alpha + \lambda_i(t)}$$

where α and β are constant and $\lambda_i(t)$ is the difference between the maximum and minimum expected payoff from each strategy i, given the current opponents' strategies. When this difference is zero, as is the case for responders at the subgame-perfect equilibrium, the noise level takes its highest value of β. If the difference could increase all the way to infinity, $\delta_i(t)$ would decrease to zero.

Figure 4(d) shows the trajectories of the perturbed replicator dynamics with such endogenized noise. The immediate point is that Figure 4(d) resembles Figure 4(c). In particular, when the noise is endogenized, the equilibrium noise levels require the responding population be significantly noisier than the proposing population. The same phenomenon occurs in our simulations of the full Ultimatum Game with even more striking conclusions.

The preceding argument shows backward induction is at best dubious in an evolutive context — even in the very simple Chain-Store Game in which a unique subgame-perfect equilibrium is obtained after only two rounds of deleting weakly and strongly dominated strategies. However, the use of rational expectations equilibria in large models is a staple of macroeconomic theory. Similarly, the successive deletion of weakly dominated strategies is a standard tool in the industrial organization literature when considering complicated games with multiple equilibria. The use of these tools does not lead to successful predictions in laboratory experiments on the Ultimatum Game. Perhaps they fail to lead to successful predictions when applied on the grand scale for similar reasons.

6. Conclusion

As noted earlier, Aumann predicted that some of his audience would categorize his paper as wrong and others as trivial. In saying this, he hit an important nail on the head. In treating the eductive argument for backward induction as trivial, game theorists have gone badly wrong. The interpretation of subjunctive conditionals is anything but trivial — otherwise it would not be a subject of controversy among logicians. Game theorists have also gone badly wrong in treating as trivial the fact that the equilibria achieved by evolutive processes will necessarily resemble those achieved by eductive argumentation.

The moral seems quite plain. If the foundations of game theory are to escape the fate of Sisyphus, we have to learn that the interpretation of mathematical models needs as much care and attention as their analysis. However, our guess is that we still have a long time to wait before interpretive issues begin to get the attention that they deserve. In the meantime, that stone will keep rolling down the hill.

References

Aumann, R., 1976, 'Agreeing to Disagree', *The Annals of Statistics* 4, 1236–9 [Chapter 2].

Aumann, R., 1995, 'Backward Induction and Common Knowledge of Rationality', *Games and Economic Behaviour*, 8, 6–19 [Chapter 11].

Bicchieri, C., 1988, 'Common Knowledge and Backwards Induction: A Solution to the Paradox', in M. Vardi (ed.), *Theoretical Aspects of Reasoning About Knowledge* (Los Altos, Calif.: Morgan Kaufmann).

Binmore, K., 1987, 'Modeling Rational Players I', *Economics and Philosophy* 3, 9–55.

Binmore, K., 1990, *Essays on Foundations of Game Theory* (Oxford: Basil Blackwell).

Binmore, K., 1993, *Playing Fair: Game Theory and the Social Contract I*, (Cambridge, Mass.: MIT Press).

Binmore, K., J. Gale and L. Samuelson, 1993, 'Learning and Subgame-Perfection', University of Wisconsin Discussion Paper.

Bolton, G. and R. Zwick, 1993, 'Anonymity versus Punishment in Ultimatum Bargaining', Pennsylvania State University Discussion Paper.

Frank, R., 1988, *Passions within Reason* (New York: Norton).

Güth, W., R. Schmittberger and B. Schwarze, 1982, 'An Experimental Analysis of Ultimatum Bargaining', *Journal of Behaviour and Organization* 3, 367–88.

Güth, W. and R. Tietz, 1990, 'Ultimatum Bargaining Behavior: A Survey and Comparison of Experimental Results', *Journal of Economic Psychology* 11, 417–49.

Harsanyi, J. and R. Selten, 1988, *A General Theory of Equilibrium Selection in Games* (Cambridge: Mass.: MIT Press).

Kohlberg, E. and J. Mertens, 1986, 'On the Strategic Stability of Equilibria', *Econometrica* 54, 1003–37.

Kreps, D., P. Milgrom, J. Roberts and R. Wilson, 1982, 'Rational Cooperation in the Finitely Repeated Prisoners' Dilemma', *Journal of Economic Theory* 27, 245–52.

Lewis, C.I., 1946, *An Analysis of Knowledge and Valuation* (La Salle, Ill.: Open Court).

Lewis, D., 1969, *Conventions: A Philosophical Study* (Cambridge, Mass.: Harvard University Press).

Lewis, D., 1976, *Counterfactuals* (Oxford: Basil Blackwell).

Reny, P., 1990, 'Common Belief and the Theory of Games with Perfect Information', *Journal of Economic Theory* 59, 257–74.

Roth, A., 1991, 'Bargaining Experiments', in J. Kagel and A. Roth (eds), *Handbook of Experimental Economics* (Princeton: Princeton University Press).

Samuelson, L., 1993, 'Does Evolution Eliminate Dominated Strategies?', in K. Binmore, A. Kirman and P. Tani (eds), *Frontiers of Game Theory* (Cambridge, Mass.: MIT Press).

Samuelson, L. and J. Zhang, 1992, 'Evolutionary Stability in Asymmetric Games', *Journal of Economic Theory* 57, 364–91.

Sandford, D., 1989, *If P, Then Q* (London: Routledge).

Selten, R., 1975, 'Reexamination of the Perfectness Concept for Equilibrium Points in Extensive-Games', *International Journal of Game Theory* 4, 25–55.

Selten, R., 1978, 'The Chain-Store Paradox', *Theory and Decision* 9, 127–59.

Selten, R. and U. Leopold, 1982, 'Subjunctive Conditionals in Decision Theory and Game Theory', in W. Stegmuller, W. Balzer and W. Spohn (eds), *Studies in Contemporary Economics, Vol, 2: Philosophy of Economics* (Berlin: Springer-Verlag).

Thaler, R., 1988, 'Anomalies: The Ultimatum Game', *Journal of Economic Perspectives* 2, 195–206.

von Neumann, J. and O. Morgenstern, 1994, *The Theory of Games and Economic Behavior* (Princeton: Princeton University Press).

Chapter 18

Reply to Binmore and Samuelson*

I heartily agree with many of the points made by Binmore and Samuelson. First, that the evolutionary approach to game theory is very important, though perhaps not to the exclusion of all other approaches. Second, that in perfect information (PI) games, backward induction (BI) may yield choices that are not only unwise and unreasonable, but quite simply irrational. Third, that interpretational issues are very important in these matters, and that in discussing them, one cannot rely exclusively on mathematics. Fourth, that in game theory and decision theory in general, and in the matter at hand in particular, one cannot restrict oneself to material implication, but must use what Binmore and Samuelson call 'subjunctive conditionals'. Fifth, that deleting weakly dominated strategies is not 'harmless'. Sixth, that in considering equilibria, one should not restrict attention to those that are 'trembling hand' perfect. Seventh, that the experimental results in the Ultimatum Game constitute an important phenomenon that cannot and should not be ignored or dismissed, and on which game theory has much of importance to say. And I could go on, listing many more points of agreement with their positions.

*Reprinted from *The Rational Foundations of Economic Behavior* (1996), edited by K. J. Arrow, E. Colombatto, M. Perlman and C. Schmidt, 130–131, with permission from Palgrave Macmillan.

These positions are argued by Binmore and Samuelson at great length, with fervour and flair and even some reasoned arguments. I have promoted many of them myself — some in the very paper they are attacking (Aumann, 1995) and others previously (Aumann, 1985, 1987, 1992a, 1992b). Indeed, the point about 'subjunctive conditionals' is absolutely central to my position (see Aumann, 1995, section 4b). I am delighted to have Binmore and Samuelson on my side in this matter, as well as in the others listed above.

The one cardinal point on which I disagree with them is my contention that common knowledge of rationality (CKR) implies backward induction. Wisely, they have made their position on this impregnable. Their arguments cannot be refuted, as they make no arguments. To be sure, they do *assert* in one place that CKR does not imply BI, and in another that there are flaws in my reasoning. But nowhere do they *show* that CKR does not imply BI, or even attempt a reasoned argument to that effect; and nowhere do they point to a single flaw, either logical or conceptual, in *my* argument.

To challenge the result that CKR implies BI, one must either find a logical flaw in my demonstration, or challenge my formulations of the underlying concepts — rationality and knowledge. Binmore and Samuelson do neither. Instead, they devote all their energy to arguing that in certain PI games, the BI choices may be (or are) unreasonable. That is correct; but it does not preclude CKR implying BI. You cannot discredit 'p implies q' by questioning q; perhaps p is also questionable. People who chide others — wrongly! — for confusing subjunctive conditionals with material implications should not themselves fall into the much more elementary error of confusing an implication with its consequent. Physician, heal thyself!

The fact of the matter is that there is a big difference between rationality and CKR, a point that Binmore and Samuelson consistently slur over. CKR is a very strong assumption, much stronger than simple rationality, and in some situations may just be too much to ask for (Aumann, 1992b). It is this, and this only, that accounts for the strangeness of the BI outcome in some PI games.

There is nothing more to say; I cannot defend myself against an attack that has no substance — is all smoke and no fire. A more detailed discussion of the issues may be found in Aumann (1995). As for the question in Binmore and Samuelson's title — 'Rationalizing Backward Induction?' — my answer is 'no; showing that CKR implies BI'.

References

Aumann, R. J., 1985, 'What Is Game Theory Trying to Accomplish?', in K. Arrow and S. Honkapohja (eds), *Frontiers of Economics* (Oxford: Basil Blackwell) 28–76.

Aumann, R. J., 1987, 'Game Theory', in J. Eatwell, M. Milgate and P. Newman (eds), *The New Palgrave, A Dictionary of Economics* (London: Macmillan) vol. 2, 460–82.

Aumann, R. J., 1992a, 'Perspectives on Bounded Rationality', in Yoram Moses (ed.), *Theoretical Aspects of Reasoning About Knowledge,* Proceedings of the Fourth Conference, TARK, 1992 (San Mateo, Calif.: Kaufmann) 108–17.

Aumann, R. J., 1992b, 'Irrationality in Game Theory', in P. Dasgupta, D. Gale, O. Hart and E. Maskin (eds), *Economic Analysis of Markets and Games* (Essays in Honor of Frank Hahn) (Cambridge, Mass.: MIT Press) 214–27 [Chapter 14].

Aumann, R. J., 1995, 'Backward Induction and Common Knowledge of Rationality', *Games and Economic Behavior,* 8, 6–19 [Chapter 11].

Chapter 19

Rationality and Comprehension*,†

Avishai Margalit and Menahem Yaari

1. Introduction

Economists and game theorists have recently been devoting a great deal of attention to laying down a theory of knowledge for decision-making units. (We shall often refer to decision-making units as 'agents'). What does the agent know about 'the world'? What does the agent know about other agents? And finally, when can we say that a given fact, event, or proposition is common knowledge among two or more agents? Some readers may find this kind of exploration rather curious, in view of the fact that 'decision-making units' are theoretical entities. It should be noted, however, that the purpose of the exercise is normative rather than descriptive. Basically, the question being asked concerns the structure of knowledge being *required* for the agents, if this or that theory of interaction (e.g., Nash equilibrium) is to be upheld. A detailed account of the recently developed models of knowledge for interacting agents may be found in Geanakoplos (1992).

*Reprinted from *The Rational Foundations of Economic Behavior* (1996), edited by K. J. Arrow, E. Colombatto, M. Perlman and C. Schmidt, Chapter 4, 89–100, with permission from Palgrave Macmillan.

†We are very much indebted to Kenneth J. Arrow, Kenneth G. Binmore and Amartya K. Sen for their comments. We also wish to thank Robert J. Aumann for giving us permission to refer to his unpublished work.

In this chapter, we shall argue that the concept of knowledge that has emerged in these discussions is unreasonably narrow and confining. The framework which we criticize and which, we claim, lies at the basis of today's theories of knowledge for interacting agents, is characterized by the following three principles:

(1) *Dichotomy.* There are two, and only two, types of knowledge: factual and analytic.
(2) *Factual= Sensory.* Knowledge is factual if, and only if, it is acquired through the receipt of a sensory signal. The agent's factual knowledge at any given state is defined to coincide with the sensory signal received by the agent at that state.
(3) *Logical Omniscience.* Analytic knowledge is innate, perfect, and complete. All tautologies and contradictions are known for what they are; knowing a tautology is itself a tautology; knowing p implies knowing all p's logical consequences; if p is not a contradiction, then p is known to be possible.

We regard these three percepts as a vestige of a naive positivist orthodoxy which, for some reason, microeconomists and game theorists have chosen to embrace. Why some of today's finest economic theorists should submit to such an orthodoxy is a fascinating question in the sociology of science. Perhaps it has something to do with the cult of free market economics which tends to view the economic agent as an organism relentlessly engaged in gratification-seeking. Be that as it may, our purpose here is merely to point out that the three principles stated above provide an inadequate basis for the theory of knowledge that is needed in the study of interaction among agents.

2. Interactive Epistemology

Among the many contributions made recently on this topic of knowledge in rational decision-making, there is as far as we know only one where an attempt is made to develop the decision-makers' information structures from basic principles. This is Robert J.

Aumann's (1992) remarkable essay. Aumann's construction uses the following building-blocks:

(a) There is a (finite non-empty) set of *individuals*. Their number is n.
(b) A *language* is given, where the symbols are letters from a (finite or denumerable) alphabet, to which are added $n + 4$ further symbols, viz. $\vee$, $\neg$, (,), $k_1, k_2, \ldots, k_n$.

The symbols of the language are given the following interpretations. Each letter in the alphabet is a 'natural occurrence'. The symbol $\vee$ means 'or', the symbol $\neg$ means 'it is not true that...', the symbols (and) have the usual meaning of parentheses, and, for $i = 1, 2, \ldots, n$, the symbol k_i means 'individual i knows that...'. The *formulas* of the language are given by the rules that each letter of the alphabet is a formula and that, given two formulas f and g, $f \vee g$, $\neg f$, $k_i f$ (for $i = 1, 2, \ldots, n$) are also formulas. On this basis, a system of modal logic is now constructed, using the axioms of propositional calculus plus $4n$ further axioms, viz.

$$(k_i f) \Rightarrow f$$
$$(k_i(f \Rightarrow g)) \Rightarrow ((k_i f) \Rightarrow (k_i g))$$
$$(k_i f) \Rightarrow (k_i k_i f)$$
$$(\neg k_i f) \Rightarrow (k_i \neg k_i f)$$

where $i = 1, \ldots, n$, f and g are formulas, and $f \Rightarrow g$ means $(\neg f) \vee g$. A *thesis* (or a *tautology*) is now defined by the conditions:

every axiom is a thesis;
if f and $(f \Rightarrow g)$ are theses, then g is a thesis;
for $i = 1, \ldots, n$, if f is a thesis, then $k_i f$ is a thesis.

The resulting system is a multi-agent version of the modal logic known as *S5*, originally introduced by Lewis and Langford (1932) in the exploration of possibility and necessity. Aumann now defines a *state of the world* as a list of formulas that contains all the theses and is inference-complete (i.e., if f and $f \Rightarrow g$ are in the list, so is g) such that a formula f is in the list if, and only if, its negation $\neg f$ is *not* in the list. The *signal* received by agent i at state S is the set of all formulas f such that f is not a thesis and $k_i f$ belongs to the list S.

Agent i's signal at a given state S carries two different kinds of information. First, there are the letters α of the alphabet for which $k_i\alpha$ belongs to S. This is what agent i knows at S about what Aumann calls 'natural occurrences'. This part of the signal is clearly sensory. Secondly, agent i's signal contains information about what *other agents* know, i.e., it includes formulas of the form $k_j f$ such that $k_i k_j f$ belongs to S, for some other agent j. How agent i can ever come to possess this kind of information turns out to be a very thorny issue. Note, in particular, that as a consequence of the axioms, the implication $k_i k_j f \Rightarrow k_i f$ always holds; i's sensory knowledge of f is a necessary condition for i's ability to know that j knows f. All this is discussed at greater length in Section 3, below.

Aumann's essay contains a curious distinction between knowledge (without quotation marks) and 'knowledge' (with quotation marks). If at some state S, f is a fact (i.e., a *formula* which is not a thesis and belongs to S) then agent i either knows f (this is written $k_i f \in S$) or else agent i does not know f ($\neg\, k_i f \in S$). This is factual knowledge. For this to be at all meaningful, agent i must 'know' the *language* in which f and $k_i f$ appear as formulas. Knowledge that is embodied in the structure of the language is normally called *analytic.* Aumann calls it 'knowledge' (with quotation marks). Notice that, in Aumann, a great many things are worked into the structure of the language, thus becoming 'known' (with quotation marks) to all agents, as part of their analytic tool-kit. For example, the state space, i.e., the complete account of all the possible states that the world can be in, is 'known' and therefore analytic. Who the other agents are, how many of them, and what their information structures are: all this is 'known' and therefore analytic — to say nothing of all theses, which are (tautologically) 'known', thus obviously analytic. Now, from the point of view of decision-making, knowledge and 'knowledge' are of course equally applicable. In choosing actions, agents will bring to bear all the information they have, whether factual or analytic. The main difference between the two is that factual information possessed by one agent may not become available to other agents (due to differences in signals received), whereas analytic information is common to all agents, and this is itself commonly known. Some simple consequences of all this will now be explored.

3. Knowledge at the Lowest Common Denominator

In examples of two-agent interactive situations it has recently become fashionable to refer to the two agents as Alice and Bob. Onto this bandwagon we are delighted to jump. Alice and Bob are travelling in a car. Alice is driving and Bob is at her side, in the passenger's seat. They approach an intersection with a traffic light. It is a special kind of traffic light: instead of being made up of three separate lighting elements — one red, one amber and one green — this traffic light is a high-tech job, with a single lighting element that changes colours. When Alice and Bob reach the intersection the light is red, so Alice stops the car. She can do this because she can see the red light for what it is (namely red), i.e., she is colour-cognizant. Bob, on the other hand, is colour-blind. The light changes to green. Alice knows (sees) that now the light is green. Bob is colour-blind, so he does not know this. So far, so good. Now, what does Bob know about what Alice knows? Bob certainly knows that Alice knows the colour of the light, i.e. Bob knows that Alice is not colour-blind, and this knowledge is *analytic*. Indeed, Alice's being colour-cognizant (i.e., her information structure) is part of the 'language'. If Bob had any doubt about whether or not Alice can see colours, he would have to move to a new world, and a new language, with the number of agents increased to include 'Alice$_1$' and 'Alice$_2$' in place of what used to be simply 'Alice', Alice$_1$ being colour-cognizant and Alice$_2$ being colour-blind. He would then have to proceed from some prior probability distribution on who it is that he is driving with (Alice$_1$ or Alice$_2$), which he would have updated, using Bayes' Rule, to take account of the evidence that, whoever it is that he is driving with, this person did in fact stop at the intersection. ('Did she stop because she saw a red light?') So, to keep matters simple, let us go back to just one Alice, good old colour-seeing Alice, and to Bob knowing this. Alice knows that now the light is green and Bob does not. Can Bob know that Alice knows that the light is now green? Absolutely not! While he does know (analytically) that Alice can see colours, he cannot know (factually) that right now she sees green. Why? Because the event 'Alice sees green' is contained in the event 'the light is green', and so if Bob, who is colour-blind, cannot know the latter, he certainly cannot know the former. (In symbols, let g be the formula 'the light is green'. $K_Ag \Rightarrow g$ is a thesis, so $K_B(K_Ag \Rightarrow g)$ is true. It therefore follows from the second axiom that $K_BK_Ag \Rightarrow K_Bg$ and since the consequent is false, so is the antecedent.) Well, you might say, Bob obviously cannot know that Alice knows that the light is green, because Bob, being colour-blind, simply does not know what 'green' *is*. This argument sounds good but it is invalid. For Bob knows *exactly* what 'green' is. Recall that Bob knows Alice's information structure. In fact, he knows Alice's information structure *analytically*, as part of his knowledge of the language. Alice can see colours and Bob knows this. He knows exactly which visual signal Alice receives at every state of the world and, in particular, he knows exactly at which states she receives the signal 'green'. But the set of states at which she receives the signal 'green' is precisely the set *defining* the colour green. This, after all, is the meaning of Alice's being colour-cognizant: she can recognize green for what it is. Hence Bob knows exactly what 'green' means, yet he cannot know that Alice knows that the light is green. Why? Bob cannot acquire the knowledge that Alice knows that the light is green, because knowledge is only acquired through the receipt of a sensory signal.

The problem seems to lie in the fact that people do not have sensory access to what other people know, which, under the sensory/analytic dichotomy, would appear to rule out any possibility for knowledge to be conveyed between individuals. Yet, much of what people know is, in fact, knowledge that had been conveyed to them from other people. Alice cannot arrange for Bob to know what she knows, no matter how hard she might try. Certainly, no oral pronouncement can ever make Bob know that she sees a green light. If she were to utter the words 'I see a green light', all Bob would know would be 'Alice says she sees a green light'. This newly acquired knowledge may affect Bob's *beliefs* concerning Alice actually seeing a green light, but not his knowledge of it. Bob's beliefs depend, among other things, on Bob's theory regarding Alice's *motives* in making her pronouncement, whereas Bob's knowledge should not.

Things get worse as Alice and Bob prepare to move. (Imagine a dozen or so cars lined up behind Alice and Bob, with the drivers impatiently hooting their horns.) As soon as Alice sees the light changing to green, she can of course put the car in gear and proceed to cross the intersection. But Alice wants Bob to know what she is doing. She wants him to know that the policy 'move when the light is green' has been adopted (or is being considered). To her dismay, she discovers, however, that Bob can never know this policy. For, in order for Bob to know any policy of action, it must be the case that this policy of action is *measurable* with respect to Bob's information structure. The policy 'move when the light is green' does not satisfy this requirement. There are in fact only two policies which Alice can adopt with Bob's knowledge, namely 'move, no matter what colour the light' and 'stay put, no matter what colour the light'. And if both Alice and Bob subscribe to the rule that peril must be avoided, then they will agree that 'stay put, no matter what' is the policy to be adopted. Just imagine the frustration of those drivers in the cars behind.

This is, of course, none other than Aumann's (1976) celebrated 'Agreeing to Disagree' result. Suppose that Alice, after receiving a signal, uses this signal to update her prior probability distribution (i.e., her prior *beliefs*) over some sample space. If Bob is to know Alice's posterior distribution, then Alice must take care not to condition on anything that Bob cannot know. She must, in other words, restrict the evidence to be used for updating her beliefs to publicly known events. So, if Alice and Bob share a common prior and if both use the same decision rule (Bayes' updating rule, say) then restricting the evidence to publicly known events will obviously result in Alice and Bob reaching the same posterior distribution. They cannot agree to disagree. (Note that this coincidence of posteriors is here a consequence merely of Bob's knowing Alice's posterior distribution. This is because we are dealing with the special case where one agent's — Alice's — information structure is a *refinement* of the other agent's — Bob's — information structure. In the more general case, with no such relationship between the information structures, to obtain the coincidence of posteriors one must postulate that these posteriors are *common knowledge* among the agents. The argument, however, is basically the same: in order for the posteriors to be common knowledge, agents must restrict their updating to publicly known events, so agreement on the posteriors follows from agreement on the priors and on the updating rule.)

Where does all this leave us? It leaves us with the awkward conclusion that, under the sensory/analytic dichotomy, the only knowledge that agents can *share* is knowledge at the *lowest common denominator*. If you want me to know that you know something, then you must take care not to know too much. If Alice wants Bob to know what she knows, then she must take care not to know that the light has turned green. This awkward conclusion follows, we maintain, from an uncritical embrace of the principle that knowledge is either sensory or else analytic. How can Bob know that Alice knows that the light is green? Obviously, he cannot know this analytically, as part of the 'language', so this knowledge must in fact be sensory. Bob's information on what Alice knows must be obtained through the receipt of a sensory signal, and this can only happen when that information is consistent with Bob's capacity for receiving sensory signals.

These remarks apply also to the much-discussed notion of common knowledge of rationality. If you and I are rational, then for our rationality to be common knowledge between us, we must restrict our behaviour in such a way that an observer who can only see public events will know that we are rational. Our rationality must, so to speak, be evident at the lowest common denominator.

All this points to a theory of knowledge which seems to us too confining. Now the obvious retort to this criticism is to say that for a theory to have explanatory power, it must be confining. But this, we maintain, is more a case of embracing a dogma than of seeking reasonable explanatory power. We would argue, following Hintikka (1973), that the possibility of knowledge which is neither analytic nor sensory must be allowed for. Agents must be allowed to possess knowledge which, on the one hand, is knowledge about the world (and in this sense 'factual') but, on the other hand, does not depend on the receipt of a sensory signal. We will maintain, for example, that knowing what states the world can possibly be in — i.e., knowledge of the 'state space' — is necessarily knowledge of this kind. (In our opinion, writing the state-space into the language, thereby making its knowledge analytic, is a ploy that cannot seriously be defended.) We propose that the word *comprehension* be used to designate this kind of knowledge which is neither analytic nor sensory. Thus, Bob, who is colour-blind, should nevertheless be able to *comprehend* the fact that Alice knows that the light is green. Similarly, agent A should be able to *comprehend* that agent B is rational without B's rationality necessarily being measurable with respect to the information structure that arises from writing down the sensory signal received by A at every state of the world.

4. The Boy-Scout Version of the Hangman's Paradox

Think of a group of boy-scouts (say n of them) forming a single file, i.e., standing in a straight line one behind the other, each (except the first) facing the back of the boy directly in front. Of course, the boy-scouts in the line all wear caps on their heads. Among these caps, all but one are white and the remaining one — exactly one cap — is red. None of the boys is near-sighted or colour-blind, so each boy can see all the caps worn by the boys who are ahead of him in line, and recognize their colours. He can't see his own cap, nor of course the caps of those behind him. This is, so to speak, the physics of the situation, and we shall assume that all the boys know it. How did they come to know it? In what sense do they know it? How thoroughly do they know it (do they know, for example, the underlying physical and biological laws)? These questions are all relevant and difficult, but we are here following Aumann and saying that the boy-scouts have a common 'language', in which their knowledge of what we have called the physics of the situation is somehow embedded. It should be noted that through knowing the physics of the situation, each boy also knows something about what the other boys know. For example, the boy who is fifth in line knows what it means (physically) to be, say, eighth in line, and in particular what being eighth in line allows one to see. The fifth boy thus knows something about what the eighth boy knows. Basically, this knowledge rests upon *counterfactual* reasoning: If I *were* eighth in line, this is what I *would* see, so says the boy who is fifth. Counterfactual knowledge generally plays a major role in economic and game-theoretic reasoning, and this case is no exception. Note, however, that under the sensory/analytic dichotomy, all counterfactual knowledge is necessarily analytic since the *counter*-factual cannot be factual.

We shall now consider a world with n possible states, defined by who is wearing the red cap. Formally, a state-space Ω may be defined by writing $\Omega = \{1, 2, \ldots, n\}$, where the i-th state ($i \in \Omega$) is identified by the assertion 'the red cap is on the head of the boy who is i-th in line'. We assume, with Aumann, that all the boys know Ω, and that this knowledge is analytic.

Let $s_i(j)$ be the sensory signal which the i-th boy (i.e., the boy who is i-th in line) receives when the state of the world is j (i.e., when the j-th boy is the one wearing the red cap). We have:

$$s_i(j) = \begin{cases} j & \text{if } j < i \\ \neg(1 \vee 2 \vee \cdots \vee i-1) & \text{if } j \geq i. \end{cases}$$

The values which the function $s_i()$ can take are sentences (or propositions). When $j < i$, $s_i(j)$ is the sentence 'the red cap is on j's head', i.e., when $j < i$, the signal received by the i-th boy tells him exactly what the state of the world is. When $j \geq i$, i's signal tells him only that the red cap is neither on 1's head, nor on 2's head, ..., nor on $(i-1)$'s head. Note that when $j \geq i$ the values of $s_i(j)$ are constant, i.e., i receives the same signal at all j, so long as $j \geq i$. Let $\prod_i(j)$ be the set of all states at which the signal received by i would be the same as that received at j. In other words, $\prod_i(j)$ is the set of those states in Ω which i cannot distinguish from state j:

$$\prod_i(j) = \{j' \in \Omega \mid s_i(j') = s_i(j)\}$$
$$= \begin{cases} \{j\} & \text{if } j < i \\ \{i, i+1, \ldots, n\} & \text{if } j \geq i. \end{cases}$$

This definition gives rise to the following important remark. In defining the set $\prod_i(j)$, one uses a condition of the form $s_i(j') = s_i(j)$. Now the values of the function $s_i(\,)$ are *sentences*, so in order to define $\prod_i(\,)$, one must first settle the question of what it means for two sentences to be equal. In a formal language, sentences are equal when they are logically equivalent, and logical equivalence is well defined within the language. Normally, however, people do not receive signals dressed as formal propositions, nor do they normally have a Robert Aumann on hand to transform for them all facts and all knowledge of facts into formulas in some pre-constructed formal language. People normally receive signals in the form of sentences in some *natural* language. More precisely, the signals which an individual receives, if they are not themselves sentences in some natural language, are *processed* by the receiving individual into sentences in some natural language. In either case, the assertion $s_i(j') = s_i(j)$ is now to be understood as saying that individual i regards (or understands, or comprehends) the two natural-language sentences $s_i(j')$ and $s_i(j)$ as equivalent to each other, i.e., that from individual i's point-of-view the sentences $s_i(j')$ and $s_i(j)$ 'say the same thing'. At this point, one immediately faces a whole host of issues having to do with the status and possible indeterminacy of meaning in natural languages and with how information which is formulated in a natural language is comprehended and conveyed. These are precisely the questions which Donald Davidson (1984) and others (see, e.g., Lewis (1983)) have been discussing under the heading of 'Radical Interpretation'. Thus, going from the function $s_i(\,)$ to the function $\prod_i(\,)$ is far from a trivial matter.

The set $\prod_i(j)$ tells us what the i-th boy knows about the state of the world when the true state is j. Specifically, when the true state is j, what the i-th boy knows is that the world is in one of the states in $\prod_i(j)$. Unlike $s_i(j)$ which is a sensory signal and hence represents *factual* knowledge, $\prod_i(j)$ spells out knowledge which in general is not factual (or not *merely* factual). In particular, when $j \geq i$ we have $\prod_i(j) = \{i, i+1, \ldots, n\}$ which says that i knows the true state to be one of the states i, $i+1, \ldots, n$. In order to arrive at this knowledge, the i-th boy must reason as follows: (i) I can see (factual knowledge) that none of the boys ahead of me wears the red cap, i.e., that the true state is not in the set $\{1, 2, \ldots, i-1\}$. (ii) I know (analytically) that the state-space is Ω, which is given by the set $\{1, 2, \ldots, n\}$. (iii) From the fact that the true state must be in Ω but is not in $\{1, 2, \ldots, i-1\}$ I *deduce* (analytically) that the true state is in $\{i, i+1, \ldots, n\}$. Thus, in order to arrive at $\prod_i(j)$, the i-th boy uses both factual and analytic knowledge, plus logical deductions which are also defined to be part of analytic knowledge. Now the logical inference which the i-th boy uses to arrive at $\prod_i(j)$ is a very primitive one, and it is hard to object to the assumption — and an assumption it is — that he is capable of performing such inferences. Recall, however, that under Aumann's theory, agents are assumed capable of correctly carrying out *all* logical reasoning, no matter how complex. Once the axioms are in the language, so are all the theorems. This is the so-called Logical Omniscience, mentioned briefly in Section 1, above. The questions arising in this connection are extremely difficult. Is a capacity for omniscient logical reasoning a precondition for rationality? If it is, then nobody is rational. If it is not, then one must decide what would be the minimal capacity for logical reasoning required for rationality. For it is not even meaningful, let alone useful, to speak of rationality for an agent who does not possess *some* capacity for logical inference. And what about computational omniscience, which is a consequence of logical omniscience? Does inability to solve a given problem in polynomial time imply that full rationality is unattainable? We do not pretend to have a theory of knowledge for rational decision-making that gives satisfactory answers to these questions. Our claim is merely that going for logical omniscience, as the existing theory does, is not likely to be the right way.

The function $\prod_i()$ leads us immediately to the i-th boy-scout's information structure. Specifically, since $\prod_i(j)$ tells us what i knows when the state is j, letting j run through the entire set Ω would give us a description of what i knows at any given state, which is i's information structure. Accordingly, letting $\prod_i$ be defined by $\prod_i = \{\prod_i(1), \prod_i(2), \ldots, \prod_i(n)\}$, we get

$$\prod_i = \{\{1\}, \{2\}, \ldots, \{i-1\}, \{i, i+1, \ldots, n\}\}$$

for $i = 1, 2, \ldots, n$. The function $\prod_i$, which is indeed referred to as i's *information structure*, is clearly a *partition* of the state-space Ω.

In the previous section there were two agents, Alice and Bob, with information structures such that Alice could always know what Bob knows, but Bob could not always know what Alice knows. Alice's information partition was a *refinement* of Bob's. Here the situation is similar, albeit with possibly more than two agents. Each boy-scout in the line knows more than the boys ahead of him and less than the boys behind him. For any two boy-scouts in the file, the information partition of the one who is behind is a refinement of the information partition of the one who is ahead. In particular for the first and last boys we have:

$$\prod_1 = \{1, 2, \ldots, n\}$$

and

$$\prod_n = \{\{1\}, \{2\}, \ldots, \{n\}\}.$$

The first in line knows nothing (about who is wearing the red cap) and the last in line knows everything, in the sense that no matter who wears the red cap, n knows it.

We are now, at long last, ready to introduce a version of the so-called Hangman's Paradox. (See Sorenson, 1982 for a related discussion.) Suppose that the boy in the t-th place in the line is in fact the one wearing the red cap, i.e., let the state of the world which actually obtains be denoted t ($t \in \Omega$). Consider the condition

$$\{t\} \notin \prod_t \qquad (*)$$

What (*) says is: he who wears the red cap does not know that he is wearing it.

Suppose that (*) becomes known to those poor boy-scouts standing in line. That is, assume that the boys *know* (*) to be true. Obviously, this knowledge cannot be sensory, so we have to assume that the boys know (*) *analytically*, in the same way that they known Ω and the $\prod_i$'s. (Note that(*) being known analytically makes (*) *common knowledge* among the boys.) We shall say nothing about how the boys could have come to know (*), even though obviously this is a question of considerable importance.

As soon as (*) is known, the boy who is 17th in line raises his hand and, when given permission to speak, says: 'Making us stand in line like this for hours on end is nothing but a cruel hoax. There's no one here with a red cap on his head!' This proclamation obviously causes some alarm in certain quarters, so no. 17 is ordered to explain. 'Well,' he says, 'the red cap — assuming there is one — cannot possibly be on n's head, because if it were n would know it. Now, $n-1$ cannot possibly have the red cap on his head, because if he did, he would see all the boys ahead of him wearing white caps so he would know that the red cap is either on his own head or on n's. But $n-1$ knows that the red cap cannot be on n's head (if it were, n would know it), therefore it must be he, $n-1$, who is wearing it. Thus, if he himself had a red cap on his head he would know it. Continuing recursively in this manner, we find that if any one of us had the red cap on his head he would know it, and this would be true in particular for the boy t, whoever he might be.' Having thus completed his argument, no. 17 is asked to please take off his cap. 'What colour is your cap?' he is asked. 'Red.' 'Did you know you were wearing the red cap?' 'No.'

Let us examine this story carefully. Checking the condition (*) against the definition of the information partitions $\prod_i$, we find that (*) is true if, and only if, $t < n$. Repeating, for the sake of emphasis, we have that the assertions $\{t\} \notin \prod_t$ and $t < n$ are *equivalent* to each other. Now suppose that at the outset we were to assume that the boy-scouts somehow came to know $t < n$ instead of assuming, as we had, that what they came to know was (*). Surely, since $t < n$ and (*) are equivalent, there can be no difference between the two settings. Yet think of that smart kid, no. 17. If $t < n$ were the assertion that was known to be true, he would no doubt have held his peace thus sparing himself an embarrassment. There simply is no hope for a recursive argument based on $t < n$, an inequality which says merely that the red cap is not on the last boy's head. Something is amiss.

Note that in recounting no. 17's argument we did not use (*) directly. Instead we used the English sentence 'he who wears the red cap does not know that he is wearing it'. Is it indeed the case that this sentence expresses the same reality that the formula (*) does? Not quite. A formula is only meaningful insofar as the symbols comprising it are well-defined. In particular, both the meaningfulness and the meaning of the formula

$$\{t\} \notin \prod_t$$

depend on the definitions of the various symbols appearing in it, and primarily on the definitions of the information partitions $\prod_1, \prod_2, \ldots, \prod_n$. These, we recall, are defined as follows:

$$\prod_i = \{\{1\}, \ldots, \{i-1\}, \{i, \ldots, n\}\}$$

for $i = 1, \ldots, n$. The $\prod_i$ are only well defined given the definition of the state-space Ω, i.e. given $\Omega = \{1, 2, \ldots, n\}$. Thus (*) is only meaningful — and only applicable — for this particular state-space and for these particular information structures. The English-language phrase 'he who wears the red cap does not know that he is wearing it' is not so tightly tied down. In fact, what no. 17 did was to use this phrase while constantly *changing* the state-space and the corresponding information structures. Here is exactly what he did:

(1) We all know (*), and (*) is equivalent to $t < n$.
(2) $t < n$ means that n cannot be the true state of the world, so $\Omega = \{1, 2, \ldots, n\}$ is *not* the correct state-space. Rather, the correct state-space is $\Omega^{n-1} = \{1, 2, \ldots, n-1\}$.

(3) If Ω^{n-1} is the correct state-space, then the correct information structures are not $\prod_1, \ldots, \prod_n$ but $\prod'_1, \ldots, \prod'_n$ defined by

$$\prod'_i = \{\{1\}, \ldots, \{i-1\}, \{i, \ldots, n-1\}\} \quad \text{for } i = 1, \ldots, n-1$$
$$\prod'_n = \prod'_{n-1}$$

(4) Letting t be the true state and noting that t can only take on the values $1, 2, \ldots, n-1$, we must now re-write (*) for the new setting, as follows:

$$(*)^{n-1} \quad \{t\} \notin \prod'_t$$

Translated into English, what $(*)^{n-1}$ says is 'he who wears the red cap does not know that he is wearing it'.

(5) The condition $(*)^{n-1}$ is equivalent to $t < n-1$. If $(*)^{n-1}$ is known to be true, then $n-1$ can never be the state of the world, so Ω^{n-1} is not the correct state space but rather $\Omega^{n-2} = \{1, 2, \ldots, n-2\}$.

and so forth.

What this shows is that in order to obtain a proper version of the Hangman's Paradox (or the Surprise Test Paradox) one needs a condition which is stronger than (*). Specifically, the condition that will give us the paradox, and provide the proper foundation for no. 17's argument, is this:

(**) Whatever the appropriate state-space and corresponding information structures $\prod_i$, the true state t shall satisfy

$$\{t\} \notin \prod_t$$

Given (**), no. 17's argument seems flawless: The appropriate state-space keeps shrinking until the empty state-space (no one's got a red cap) is reached, where the condition $\{t\} \notin \prod_t$ can be said to hold vacuously. Yet, when no. 17 takes a look at his own cap he finds that it is red, admitting that he did not know this when the cap was still on his head. Something must have gone wrong in his reasoning after all.

As we have seen, no. 17's backward induction argument works through the manipulation of the state-space. Well, it turns out that manipulating the state-space is a very tricky business. In order to find out where the crux of the matter lies, let us reconstruct no. 17's argument in such a way that his conclusion will in fact be correct.

We start with $\Omega = \{1, 2, ., n\}$, together with the condition $\{t\} \notin \prod_t$ which, as we know, is equivalent to $t < n$. At this point, no. 17 makes the following suggestion: 'Since $t < n$, it is certain that the n-th boy cannot be wearing the red cap. So, what is the point of keeping no. n stupidly standing in line like this?' This leads to no. n being told that he can put his cap in his pocket and go to the cafeteria for a cup of hot chocolate. We are now left with just $n - 1$ boys standing in line, the n-th having left for the cafeteria. The new state-space is given (*physically*) by $\Omega^{n-1} = \{1, 2, \ldots, n-1\}$ and $\{t\} \notin \prod_t$ tells us that the red cap cannot be on $(n-1)$'s head. So, $n-1$, who no longer has any relevance for who is wearing the red cap, is excused and goes to the cafeteria for hot chocolate. The line has physically shrunk once again, the new state space is $\Omega^{n-2} = \{1, \ldots, n-2\}$ and the process can continue. No. 17, who will be completing his argument in the cafeteria, is now absolutely right: the state-space has been reduced to nought and the condition $\{t\} \notin \prod_t$, if at all meaningful, holds vacuously.

In this version of the story, the shrinking of the state-space is *physical.* It becomes part of what we have called 'the physics of the situation'. In the previous version, with all the boys staying in line with their caps on their heads, the shrinking of the state-space was *virtual.* The very same argument can be sound when the revisions of the state-space are physical, and faulty when these revisions are virtual. It thus becomes a matter of utmost importance for agents to know the precise grounds for admitting a candidate to membership in the state-space or denying it. This kind of knowledge can be neither purely factual nor purely analytic. We call it comprehension.

5. Conclusion

The most consistent and eloquent advocate of the view that knowledge must be either sensory or else analytic was, of course, David Hume. From the very start, however, one of the nagging questions which Hume's analysis did not appear to resolve was how to deal with knowledge of 'other selves'. Some critics went so far as to assert that Hume's position must necessarily lead to solipsism. It would not be incorrect, we think, to describe this essay as an echo of that criticism of David Hume: in the study of interaction among agents, the requirement that agents' knowledge be subject to sensory/analytic dichotomy cannot be sustained. Our suggestion for relaxing this dichotomy involves the introduction of what we have called 'comprehension'. Whether or not 'comprehension' can be modelled explicitly remains to be seen.

References

Aumann, R. J., 1976, Agreeing to disagree, *The Annals of Statistics* 4, 1236–9 [Chapter 2].

Aumann, R. J., 1992, Notes on interactive epistemology, version of 17 July 1992, unpublished.[1]

Davidson, D., 1984, Radical Interpretation, in D. Davidson, *Inquiries into Truth and Interpretation* (Oxford: Clarendon Press) pp. 125–39.

Geanakoplos, J., 1992, Common knowledge, *Journal of Economic Perspectives* 6(4), 53–82.

Hintikka, J., 1973, Information, deduction, and the a-priori, in J. Hintikka, *Logic, Language-Games and Information* (Oxford: Clarendon Press) pp. 222–41.

Lewis, C. L. and C. H. Langford, 1932, *Symbolic Logic* (New York: Dover) (2nd edn, 1959).

Lewis, D., 1983, Radical interpretation, in D. Lewis, *Philosophical Papers*, vol. 1 (New York: Oxford University Press), pp. 108–22.

Sorenson, R. A., 1982, Recalcitrant variations of the prediction paradox, *Australasian Journal of Philosophy* 60, 355–62.

[1]Subsequently published; see Chapter 3.

Chapter 20

Reply to Margalit and Yaari*

On the issue of 'logical omniscience' — the assumption that if one knows something, then one knows all its logical consequences — I am in complete agreement with Margalit and Yaari. There is no question that this is an important, far-reaching, and rather unreasonable assumption, and that it would be highly desirable to get rid of it. Unfortunately, I know of no coherent system of epistemic logic that does so, even in the one-agent case. One could take the position that this problem is so central that until it is solved, there is no point in bothering with the epistemic foundations of interactive decision theory at all. In the 'Notes on Interactive Epistemology' (Aumann, 1992) to which Margalit and Yaari refer, I chose not to take that position, but to set forth the epistemic foundations of game theory and rational economics as they appear today, i.e., with the assumption of logical omniscience.

Also, I agree entirely that the 'sensory — analytic dichotomy' is not useful or appropriate. The word 'sensory' does not appear in Aumann (1992): indeed, there is nothing there about the source of an agent's knowledge. The main point of Aumann (1992) is to give a coherent foundation for the representation of non-tautological

*Reprinted from *The Rational Foundations of Economic Behavior* (1996), edited by K. J. Arrow, E. Colombatto, M. Perlman and C. Schmidt, 106–107, with permission from Palgrave Macmillan.

knowledge that agents may have about each other's knowledge. If, as Margalit and Yaari claim, the dichotomy precludes agents from acquiring such knowledge, I am certainly with them in rejecting it.

On the other hand, the interpretation of 'Agreeing to Disagree' (Aumann, 1976) in Margalit and Yaari misses the whole point of that result. They write that 'Alice must take care not to condition on anything that Bob does not know'. I had hoped to have made it clear — both in the 1992 notes and in the original paper (1976) — that that is not so! The first two sentences of Aumann (1976) read, 'If two people have the same priors, and their posteriors for a given event A are common knowledge, then these two posteriors must be equal. *This is so even though they may base their posteriors on quite different information.*' See also Section 5 of Aumann (1992).

As for the 'Hangman's Paradox', the paradox seems to have nothing to do with *multiple* periods: it works just as well for one. Suppose one tells a class, 'Our next scheduled meeting will be devoted to an exam, but you will not know this beforehand'. Obviously, this involves a contradiction, so the students will not know what to make of it. At the next scheduled meeting, the exam is given, so the first part of the announcement was correct. The second part was also correct: since the announcement was gibberish, it couldn't be taken seriously, so the students indeed did not know about the exam.

With 17 periods, it is the same: though the announcement is more complicated to think through, in the end it is still (i) gibberish, and (ii) correct.

More precisely, it is not the content of the announcement that is gibberish, but its being an announcement — something that the listeners are meant to know after hearing. Some propositions simply cannot be known, though they may well be true — for example, any proposition of the form 'x and not kx' (of which the one-period Hangman's Paradox is an instance). If we call this f, then kf is equivalent to 'kx and not kx', which is tautologically false.

While I agree with Margalit and Yaari on the 'sensory — analytic dichotomy', I must admit to being puzzled as to the nature of the point they are trying to make. If Alice tells Bob that the light turned green, why doesn't he know this? They say that he only knows that she said it: but that sounds like a quibble. If one wishes to go that route, one may as well say that she herself doesn't know that the light is green, only that she sees it as green; perhaps she is hallucinating or dreaming, or has developed a fever that affects her colour perception. Alternatively put, why do Margalit and Yaari not consider hearing as one of the senses? This whole line of argument is unconvincing. In particular, the conclusion that knowledge cannot be conveyed between individuals seems farfetched indeed.

It appears from several places in their chapter (e.g., p. 91, lines 25–31; p. 92, lines 30–32; p. 94, lines 16–18)[1] that Margalit and Yaari have a basic misunderstanding of the construction in Aumann (1992). I *assume* no analytic knowledge other than that which is embodied in the axiom schema of the propositional calculus and of knowledge, and the *modus ponens* rule. All other analytic knowledge is *derived*, not assumed. Given the number of agents, the state space is *categoric*. And if one considers the number of agents an issue, it may be taken to be a denumerable infinity (i.e., a pool large enough to cover all agents); then this, too, is categoric, and there is no substantive knowledge at all in the state space. In a sense, that is the whole point of the construction in Aumann (1992) — to *derive* the state space, so that it need *not* be assumed as analytic. The problems that Margalit and Yaari raise are discussed in Section 5 of my 1992 notes; the subsequent construction solves these problems.

One may also think of this in another way: that the state space is not a part of the agent's knowledge at all, but is only in the analyst's mind. All that the agent knows is a list of formulas. The rest is a construction that is useful for the analyst, but that the agent does not need.

Finally, it may be that the disagreement between the authors and me is largely semantic — I use the term 'knowledge' in a more comprehensive way than they, to include what they call 'comprehension'.

---

[1]The references to the original paper correspond respectively to p. 398, lines 26–33; p. 400, lines 17–19; p. 403, lines 10–12, of Chapter 19 in this book.

There is also a difference in emphasis and direction between us. They are interested in the sources and meaning of knowledge — how things get to be known, and what it 'really means' for them to be known. My approach is less philosophical and more pragmatic; basically, I wish only to provide a coherent formalization of those aspects of knowledge that are relevant to interactive decision theory and related disciplines.

References

Aumann, R. J., 1976, 'Agreeing to Disagree', *The Annals of Statistics* 4, 1236–9 [Chapter 2].

Aumann, R. J., 1992, 'Notes on Interactive Epistemology', version of 17 July 1992; available as DP 67 at the Center for Rationality and Interactive Decision Theory, the Hebrew University of Jerusalem, February 1995.[2]

[2]Subsequently published; See Chapter 3.

Chapter 21

A Comment on Aumann's Bayesian View*,†

Faruk Gul

Abstract: In Aumann (1987), it is asserted that for those who adhere to the "... Bayesian view of the world, the notion of equilibrium is an unavoidable consequence..." I discuss two possible interpretations of the information model and show that neither interpretation supports this assertion. The *hierarchy representation* interpretation renders the prior stage meaningless and hence both the key assumption of Aumann's theory and its conclusion become impossible to interpret. The *prior* interpretation, on the other hand, is distinctively non-Bayesian. Furthermore, both the common prior assumption and the notion of having beliefs over one's own actions are problematic in the latter interpretation.

Aumann (1987) presents a result which he interprets as establishing that, for those who adhere to the "... Bayesian view of the world, the notion of equilibrium is an unavoidable consequence..."[1] The purpose of this comment is to refute this claim.

*Reprinted from *Econometrica* (1998), 66, 923–927, with permission from Wiley.
†I am indebted to Eddie Dekel-Tabak, David Kreps, and Robert Wilson for their help. Financial support from the Alfred P. Sloan Foundation and the National Science Foundation is gratefully acknowledged.
[1]Aumann (1987), p. 2.

An information model $I = \{\Omega, (T_i, p_i)_{i=1}^n, \tilde{x}\}$ consists of a set of states of nature Ω, partitions T_i of Ω, prior probability distributions p_i on Ω,[2] and a function $\tilde{x} : \Omega \to X$, where X is the set of relevant parameter values for the underlying problem. Let $t_i(s)$ denote $t_i \in T_i$ such that $s \in t_i$.

Aumann (1987) considers an information model in which $X = A \times Y$, where $A = \Pi_{i=1}^n A_i$ is the set of pure strategy profiles for some finite normal form game of complete information, $G = \{(A_i, u_i)_{i=1}^n\}$, and Y is the set of all other relevant parameters. Let $\tilde{x}^n$ denote the first n coordinates of $\tilde{x}$. Aumann makes the following assumptions:

Assumption 1 (Common Priors). *$p = p_i$ for all i.*

Assumption 2 (Bayesian Rationality). *For all i, $s \in \Omega$, and $z_i \in A_i$,*

$$Eu_i(\tilde{x}^n | t_i(s)) \geq Eu_i(z_i, \tilde{x}_{-i}^n | t_i(s)).$$

Theorem (Aumann (1987)). *If $\tilde{x}_i^n$ is measurable with respect to T_i for all i (i.e., each player knows his own actions) and Assumptions 1 and 2 are satisfied, then the distribution of $\tilde{x}^n$ is a correlated equilibrium distribution.*

Aumann's defense of his assumptions includes the following claims:

(1) The statement, "*I is common knowledge*" is a tautology. Hence all players know I.[3]
(2) The common prior assumption reflects a "reasonable" philosophical position, and nearly all of information economics is predicated on this assumption: "... [P]eople with different information may legitimately entertain different probabilities but there is no

[2]For the sake of simplicity, consider only finite Ω's. The papers cited below by Mertens and Zamir (1985) and Brandenburger and Dekel (1993) do not guarantee the finiteness of Ω.

[3]In the discussion of the prior view below, I challenge even the weaker assertion that players know I (i.e., each other's beliefs, for example), not just the common knowledge assumption.

rational basis for people who have always been fed the same information to do so."[4]

There are two possible ways to interpret the information model. In the first of these, we imagine a situation prior to the economic problem to be considered. We assume that the p_i's described the beliefs of players and were common knowledge at this prior stage. At a subsequent stage, a state of nature is realized, agents receive their information $t_i(s)$, update their priors, and make the appropriate adjustments in their beliefs and behavior (as embodied in the function $\tilde{x}$). In this interpretation, the prior stage represents a situation which actually occurred at some previous time. The distribution of the random variable $\tilde{x}$ implied by any one of the existing prior distributions p_i is a meaningful vehicle for stating predictions or making welfare comparisons.

For example, in this interpretation, statements of the form "*ex ante* everyone would be better off if..." or "the marginal prior distribution of agent i's beliefs on the set of action profiles is a correlated distribution" are statements that are independent of the particular representation of the underlying problem. In this interpretation, all states of nature describe contingencies that at a prior stage were considered as possible resolutions of the uncertainty. I will call this interpretation the *prior* view. It is evident that much of information economics is predicated on this view.

The prior view outlined above is an inherently dynamic story. It forces us to think of a prior stage. Note that *if* a prior stage exists, it is certainly not a tautology (but often boldy assumed in information economics models) that agents know each other's beliefs and how these beliefs will be revised. When priors include beliefs about one's own action as in Aumann's Theorem, the knowledge and common prior assumptions become even more onerous: it is particularly difficult to imagine a moment in time where Players 1 and 2 have the same beliefs about Player 1's future actions. Moreover, the assumption of common priors in this context is antithetical to

---

[4]Aumann (1987), pp. 13–14.

the Savage-established foundations of statistics (i.e., the "Bayesian view"), since it amounts to asserting that at some moment in time everyone must have identical beliefs.[5]

The second interpretation of the model (which I will call the *hierarchy representation* interpretation) is based on a result due to Mertens and Zamir (1985) and Brandenburger and Dekel (1993). These two papers show that given any collection of infinite hierarchies of beliefs (one for each player), one can construct an information model $I = \{\Omega, (T_i, p_i)_{i=1}^n, \tilde{x}\}$ such that at the true state of nature $s^* \in \Omega$, the posterior of each player i represents the same beliefs as the infinite hierarchy of beliefs of player i over X. Thus, in this interpretation, an information model is simply a notational device for representing the n-tuple of infinite hierarchies of beliefs over X. To fix ideas, consider the following simple pair of infinite hierarchies of beliefs:

Let $X = \{x, y\}$ denote the set of parameters. In particular assume that x, y are the two strategy choices of Player 1. Let $[x]$, $[y]$ denote the "events" x is realized and y is realized respectively. (Note that (1a)–(1d) define Player 1's and (2a)–(2d) define Player 2's hierarchy.)

(1a) Player believes with probability 1 that $[x]$ (henceforth, I will use BFC, believes with certainty, as short-hand for "believes with probability 1"). (1b) 1 BFC that 2 BFC that if $[x]$ then 1 BFC $[x]$ and if $[y]$ then 1 BFC $[y]$. (1c) 1 assigns probability .5 to the events E_1 and E_2 where $E_1 = \{$2 assigns probability .4 to $[x]$ and .6 to $[y]\}$ and $E_2 = \{$2 assigns probability .5 to $[x]$ and .5 to $[y]\}$. (1d) 1 BFC

[5]"The criteria incorporated in the personalistic view do not guarantee agreement on all questions among all honest and freely communicating people, even in principle. That incompleteness, if one will call it such, does not distress me, for I think that at least some of the disagreement we see around us is due neither to dishonesty, to errors in reasoning, nor to friction in communication, though the harmful effects of the latter are almost incapable of exaggeration." (Savage (1954) p. 67). Here, Savage appears to be rejecting not only the idea of "neutral" common probabilities at any stage, but also the idea that "difference in probabilities should reflect differences in information only". I am grateful to an anonymous referee for this citation. Compare with the citation from Aumann in (2) above. For another analysis of Savage's views and the common prior assumption, see Morris (1995).

that 2 BFC (1b) and (1c), 1 BFC that 2 BFC that 1 BFC that 2 BFC (1b) and (1c) and so forth.

(2a) 2 assigns probability .4 to $[x]$ and .6 to $[y]$. (2b) 2 BFC that if $[x]$, 1 BFC $[x]$, and if $[y]$, 1 BFC $[y]$. (2c) 2 BFC that 1 assigns probability .5 to E_1 and .5 to E_2. (2d) 2 BFC that 1 BFC (2b) and (2c), 2 BFC that 1 BFC that 2 BFC that 1 BFC (2b) and (2c) and so forth.

The following information model represents these two infinite hierarchies:

$I = \{\Omega, (T_i, p_i)_{i=1}^n, \tilde{x}\}$ where $\Omega = \{s_1, s_2, s_3, s_4\}$, $T_1 = \{\{s_1, s_2\}, \{s_3, s_4\}\}$, $T_2 = \{\{s_1, s_3\}, \{s_2, s_4\}\}$, $\tilde{x}(s_1) = \tilde{x}(s_2) = x$, $\tilde{x}(s_3) = \tilde{x}(s_4) = y$, $p_1(s_1) = p_1(s_2) = .5\alpha$, $p_1(s_3) = p_1(s_4) = .5\beta$, $p_2(s_1) = .4\delta$, $p_2(s_3) = .6\delta$, $p_2(s_2) = p_2(s_4) = .5\gamma$, for any $\alpha, \beta, \delta, \gamma > 0$ such that $\alpha + \beta = \delta + \gamma = 1$ and $s^* = s_1$ is the true state of nature.

Aumann's remarks regarding the common knowledge assumptions being tautologies are valid in this context. That is, any conclusion a player can draw from I and his true type, he can also draw from his infinite hierarchy of beliefs over X. However, there is no prior stage and hence no possible interpretation of the distribution of $\tilde{x}$ with respect to any one of the priors. There is also no way to talk about one player being more or less informed than another or an outside observer since such comparisons necessitate a dynamic framework in which information is actually acquired.[6] The priors are artifacts of a notational device to represent the infinite hierarchies of beliefs on X of the players, i.e., their "posteriors" at the true

[6]Aumann in his reply proposes that if, in the model representing the infinite hierarchies of beliefs, 1's partition element is fully contained in 2's, then 1 is better informed at any state in this partition element of 1. He states that this test "nicely captures the intuitive idea of being more informed" (Aumann 1998, p. 935, footnote 13). However, the hierarchy representation view offers no means of determining if the greater confidence of Player 1, implied by his finer information partition, represents better information, unjustified over-confidence, or a legitimate disagreement between reasonable people. One could resolve the issue by *asserting* that 1's belief is in fact knowledge (i.e. implies truth). The usefulness of this option in developing a subjectivist Bayesian view of the world is, however, questionable.

state of nature.[7] The states of Ω other than s_1 never represented contingencies that were considered possible as realizations of the uncertainty; there was never a moment in time at which either player thought s_2 could have occurred. In fact, the occurrence of the state s_2 or the idea of "giving" Player 2 the information $\{s_2\}$ does not correspond to meaningful thought experiment. "Conditioning" p_2 on $\{s_2\}$ cannot be viewed as giving the information $\{s_2\}$ to Player 2. To see this, note that we cannot change Player 2's partition without changing the infinite hierarchy of beliefs for 1 as well.[8]

The fallacy of viewing the "priors" in the above representation as beliefs at some hypothetical prior stage becomes clear, if we remember that the information model above is nothing more than an equivalent representation of the infinite hierarchies of beliefs (i.e., (1a)–(1c) and (2a)–(2c)). Yet there is no data in either of these hierarchies regarding any "prior" stage. Nor is there any data in the infinite hierarchies regarding what the agents *would have believed* had their information been "less" or "more" than what it in fact is. Hence, no such data can be present in the equivalent representation of these hierarchies of beliefs. The fact that the infinite hierarchies of beliefs contain no data about any prior stage can also be verified by observing that $\alpha = p_1(\{s_1, s_2\})$ is indeterminate (i.e., the infinite hierarchy of beliefs of a player does not pin down his own prior for his own types). Thus, it is clear that insisting on $p_1(\{s_1, s_2\}) = p_2(\{s_1, s_2\})$ has nothing to do with the view that "differences in probabilities reflect differences in information only" even if we could understand what this view means within the hierarchy representation interpretation.

Finally, it can be shown that no information model that represents the infinite hierarchy of beliefs for 1 defined by (1a)–(1c) can have a common prior, irrespective of the infinite hierarchy of

---

[7]Brandenburger and Dekel (1993) explicitly avoid any reference to the prior in their representation theorem mentioned above.

[8]Note Axiom 2 in the reply.

beliefs of 2.[9] How can it be that insisting on a common prior reflects the view that "differences in probabilities reflect differences in information only" if the beliefs of Player 1 *alone* without any mention of Player 2's beliefs and presumably his information, can preclude a common prior? Since Ω and the priors are not primitives, ultimately, the meaning of any assumptions or conclusions regarding them (i.e., statements such as "the priors are common" or "the prior distribution of actions is a correlated equilibrium distribution") can be understood only with respect to their implications on the posteriors of the players at the true state of nature (i.e., the infinite hierarchies of beliefs over X). The exact implications of the common prior assumption on the infinite hierarchy of beliefs are not known.[10] Thus, within the hierarchy representation interpretation, we do not know what it is that we would be accepting if we were to accept the common prior assumption. Arguing for common priors in the hierarchy representation interpretation on the grounds that people with the same level of information should have the same beliefs is analogous to arguing for risk aversion on the grounds that the incremental units of money give less and less satisfaction. It amounts to an abuse of the formal similarity of two objects (prior and hierarchy representation interpretations of the information model in one case and the von Neumann–Morgenstern utility function versus some cardinal hedonic measure in the other).

Of the two possible interpretations of the information model, only the hierarchy representation interpretation supports the claim that the information model itself is common knowledge among the players. However, this interpretation renders the prior stage meaningless (i.e., it becomes impossible to associate the prior stage with a sensible thought experiment), and hence both the common prior assumption and the conclusion of Aumann's theorem, that the prior distribution of action profiles is a correlated equilibrium, become uninterpretable.

---

[9]To see this observe that (1b)–(1d) imply E_1 and $[x]$ must be p_1 independent. Obviously, E_1 and $[x]$ can not be p_2 independent.

[10]I am grateful to an anonymous referee for pointing this out.

Moreover, the hierarchy representation interpretation offers no argument for identifying the "priors" of the representation with beliefs at any prior stage. Finally, insisting that priors be common does not correspond to anything we might mean by the phrase "differences in probabilities reflect differences in information only", but rather constitutes a complex and unintuitive restriction on *each* infinite hierarchy. Even if we were to impose common priors, this would not render the prior stage relevant, nor would it render the prior distribution meaningful, nor would it justify identifying this prior with the beliefs of a heretofore unmentioned outside observer within the hierarchy representation interpretation. If an outside observer existed, we would have to model her beliefs the same way we model the players' beliefs. It can be shown that if the outside observer were modeled as an additional player, the common prior assumption alone would not enable us to conclude that his beliefs over the behavior of the actual players must constitute a correlated equilibrium. In fact, if the underlying game were a 2×2 game, *any* belief for the outside observer that placed zero probability on non-rationalizable actions would be consistent with all of Aumann's assumptions.

On the other hand, with the prior view, it is not a tautology that players know each other's priors. With this view, the assumption that players have priors over their own actions is problematic. Assuming that these priors are commonly known and identical is all the more so. Literally, with the prior view, Aumann's theorem amounts to noting that if actions are generated by some randomization device, and if every action in the support of the prior distribution is conditionally optimal (i.e., conditional on that action being played), then the prior distribution of the action profiles is a correlated equilibrium (i.e., simply a restatement of the definition of correlated equilibrium). Neither the theorem nor the analysis provides any new argument for why one would expect actions to be generated in this way nor why beliefs for the players (or an outside observer) should be as if behavior were generated in this manner.

Ultimately, Aumann's defense of the assumptions of his theorem boils down to a peculiar philosophical position. He states, in his reply (Aumann (1998, p. 937)) that assumptions (or axioms) are to be intuitive but not compelling, that we do not "believe" assumptions, that they are not articles of faith, and that in the end they will be judged by where they lead rather than considerations of innate plausibility. This is a strange defense of an axiomatization that claims to establish that for those who adhere to the "... Bayesian view of the world, the notion of equilibrium is an unavoidable consequence ...".

References

Aumann, R., 1987, "Correlated Equilibrium as an Expression of Bayesian Rationality," *Econometrica* 55, 1–18. [Chapter 8]

Aumann, R. and Brandenburger, A., 1995, "Epistemic Conditions for Nash Equilibrium," *Econometrica* 63, 1161–1180. [Chapter 10]

Brandenburger, A. and Dekel, E., 1993, "Hierarchies of Beliefs and Common Knowledge," *Journal of Economic Theory* 59, 189–198.

Mertens, J. F. and Zamir, S., 1985, "Formulation of Bayesian Analysis for Games with Incomplete Information," *International Journal of Game Theory* 19, 1–29.

Morris, S., 1995, "The Common Prior Assumption in Economic Theory," *Economics and Philosophy* 11, 1–27.

Savage, L., 1954, *The Foundations of Statistics*, New York: Wiley.

Chapter 22

Common Priors: A Reply to Gul*,†

1. Introduction

Gul (1998) (henceforth simply Gul) attacks the conceptual foundation of the Common Prior Assumption (CPA), which is essential for the derivation of correlated equilibrium in Aumann (1987) (henceforth [A]). We are grateful for the opportunity to discuss the CPA and the underlying information model in more detail; evidently, our 1987 discussion was too sketchy.

To avoid misunderstanding, we stress that we do not consider the CPA "true;" the concept of truth does not apply here. We do think that it embodies a reasonable and useful approach to interactive

*Reprinted from *Econometrica* (1998), 66(4), 929–938, with permission from Wiley.

†Research support from NSF Grant SES-9209277, and from the Game Theory Program at SUNY-Stony Brook, is gratefully acknowledged. Also, we heartily thank Professor Dov Samet for several important discussions regarding this material. Finally, we wish to express our gratitude, appreciation, and admiration to the co-editor of *Econometrica* in charge of this note, and to two anonymous referees. Over a period of years, they have invested an unusually large amount of time, effort, and energy in the processing of this note, far beyond the call of duty, and so have played a large role in shaping its current form.

decision problems, though by no means the only such approach; and that it does not suffer from the deficiencies attributed to it by Professor Gul.[1]

Section 2 is devoted to technical preliminaries, and can perhaps be omitted or only briefly scanned at a first reading. In Sections 3 through 6, we flesh out an argument for the CPA that was presented sketchily in [A]. This is then used in Sections 7 and 8 to respond to Gul's points.

2. Partition Structures and Hierarchies

There are several representations of information in n-person environments. One consists of a space X of parameter values, a finite[2] space Ω of "states of the world," a function $\mathbf{x}\colon \Omega \to X$, and for each of the n players i, an information partition of Ω and a probability distribution $p(\cdot; i, P)$ on each atom P of his partition; call this a *partition structure*. In such a structure, the meet[3] of the information partitions is called the *common knowledge* (*ck*) partition; its atoms are the *ck components* of the structure. A *connected*[4] structure is one with a single *ck* component; since at any state ω, the "true" *ck* component is commonly known by the players, one may for many purposes limit discussion to connected structures.

[1]Gul starts by disputing our claim, in the introduction to [A], that "the notion of equilibrium is an unavoidable consequence of (Bayesianism)." We readily agree that (objective) correlated equilibrium is not literally an *unavoidable* consequence of Bayesianism alone; one also needs the CPA. This is made abundantly clear at several places in [A] (Sections 3, 4b, and 5).

Even with the CPA, Bayesianism itself is not enough for correlated equilibrium; one needs *common knowledge* of Bayesianism, which is a different kettle of fish altogether. We are sorry if anyone was misled.

[2]The finiteness restriction is not without loss of generality, as noted both in [A] and by Gul.

[3]Finest common coarsening.

[4]With a given partition structure $\mathbf{P}$, one can associate a graph G, whose vertices are the states ω, and whose edges are pairs of states lying in the same information set for some player. Then $\mathbf{P}$ is connected iff G is.

Information may also be represented by an n-tuple of knowledge-belief hierarchies like[5] those in Harsanyi (1967–68), Mertens–Zamir (1985), and others; call this a *hierarchy n-tuple.*

These two representations of information (by partitions and by knowledge-belief hierarchies) are closely related; they are two ways of looking at the same thing, two sides of the same coin. Thus, each state ω in a partition structure $\mathbf{P}$ induces a unique hierarchy n-tuple in a natural way; we call it the hierarchy n-tuple *at* ω. Conversely,[6] given a hierarchy n-tuple h, one may find a connected partition structure $\mathbf{P}$ with a unique state ω at which h is the hierarchy n-tuple. If, moreover, one asks that $\mathbf{P}$ be *reduced* — i.e., that each two different states in $\mathbf{P}$ induce different hierarchy n-tuples — then $\mathbf{P}$ is uniquely determined.[7]

Partition structures look much like the model of [A] and Gul's "information model," but there is a noteworthy difference. There each player i starts out with a prior on all of Ω; his posterior

[5]But not identical with them. They deal with beliefs — probabilities — only; we are interested also in knowledge, in the sense of absolute certainty (as distinguished from probability 1). Already in the two-player case, a pair of knowledge-belief hierarchies is an awesomely complex object. At the first level of the hierarchy, each player has a knowledge-belief profile about X; that is, he knows that the true parameter value is in a certain subset B of X, and he has a probability distribution on B. The knowledge of the two players must be *consistent*; one player cannot know something that the other knows to be false. At the second level of the hierarchy, each player has some knowledge and beliefs about pairs consisting of elements of X and the other players' first-level knowledge and beliefs; these second-level knowledge-belief profiles of the two players must be consistent with each other in a sense like that described for the first level, and each player's second stage profile must also be consistent with his first level profile (e.g., the first level must be the marginal of the second level when projected onto the first level). And so on, ad infinitum.

[6]See, for example, Mertens and Zamir (1985) — though we stress again that their set-up is a little different, in that they do not deal with absolute certainty (as distinguished from probability 1 belief).

[7]Indeed, not only each hierarchy n-tuple, but even just the hierarchy of one player alone, uniquely determines the associated partition structure. Since a player may always be presumed to know his own knowledge-belief hierarchy, it follows that he also knows precisely the relevant partition structure.

probabilities given his information can then be *derived*, using ordinary conditional probability calculations. Here, we *start* with the posteriors. Mathematically, the two kinds of model are equivalent; each can easily be derived from the other. Here we have chosen to avoid defining the basic model in terms of a prior on the entire state space, in order to emphasize our primary concern with the players' actual information and probability assessments — not with how the information and assessments were derived, and not with the situation at any previous time.

3. The Intuition for Common Priors

A *common prior* for a partition structure **P** is defined as a probability measure q on Ω such that $p(E; i, P)q(P) = q(E \cap P)$ whenever E is an *event* (subset of Ω), i a player, and P an atom of i's information partition. In words, each player's probability is derived from q by conditioning on the information in his partition. The *common prior assumption* (for **P**) says that **P** is endowed with a common prior.

The basic intuition for the CPA, prominently cited by Gul, was set forth in [A, pp. 13–14] as follows: "... the CPA expresses the view that probabilities should be based on information; that people with different information may legitimately entertain different probabilities, but there is no rational basis for people who have always been fed precisely the same information to do so.... Under the CPA, differences in probabilities express differences in information *only*."

A decade later, we must admit that we could have been more explicit here. After all, the players do *not* in general have the same information; why is the argument relevant for them?

To answer this, let us imagine that the players forget all their differential information; formally, this is represented by a partition structure in which each of the partitions is replaced by the trivial partition (consisting of Ω only). In this new situation, the players *do* have precisely the same information. So we *can* apply the above argument from [A], and conclude that then they all *do* have the same probability; denote it q.

Now, suppose the players are reminded of what they forgot; formally, return to the original partitions. Being reminded is a way of acquiring information; so each player's current probabilities may be derived from q by conditioning on his information. Since we are now back where we started, it is reasonable to suppose that also the probabilities are the same as those with which we started; that is, they are all derived from q by conditioning on the private information. But this means that q is a common prior.

This argument is informal. *If* we wish to formalize it, we must expand the framework to a dynamic one, in which a player's information can change. And, we must formulate axioms that embody the underlying principles that

(1) players with the same information have the same probabilities; and
(2) when information is acquired, probabilities are updated by the usual rules of conditioning.

Do we wish to formalize it? We think yes. In conceptual discussion, it is easier to come to grips with an argument — to identify the essential points, to separate the difficulties — if it is formal. Nevertheless, the "theorem" below is nothing more than a precise formulation of the above informal argument from [A].

It appears that our main difference with Gul revolves around the dynamic framework. He views the given informational situation as static, and considers it inappropriate to ask, "where did we come from, what might we have known before?" Imbedding the given set-up in a larger one with hypothetical elements bothers Gul, even though such imbeddings are standard in axiomatic analyses (see Section 8a).

Note that the argument in this section depends basically on the substantive notion of "acquiring information" rather than on this or that formalism.

4. Formal Treatment

Define a *dynamic framework* as a family $\Im$ of partition structures $\mathbf{P}$, with the same state space Ω and the same player set, that is closed under coarsening; i.e.,

(0) *If $\mathscr{P}$ is the partition profile*[8] *in some structure* $\mathbf{P}$ *in the family* $\Im$, *and* $\mathscr{Q}$ *is obtained by coarsening*[9] *one or more of the partitions in* $\mathscr{P}$, *then there is a structure* $\mathbf{Q}$ *in* $\Im$ *with partition profile* $\mathscr{Q}$.

The structures in a dynamic framework $\Im$ represent different situations that may arise as time progresses and the players acquire more and more information. Each $\mathbf{P}$ in $\Im$ is viewed as resulting from some history; we ask that $\Im$ contain all possible structures that may have preceded $\mathbf{P}$ in this history. Call $\Im$ *consistent* if for all $\mathbf{P}$ and $\mathbf{Q}$ in $\Im$, events E, and players i and j, we have

(1) *If the same event P is an atom of the partitions of both i and j in* $\mathbf{P}$, *then* $p_{\mathbf{P}}(\cdot; i, P) = p_{\mathbf{P}}(\cdot; j, P)$, *where* $p_{\mathbf{P}}$ *denotes the probabilities in* $\mathbf{P}$; *and*

(2) *Suppose that i's partition in* $\mathbf{P}$ *refines his partition in* $\mathbf{Q}$, *while each other player's partition is the same in* $\mathbf{P}$ *as in* $\mathbf{Q}$. *Let P be an atom of i's partition in* $\mathbf{P}$, *and Q that atom of i's partition in* $\mathbf{Q}$ *that includes P. Then* $p_{\mathbf{P}}(E; i, P)p_{\mathbf{Q}}(P; i, Q) = p_{\mathbf{Q}}(E \cap P; i, Q)$, *and* $p_{\mathbf{P}}(\cdot; j, \cdot) = p_{\mathbf{Q}}(\cdot; j, \cdot)$ *for* $j \neq i$.

These two axioms embody the two numbered "principles" in Section 3. Note that (1) yields

(la) *If each player's partition has just one atom — namely all of* Ω *— then there is a single probability q on* Ω *that is the same for all players and represents all their probabilities.*

This means that if the players know "nothing," they must have the same probabilities.

---

[8] n-tuple of information partitions.

[9] One partition *coarsens* another if each atom of the coarser partition is a union of atoms of the finer one.

Theorem. *In a consistent dynamic framework, each partition structure* **P** *has a common prior.*

Proof. For simplicity, take $n = 2$; the case of general n is similar. Call the players 1 and 2.

Starting from the partition profile $\mathscr{P} = (\mathscr{P}^1, \mathscr{P}^2)$ in $\mathbf{P}$, construct two auxiliary profiles $\mathscr{Q}$ and $\mathscr{R}$. Define $\mathscr{Q}$ as the trivial profile, in which $\mathscr{Q}^1$ and $\mathscr{Q}^2$ have only one atom each, namely all of Ω. Define $\mathscr{R}$ by $\mathscr{R}^1 := \mathscr{P}^1$ and $\mathscr{R}^2 := \mathscr{Q}^2$. Thus $\mathscr{Q}$ arises from $\mathscr{P}$ when both players "forget" their private information; $\mathscr{R}$ from $\mathscr{Q}$, when 1 is then "reminded" of her information, but 2 is not. One may also think of $\mathscr{P}$ as arising from $\mathscr{R}$ when 2 is *then* reminded of *his* information.

By (0), there are partition structures **Q** and **R** in $\Im$ whose partition profiles are $\mathscr{Q}$ and $\mathscr{R}$ respectively. By (la), there is a single probability distribution q on Ω that represents both players' probabilities in **Q**. Applying (2) twice, first to go from **Q** to **R**, then from **R** to **P**, we find that the probabilities in **P** are the conditionals of q given the information of each player in **P**. Thus **P** has the common prior q, so the proof is complete.

5. Discussion

It is worthwhile to be a little more explicit about the motivation for our treatment.

As we have said, the CPA expresses the idea that differences in probabilities should reflect differences in information *only.* If one sets forth all relevant information in sufficient detail, then in principle, there should be no room for differing probabilities. When we say all relevant information, we mean *all*: the schools the players attended, their childhood experiences, even their genes (which indirectly reflect the experience of previous generations). Of course, the players do not need to know all this information; indeed, usually they know very little. What we are saying is that if people have precisely the *same* information about all these factors — no matter how much or how little it is — then it is not unreasonable to assume that they entertain the same beliefs.

Admittedly, in concrete instances it is far beyond anybody's power to write down an explicit model of this kind. Yet solid, down-to-earth conclusions are routinely drawn from theoretical models whose complexity — or simply sheer size — defies the imagination. General equilibrium theory requires that economic agents have complete preferences over commodity spaces whose *dimension* may run into the tens of thousands. The first theorem in game theory (Zermelo (1913)) says that chess has a pure strategy saddle point; it cannot even be *stated* — much less proved — without considering strategies that are beyond anyone's power to describe or even imagine in any concrete sense. Using Zermelo's theorem, one can show that in the game of Hex, the *first* player has a winning strategy (Gale (1979)); nobody knows what it is, and probably it cannot be described in any practical sense. The infinite hierarchies of beliefs to which Gul refers are objects of astounding complexity, which it is utterly unrealistic to ascribe to human agents. One could adduce more and more examples.

In all these cases, the theoretical models have important, widely recognized implications. We suggest that here too, it is perfectly legitimate to see where we are led when we allow the states to include *all* relevant information, without providing details.

6. A Question About Axiom (2)

Though the partitions of players other than i are the same in **P** and **Q**, nevertheless it does not seem that only i's information is changed in going from **Q** to **P**. Let $\mathscr{P}^i$ and $\mathscr{Q}^i$ be i's partitions in **P** and **Q** respectively. Suppose the true state ω of the world lies in an atom of $\mathscr{Q}^i$ that is nontrivially partitioned by $\mathscr{P}^i$. Let j be a player other than i. In **Q**, Player i does not know the element of $\mathscr{P}^i$ in which ω lies, and j knows that i does not know this. In **P**, Player i does know the element of $\mathscr{P}^i$ in which ω lies, and j knows that i knows this. Thus in the passage from **Q** to **P**, both i and j have learned something; i has learned the element of $\mathscr{P}^i$, and j has learned that i has learned the element of $\mathscr{P}^i$. Indeed, in **P** it is common knowledge that i knows the element of $\mathscr{P}^i$, so i has learned more than just the element of $\mathscr{P}^i$; she has, for example, learned that j has learned that she has learned the element of $\mathscr{P}^i$. Under these circumstances, is it still true that in going from $\mathbf{Q}$ to $\mathbf{P}$, Player j should not change his probabilities, and i should simply use the ordinary rules of conditioning?

To answer this, we must look more closely at the meaning of the partition structures $\mathbf{P}$ and $\mathbf{Q}$. Imagine that the players are called into a room, and in each other's presence are told Ω, $\mathbf{P}$, and $\mathbf{Q}$, that upon leaving the room, i will be told the true element of $\mathscr{Q}^i$, each other player will be told the true element of his partition, that i will be told the true element of $\mathscr{P}^i$ at a specified time t in the future, and that nobody will find out anything else.[10] Then $\mathbf{Q}$ and $\mathbf{P}$ represent the situations before and after t respectively. Clearly i learns something new at time t, but does any other player j learn anything that he did not already know?

We claim that he does not. It is true that j gets to know at time t that i knows the element of $\mathscr{P}^i$, but he knew beforehand that he would get to know this. It is as if j is taking a train from Basel to Zürich. As the train pulls out of the Basel station, he knows that he is in Basel, and later he knows that he is in Zürich. But that is not "learning." He knew already in Basel that he would get to Zürich; that he indeed did so should not make him revise his probabilities. Similarly, i *knew* that j will know that she (i) will know the element of $\mathscr{P}^i$, so what she really learns at time t is *only* the actual element of $\mathscr{P}^i$. Therefore, i should indeed apply the ordinary rules of conditioning in passing from $\mathbf{Q}$ to $\mathbf{P}$.

Differently put: the elements of Ω describe the situation in $\mathbf{P}$ — that after time t. The partitions in $\mathbf{Q}$ describe what the players know before t about what they will know after t. Clearly, then, only i learns anything at time t; what she learns is *only* the true element of $\mathscr{P}^i$.

---

[10]The story about the room is for vividness only; it should not be taken too literally.

7. Gul's "Prior Interpretation"

This interpretation of Gul's "information model" (essentially our "partition structure") involves two stages: "prior" and "current." The given partition structure represents the current stage. At the prior stage — which is meant to model "a situation that actually occurred at some previous time" — there is no differential information; all players consider all elements of Ω possible. As Gul points out, this implies that the agents know each others' beliefs. He says that "much of information economics is predicated on this view" and it "is often boldly assumed," but is "certainly not a tautology." It appears from this that he considers his "prior interpretation" as dubious, even without common priors.

We agree. Though it *may* happen that there is an "actual" prior stage at which beliefs are commonly known, this is the exception rather than the rule. If there is, then the analysis in the foregoing sections applies, and we conclude that at that stage the beliefs must be the same — i.e., we have a common prior. If, as seems more likely, the beliefs at an "actual" prior stage are different and *not* commonly known, then there must be differential information already at that stage; and then again, the foregoing analysis leads us to a common prior at a hypothetical stage that precedes the "prior stage," and so also at the "current" stage. The only case that *would* be inconsistent with the CPA is if the beliefs at the prior stage were commonly known and different; but Gul has adduced no evidence or even argument that such a situation is tenable.[11]

[11]The passage from Savage (1954) cited by Gul in his footnote 6 must be read in context. As his book's title indicates, Savage's primary concern was not decision theory but statistics; specifically, statistics as a tool for scientific induction. Here Savage sensed a difficulty. His theory was personal. It depended on the individual; in principle, *based on the same evidence*, different individuals could legitimately reach different conclusions on, say, the temperature of the sun. This personal approach does not seem to jibe with generally accepted views of science. Many of us view science as an attempt to get at the truth, and that seems unrelated to our personal preferences for tea or coffee.

The whole of Savage's Section 4.6 (from which the passage is quoted) is devoted to grappling with this problem, to trying to bridge this gap. On the one hand, Savage does *not*, in fact, include anything like the CPA or our Axiom (1) — his formal apparatus really is purely personal. On the other, he did consider this

8. Gul's "Hierarchy Interpretation"

This is basically what is presented in Section 2 above. Let us start by noting that Gul does not challenge the formal correctness of [A]; the issues he raises are all interpretive. An axiomatic development, like that in Sections 2–6 above, is ideally suited to deal with such matters: By separating sharply between assumptions and the formal process of deducing conclusions from them, it enables us to focus and clarify the interpretive discussion.

We agree with Gul that the above development of common priors is essentially dynamic, that it depends on the idea of acquiring information and using it to update one's probabilities. And though we consider this perfectly legitimate and intuitive, we also agree that it *would* be desirable to characterize common priors and/or the CPA directly in terms of the "current," posterior probabilities, without any reference, either implicit or explicit, to any prior stage.[12]

---

a problem, and was looking for ways around it. See footnote 13 in [A] (footnote 12 in Chapter 8), which describes some of Savage's approaches to this problem (and concludes, quite mildly, that "it's just possible that he would have welcomed the CPA").

So there is some ambivalence in this section. In the cited passage, Savage says that the "incompleteness" (the personalistic nature of the probabilities) does not "distress" him. It *does*, however, bother him enough to address; and he *is* willing to call it an "incompleteness." One can read this as saying that though inconsistent beliefs are an embarrassment, they are something one can live with, are not unacceptable, not a reason to reject the theory. But that doesn't mean that he would not have welcomed a more "complete" theory, as [A] suggests.

Note the end of the quote: "... though the harmful effects of (friction in communication) are almost incapable of exaggeration." This is typical of his ambivalence; he seems to be backing away from what he just said — to be saying, "well, maybe disagreements are, after all, the result of 'friction in communication.' "

[12]Nevertheless, we disagree with Gul's assertion that "to talk about one player being more ... informed than another ... necessitate(s) a dynamic framework in which information is actually acquired." In fact, no dynamics are required for this, in either representation of information. With partitions, 1 is more informed than 2 at the state ω if and only if the atom of $\mathscr{P}^1$ containing ω is strictly included in an atom of $\mathscr{P}^2$. This nicely captures the intuitive idea of being "more informed:" 1 knows everything that 2 knows, but 2 does not know everything that 1 knows. With hierarchies, 1 is more informed than 2 if and only if 1 knows 2's hierarchy

We now list Gul's arguments, together with our responses:

(a) *A hierarchy n-tuple does not refer to any prior stage. So the prior stage is irrelevant, and any arguments using a hypothetical, artificially constructed prior stage are inappropriate.*

What Gul fails to realize is that in *any* axiomatic system, the arguments depend crucially on hypothetical, artificial situations that never existed. The essence of the axiomatic approach is that it works with an entire system, and with the relations between the objects in it. In particular, it relates the given, "real," situation to a whole lot of other situations, all of them hypothetical. This happens constantly — in Arrow's (1951) social welfare theory, in the Shapley value (1953), in Nash's (1950) bargaining solution, indeed even in Savage's (1954) development of probabilities themselves! Thus to derive Nash's solution of a given unsymmetric bargaining problem, one *must* consider a whole lot of other problems, including a symmetric one. That is, one must say how the players *would* divide the payoff if they were in this other situation, even though they are not, never were, and never will be. In Savage's theory, to deal with a single "real" choice problem, one must consider a host of other, hypothetical ones.[13] Similarly for Arrow, Shapley, and indeed almost any axiomatic system.

(i.e., 1's hierarchy allows for only one hierarchy of 2, and so ascribes probability 1 to it), but 2 does not know 1's.

[13]Savage himself was very much aware of the crucial role played in probability by hypothetical constructs that never existed and never will. In discussing a medical decision problem, Savage (1971) wrote, "It is quite usual in this theory to contemplate acts that are not actually available. These serve something like construction lines in geometry. A typical decision theoretic argument runs, 'If B were available, I would clearly prefer A to B and B to C; therefore, my momentary impression that C is more attractive than A will not bear inspection.' In particular, I can contemplate the possibility that the lady dies medically and yet is restored in good health to her husband." In referring to a different problem in the same letter, he wrote, "I would regard it as fanciful but not as nonsense to say, 'You experience sunshine if it rains, and rain otherwise.'" Hypothetical, artificial constructs were bread and butter to Savage.

(b) *Since there never was a prior stage, the prior distribution is meaningless. In particular, a common prior — if there is one — is "uninterpretable."*

Whereas point (a) challenged the conceptual *validity of the theorem* and/or its derivation, here it is the conceptual *meaningfulness of the conclusion* that is challenged.

In response, we note first that the conclusion does have at least one important practical implication not involving the prior at all, and so not requiring "interpretation" of the prior: When knowledge and probability 1 are the same,[14] the action profile at any state must be among those occurring with positive probability in some correlated equilibrium. Since the correlated equilibria often constitute a rather circumscribed set, which can be explicitly calculated by solving a finite family of linear inequalities, this has considerable "predictive" content.

Second, we hold that the conclusion *does* have clear intuitive meaning, even as stated. We do not agree that a common prior has no "meaning" or "interpretation" unless there actually was a time at which some particular person held this prior as his probability distribution. The interpretation of a common prior derives naturally from the axioms: It represents the "correct" or "appropriate" probabilities — what people would or should believe — if there were no private information. Admittedly, the existence of such "neutral" probabilities is not obvious. But that is what the axioms yield; and in any case, the *meaning* or interpretation of this concept is clear.

(c) *A state ω in Ω represents an n-tuple of infinite hierarchies of beliefs of the players over the space X of relevant parameter values. A partition structure is only a "notational device" for representing these hierarchies. Therefore, the CPA can be defended only by defending its implications for these infinite hierarchies.*

[14]I.e., at each state, each player assigns probability 1 to an event if and only if he knows it. When this is not the case, a similar but more complicated conclusion holds.

These implications are unclear. Therefore, the CPA cannot be defended; it must be rejected.

First, Gul's claim is not quite correct; a state ω represents an n-tuple of *knowledge*-belief hierarchies, not just of belief hierarchies (see Section 2). While this is not very important, it helps us to see why some of Gul's other claims may be problematic (see Section 8d).

Second, we do not agree that partition structures are merely "notational devices" to represent hierarchies. The two models are simply equivalent. The hierarchy model has the advantage that its tautological nature is more apparent. For other purposes, including ours, the partition model is more useful; it is more transparent and less cumbersome. Since the models are equivalent, one may choose the more convenient one for any particular task that comes to hand; for our task, the partition model is more convenient.

Third, even if we would grant that the hierarchy model is the "primitive," our argument would not be affected. We could still construct Ω and the various partition structures $\mathbf{P}$ (see the scenario in Section 6), still assume the axioms in Section 4, and still deduce common priors. If the originally given hierarchies do not admit common priors, the axioms are violated. Thus if Gul wishes to challenge the CPA, he *must* come to grips with the axioms.

Fourth, the idea that interpretations must be directly in terms of primitives is strange. We do not go back to Dedekind cuts every time we think about real numbers, nor to ϵ, δ every time we think of continuity. Savage derives probabilities from preferences, but surely we do not return to preferences every time we formulate an idea about probability.

Try "interpreting" covariance 0, or even just independence, directly in terms of preferences!

(d) *How can common priors reflect the view that "differences in probabilities reflect differences in information only" if the beliefs of Player* 1 alone *can preclude a common prior?*

The force of this argument eludes us. First, it is *always* the case that the hierarchy of one player alone determines the entire associated partition structure, and therefore also whether or not the CPA applies; see footnote 7. Second, our position can be roughly summarized by "CPA iff (differences in probabilities imply differences in information)." Gul's example has "*not* CPA." How is our position contradicted?

(e) *The CPA does not imply that the beliefs of an "outside observer" over the players' action profiles constitute a correlated equilibrium.*

This sounds incorrect, at least when the term "outside" has its straightforward, usual meaning, as in [A] — that the observer has no private information.[15] If, as Gul suggests, we take him as an ordinary person with his own beliefs, then our axioms (i.e., the CPA) apply to him as well as the players; so since he has no private information, his probability must be a common prior of the players. By [A], this is a correlated equilibrium.

In any case, outside observers are not central to our view; in [A] they appear only once, and then not in connection with the CPA.

(f) *Arguing for common priors on the grounds that people with the same information should have the same beliefs is like arguing for risk aversion on grounds of decreasing marginal utility.*

The comparison with risk aversion is quite apt in a number of ways. In both cases there are three modes of formulation:

the purely conceptual, as in "people dislike taking risks" and "beliefs are based on information;"

the abstract formal, as in "a sum of money is preferred to a lottery whose expectation is that sum" and Axiom (1) in Section 4; and

the concrete formal, as in "the marginal utility of money is decreasing" and "there exists a common prior."

[15]By this we mean that it is common knowledge that each player knows what the observer knows; i.e., the observer's partition coarsens each player's partition.

We don't believe in one formulation "because" we believe in another; the three modes simply express the same ideas in different ways. Indeed, we don't "believe" in these axioms at all; they are not articles of faith. Like Euclid's parallel postulate, they have intuitive appeal, but are not "compelling." Their importance stems from their pulling together a large body of theory, while maintaining a certain simplicity and spareness. Like other scientific hypotheses, they must be judged by where they lead rather than by considerations of innate plausibility.

References

Arrow, K. J., 1951, *Social Choice and Individual Values*, New York: John Wiley and Sons.

Aumann, R. J., 1987, "Correlated Equilibrium as an Expression of Bayesian Rationality," *Econometrica* 55, 1–18 ([A] in the text) [Chapter 8].

Gale, D., 1979, "The Game of Hex and the Brouwer Fixed Point Theorem," *American Mathematical Monthly* 86, 818–827.

Gul, F., 1998, "A Comment on Aumann's Bayesian View," *Econometrica* 66, 923–927 [Chapter 21].

Harsanyi, J. C., 1967–68, "Games with Incomplete Information Played by Bayesian Players," *Management Science* 14, 159–183, 320–334, 486–502.

Mertens, J.-F., and S. Zamir, 1985, "Formulation of Bayesian Analysis for Games with Incomplete Information," *International Journal of Game Theory* 14, 1–29.

Nash, J. F., 1950, "The Bargaining Problem," *Econometrica* 18, 155–162.

Savage, L. J., 1954, *The Foundations of Statistics.* New York: John Wiley and Sons.

——— 1971, "Letter from Leonard Savage to Robert Aumann," in *Essays on Economic Decisions Under Uncertainty*, by J. H. Dreze. Cambridge: Cambridge University Press (1987), 78–81.

Shapley, L. S., 1953, "A Value for n-person Games," in *Contributions to the Theory of Games*, Vol. II, ed. by H. W. Kuhn and A. W. Tucker. Princeton: Princeton University Press, 305–317.

Zermelo, E., 1913, "Über eine Anwendung der Mengenlehre auf die Theorie des Schachspiels," *Proceedings of the Fifth International Congress of Mathematicians (1912)*, 2, 501–504.

Subject Index

O

P

R

S

T

U

V

Y

Name Index